The Trauma Question

'Roger Luckhurst's *Trauma Question* is a tour de force ... His prose is lucid, his choice of examples illuminating, and his analyses consistently informative and well developed.'

—*Dominick LaCapra, Cornell University*

'This is the most comprehensive, intellectually exciting and elegantly written book that I have read in the field.'

—*Patricia Waugh, Durham University*

'Luckhurst's *The Trauma Question* covers an extraordinary range of materials in a most thorough and competent manner.'

—*Sander Gilman, Emory University*

In this book Roger Luckhurst introduces and advances the fields of cultural memory and trauma studies, tracing the ways in which ideas of trauma have become a major element in contemporary Western conceptions of the self.

Luckhurst outlines the origins of the concept of trauma across psychiatric, legal and cultural-political sources, from the 1860s to the coining of Post-Traumatic Stress Disorder in 1980. He then explores the nature and extent of 'trauma culture' through English and American sources from 1980 to the present, drawing upon a range of cultural practices from literature, memoirs and confessional journalism through to photography and film. The study covers a diverse range of cultural works from writers Toni Morrison, Stephen King and W. G. Sebald to artists like Tracey Emin, Christian Boltanski and Tracey Moffatt and film-makers David Lynch and Atom Egoyan.

The Trauma Question represents an important step forward for those seeking a greater understanding of this controversial and ever-expanding area of research.

Roger Luckhurst teaches in the School of English and Humanities, Birkbeck College, University of London. He is the author of *'The Angle Between the Walls': The Fiction of J. G. Ballard* (1997), *The Invention of Telepathy* (2002) and *Science Fiction* (2005).

The Trauma Question

Roger Luckhurst

 Routledge
Taylor & Francis Group

LONDON AND NEW YORK

First published 2008
by Routledge
2 Park Square, Milton Park, Abingdon OX14 4RN

Simultaneously published in the USA and Canada
by Routledge
270 Madison Ave, New York, NY 10016

Routledge is an imprint of the Taylor & Francis Group, an informa business

Typeset in Baskerville by
Book Now Ltd, London
Printed and bound in Great Britain by
Antony Rowe Ltd, Chippenham, Wiltshire

British Library Cataloguing in Publication Data
A catalogue record for this book is available from the British Library

Library of Congress Cataloging in Publication Data
Luckhurst, Roger.
The trauma question / Roger Luckhurst—1st ed.
    p. cm.
Includes bibliographical references.
1. Arts, Modern—Psychological aspects. 2. Psychic trauma in art.
3. Psychic trauma—Social aspects. I. Title.
NX449.5.L83 2008
709.04001′9—dc22   2007047897

ISBN10: 0–415–40272–7 (hbk)
ISBN10: 0–415–40271–9 (pbk)

ISBN13: 978–0–415–40272–9 (hbk)
ISBN13: 978–0–415–40271–2 (pbk)

Contents

Figures

Every effort has been made to trace and contact copyright holders. The publishers would be pleased to hear from any copyright holders not acknowledged here, so that this acknowledgement page may be amended at the earliest opportunity.

Acknowledgements

Thanks, as always, to the gang for putting up with this for too many years: Julie, Simon, Francis, Mark, Sally and Mary.

This book could not have been completed without the enlightened atmosphere of respect for every kind of research in the School of English and Humanities at Birkbeck. For lively dialogue and assistance, my colleagues at Birkbeck Joe Brooker, Sally Ledger, Laura Salisbury, Carol Watts and Jo Winning have been consistently inspirational.

I've been helped along the way by Isobel Armstrong, John Beck, Fred Botting, Mark Bould, Jenny Bourne-Taylor, Peter Brooker, Carolyn Burdett, Steve Burwood, Rick Crownshaw, Istvan Csicsery-Ronay Jr., Robert Eaglestone, Claire Feehily, Arthur Frank, David James, Cora Kaplan, Nicola King, Richard Kirkland, Dominick LaCapra, Rob Latham, Laura Marcus, Catherine Maxwell, Ulrika Maude, Jo McDonagh, Keith McDonald, Aris Mousoutzanis, Peter Middleton, Peter Nicholls, Daniel Pick, Adam Roberts, Antony Rowland, Lynne Segal, Marq Smith, Pam Thurschwell, Marina Warner, Pat Waugh, Tim West (who kept me moving), Wendy Wheeler, Anne Whitehead and Anne Witchard.

I was lucky enough to get expert advice from Mark Flynn, Clinical Psychologist at the Tower Hamlets Mental Health Care Trust on current psychiatric thinking about the treatment of trauma and I unashamedly plundered his reading lists. Mark Reid of the British Film Institute and Stephen Hughes of BBC Radio 4's 'Film Programme' took me for monthly lunches at Marino's in Rathbone Place, where I also dined on their amazing knowledge of film. Stephen has also given me lots of opportunities to think about trauma and film for radio pieces, for which I'm very grateful. Julie Crofts conveniently studied law whilst I was working on this project and was able to assist my stumbling attempts in this field. There is no chapter on drama in this book largely because I could not hope to compete with Professor Mary Luckhurst's expertise in this area. She's also my big sister and could still beat me up. I wholeheartedly recommend her work on the 'shock' drama of the 1990s by Sarah Kane, Martin McDonagh and others.

I've been able to think this project through with successive generations of students on my MA course on trauma and cultural identity and on the short course for the Cultural Memory MA at the Institute of German and Romance

Studies at the School of Advanced Studies. I am lucky to have such brilliant and disputatious students and I particularly want to mention Rob Harding, Anne Holloway, and Frances Gertler for helpful references and discussion.

Portions of this book, in early and halting form, have appeared in *Critique, Science Fiction Studies, New Formations, Literature and the Contemporary*, edited by Roger Luckhurst and Peter Marks, *Literary Theory and Criticism: An Oxford Guide*, edited by Patricia Waugh, and *Uncanny Modernity* edited by Jo Collins and John Jervis. Although I've transformed nearly every word since, I want to thank everyone involved for the opportunities to develop this project.

This book is, as always, for Julie. Julie has endured this project under her roof for many years and has been its unstinting supporter, recommending reading, lighting out for obscure art shows and unblinkingly knitting through whatever trauma film came up next. This support was only mildly undermined by a tendency to conduct discussions of trauma in a sort of cod-Marlene Dietrich accent on the grounds it sounded suitably tragic and burdened by history.

>Sigh<

Still, this comes your way with unbounded love.

Introduction

In 1980, the American Psychiatric Association included in the new edition of its official diagnostic manual the symptom indicators for a new illness: Post-Traumatic Stress Disorder. Those confronted with an experience involving 'actual or threatened death or serious injury, or a physical threat to the physical integrity of the self' considered to be outside the range of normal experience are diagnosed with PTSD if they present certain clusters of symptoms. Individuals who experience wars, disasters, accidents or other extreme 'stressor' events seem to produce certain identifiable somatic and psycho-somatic disturbances. Aside from myriad physical symptoms, trauma disrupts memory, and therefore identity, in peculiar ways. The first cluster of symptoms relate to the ways in which 'the traumatic event is persistently re-experienced' – through intrusive flashbacks, recurring dreams, or later situations that repeat or echo the original. Weirdly, the second set of symptoms suggests the complete opposite: 'persistent avoidance of stimuli associated with the trauma' that can range from avoidance of thoughts or feelings related to the event to a general sense of emotional numbing to the total absence of recall of the significant event. A third set of symptoms points to 'increased arousal', including loss of temper control, hyper-vigilance or 'exaggerated startle response'. Symptoms can come on acutely, persist chronically, or, in another strange effect, appear belatedly, months or years after the precipitating event (American Psychiatric Association 2000: 467–8).

The arrival of PTSD helped consolidate a trauma paradigm that has come to pervade the understanding of subjectivity and experience in the advanced industrial world. Each successive edition of the *Diagnostic Manual* has expanded the categories of those who might be diagnosed with PTSD. At first PTSD was only attributable to those directly involved, but 'secondary' victim status now includes witnesses, bystanders, rescue workers, relatives caught up in the immediate aftermath, a proximity now extended to include receiving news of the death or injury of a relative. An understanding of the psychological consequences of trauma has percolated into many different contexts, and Western cultures have convulsed around iconic trauma events. Families might be found to conceal histories of domestic abuse, as recovered memory treatments dissolve the psychic defences of denial and amnesia and whole sections of traumatic childhoods return to consciousness in full, horrific technicolour. Collectives, whether they are political activists, survivor groups, or ethnic, regional or national formations unite around the re-experiencing of their woundedness. Histories of gender, sexual or racial violence have indubitable reasons for finding explanatory power in ideas of trauma, yet traumatic identity is now also commonly argued to be at the root of many national collective memories. From Sigmund Freud's speculations on the buried trauma at the origin of Jewish history, one can now read up on the traumas that drive post-war Germany, post-9/11 America, Eastern Europe after Communism, or post-colonial Britain (see Santner 1990, Kaplan 2005, Butler 2004, Eyal 2004, Lindsay 2004, Howe 2003). To Andreas Huyssen, it seemed as if the entire twentieth century was marked under the sign of 'historical trauma' (Huyssen 2003: 8).

In this cultural context, extremity and survival are privileged markers of identity. Concentration camp inmates, Vietnam and Gulf War veterans, victims of atrocities, traumatized parents and survivors of disaster are the subject of intensive political, sociological, biological, psychiatric, therapeutic and legal investigation and dispute. Government inquiries, medical task forces, newspaper leader columns and grass-roots pressure groups contest the nature and extent – or even the basic reality – of traumatic impacts. Best-seller lists have carried sagas detailing extremities of domestic violence, rape, war atrocity, terminal illness, family deaths or the tragi-comic eccentricities of traumatic memory. Academic monographs have proliferated, often appearing to subsume the whole area of Memory Studies under the sign of trauma. 'Increasingly, memory worth talking about – worth remembering – is memory of trauma' (Antze and Lambek 1996: xii). Meanwhile, in the curious world of celebrity culture, trauma can amplify or even become the sole reason for fame. What Mark Seltzer has termed the 'pathological public sphere' (Seltzer 1997: 3) periodically develops around moments of trauma and engenders a particular kind of community. Instances might include the death of Princess Diana, cruel or unusual child murders, the inauguration of Holocaust Memorial Days, or terrorist attacks on New York, Madrid, or London. One recent commentary skirts close to open nostalgia for the New York of September 2001, when, in the wake of the terrorist attacks, there was 'the real creation of new public-sphere communities': 'I felt a connection to strangers I had never felt before' (Kaplan 2005: 2, 9). For another of the leading cultural theorists of recent years writing explicitly in the wake of 9/11, grief is now one of the best means for thinking about social collectives since it 'furnishes a sense of political community of a complex order, and it does this first of all by bringing to the fore the relational ties that have implications for theorizing fundamental dependency and ethical responsibility' (Butler 2004: 22). Welcome to contemporary trauma culture.

Trauma derives from the Greek word meaning wound. First used in English in the seventeenth century in medicine, it referred to a bodily injury caused by an external agent. What wounded and what cured shared the same term: physicians applied traumatic herbs or balsams to injuries. In early editions of the *Oxford English Dictionary* the entries for trauma, traumatic, traumatism and the prefix traumato- cite solely from sources concerning physical wounds. The one exception comes from an 1895 edition of *Popular Science Monthly*: 'We have named this psychical trauma, a morbid nervous condition'. This is an early indication of the drift of trauma from the physical to the mental realm that would start taking place in the late nineteenth century. In the current edition of the *OED*, citations to physical wounds are reduced to three and are substantially outnumbered by those from psychoanalysis and psychiatry. The predominant popular connotations of trauma now circle around metaphors of psychic scars and mental wounds. The metaphor of a psychological 'impact' still retains the sense of a wound caused by an exterior agent. The *OED* also records a further drift into general usage of the adjective 'traumatic' for any difficult or untoward event. Trauma, however, still refers to bodily injury in medicine and, as Steven Connor observes, the focus on the boundary of the skin in ritual piercing, cutting or scarification continues to play with powerful taboos in many cultures. Trauma culture has emerged whilst the skin has been 'the visible object of many different forms of imaginary or actual assault' in the modern world (Connor 2004: 65).

Indeed, it is useful to retain a sense that meanings of trauma have stalled somewhere between the physical and the psychical. Virtually every traumatic disorder has been the occasion for violent dispute over its ultimate origin, whether industrial accident, hysteria, shell shock, survivor syndrome, combat fatigue or PTSD. Are the symptoms the result of a physical, organic disease produced by identifiable external agents, or a wholly psychical disorder constructed by simulation, suggestion, mental breakdown or inherent mental weakness? Or does it emerge from the 'nerves', that uncertain, interstitial locale somewhere between the body and mind? Nervous shock or nervous exhaustion were self-consciously produced by Victorian doctors seeking for a third term to lie between the organic and the mental realms, a switching point where the physiological and psychological converged and conversed in unpredictable ways. As Janet Oppenheim commented, 'metaphor permeated all Victorian and Edwardian discussion of the nerves' (Oppenheim 1991: 83). Arguments over the physical or psychical nature of trauma regularly refresh their grounds of argumentative authority, yet the structure of the dispute has not substantially changed for a hundred years.

Trauma is a piercing or breach of a border that puts inside and outside into a strange communication. Trauma violently opens passageways between systems that were once discrete, making unforeseen connections that distress or confound. Trauma also appears to be worryingly transmissible: it leaks between mental and physical symptoms, between patients (as in the 'contagions' of hysteria or shell shock), between patients and doctors via the mysterious processes of transference or suggestion, and between victims and their listeners or viewers who are commonly moved to forms of overwhelming sympathy, even to the extent of claiming secondary victimhood. Therapists have discussed the problem of developing 'vicarious traumatization' from listening to difficult patient material; E. Ann Kaplan has used this idea to suggest a wider problematic of the 'translation' (through the media and other routes) of trauma across different communities. Transmissibility has become a central ethical concern about the representation and response to traumatic narratives and images. Can or should the right to speak of trauma be limited to its primary victims? Who can claim 'secondary' status without risking appropriation? Dominick LaCapra, recognizing trauma's potential 'to confuse self and other, and collapse all distinctions' has suggested a distinction for criticism between identification, which falls into this dangerous confusion, and empathy, which preserves distance (LaCapra 2001: 21). His reiteration of this divide suggests that it is constantly under threat of being overrun.

This uncertain, unbounded outward movement of trauma from its original wound is dramatically demonstrated by the very reach the term has now attained. To grasp its full resonances, one needs to be at least minimally aware of the history of psychodynamic psychology in the late nineteenth century including, but far from exclusively, the work of Sigmund Freud, and then the progress of the law of tort regarding recovery of damages relating to the negligent infliction of 'nervous shock' since 1901, and then the role of military psychiatry and pension agencies across successive wars of the twentieth century, and then the place of trauma in deconstruction and post-structuralist philosophy since about 1990, and then sociological theories of trauma as 'a socially mediated attribution', a form of collective memorial practice that therefore rejects the 'naturalistic fallacy' of psychologists (Alexander 2004: 8), and then recent studies of the brain physiology of the *locus coeruleus* and the effects on memory and emotion of catacholamines like norepinephrine when under severe stress, and then, finally, the revolution in treatments of traumatic stress using a combination of drugs focused on serotonin and cognitive behavioural therapy. Given the specialization of knowledge and the sheer volume of discipline-specific scholarship, it is a severe stretch to acquire this range of expertise, with almost inevitable lapses of knowledge and understanding. As LaCapra observes, 'No genre or discipline "owns" trauma as a problem or can provide definitive boundaries for it' (LaCapra 2001: 96). Trauma is also always a breaching of disciplines.

However, the dominant model for cultural trauma, my principal concern in this book, derives from a relatively narrow segment of this complex, multi-disciplinary history. The work of Cathy Caruth, one of the central figures who helped foster the boom in cultural trauma theory in the early 1990s, turns on the device of *aporia*, or unresolvable paradox. Trauma, Caruth suggested in an introduction to a special issue on 'Psychoanalysis, Culture and Trauma' in 1991, 'extends beyond the bounds of a marginal pathology and has become a central characteristic of the survivor experience of our time' (Caruth 1991b: 417). Even so, trauma was an inherently 'paradoxical experience' (Caruth 1991b: 417). An event might be considered traumatic to the extent that it overwhelmed the psychic defences and normal processes of registering memory traces. Trauma somehow is seared directly into the psyche, almost like a piece of shrapnel, and is not subject to the distortions of subjective memory: it is 'a symptom of history' (Caruth 1991a: 3). Yet precisely because of this unusual memory registration, it may be that what is most traumatic is that which does not appear in conscious memory. 'Traumatic experience', as Caruth formulates it, 'suggests a certain paradox: that the most direct seeing of a violent event may occur as an absolute inability to know it' (Caruth 1996a: 91–2). Paradoxes intensify around this critical instant of a defining yet unknowable memory lodged in the mind: under the sign of trauma, 'a history can be grasped only in the very inaccessibility of its occurrence', 'its truth is bound up with its crisis of truth' (Caruth 1991a: 7). A further Freudian paradox is the strange temporality of traumatic memory: an event can only be understood as traumatic *after* the fact, through the symptoms and flashbacks and the delayed attempts at understanding that these signs of disturbance produce. The 'peculiar, temporal structure, the belatedness of trauma' is another aporia: 'since the traumatic event is not experienced as it occurs, it is fully evident only in connection with another place, and in another time' (Caruth 1991a: 7). For Caruth, trauma is therefore a crisis of representation, of history and truth, and of narrative time. Repeatedly, there is the claim that psychoanalysis and literature are particularly privileged forms of writing that can attend to these perplexing paradoxes of trauma.

Caruth's small body of work has been extremely influential, and it is worth spending some time on elaborating the elements it manages so effectively to condense. It could be said to derive from three distinct lines of thought. The first invokes the work of the German–Jewish Marxist philosopher Theodor Adorno on the ruination of Western philosophy by the traumatic facts of Nazism, encompassed for him in one proper name: Auschwitz. In 1949, Adorno declared, in a famous and much misquoted statement, that 'To write poetry after Auschwitz is barbaric' (Adorno 1981: 34). Within his broader attempt to maintain cultural critique within a remorselessly expropriative capitalism, Adorno kept returning to, and modulating, a declaration which had begun to circulate beyond his control. In *Negative Dialectics*, he saw Auschwitz as a challenge to the very act of thought itself. 'Our metaphysical faculty is paralysed because actual events have shattered the basis on which speculative thought could be reconciled with experience … After Auschwitz there is no word tinged from on high, not even a theological one, that has any right unless it underwent a transformation' (Adorno 1973: 362, 367). For Adorno, all Western culture is at once contaminated by and complicit with Auschwitz, yet the denial of culture is equally barbaric. If silence is no option either, Adorno sets art and cultural criticism the severe, and paradoxical, imperative of finding ways of representing the unrepresentable.

In Adorno's wake, the 'problem' of Auschwitz is the determining catastrophe that inaugurates the trauma paradigm, for after 1945 all culture must address this question. 'We come after', was George Steiner's abrupt statement (Steiner 1967: ix). Giorgio Agamben has reiterated 'the aporia of Auschwitz' as 'the very aporia of historical knowledge: a non-coincidence between facts and truth, between verification and comprehension' (Agamben 1999: 12). Jean-Francois Lyotard similarly regarded Auschwitz as a 'sign of history', a ruptural moment of such extremity that it challenged the premises of conventional historiography. Instead, the historian 'must break with the monopoly of history granted to the cognitive regimen of phrases, and he or she must venture forth by lending his or her ear to what is not presentable under the rules of knowledge' (Lyotard 1988: 57). Lyotard explicitly evoked the Freudian idea of the paradoxically registered yet unregistered trauma, portraying modernity as something insistently haunted by what it had violently suppressed or forgotten in the symptom that 'would signal itself even in the present as a spectre' (Lyotard 1990: 11). For post-trauma aesthetics, Lyotard turned to the theory of the sublime, where representing the very failure to process the overwhelming event paradoxically figures its success as a work of art. Lyotard gave avant-garde art a privileged place in articulating this paradox: 'What art can do is bear witness not to the sublime, but to this aporia of art and to its pain. It does not say the unsayable, but says that it cannot say it' (Lyotard 1990: 47).

The second main reference for this aporetic thinking came from Jacques Derrida's deconstruction of philosophy and its important place in literary theory in the American academy in the 1970s and 1980s. In a late lecture called *Aporias,* Derrida reflected on how his readings had always sought out significant moments of apparent contradiction or irresolution, 'so many aporetic places or dislocations' that each text tended to reveal (Derrida 1993: 15). Derrida figured the aporia as a blocking of passage, a stalling or hesitation, a foot hovering on the threshold, caught between advancing and falling back, between the possible and the impossible. Derrida had pursued the possibility and impossibility of mourning in Paul de Man's work, the paradoxes of memory in Freud's models of psychic inscription, burnt traces or cinders of memory, and the aporia of the wound in Paul Celan's poetry (Derrida 1986, 1991, 2001, 2005). Preserving the traces of these aporia was central to Derrida's commitment to responsible thought, ethics and politics: the trauma was that most Western thought suppressed this passage of undecidability, that all metaphysics enacted a kind of violence.

Derrida's principal avenue into the American academy was through the so-called Yale School from the mid-1970s. The linch-pin of this grouping was Paul de Man, who developed a particular deconstructive reading of language. In the gap between reference and representation at least some of what we intended to mean was always open to misinterpretation or error; literature in particular seemed to foreground the slippages inherent in the act of representation, and often came to be *about* this erring. To de Man, this inevitably affected the work of literary interpretation too, which he formulated in the pithy paradox: 'The allegory of reading narrates the impossibility of reading' (de Man 1979: 77). De Man's errings and slippages between reference and representation clearly informed Caruth's formulation of the paradoxes of traumatic representation (there is a whole chapter on his theories of referentiality and language in *Unclaimed Experience* and her theory of traumatic aporia was first formulated when at the Yale English department). Yet this reading of de Man was only part of a wider move by Yale critics to trauma theory. Geoffrey Hartman, whose deconstructive rereadings of Romantic literature and expositions of Derrida's work were prominent in establishing the influence of the Yale School, started to turn his interest to the remembrance and representation of the Holocaust in the early 1990s. The Fortunoff Holocaust Video Archives at Yale, which collects the testimony of Holocaust survivors, and which Hartman co-founded, prompted him to explore this area both theoretically and autobiographically (Hartman had escaped the persecution and murder of the European Jews by travelling from Germany first to England and then America as a child). By 1995, Hartman had effectively translated his long critical career into variations on the study of trauma. If trauma marks the disjunction between the event and the forever belated, incomplete understanding of the event, then Hartman argued that this was at the heart of Romantic poetry. Figurative language is a form of 'perpetual troping' around a primary experience that can never be captured. Whether it is Coleridge's Ancient Mariner compulsively repeating his tale, or William Wordsworth's account in *The Prelude* of how poetic subjectivity is created through wounding events, Hartman proposed that trauma theory was a key expository device. Hartman had always emphasized that poetic discourse induced a proliferation of meanings; trauma was now the motivating 'nature of the negative that provokes symbolic language and its surplus of signifiers' (Hartman 1995: 540). An interview with Caruth confirmed this reorientation of his work around trauma (Caruth 1996b). Another important Yale critic, Shoshana Felman, also undertook this translation of deconstruction into trauma theory at about the same time. Felman is justly famous for her 1977 essay on Henry James's *The Turn of the Screw*, which explored how this ghost story had driven successive generations of literary critics to a form of interpretive madness. Rather than attempting to solve the enigma, Felman examined how the text generated ambiguity, placing the emphasis not on positive knowledge but on where 'meaning in the text *does not come off*, that which in the text, and through which the text, *fails to mean*' (Felman 1977: 112). In 1991, Felman was still writing about the limits of interpretive knowledge, but this time in relation to Holocaust testimony, publishing a study of Claude Lanzmann's nine-hour film, *Shoah*, a collation of survivor testimony that builds up a picture of how the genocidal machine of Nazism carried out the 'Final Solution'. Felman was still interested in paradoxes and the limits of knowledge, but this time there was a language of crisis and urgency about taking responsibility for the historical truth, given that ours is 'an *age of testimony*, an age in which witnessing itself has undergone a major trauma' (Felman 1991: 41). She understands Lanzmann's documentary project to capture the fragility of surviving witness in now familiar aporetic terms: it is 'to make the referent come back, paradoxically, as something heretofore unseen by history; to reveal the real as the impact of a literality that history cannot assimilate or integrate, as knowledge, but that it keeps encountering' (Felman 1991: 76). The following year, Felman published *Testimony* with the psychoanalyst Dori Laub, a text in which the trauma of the Holocaust prompts almost obsessively repeated and anxiously underlined aporetic formulae. The Holocaust is presented as 'a radical historical *crisis of witnessing* ... an event eliminating its own witness' (Felman and Laub 1992: xvii). 'The *necessity of testimony* ... derives ... from the *impossibility of testimony*', they reiterated (Felman and Laub 1992: 224).

Felman also theorized a new pedagogy of trauma, in which the effectiveness of the textual material was measured by its ability to '*break the very framework of the class*' (Felman and Laub 1992: 48). Felman discovered that she had inadvertently induced a 'crisis' in her students, but then actively sought this disturbance as a measure of the material in communicating trauma. 'Teaching', Felman argued, 'must in turn *testify*, make something *happen*' (Felman and Laub 1992: 53). This activism presumably aimed to incite affect in students for the ultimately cognitive ends of learning, even though trauma was defined as an aporia that disarmed cognitive grasp. The classroom was a significant space through which to theorize the affective transmission and circulation of traumatic emotions: *Testimony* headed the boom in the transformation of Yale deconstruction into trauma theory which then travelled across literary and cultural studies. Felman's theory of education appeared first in Caruth's special issues of *American Imago*, where Caruth spoke approvingly of 'the possibility of a truly pedagogical encounter ... [which] creates new ways of gaining access to a historical catastrophe for those who attempt to witness it from afar' (Caruth 1991b: 422). The academic influence of these works actively demonstrated the transmissibility of traumatic affect.

The third and most explicit source for theories of cultural trauma is psychoanalysis. That Lyotard, Derrida, Felman and Caruth all engage with trauma via Freud suggests that his work is the unavoidable foundation for theories of trauma, and this is undoubtedly the case for cultural studies. Freud's engagement with the traumatic neuroses was actually rather intermittent, and Ruth Leys comments that 'Freud's writings on trauma and the mechanisms of defence are disorganized in ways that seem to invite, or necessitate, critical discussion' (Leys 2000: 274). As a result, Freud's three major interventions have each provided models that are not always compatible but which persist into contemporary discussions. 'On the Psychical Mechanism of Hysterical Phenomena', co-authored with Joseph Breuer in 1893, regarded traumatic hysteria as a psychical disorder of memory, encapsulated in the famous epigram '*Hysterics suffer mainly from reminiscences*' (Freud 1895: 58). Traumatic memory is puzzling, '*completely absent from the patient's memory when they are in a normal psychological state*', but which persists below the threshold of consciousness 'astonishingly intact' and with 'remarkable sensory force' (Freud 1895: 60). The sketch of their treatment turned the hysteric's body into a cryptogram, each bodily or mental symptom to be traced back to a 'tormenting secret' and to be cured by '*bringing clearly to light the memory of the event ... and in arousing its accompanying affect, and when the patient had described that event in the greatest possible detail and had put the affect into words*' (Freud 1895: 57). In *Studies on Hysteria* these traumatic events related, as in the famous case of 'Anna O.', to the death of the father and repressed guilt. Three years later Freud insisted that these traumatic secrets 'in the end ... infallibly come to the field of sexual experience' (Freud 1896: 199), a position inextricably linked to the origins of psychoanalysis itself, the term Freud coined in 1896. This produced a different emphasis in theorizing the traumatic origins of hysteria. Freud's sexual theories supposed a two-stage development, an early phase of infantile sexuality that was repressed for a period of childhood 'latency' and which returned with puberty and the emergence of adult sexuality. Sexual neuroses and perversions were ascribed to deviations of the sexual aims that resulted from infantile disturbances (this normative language is Freud's own, in his *Three Essays on Sexuality*). In other words, early traumas in childhood would be forgotten in latency, but re-emerge in adults. Sexual disorders therefore acted like clues hinting at a hidden crime buried in infancy: interpretive excavations to uncover the sexual secret became the basis of Freud's case histories. This two-stage theory of trauma, the first forgotten impact making a belated return after a hiatus, has been central to cultural trauma theory. The psychoanalyst Jean Laplanche has translated Freud's term for belated or deferred action as 'afterwardsness', a deliberately awkward word that foregrounds the odd temporality of an event not understood as traumatic until its return (Laplanche 1999). No narrative of trauma can be told in a linear way: it has a time signature that must fracture conventional causality.

Freud's sexual economy of psychic life reached an impasse in 1918, when he was forced to return to the problem of trauma a second time, at the end of the Great War. His dynamic model of the psyche could not apparently account for the symptoms of war neurosis in soldiers, which was typically marked by an obsessive return in waking thoughts and nightmares, to the pain and terror of traumatic battle scenes. This active pursuit of unpleasure forced Freud reluctantly to return to what he called 'the dark and dismal subject of traumatic neurosis' (Freud 1920a: 283). *Beyond the Pleasure Principle*, first published in 1920, was Freud's highly speculative attempt to understand what he termed this 'repetition compulsion'. In essence, the psyche constantly returned to scenes of unpleasure because, by restaging the traumatic moment over and over again, it hoped belatedly to process the unassimilable material, to find ways of mastering the trauma retroactively. In a lucid metaphor, Freud envisaged the mind as a single cell with an outer membrane that does the work of filtering material from the outside world, processing nutrients, repelling toxins, and retaining the integrity of its borders – just as the conscious mind did. A traumatic event is something unprecedented that blasts open the membrane and floods the cell with foreign matter, leaving the cell overwhelmed and trying to repair the damage. 'We describe as "traumatic" any excitations from outside which are powerful enough to break through the protective shield', Freud said.

> Such an event as an external trauma is bound to provoke a disturbance on a large scale in the functioning of the organism's energy and to set in motion every possible defence measure. At the same time … there is no longer any possibility of preventing the mental apparatus from being flooded with large amounts of stimulus, and another problem arises instead – the problem of mastering the amounts of stimulus which have broken in and of binding them, in the psychical sense, so that they can be disposed of.
>
> (Freud 1920a: 301)

The compulsion to repeat was a rearguard action to manage the traumatic impact, Freud reverting to the original sense of trauma as a wounding intrusion from outside. Observed in children (who staged the distressing absence and return of the mother in obsessive games), Freud conjectured 'that children repeat unpleasurable experiences for the additional reason that they can master a powerful impression far more thoroughly by being active than they could by merely experiencing it passively' (Freud 1920a: 307). Repetition compulsion has become a cultural shorthand for the consequences of traumatic events: individuals, collectives and nations risk trapping themselves in cycles of uncomprehending repetition unless the traumatic event is translated from repetition to the healthy analytic process of 'working through' (see Freud 1914).

Third, Freud's late work, *Moses and Monotheism* (1939), was given over to Freud's speculations on the origin of Judaism by using the analogy of the effect of trauma on the individual for an entire race. Freud proposed that the Jews carried a hidden traumatic secret in their infancy, the murder of their founder and law-giver Moses. After a period of latency, the Mosaic law of the one vengeful god returned, reaffirming Judaism as a monotheistic religion, which for Freud was the ambiguous onset of civilization. Largely ungrounded speculations such as this on prehistory were typical of Victorian anthropology, but Freud pressed for a structure of explanation from a 'remote field', applying the traumatic neuroses of the individual to the group. 'In it we once more come upon the phenomenon of latency, the emergence of unintelligible manifestations calling for an explanation and an early, and later forgotten, event as a necessary determinant. We also find the characteristic of compulsion' (Freud 1939: 72). In one of his clearest summations of the aetiology of traumatic neurosis, Freud argued that the compulsions deriving from a forgotten traumatic kernel displayed 'great psychical intensity and at the same time exhibit a far-reaching independence of the organisation of the other mental processes'. They act, he claimed, 'like a State within a State' (Freud 1939: 76). This analogy evoked the prejudice against Jews as unassimilated foreign bodies in European nations, and *Moses and Monotheism* was explicitly marked by the disruptions to writing caused by the rise of Nazism in Germany, the invasion of Austria, and Freud's exile in London. The book has been read as a barely encrypted autobiographical reflection on expulsion and exile.

For Caruth, *Moses and Monotheism* 'can help us understand our own catastrophic era, as well as the difficulties of writing a history from within it' (Caruth 1996a: 12). Whilst Caruth emphasizes the aporia of a history driven by an inaccessible traumatic pre-history, general notions of collective cultural traumas derive in large part from Freud's speculations. Kai Erikson defined 'collective trauma' as 'a blow to the basic tissues of social life that damages the bonds attaching people together and impairs the prevailing sense of communality' (Erikson 1991: 460). 'The communal dimension of trauma', Erikson concludes, 'is one of its distinctive clinical signatures' (Erikson 1991: 471). There is a strong counter-tradition in sociology that objects to modelling societies on the individual psyche: starting with Maurice Halbwachs, and continued with work by Paul Connerton and Jeffrey Alexander, collective memory is regarded as a set of changing social practices rather than exteriorizations of psychic structures. Yet Freud's elision of neurotic and national history has been another important place where psychical trauma has become delimited and easily transmissible by analogy, providing a set of models in general circulation.

It is striking that whilst the trauma theory pursued by Felman, Caruth and others excavated and redeployed these models from the history of psychoanalysis, there is little acknowledgement in their work of the violent disputes that erupted around Freud in the 1980s and 1990s, arguments that fundamentally re-examined the contribution of psychoanalysis and inevitably coloured the reception of any theory of trauma tinged with Freudianism. In these years, Freud was never far from the controversies over the nature of traumatic memory. In 1984, as feminist theorists advanced the thesis that sexual abuse was widespread and structural within the patriarchal family, Jeffrey Masson published his interpretation of previously unpublished materials in the Freud archive. Masson's *Assault on Truth: Freud and Child Sexual Abuse* argued that Freud had come to the realization that all of his women patients had been sexually abused by their fathers. Although Freud had published these findings in 'The Aetiology of Hysteria' in 1896, Masson suggested that this paper had precipitated a professional and theoretical crisis, played out mainly in letters to his friend Wilhelm Fliess. Over the next two years Freud discarded the so-called 'seduction theory' for an account of the universal sexual *fantasies* of sons and daughters – the seed of the Oedipus complex that would be Freud's foundation for his psychodynamic theory of the universal development of the subject. In Masson's melodramatic account, Freud had come across a traumatic truth that he could not countenance and suppressed with a theory that turned actual abuse into structural fantasy if not fabrication. A significant strand of feminist cultural theory had relied on psychoanalysis, but Masson's Freud was a patriarch intent on suppressing the truth of women's experience. Masson's thesis generated an outpouring of heavily invested attacks and defences (see, for instance, Borch-Jacobsen 1996, A. Scott 1996, Malcolm 1997).

A corollary to this dispute began to develop in the late 1980s, when advocates of recovered memory therapies claimed to be unearthing pristine memories of repressed or dissociated childhood traumas many years after the fact in vast numbers of patients. This relied on the conviction that traumatic memory was preserved in pristine form outside conscious recall, but could be recovered complete with appropriate therapeutic intervention (called Recovered Memory Therapy, or RMT). Some claimed this to be based on Freud's model of the repression of traumatic memory. Recovered memories of abuse led to criminal proceedings and imprisonments, even changes to the statutes on limitation in some American states, the legal arguments often hinging on psychiatric expertise about the specific peculiarities of traumatic memory. The iconic legal case was the imprisonment of George Franklin in California in 1990, on the sole evidence of his daughter who had, with her therapist, recovered repressed memories of the murder of a childhood friend from 1969. Psychiatric expertise that confirmed the ability to recover repressed memories in pristine form was presented by Lenore Terr; equal and opposite psychiatric expertise that traumatic memories were unusually malleable and open to revision was presented by Elizabeth Loftus. Both published popular accounts of their involvement in medico-legal wranglings over recovered memory, part of a vast psychiatric literature (Loftus and Ketcham 1996, Terr 1994).

Already highly controversial, RMT techniques were thrown further into question by a series of cases that alleged to recover extensive networks of ritual or 'satanic' abuse. At its peak, passionate advocates claimed that 50,000 babies had been murdered in black magic rituals in America. Lawrence Wright attacked the basis of Paul Ingram's imprisonment for ritual abuse of his daughters in the *New Yorker* in 1993, his book *Remembering Satan* appearing a year later. Two high-profile cases in England claiming organized Satanic abuse collapsed in Rochdale in 1990 and Orkney in 1991. Meanwhile, at the outer fringes of this cultural imaginary, Whitley Strieber published his best-seller *Communion* at the height of these disputes, detailing his hypnotic recovery of profoundly traumatic memories of kidnap and sexual abuse by alien creatures. A slew of alien abduction narratives followed, including the globally successful television series, the *X Files* (see Luckhurst 1998). Because therapists were anxious not to deny the reality of traumatic testimony, and thus place themselves in the position of the reality-denying Freud, these efflorescences had to be upheld as literally true. This helped the cause of counter-movements like the False Memory Syndrome Foundation (set up in 1994), which argued that traumatic memory might be iatrogenic, the product of the very therapy used to treat it.

Freud's name was regularly if often inaccurately invoked in these disputes. The campaigning anti-Freudian, Frederick Crews, regarded recovered memory as the 'stepchild' of Freudianism and which helped confirm that 'psychoanalysis was the paradigmatic pseudoscience of our epoch' (Crews 1997: 14, 9). Crews' attacks tended to be scattergun, constantly shifting their ground. Freud might indeed have figured traumatic memory as a hidden truth that could be released from repression and brought to light. However, as Richard Terdiman has pointed out, there are two models of memory that exist in productive tension in Freud's work. The unconscious might seem to preserve pristine memories, but as soon as that 'eerie fixity' reached consciousness the traumatic memory 'exhibits a positively wanton disloyalty to the truth' (Terdiman 1993: 290). As early as 'Screen Memories', Freud recognized that childhood memories were highly malleable, subject to ceaseless revision and interpretation:

> It may indeed be questioned whether we have any memories at all *from* our childhood: memories *relating to* our childhood may be all that we possess. Our childhood memories show us our earliest years not as they were but as they appeared at later periods when the memories were aroused.
>
> (Freud 1899: 322)

The difficulty that recovered memories could be constructions or confabulations had already been anticipated by Freud. However, Crews' tendentious anti-Freudian journalism was backed by a host of serious scholarly and scientific interrogations into the founding premises of psychoanalysis at this time (Sulloway 1992, Kitcher 1992, Webster 1995). Reflecting the shift away from the kind of psychodynamic models that underpinned Freud's thinking, psychiatry began to legitimate itself by an appeal to the biochemistry and neuroendocrinology of the brain from the 1970s on. This biologization, Allan Young has argued, in fact helped produce the very term 'post-traumatic stress disorder', and certainly its key symptom clusters. In fundamental ways the scientific basis for PTSD was incompatible with psychoanalysis. Thus, whilst archivists and historians exploded the myths of the origins of psychoanalysis, the reorientation of psychiatry had also marginalized Freud.

Freud's pervasion of certain parts of the humanities and his effective absence in the social and natural sciences has led to strands of trauma theory that continue along parallel tracks with only the vaguest (usually contemptuous) awareness of each other. For Caruth at least, trauma is a challenge because it is an aporia that tests the limits of the psychoanalytic frame, even if Freud's work remains the central corpus through which to articulate the traumatic paradox. Yet, to her credit, there are signs that Caruth acknowledged the changing locus of authority. Her view of traumatic memory as a registration 'outside' registration in fact owed much to the neurobiological speculations of Bessel van der Kolk, whose work on the literal 'engraving of trauma' on the mind Caruth included in her *American Imago* special. Van der Kolk has attempted to isolate the physiological basis for the peculiar, eidetic intensity of traumatic memories and their location outside conscious recall by tracking the release of hormones in the brain at times of extreme stress. The hypothesis is that these discharges intensify emotional states (which can be re-experienced later as terrifying returns to the initial traumatic scene), but block cognitive processing and so are unavailable to narrative memory. Caruth suggests parallels to her own theorization of the unknowable fragment of history lodged in the unconscious. In a forceful critique, Ruth Leys has taken aim at Caruth's unlikely elision of poststructuralist literary theory, neurophysiology and psychoanalysis, arguing that Caruth and Van der Kolk reference circularly to each other's speculations in order to bolster up a naively literal model of trauma's psychic imprint. Leys places Caruth and Van der Kolk at the 'mimetic' pole of trauma theory, in which trauma is the unprocessed fragment of the thing itself. It is undermined by the 'antimimetic' pole, in which traumatic memory is always representational, available to memory, and therefore open to constant revision. The oscillation of these poles dominates the history of trauma back to its genealogical origins in the nineteenth century. For Leys, it means 'current debates over trauma are fated to end in an impasse' (Leys 2000: 305) since equal and opposite theories hold court. After this mauling, it might be tempting to discard Caruth, were it not that the length of Leys' critique acts as a strange sort of monument to its importance. It is still the work where the lines feeding notions of cultural trauma converge: the problem of aesthetics 'after Auschwitz'; the aporia of representation in poststructuralism; the diverse models of trauma developed by, and in the wake of, Freud.

In another 'genealogical' study, Wulf Kansteiner has charged that 'the most severe abuses of the trauma concept currently occur in the abstract, metaphorical language of cultural criticism' (Kansteiner 2004: 215). He takes aim at the 'aestheticiscd, morally and politically imprecise concept of cultural trauma', a loose notion that 'turns us all into accomplished survivors' (Kansteiner 2004: 194, 203). He examines a critical trajectory from Adorno through Lyotard to Caruth and into cultural studies that generalizes traumatic experiences and turns it into a problem of media signification: 'Just because trauma is inevitably a problem of representation in memory and communication does not imply the reverse, i.e. that problems of representation are always partaking in the traumatic' (Kansteiner 2004: 205). It is this reversal that has allowed trauma to saturate contemporary culture. Kansteiner's outrage is driven by his sense that there has been an appropriation of the epoch's inaugural historical trauma: the Holocaust. Any comparisons, any sense of trauma's transmissibility, its outward movement from the wound, turns brute historical fact into cheaply traded tokens of degraded 'survivor culture'. This exceptionalist stance has been a significant strand in writing on the Holocaust, understandably where the difficulty of witness has been harried by Holocaust revisionism. It is most often associated with the survivor Elie Wiesel's insistence on the ethical and political demands produced by unprecedented violence against the Jews. Yet exceptionalism has also become controversial, some claiming that the elevation of the Jewish catastrophe silences other genocidal acts and has been used for reactionary political ends. These debates need time and care (and are treated in the first chapter): here, the point is more about disciplinarity. Kansteiner privileges history over cultural studies, yet his genealogy is ignorant of the history of trauma in psychology and law since the 1860s, discourses that have shaped how Holocaust survival has been constructed. Without a multi-disciplinary knowledge, there can only be an unappetizing competition between disciplines to impose their specific conception of trauma. We need another model for understanding the tortuous history and bewildering contemporary extent of a paradigm that is an intrinsically inter-disciplinary conjuncture.

The dead metaphor in Kansteiner's essay is 'genealogy'. Foucault's proposal for a historical genealogy was to suspect 'all-encompassing and global theories' in order to attend to the 'discontinuous, particular, and local', all those 'historical contents that have been buried or masked in functional coherences or formal systematizations' (Foucault 2003: 6–7). He was also concerned to recover 'subjugated knowledges', that 'whole series of knowledges that have been disqualified as nonconceptual knowleges, as insufficiently elaborated knowledges' (Foucault 2003: 7). This might be more rigorously pursued. But even more useful for this project is Bruno Latour's attempts to rethink science and its history as inextricably connected to culture, politics and society. Latour's theory does not put knowledge into hierarchies but sees knowledges and practices as forming complicated networks. A successful statement can be measured by how many links or associations it makes, not only within the rigours of its own discipline but far beyond it too, as it loops through different knowledges, institutions, practices, social, political and cultural forums. A scientific concept therefore succeeds through its heterogeneity rather than its purity, 'the number of points linked, the length and strength of the linkage' (Latour 1987: 201). In this network, Latour prefers to call a concept a *knot* because it helps to visualize the many heterogeneous elements it binds together. The history of such a knot would be an act of unravelling, revealing how the knot is 'intensely connected to a much larger repertoire of resources' (Latour 1999: 108).

It seems to me that the rise of the concept of trauma suggests itself as an exemplary conceptual knot whose successful permeation must be understood by the impressive range of elements that it ties together and which allows it to travel to such diverse places in the network of knowledge. Even more relevantly, I see trauma as one of those distinctive 'hybrid assemblages' that Latour suggests confront us in the contemporary world. Increasingly, we have to deal with 'tangled objects', imbroglios that mess up our fundamental categories of subject and object, human and non-human, society and nature. Latour's examples include ozone holes, global warming, 'mad cow disease' or immuno-deficiency diseases – things that seem to emerge somewhere between the natural and the man-made and that tangle up questions of science, law, technology, capitalism, politics, medicine and risk. These have 'no clear boundaries, no sharp separation between their own hard kernel and their environment' (Latour 2004: 24). Fundamentally, they are not yet settled as 'matters of fact'; they are contentious precisely because the facts cannot be decided by competing claims, where facts are enrolled for different kinds of social and political investments. Instead, these tangled objects 'first appear as matters of concern, as new entities that provoke perplexity and thus speech in those who gather around them, and argue over them' (Latour 2004: 66). Rival theories proliferate around the notion of trauma because it is one of these 'tangled objects' whose enigmatic causation and strange effects that bridge the mental and the physical, the individual and collective, and use in many diverse disciplinary languages consequently provoke perplexed, contentious debate. Rather than offer another invested polemic, I propose we need to begin by unravelling the complex elements that have been knotted into the notion of trauma.

To this end, the first half of this book is a historical genealogy that tries to make sense of the divergent resources that have been knotted into the concept of trauma across its peculiarly disrupted, discontinuous history. This genealogy will track the multi-disciplinary origin of trauma in the nineteenth century through industrialization and bureaucratization, law and psychology, military and government welfare policies, before suggesting that our current conjuncture begins to knot these diverse and discontinuous elements together in the identity politics of the 1970s. Tracing this history means it becomes easier to discern the strands that thread through the cultural materials examined in Part II. I want to make the strong claim that cultural narratives have been integral not just in consolidating the idea of post-traumatic subjectivity, but have actively helped form it since 1980. The transmissibility of trauma has meant that many aspects of cultural life in advanced capitalist societies have become part of the imbroglio of the post-traumatic self. In four chapters, I examine literary and popular fiction, the revaluation of memoir around extreme experience, debates on the photography of atrocity and the way narrative disruptions in cinema convey traumatic experience. Visual culture in particular can demonstrate how the impact of culture can alter psychiatric diagnostics: the ideas of flashbulb memories or intrusive flashbacks have emerged in psychiatry long after the grammar and narrative possibilities of these notions have been worked out in cultural forms. I have deliberately sought to extend the range of cultural reference from the relatively narrow body of texts that typically feature in cultural trauma theory: I wanted to move beyond Modernist aesthetics of fragmentation and aporia and into popular culture to demonstrate not just pervasiveness of trauma but also the reiteration of traumatic subjectivity in different kinds of register. In a brief afterword, I suggest the ways in which the trauma paradigm might meet its limits.

Part I
Aetiology

1 The genealogy of a concept

> The history of a concept is not wholly and entirely that of its progressive refinement … but that of its various fields of constitution and validity, that of its successive rules of use, that of the many theoretical contexts in which it developed and matured.
>
> (Foucault 1974: 4)

This chapter will attempt to follow this programme, aware that trauma offers particular challenges in bringing together far-flung and heterogeneous resources. Authorities in the field have recognized that 'a continuous history would be impossible to establish', since historicism puts into question 'the idea of a single, uniform, transhistorically valid concept of psychological trauma' (Micale and Lerner 2001: 24, 25). For Judith Herman, the history of trauma is *itself* traumatized, being singularly marked by 'episodic amnesia': 'Periods of active investigation have alternated with periods of oblivion. Repeatedly in the past century, similar lines of inquiry have been taken up and abruptly abandoned, only to be rediscovered later' (Herman 1994: 7). Foucault's proposal, that histories need to be aware that concepts emerge across dispersed sites and in discontinuous ways, comes ready built into trauma. The challenge is to construct something coherent from the different elements that need to be put into play.

What follows is in five sections. I want to put some flesh on the truism that trauma is a concept that can only emerge within modernity, tracing it as an effect of the rise, in the nineteenth century, of the technological and statistical society that can generate, multiply and quantify the 'shocks' of modern life. This broad context is the frame that produces the conditions of emergence for trauma in specific disciplines from about 1870 to the Second World War: law, psychiatry and industrialized warfare. After elaborating the notions of trauma that develop from these distinct, but overlapping knowledges, the last section will examine how these languages were reformulated in the linkage of trauma and the politics of identity from the 1960s, looking particularly at the formation of 'survivor syndromes' for victims of nuclear war and Nazi persecution, the politicization of illness in Vietnam war veterans, and the transformed understanding of women's experience by feminism.

Trauma and modernity

Trauma is typically held to be 'responsive to and constitutive of "modernity"' (Micale and Lerner 2001: 10). 'Modernity', Seltzer confirms, 'has come to be understood under the sign of the wound': 'the modern subject has become inseparable from the categories of shock and trauma' (Seltzer 1997: 18). Modernity, often loosely dated to the rise of the modern nation state in the eighteenth century, is identified with a series of contradictory transformations of the rela- tions of so-called traditional society. The fixity of place, the dense network of social relations and local traditions typical of the village, for instance, is dislocated by a new orientation of the individual to an abstract, national and increasingly international space. Similarly, the local rhythms of time are replaced by a stan- dardized time that routinizes labour time and co-ordinates national economies and transport systems. Individuals are 'disembedded' from cyclical rituals and tra- ditions and experience a release from narrow expectations that is at once liberat- ing and angst-ridden. Self-identity, in other words, is uprooted from traditional verities and subject to a kind of permanent revolution: all that is solid melts into air (Berman 1983).

The classic site of modernity is the city, which by the end of the nineteenth century had swallowed the majority of the British population, turning an agrar- ian nation into an urban one. In these sprawling, artificial terrains, divorced from nature, commentators began to worry about the overstimulation and exhaustion caused by prolonged immersion in the city. 'New machines had come in to make life still more complicated', Grant Allen wrote in 1894: 'sixpenny telegrams, Bell and Edison, submarine cables, evening papers, perturbations coming in from all sides incessantly; suburbs growing, the hubbub increasing, Metropolitan railways, trams, bicycles, innumerable' (Allen 1894: 119–20). Walter Benjamin's account of Paris as the capital of the nineteenth century explicitly theorized urban experi- ence as 'a series of shocks and collisions', regarding the overwhelming rush of street transport, advertising, telephones, films and crowds as subjecting 'the human sensorium to a complex kind of training', in effect an engineering of new urban selves (Benjamin 1973: 171). Explicitly relying on Freud's ideas of the shock that overwhelms psychic defences, Benjamin saw Paris as a city of traumatic encounters, rewriting the very notion of experience. Charles Baudelaire was Paris' great poet because he was a traumatophile, seeking out the shocking encounter, traversing the streets like a fencer, welcoming every shock and parry.

The intrinsic ambivalences of modernity – progress and ruin, liberation and constraint, individualization and massification – are perhaps best concretized by technology. Technology can be seen as the instrumental vehicle for the liberations of modern space-time, but it can also be the 'demonic' force that reduces humans to 'the conscious limbs of the automaton,' as Marx evocatively put it (Marx 1980: 141). Humans might regard technology as the prosthetic extension of their will to mastery, yet nearly every new technology hailed in this way also attracts a com- mentary that regards it as a violent assault on agency and self-determination. This ambivalent commentary nearly always invokes the traumatic. The mythic origin of the cinematograph has an apocryphal story of audiences running from the Lumière brothers' film of an oncoming train, prompting Tom Gunning to call early cinema 'the cinema of attractions, which envisioned cinema as a series of visual shocks' (Gunning 1999: 820). Similarly, the global network of telegraphy and telephony, the 'nerves of empire', was soon haunted by the spectral voices of the dead that travelled along the wire at the same speed as the electrical spark (Luckhurst 2002). It should come as no surprise, then, that the general scholarly consensus is that the origin of the idea of trauma was inextricably linked to the expansion of the railways in the 1860s.

The railway was the icon of British modernity: widely held to exemplify engineering genius, it also heralded what contemporaries called 'the annihilation of space and time', compressing travel length and distance. Whilst British clock-time was eventually standardized across the country in order to integrate the railway timetable, it remained a dangerous and chaotic industry. From the very first public run of Stephenson's Rocket in September 1830, death attended the operation of the railway: the MP William Huskisson was struck on the tracks. With the 1871 Railways Regulation Act, records of fatal accidents were properly reported and for the next thirty years, there were never less than 200 passenger deaths a year, with the peak in 1874 of 758 deaths (Bartrip and Burman 1983).

Wolfgang Schivelbusch has influentially suggested that the effect of 'the industrialisation of the means of transport' was 'to alter the consciousness of passengers: they developed a new set of perceptions' (Schivelbusch 1986: 14). This extended beyond the denatured terrain now processed through the window of the 'machine ensemble', for the railway accident was the site of the 'first attempt to explain industrial traumata' (Schivelbusch 1986: 24, 136) as it exposed the travelling middle and upper classes to the kinds of technological violence previously restricted to factories. The speed of collisions often rendered these accidents particularly gruesome events. Yet even those who survived without apparent physical injury began to report strange effects on their nerves. In 1862, *The Lancet* (the journal of the British Medical Association) carried a supplement on 'The Influence of Railway Travelling on Public Health', which included medical speculations that travelling at speed might have concussive effect on the nervous system, whilst the violent jarring of the body in an accident might induce permanent but invisible damage. Because the fevered expansion of the railways from the 1840s was driven by free market companies, the medical question of injury was always also a legal question of liability. Could those who bore no physical mark nevertheless claim damages for nervous debility that often began to develop some time after the accident? In 1862, a Mr Shepherd was awarded £700 in compensation for the detrimental effects on his ability to conduct business, after testifying that since his involvement in a railway accident in 1858 his 'chief complaint' was 'a feeling of nervous depression, and particularly that the countenances of his fellow-passengers, with terrified eyes, would come before him whenever he attempted to do any reading or writing' (cited Harrington 2003: 212). Thus was the medico-legal notion of 'railway spine' inaugurated. This is what Charles Dickens suffered after his 'terribly destructive accident' in 1865, in which he assisted the badly injured at a bridge derailment, and later rescued his manuscript of *Our Mutual Friend* (Dickens 1865: 799). Dickens suffered all manner of subjective disturbances in the following months: he wrote 'I am not quite right within, but believe it to be an effect of the railway shaking' (cited Trimble 1981, 28). This has led some critics to regard Dickens as a victim of PTSD (Matus 2001). In the 1870s, *The Lancet* alarmingly announced that 'we may be said to have supped full of railway horrors, and railway travelling has become almost insupportable to persons of a nervous temperament' (cited Harrington 1994: 17). Later still, Max Nordau decried modernity's degeneration as a result of nervous overstimulation, including in his principal causes 'the little shocks of railway travelling, not perceived by consciousness' and the mental overload of 'every scene we perceive through the window of the flying express' (Nordau 1895: 39).

Railway spine was the first instance of a theory of trauma that became contentious because rival theories placed it at opposing ends of the spectrum from physical to psychical etiologies. The surgeon John Erichsen published a series of lectures in 1866 on railway spine which was successful in linking the term to a physical theory. The violent jolt of an accident resulted in concussion of the spine:

> a certain state of the spinal cord occasioned by external violence; a state that is independent of, and usually, but not necessarily, uncomplicated by any obvious lesion of the vertebral column ... – a condition that is supposed to depend upon a shake or jar received by the cord, in consequence of which its intimate organic structure may be more or less deranged, and by which its functions are greatly disturbed.
>
> (Erichsen 1875: 15)

In the absence of certain medical knowledge about the physiology of the nervous system, Erichsen speculated that jarring caused molecular changes in the spinal fluid, yet he also resorted to analogy, as

> when a magnet is struck a heavy blow with a hammer, the magnetic force is jarred, shaken, or concussed out of the horse-shoe ... . So, if the spine is badly jarred, shaken or concussed by a blow or shock ... we find that the nervous force is to a certain extent shaken out of the man, and that he has in some way lost nerve-power.
>
> (Erichsen 1875: 156–7)

The case histories presented offered portraits of disordered memory, disturbed sleep and frightful dreams, and various types of paralysis, melancholia and impotence, with a particular emphasis on the sudden loss of business sense. The most 'remarkable' detail for Erichsen was the belated onset of these symptoms: 'at the time of the occurrence of the injury the sufferer is usually quite unconscious that any serious accident has happened to him' (Erichsen 1875: 157). The physical and mental effects seemed to ramify and worsen over time: Erichsen's prognosis for amelioration was pessimistic.

Erichsen's organic basis appealed to simple mechanical cause and effect and gained popular and professional currency, but it was also subject to critique. The most sustained attack was by Herbert Page, who regarded Erichsen's evidence as 'lamentable' and despaired that '"concussion of the spine" is used almost indiscriminately both in and outside the medical profession' (Page 1883: 74). Page pointed to studies of post-mortem pathology that could present no evidence in support of organic lesions. Instead, Page tried to shift railway spine onto a different premise: 'we shall see that the course, history, and general symptoms indicate some functional disturbance of the whole nervous balance or tone rather than structural damage to any organ of the body' (Page 1883: 143). The functional disorders were the product of the profound shock of the collision:

> The vastness of the destructive forces, the magnitude of the results, the imminent danger to the lives of numbers of human beings, and the hopelessness of escape from the danger, give rise to emotions which in themselves are quite sufficient to produce shock.
>
> (Page 1883: 148)

To Page, this also explained how symptoms arrived belatedly: 'Warded off in the first place by the excitement of the scene, the shock is gathering, in the very delay itself' (Page 1883: 148). This was Page's formulation of what he called *nervous shock*. Erichsen had in fact already acknowledged shock in the considerably expanded edition of his lectures in 1875, conceding that

> terror has much to do with its production. It must be remembered that railway accidents have this peculiarity, that they come upon the sufferers instantaneously and without warning, or with but a few seconds for preparation, and that the utter helplessness of a human being in the midst of the great masses in motion renders these accidents peculiarly terrible.
>
> (Erichsen 1875: 196)

Yet Erichsen regarded these functional conditions as a distinct but lesser type of response to accidents; organic impacts still occurred, and were the more serious illnesses. In contrast, Page saw all of these nervous disorders as resulting from 'purely psychical causes' (Page 1883: 148).

If Page seems the closer to modern conceptions, it is important to realize that his insistence that the psychical traumas of railway accidents were forms of hysteria came from transparently pecuniary motives. Page had been the surgeon for the London and North Western Railway Company for nine years when he wrote his book. Erichsen's argument had to be defeated because an organic origin for railway spine nearly always resulted in huge payments for damages to those caught up in railway accidents, and this was being worryingly extended to those without any visible physical injury. To associate nervous shock with hysteria was to equate it with a shameful, effeminate disorder, often dismissed as a form of disease *imitation* (what was called 'neuromimesis') or malingering. Accident victims who presented these symptoms could now be suspected of feigning illness for financial advantage. After a chapter devoted to spotting cases of 'Malingering', Page proposed that the prospect of legal compensation was fuelling and prolonging forms of hysteria:

> the knowledge that compensation is a certainty for the injuries received, tends, almost from the first moment of illness, to colour the course and aspect of the case, with each succeeding day to become part and parcel of the injury in the patient's mind.
>
> (Page 1883: 255)

Eric Caplan has detailed the rise of the National Association of Railway Surgeons in America in 1888 as an organization devoted to contesting any organic basis to railway spine, since rail companies were losing millions in law cases where they suspected juries were already biased to favour individual victims over large railroad corporations in an era of anti-trust agitation. Railway spine, one leading figure complained in 1894, had been 'invented by one of the most clever English surgeons', yet 'it has baffled both railway surgeons and counsel, and, vampire-like, sucked more blood of the corporate bodies and railway companies than all other cases combined' (cited Caplan 1995: 412). But Page's argument should not be dismissed as laissez-faire Victoriana: the term 'accident neurosis' was proposed in 1961 as a specific syndrome 'motivated by hopes of financial and other rewards, and which shows considerable improvement following the settlement of compensation' (Mayou 1996: 399). In 1981, Michael Trimble's historical study, *Post-Traumatic Neurosis*, foregrounded the fact that psychiatric debates 'represent the veneer of a multi-million pound enterprise', and included the chapter 'The Central Issue – Malingering'. Guides for forensic assessment of cases still outline the means to detect so-called 'factitious PTSD'.

'Railway spine' names a conjuncture of body and machine, the violent collision of technological modernity and human agency. This inaugural version of trauma is also intrinsically modern because it is, from the first, a *medico-legal* problem, which is to say it is defined in and through the institutions and discourses marking the rise of the professional society in the nineteenth century. Rival experts would henceforth seek to define the protean signs of trauma in their specific disciplinary languages, partly recognizing that the very act of definition contributed to the mobility of symptoms. I need to trace in some detail how the legal and psychiatric disciplines have formulated trauma, sometimes in concert but just as frequently in a curious kind of symbiotic conflict.

Before this, there is one significant way in which the modernity of trauma has not yet been grasped. Whilst many historians of trauma start on the railway, it is important not to fetishize these technological origins. To describe a machine, as Latour says, is not just a technical matter: it is also to describe the social relations that are bound into it (see Latour 1987). The railway accident was the encounter of the general public with the consequences of industrialization that had largely been concealed within the factory system. Early agitators for reform, like Robert Dale Owen, might describe streets full of mutilated cotton workers, but these were out of sight of metropolitan governments and opinion. The figures for much of the nineteenth century for railway fatalities were only for passengers, since rail worker deaths and injuries were initially regarded as the occupational hazard of working in high-risk environments. Workers 'chose' this work, and the pay allegedly reflected the risk, this so-called *volenti* principle barring any right to claim from employers for injury. However, the English High Court heard its first case for a claim for industrial accident in 1836, and this began a series of reforms throughout the century that eventually resulted in the Workmen's Compensation Act of 1897. The Act was intended to introduce a general form of insurance to take the sting from the new union co-ordination of negligence claims against employers. Initially it involved only a narrow selection of industries considered vital to the national interest, establishing 'work injury victims as an elite group, analogous to war pensioners, eligible for special benefits' (Bartrip 1985: 163). The range of workers was extended in 1906, and progressively extended into the 1920s. The German state had established its own Imperial Insurance Office for industrial injury in 1884, and most European states followed over the next twenty years. In England, this agitation on behalf of what Earl Fitzwilliam called 'the wounded soldiers of industry' was a significant element of the transformation of a Victorian laissez-faire economy into the beginning of a national insurance system, and thus the modern welfare state (Bartrip and Burman 1983: 5). This is the rise of what Francois Ewald calls the 'Providential State', where society is 'constructed out of myriad efforts at the administrative and personal levels to remove, predict, and repair the damages of dysfunction' (cited Rabinbach 1996: 50). The industrial accident is the juncture around which a new kind of state emerges, since it brings together 'attorneys, judges, lawmakers, government officials, medical experts, and the insurance specialists', with claims adjustors, health and safety officials and company assessors, and other subsets of expertise emerging later (Rabinbach 1996: 51). The accident was where the social, economic, political and bureaucratic elements of the state met up to determine and contest the traumatic costs of industrialization.

The key change this legislation produced was a shift from liability to an insurance system where responsibility was not an issue. Inside what Karl Figlio evocatively names the 'accident cosmology' there is no good or bad intention and therefore no blame (Figlio 1985: 197). Instead, 'social risk was considered to be a consequence of industrial modernity, recognizing that impersonal forces rather than individual wills were often the determinants of a person's destiny' (Rabinbach 1996: 58–9). Inevitably, a state-run system also resulted in fears that the intrinsically lazy working classes would exploit the system and rapidly produce a large and permanently invalided population on state salaries. By the 1890s French government experts discussed *les maladies simulées*, the Germans *Rentenneurose* or 'pension neurosis' – new forms of that alleged accident neurosis of the kind that had angered the railway surgeons.

If social relations were reorganized around the accident, it is possible to consider the accident itself as a product of modernity. From the broadest purview, trauma develops from the rise of the statistical society, those various forms of calculus that helped to process and begin to control the chaotic explosion of the industrial revolution in nineteenth century England, Europe and America. Statistical analysis of the economic and social activities of populations, Theodore Porter argues, helped marshal ways of conceiving a large-scale social entity, and was particularly good at 'uncovering causal relationships where the individual events are either concealed from view or are highly variable and subject to a host of influences' (Porter 1986: 3). From the local chaos of apparently free agents, statistics abstract larger orders and regularities of behaviour: society becomes a calculus of probabilities. Probabilism 'implies simply that our knowledge does not permit prediction, though there may be no exceptions to complete causality in the world' (Porter 1986: 12). This causality implied the possibility of rational management, reform and improvement of society, and this drove the enlightenment ambitions of the statistical movement. Yet as statistical measurements improved, so did the record of the puzzling and damaging consequences of modernity, not just of poverty, inequality and disease, but records of industrial and technological accidents. The reporting of factory accidents was uneven, and only marginal to the reformist Factory Acts of the 1840s, but better enforcement of the reporting and collating of accident statistics amplified concerns from the 1870s. Roger Cooter has proposed that late Victorian Britain was transformed by a new consciousness of the accident, which prompted the rise of the volunteer ambulance and first-aid movements. This was a quasi-military attempt to control the hazards of the city, where accidents became 'symbols of the omnipresent potential dangers of the socially destabilized late-Victorian urban context' (Cooter 1997: 123). This collation made accidents appear to be rather paradoxical events. On the one hand, they were obviously anomalous and disruptive intrusions into the norms of the factory or transport system. On the other, they were also, as statistical probabilities showed, entirely calculable. They were unforeseeably foreseeable. As government reforms, health and safety regulations and standardization (for instance, of railway timetables) mitigated the worst possibilities of industrialized modernity, these improvements of course increased the sense of cataclysm when the inevitable accident struck somewhere in the system. If subjectivity is constituted within increasingly complex technological environments, then when 'the technological base collapses, the feeling of habituation and security collapses with it' (Schivelbusch 1986: 162). The accident is therefore historically constituted by the specific kinds of risky environments typical of modernity. Trauma is inextricably tied to this accident cosmology: the psychological consequences of the accidents and disasters continue to be a substantial area of current research. Legal scholars, too, have recognized that in modern disasters 'the more complex, interactive, and opaque the system, the greater the number of latent errors it is likely to contain', making causation and attribution difficult to compute (Wells *et al.* 2000: 500). The professional discourses of modernity may shape how trauma is conceived: it does not mean that they can capture it in definitive formulations.

The law of 'nervous shock'

For Karl Figlio, the accident could only come to exist 'in a cosmology in which the common view of personal relationships had become contractual, so that obligations and injury could be seen as terms of contract' (Figlio 1985: 183). The accident must immediately invoke questions of responsibility and liability (Campbell 1997). It is for this reason that negligence claims in the law of tort have provided the dominant (although not only) way in which law has interacted with, and fundamentally helped constitute, contemporary notions of trauma. PTSD entered official psychiatric diagnostics in 1980, as we have seen. In 1989 the so-called Zeebrugge Arbitration (following the sinking of a passenger ferry outside the port) was the first case in England in which it was 'agreed on all sides that the courts would now accept that PTSD was a recognized psychiatric injury for which compensation would be recoverable at law without proof of any actual physical harm' (Pugh and Trimble 1993: 426). Yet by 1998 the English Law Commission issued a lengthy report, *Liability for Psychiatric Illness,* in recognition of the legal con-fusion and injustices in recent cases concerned with PTSD and other forms of trauma. The present law was deemed 'unsatisfactory', yet after extensive consul-tation the commissioners concluded that 'we do not think that medical knowledge has advanced to a sufficiently mature stage for the complete codification of lia-bility for psychiatric illness' (Law Commission 1998: 3). They eschewed statutory legislation in favour of allowing the law 'to develop incrementally' case by case (Law Commission 1998: 3). Case law has been the means by which the notion of 'nervous shock' developed over the past one hundred years, but it was the judge-ments in these cases that had produced the sense of arbitrariness in determining psychiatric liability, and which prompted the Law Commission report in the first place. The irresolution of legal discourse around nervous shock is central to any understanding of the contemporary trauma paradigm.

The purpose of this section, since I am very far from being a legal expert, is merely to try to outline the significant tort case law which developed the notion of 'nervous shock' and changing conceptions of psychiatric harm. I will then briefly turn from the civil law to look at the interaction of criminal law and theo-ries of trauma. Both areas of the law show the pressure produced with changing psychological conceptions of trauma in the 1980s and 1990s.

In 1888 an employee at a railway crossing in Australia mistakenly waved a horse and buggy through a barrier, nearly causing a collision with the oncoming train. A legal case was mounted on behalf of Mrs Coultas, who claimed that the severe fright of the incident had induced her later miscarriage. The judgement (*Coultas* v. *Victorian Railway Commissioners* 1888) initially found for the claimant, but was challenged all the way to the London Privy Council, which oversaw the colo-nial courts. Here, the judgement was overturned on the basis that there had been no physical injury and therefore no proof of direct causation from the incident at the railway to the later miscarriage. The appeal judges explicitly stated that the case had to be overturned, otherwise the field would be opened to a mass of 'imaginary claims' (see Mendelson 1997). This is the argument familiar from dis-putes over 'railway spine', and the law has in general been reluctant to allow dam-ages for 'invisible' psychological impacts (where causation cannot be proved by physical evidence) in order to prevent, in that perennial legal phrase, opening the floodgates of litigation.

In very similar circumstances to *Coultas* thirteen years later, a carriage was driven through a pub window in East London, causing the publican's wife severe shock and the premature birth of an 'idiot' son. This time the case, *Dulieu* v. *White* (1901), produced a landmark judgement: 'Damages which result from a nervous shock occasioned by fright unaccompanied by any actual impact may be recoverable in an action for negligence if physical injury has been caused to the plaintiff' (669). No distinction was to be made between actual impact and *fear* of impact if the physical result was the same. In passing judgement, Judge Kennedy commented explicitly on the distinction between 'nervous' and 'mental' that should have been made in *Coultas*. '"Nervous" is probably the more correct epithet where terror operates through parts of the physical organism to produce bodily illness', he said, whilst 'merely mental pain unaccompanied by any injury to the person cannot sustain an action of this kind' (672–3). Any psychological impact, in other words, had to be proven to have been stamped on the body to reach the legal threshold. To this limit on claims was added that the nervous shock could only arise from fear of immediate injury to oneself, not others, and that defendants were not bound 'to guard against an injurious result which would only happen to a person of peculiar sensitiveness' (686). This introduced what later became the 'standard of susceptibility', the intensity of nervous shock being judged normatively as an event that could not be endured by those of 'ordinary fortitude' or 'customary phlegm' (*Bourhill* v. *Young* 1943).

Dulieu established nervous shock both as a recognized illness and a strict measure of compensable traumatic impact. The limit on those who can claim nervous shock to the primary victim of the incident has been consistently challenged, and fitfully extended ever since. In *Hambrook* v. *Stokes Bros* (1925), a lorry careering out of control had left a mother so terrified for the safety of her children that she became ill and later died. A court ruled that fear for others could be grounds for compensation, if the defendant's action was reasonably foreseeable in producing such shock. The ruling therefore added secondary victims to those involved in the primary traumatic event. A restriction came with *Bourhill* v. *Young*: a woman who heard a traffic accident but did not see the impact, only the blood on the pavement, was judged to have no right to claim for nervous shock and subsequent miscarriage, as the defendant could not reasonably foresee her reaction (the predominance of miscarriage cases likely reflects the anxiety to demonstrate nervous shock had bodily rather than 'merely mental' consequences, but also of course feminizes the shock reaction). *Bourhill* v. *Young* remained a guiding judgement for over twenty years.

The central modern case determining questions of relationship and proximity to the traumatic event was *McLoughlin* v. *O'Brian* (1983). In this case, the mother was two miles away from an accident involving her husband and children. One child died at the scene, and she rushed to the remainder of her family at the hospital. Her subsequent nervous shock was held to be the result of witnessing her surviving family still covered in blood and dirt from the accident. The claim for damages was successful by extending the arena of nervous shock from the accident to the 'immediate aftermath'. This extension in time was bought at the expense of a reconfirmation of what Lord Wilberforce called 'control mechanisms' on who might claim, since 'defendants cannot be expected to compensate the world at large' (cited Giliker and Beckwith 2000: 88). Fear for others had to be fear for the death, injury or imperilment of those with whom one has a 'close tie'; bystanders, the judgement held, 'must be assumed to be possessed of sufficient fortitude to enable them to endure the calamities of modern life' (Law Commission 1998: 26).

This is the barest outline of the case law (see Giliker and Beckwith 2000 and Weir 2000 for more complete surveys). Case law has come to identify five tests for a successful claim: the event must be shocking; it must have been reasonably foreseeable that the defendant's action would cause nervous shock; the shock must breach the defences of 'ordinary fortitude'; it must produce a recognizable psychiatric illness beyond normal emotions of pain and grief (grief has to become 'pathological' to be considered an illness, as decided in *Vernon* v. *Bosley No. 1* (1997)); and secondary victims must reach strict thresholds of proximity in time and space to the event, as well as proximity of relationship to the primary victims. It is evident that whilst legal definition is propped on psychiatric expertise these tests are normative and restrictive in ways that abandon psychological understanding of trauma. Trauma is marked by strange, apparently non-causal temporal development; it can move outwards in an unpredictable proliferation from the original wound; its limits are difficult to draw. Law is determined to restrict this proliferation and insist on causation, always intent on preventing the floodgates of litigation from opening. Yet, in relying on PTSD as the privileged 'recognisable psychiatric illness', the law does not rest on a stable definition of trauma. Since 1980, PTSD has not been a fixed but a very mobile term, progressively extending the types of symptoms and categories of sufferers outwards from the initial restrictions on what constituted the traumatic event. This has been partly constitutive and partly reflective of very broad notions of 'cultural trauma', a term virtually impossible to reconcile with legal definitions. Yet the restrictive law of nervous shock came into conflict with this culture as awareness of traumatic responses entered into wider currency. Contradictory legal judgements have marked the traumatic consequences of one key event: the Hillsborough disaster.

In 1989, 95 Liverpool Football Club spectators were killed and 400 injured in the Hillsborough football ground. Scenes of the crowd being crushed against metal fences were broadcast live on television and radio, and repeated on news broadcasts. Claims for physical injuries were settled quickly, since the police admitted negligence in allowing too many fans into the stadium. In *Alcock* v. *Chief Constable of South Yorkshire* (1992), sixteen claimants brought an action for nervous shock and consequent psychiatric illness. Fifteen were relatives of those killed or injured at Hillsborough. The judgement found against the claimants on a number of points. Secondary victim status was strictly applied: hence, the judges thought relationships to spouses, parents and children could be presumed to be a close tie, whilst those of siblings, grandparents or uncles and aunts were not, and such claimants would be required to demonstrate close ties. For one Hillsborough claimant, watching a brother die might have been a trauma, but was not recoverable at law. Questions of proximity were also narrowly invoked. In terms of time, the 'immediate aftermath' was limited to an hour, so that the viewing and identification of the bodies starting eight hours later was deemed to be outside the limit of the event (bodies had also been prepared for viewing, so were held to be less shocking). In terms of space, the necessary proximity ruled out anyone who had seen the event in a mediated way, via television or by any third party report, but also distinguished between different areas inside the football ground. Lord Oliver insisted on the shock test, and therefore denied the claim because 'their discovery of the death of loved ones was gradual rather than sudden' (Law Commission 1998: 35–6). Wilberforce also concurred: 'There remains … just because "shock" in its nature is capable of affecting so wide a range of people, a real need for the law to place some limitation on the extent of admissible claims' (cited Pugh and Trimble 1993: 428). In the meantime, the judgement *McFarlane* v. *EE Caledonia* (1994), a result of the Piper Alpha oil platform fire, effectively barred claims of 'bystanders' from making nervous shock claims. *Page* v. *Smith* (1996), another case concerning psychiatric illness resulting from a car accident, was a landmark in effectively establishing that where the prospect of physical harm existed, psychiatric damage was also reasonably foreseeable and did not have to be proven separately. This parity of bodily and mental harm was restricted to primary victims only, reaffirming a clear distinction between primary victims (who have a reasonable fear for their physical safety) and secondary victims (who are only proximate to the traumatic event).

The perception that *Alcock* was a mechanical and cruel application of the law intensified when six police officers on duty at Hillbsborough claimed for post-traumatic stress in *Frost* v. *Chief Constable of South Yorkshire Police* (1997). At trial, the case was dismissed with the argument that 'traumatized professional rescuers not placed in personal peril by the accident were not to be assisted by the common law' (Mullany and Handford 1997: 411). However, the Court of Appeal by a majority upheld their claim. The ruling found in favour of officers who had tried to administer first aid by the metal pens or been in the ground, but also for those who had handled bodies in hospitals and temporary mortuaries after the event and at some distance. The judgement therefore extended claims of PTSD to 'rescuers' (four of the officers) and employees (the other two), where their duties had brought them within range of foreseeable psychiatric injury through employer negligence. The outrage of the relatives previously barred from claims resulted in the House of Lords overturning this Appeal Court ruling, and the case of the officers was reconsidered in *White* v. *Chief Constable of South Yorkshire* (1999). This judgement prompted further refinements to the categories of primary and secondary victimhood, and within that to the special cases of employees, 'unwitting agents' and rescuers. The judgement found against the officers, on the grounds that they were not primary victims, and had also failed to meet the tests for secondary status. The ruling, over-ruling and then over-over-ruling of this case demonstrated how confusing the law had become in establishing the legal parameters of a large-scale traumatic event.

In his *Alcock* judgement, Lord Oliver confessed that the law on psychiatric harm was not 'entirely satisfactory or logically defensible' (1992: 418). Commentators have been harsher: Pugh and Trimble have called the law a lottery 'in which some bystanders get spattered with blood and others with money' (Pugh and Trimble 1993: 429). It was these confusions and concerns that prompted the Law Commission report in 1998. Their reform principally focused on addressing the public perception of arbitrary and cruel divisions within secondary victimhood status, arguing for legislation that a claimant

> who suffers a reasonably foreseeable psychiatric illness as a result of the death, injury or imperilment of a person with whom he or she has a close tie of love and affection, should be entitled to recover damages ... regardless of the plaintiff's closeness (in time and space) to the accident or its aftermath or the means by which the plaintiff learns of it.
>
> (Law Commission 1998: 89)

This eased the offence of having to demonstrate a relationship was strong enough to result in a traumatic impact. It also considerably expanded the range of claimants, as the commissioners considered 'the class of relationships in which the tie is presumed is currently drawn too narrowly' (Law Commission 1998: 91). Even so the report had to counter the inevitable 'floodgates' argument, and included a projected calculation of higher insurance premiums as the result of any legal change, arguing for only a limited financial impact. Society could insure itself against wider traumatic impacts for only a two to five per cent increase in premiums.

The strongest recommendation was for the abolition of nervous shock as a test of psychiatric illness. Nervous shock, over one hundred years old and embedded in Victorian reactions to a new technological modernity, had remained important in law into the 1990s, again producing apparently cruel judgements. In *Sion* v. *Hampstead Health Authority* (1994), for instance, a mother's claim for psychiatric illness was disallowed because her son's condition deteriorated slowly into coma and eventual death: it was not speedy enough to be shocking. Nervous shock had been retained in the main to establish an immediate causation to the event itself; the report considered that courts and juries were now able to understand the more complex and variegated causations, the strange time delays or displaced symptoms, often typical of trauma-related psychiatric disorders. 'What matters is not the label on the trigger for psychiatric damage, but the fact and foreseeability of psychiatric damage', said one judge at the *Frost* appeal, recommending that nervous shock be disregarded (cited Mullany and Handford 1997: 412). The legal category of 'recognisable psychiatric illness' itself also needed some consideration: the diagnostic grid of PTSD had become the legal standard, ignoring and sometimes dismissing other psychological reactions to trauma, such as debilitating depression or anxiety. Nevertheless, the report considered it impossible to define by statute what a 'recognisable psychiatric illness' could be. The flexibility of case law would have to shadow-box with the protean nature of trauma itself.

Legal discussions often contain deferential gestures to psychiatric expertise. Considering *Frost*, Lord Steyn reaffirmed that 'Only recognisable psychiatric harm ranks for consideration. Where the line is to be drawn is a matter for expert psychiatric evidence' (cited Weir 2000: 108). Yet these knowledges have remained consistently in tension. The English Law Commission ultimately recognized that legal definitions of trauma would never be compatible with official psychiatric diagnostics, which were in any case insufficiently 'mature' to make good law. In 2004, yet another report, this time for the Scottish Law Commission called *Damages for Psychiatric Injury*, was received with frustration in some quarters because it 'prefers flexible, fact-oriented restrictions to bright-line, "legal" rules'. Psychiatry had over-influenced the commissioners, where 'in the world of litigation, certainty matters' (Nolan 2005: 995).

Tort is only one area in which trauma has come into contentious contact with the law. The most dramatic and controversial cases derive from the ways in which PTSD has been deployed within criminal law. Traumatic stressors are said to produce long-term behavioural transformation, including loss of impulse control, violent over-reactions, forms of dissociation or other amnesiac states. Each of these has been the basis of defences that post-traumatic stress undermines intent, the legal requirement of *mens rea* for any criminal act (for the English context see Adshead and Mezey 1997). PTSD thus fuses, in English law, with the McNaughton rules on insanity, or claims for diminished responsibility as a result of suffering a recognized 'abnormality of mind'. There is more controversy around dissociation or 'automatism' pleas, in which trance or other automatic states are argued to be the result of prior traumatization, and thus suspend the defendant's will from any criminal act committed during the fugue. Some of these defences have been successful: in 1990, for instance, a woman claimed to be in a state of acute PTSD following a rape and was thus without criminal responsibility for stabbing a man to death three days later. Prolonged and violent physical abuse of women has made some headway as a defence for their reactive violence, although courts demand clear lines of causation that such cases of 'complex PTSD' often resist (see Herman 1992). These arguments echo the famous legal disputes in the late nineteenth century around criminal responsibility, hysteria and hypnotism, when a series of legal cases were the public stage for rival psychological theories. In 1890, Gabrielle Bompard's defence against murder was that she had been hypnotized and compelled to act against her will. 'Criminal suggestion', propounded by the psychologist Dr Liégeois at the trial, relied on the disturbing idea that conscious will and morality could be suspended by the accomplished hypnotist who could then implant suggestions outside the conscious memory of his unwitting subject. Claiming universal applicability – everyone was suggestible rather than a susceptible few – this theory challenged legal fundamentals about responsibility and was dismissed (Laurence and Perry 1988). This trial, however, was one of a number that brought ideas of the buried suggestion, hidden compulsion and dissociated strands of multiple memory into the public realm. Liégeois learnt that the conception could not be controlled by his medical expertise but became sensationalized as it circulated through 'medico-legal experts, political theorists, and the public alike' (Harris 1985: 232).

The sensational criminal trials concerning trauma since PTSD tend to be those centred on the recovered memory of sexual abuse that have taken place in

America. In the early 1990s, courts seemed prepared to accept that a traumatic reaction to abuse could be a blanket 'dissociative amnesia' of the event which might only be recovered many years later, often by hypnotic recovery techniques. Some psychiatric experts testified to this effect, and argued that the statute of limitations for prosecutions needed to be lifted, and the 'delayed discovery' rule has been adopted in a number of states. The landmark recovered memory case was the prosecution of George Franklin in California in 1990 for a murder committed in 1969, sole proof of which came in the form of memories recovered by his daughter under hypnosis. Despite competing psychiatric views on the plausibility of these recovered memories, Franklin was found guilty. Other prosecutions followed, including the imprisonment of Paul Ingrams for ritual abuse of his daughters that they had recovered, and of which Ingrams himself had no conscious memory until hypnotized (see Wright 1994). By the mid-1990s, however, most courts had become sceptical of total amnesiac loss, and Franklin's prosecution was overturned in 1995. Psychiatric research contesting blanket repressed memory has compromised its use in the law courts. Judgements in California (*Engstrom* v. *Engstrom* 1997), Rhode Island (*State of Rhode Island* v. *Quattrocchi* 1999) and Massachusetts (*Commonwealth* v. *Frangipane* 2001) have all argued that because recovered memory is a site of psychological controversy, it is not legally admissible. In *Jane Doe et al.* v. *A Joseph Maskell* (Maryland 1996), the court refused to recognize that repression had been proven to be a distinct memory mechanism (see Loftus and Davis 2002 and Memon and Young 1997 for discussions).

Part of the problem in these cases has been the place of the psychiatric expert in the adversarial legal system. In the 1920s, the *Frye* rule established that expert testimony had to be 'generally accepted' in a particular specialism. This was changed by Federal Rules of Evidence in 1974, since *Frye* was felt to be too narrow and exclusionary. A new bias emerged 'in favour of admission of relevant evidence … leaving it to the jurors to decide between competing experts' (Shuman 2003: 6). Different theories could now be recruited adversarially, and the situation developed further with the 1993 Supreme Court ruling in *Daubert* v. *Dow Pharmaceuticals*, which reinforced the view that admissibility, to be determined by the judge, depended on 'the quality and adequacy of methodology and the theoretical soundness on which the expert's opinion was based' (Wilson and Moran 2004: 618). Now entirely incompatible theories of trauma had greater chances of receiving a legitimate hearing: it emphasized the extent to which trauma was not a 'matter of fact', as Latour puts it, but a 'matter of concern', an enigmatic thing that prompts perplexity, debate and contested opinion (Latour 2004: 66). It remains the case the psychiatric experts can be found to support the position that traumatic memory is either a highly specific and accurate form of memory registration or, on the contrary, an unusually malleable form of interpretive memory.

Although there are a growing number of handbooks for psychologists giving expert testimony (see, for instance, Simon 2003), most recognize a fundamental incompatibility between legal and psychological discourse on trauma. Michael Trimble despairs at the legal view that causation must be understood on the measure of the man in the street: 'very often the man in the street is incorrect, linking in a causal way things which scientifically have been shown to be non-causal. Perhaps nowhere is this more common than when linking accidents to subsequent medical symptoms' (Trimble 1981: 133). Yet the authority of psychology, particularly in relation to the natural sciences, is not always secure. As the new discipline took shape in the latter half of the nineteenth century, trauma was commonly at the heart of the controversies that attended its emergence. Let's now turn to this.

Trauma in psychology 1870–1914

The metaphorical drift of 'trauma' from physical damage to psychical wounding took place at the time when the treatment of the insane was transformed by new paradigms in psychology. This is not a straightforward story in which the Victorian physicalist model is displaced by a modern psychogenic one. Rather, there were new biological and neurological resources that were used to reinforce the somatic origins of mental illness, and these arrived at exactly the same time (in the 1870s and 1880s) that different groups of psychological researchers began to argue the radical case for a largely psychodynamic model of mind. As a result, the causes and consequences of trauma remained a matter of dispute between rival theories up to the onset of the Great War, when shell shock once more reinvented the terms of the debate.

In 1900, Charles Dana rehearsed the history of railway accidents and their effects on the nerves, explaining that the idea of 'concussion of the spine' had now been displaced by the term *traumatic neurosis*. This had been theorized by the German–Jewish psychiatrist Hermann Oppenheim in 1889. True to form, Oppenheim had studied the cases of railway and industrial accidents, and had concluded that the consequent symptoms were the result of 'molecular changes in the central nervous system' or in the 'vascular system of the brain' (Oppenheim 1911: 1171). This was not a simple reduction to the physical, however. Oppenheim used the term neurosis because he regarded the symptoms as *functional* rather than *organic* disorders – that is, as disorders of the *action* of the nervous system, not of the *structure* of the nerves themselves. These were transient rather than permanent disorders and thus treatable. He also recognized the emotional effect of shock was responsible for the majority of symptoms. Nevertheless, like Erichsen, Oppenheim's theory was roundly attacked and accused of legitimating fraudulent claims of malingerers and the weak-willed: unfortunately Oppenheim's monograph coincided with the decision of Bismarck's Imperial Insurance office to compensate workers for post-traumatic neurosis. A witch-hunt against *Rentenneurose* (pension neurosis) left Oppenheim later recalling that in Germany 'the traumatic neurosis was everywhere expunged and tabooed', and his work vilified as crude somatic reductionism (cited Lerner 2001: 150).

The same term was more successful in France, however, because it was associated with the most famous European neurologist of the era, Jean-Martin Charcot. Charcot was director of the Salpêtrière asylum in Paris between 1862 and his death in 1893, turning a vast rambling holding centre for misfits and the criminally insane into a laboratory for the systematic study of mental illness, 'a sort of *living pathological museum* whose resources are almost inexhaustible' (Charcot 1991: 3). In 1876, Charcot had offered his codification of *la grande hystérie*, using photography and other modern technologies to determine the progressive stages of a hysterical attack. His report to the Academie des Sciences in 1882 confirming the clinical existence of hypnotism transformed a phenomenon previously associated with fringe science, stage tricks and mesmeric charlatans into an orthodox medical pursuit. In the mid-1880s, Charcot began to examine cases of *névrose traumatique* in male patients. In his *Clinical Lectures on Diseases of the Nervous System*, Charcot presented six cases of male hysteria, linking directly to debates around the nature of railway spine, since the men's symptoms were all sequelae to industrial accidents, 'serious and obstinate nervous states which present themselves after collisions' (Charcot 1991: 221). Charcot's aggressive materialism was evident in his persistent reduction of Catholic women saints to hysterics; here, the provocation was in asserting that hysteria could be found in men, since the disease was etymologically and historically associated only with women. Male hysteria lay 'often unrecognised, even by very distinguished physicians' (Charcot 1991: 221), in part because male symptoms – in contrast to women – tended to be persistent, stubborn and stable and were therefore mistaken as organic illnesses. In acknowledging the existence of these cases, Charcot was 'alive to the disturbing effects of the work environment on the mental and physical health of the Parisian men' (Harris 1991: xxxi), and played to the 'widespread social perception that rapid, unrestrained change may be disease-inducing' (Micale 2001: 138–9). Even 'robust men presenting all the attributes of the male sex', Charcot asserted, could be disaggregated by the traumatic accident (Charcot 1991: 99). Trauma thus found itself plugged into Charcot's monumental taxonomy of hysterias.

The conditions presented the familiar mysterious trajectory. Minor accidents were capable of flowering into an elaborate range of contractures, paralyses, fainting, fugue states, or amnesia. 'The Salpêtrière's brand of trauma dealt in quite simple scenes' (Didi-Huberman 2003: 153) – a blacksmith burns his arm, a razor slips, there is a fall on the stairs. 'It is usual for these diseases to localise themselves at first in parts where the wound, the contusion, or the sprain is produced' (Charcot 1991: 33). The functional disorder propped itself on the initial physical wound, but then seemed to use this opening to travel through the nervous system and to develop diffuse and varied organic manifestations. Charcot noted that the contractures and paralyses could not be mapped onto the known physical distribution of the nerves: they were fantasies of how the body worked. These were therefore hysterical symptoms, 'psychical paralyses': 'observe, I do not say *imaginary paralyses,* for indeed these motor paralyses of psychical origin are as objectively real as those depending on an organic lesion' (Charcot 1991: 289). Psychical factors were also emphasized with the disturbances of memory. Accidents could produce *traumatic retrograde amnesia* (Charcot 1991: 376), where significant chunks of time prior to and including the accident were lost. Salpêtrière doctors also studied anterograde amnesia in which the capacity to create new memories were lost in the wake of the traumatic event (see Janet 2001). As with Erichsen, Page and the legal discussion of nervous shock, Charcot confirmed that along with the injury, there is a factor which most probably plays a much more important part in the genesis of the symptoms than the wound itself. I allude to the fright experienced by the patient at the moment of the accident.

(Charcot 1991: 231)

For all this emphasis, Charcot regarded any hysterical symptom as ultimately a marker of an inherited biological weakness. Hereditary physiological traits were the precondition, the explanation for why certain people could survive extreme events unscathed whilst others become irrecoverable hysterics over a mild distress. Charcot's case histories always situated a patient in a family history, a network of biological disorders – a nervous father, an asthmatic mother, an epileptic great-uncle, children with hystero-epilepsy, and so on. These cases play out the logic of degeneration, the theory that any morbid deviation from normal behaviour would produce biological consequences that would rapidly ramify through successive generations. An alcoholic or epileptic parent might spawn sexually deviant children, say, and then grandchildren who were criminally insane. Degeneration theory, a precipitous descent down the evolutionary ladder, was coined by Auguste Morel in 1857. By the late nineteenth century, it was 'so pervasive and seductive ... that it was all but impossible to avoid' (Greenslade 1994: 8). It was a loose schema or generative metaphor that could organize materials as diverse as sea squirts, decadent artists, rebellious working classes, African natives, the criminal residuum, and virtually every mental disorder (see Chamberlain and Gilman 1985). Charcot claimed that 70 per cent of his male traumatic hysterics suffered from maternal 'heredity of similitude' – that is, hysterical mothers begat hysterical sons with identical symptoms (Charcot 1991: 85). For Charcot, physical injury and psychical shock were immediate causes, but had flowered with the proper hereditary conditions. Traumatic neurosis was a conjuncture where the accident met destiny, modernity met blood.

This physicalist model matched the dominant thinking in English alienism too. From about 1870, the enlightenment hope that moral management might cure or ameliorate lunacy tended to be replaced with a stark biological determinism. Although there was held to be a psychophysical parallelism between body and mind, mental powers were regarded as the latest evolutionary addition and thus able to control the lower, animalistic impulses and instincts of the body. Mental illness was a failure of the will to command, in which the mind became subordinate to morbid states of the brain: 'Diseased physical processes as it were spilled over from their ordinary sphere of action in the physical organism into the normally separate and closed domain of mind' (Clark 1981: 276). The course of 'cerebro-psychical dissolution' was simple: it was

the reverse process to that of nervous evolution. The highest and latest-evolved nervous arrangements, being the most unstable, are the first to be thrown *hors de combat* by the inroads of general cerebral disease: the successive changes of dissolution retrace the path followed by those of evolution.

(Sully 1892: 321)

The pioneering neurologist Hughlings Jackson was open about the consequences of this: 'Psychical symptoms are to medical men only signs of what is wrong in a material system' (cited Clark 1981: 283). The manifest symptoms were insignificant since they were epiphenomenal, pointing to an underlying somatic pathology. As the leading alienist Henry Maudsley attested in *Body and Will*, normal psychological health was a 'physiological conception of a number of confederated nerve-centres' (Maudsley 1883: 259). The ego or Self was not metaphysical, but a result of 'the objective synthesis or unity of the organism' (Maudsley 1883: 315). If the will was 'the last expression of an hierarchical co-ordination of tendencies' then 'dissolution of the will is the absence of co-ordination, which terminates in independent, irregular and anarchical action' (Ribot 1892: 1367–8). In Maudsley's view, illness was always a disaggregation of this unity, an unbinding of this synthesis into separate parts, and he speculated that moral alienation was the result of 'minute molecular changes' in the brain (Maudsley 1883: 268). Treatment was directed at reunifying and bolstering the patient's will, the doctor, if necessary, replacing the patient's absent or perverted will with their own severe injunctions (almost literally insisting the patient 'pull themselves together' behind a unified will). In contrast to psychotherapeutic practice, doctors nearly uniformly resisted engaging with the precipitating traumatic causes of illness. James Crichton-Browne aimed to 'withdraw the patient's mind from the contemplation of an objectionable and painful past and from ferreting out verminous reminiscences, and to occupy it with prospective duties and wholesome pursuits' (cited Clark 1981: 300). Hermann Oppenheim similarly suggested that in cases of traumatic neurosis it was best 'to convince the injured man that neglect of his nervous troubles is the most effective means of getting rid of them' (Oppenheim 1911: 1179). Yet treatment was also necessarily circumscribed by heredity, since the dissolution of the will was likely predetermined by an inherent weakness that waited in the blood to seize on a moment of trauma. The degenerative taint could not be removed; it banished cure.

The marginal status of mad-doctors and alienists in Victorian society has been well recorded. For *Nature*, the official organ of the new science professionals, psychology was 'the science furthest removed from the reach of experimental means and inductive method' and was therefore the science 'which has longest remained in the trammels of … metaphysical thought' ('Charles Darwin' 1882: 169). This led to an anxiety to prop itself on authoritative discourses like biology. Yet this had contradictory results, as historian Janet Oppenheim observes. 'Psychiatry could assume the status of science only if it embraced a somatic model of mental alienation, tracing the roots of that disorder to some lesion or malfunction of the body', yet the more they insisted on their status as physiologists, the more they ceded their authority to other disciplines and 'contributed to the dilemma that challenged their professional identity' (Oppenheim 1991: 35 and 38). From the 1890s, neurological advances recategorized illnesses such as epilepsy and syphilitic paralyses from the psychological to the definitively physiological realm. Neurones were isolated in 1891. The structure of the synapse was described in 1897, ending many vague speculations about mental action (see Black 1981). Hormones, a term coined in 1905, became the basis for a new specialism, endocrinology, where chemical explanations were developed for the complex physiological effects of shock. Adrenalin was isolated in 1915: the release of adrenalin into the blood stream in situations of extreme stress has been central to most subsequent physiological theories of trauma, culminating in PTSD. No wonder that when shell-shock patients were first received by the neurology elite of London's Queen Square from 1915, psychological assessments and treatments were regarded as an utter irrelevance (see Shephard 2000: 112ff).

This physiological trajectory for traumatic neurosis rendered some psychological speculations redundant. Yet trauma was also fundamentally retheorized in another strand of psychology that emerged in the 1870s and this was also to have enduring consequences. Psychodynamic theories in the main flatly refused to prop themselves on a physiological explanation: trauma was to be understood intrapsychically, as a disorder of the mental economy alone. The range of psychodynamic theories has long been hidden by the tendency to focus solely on the psychoanalysis pursued by Freud from the 1890s, but this has recently changed with revisionist histories of psychology. This is vital, because the shadings of contemporary trauma theory can only be grasped by excavating this history. I want to outline four areas of psychodynamic theory that have had an impact on how psychic trauma has been theorized: the psychotherapeutics of suggestion associated with the Nancy School; theories of double personality; the model of dissociation developed by Pierre Janet; and lastly the psychogenic theory of traumatic hysteria proposed by Freud.

European psychology in the 1880s became engulfed in a controversy that demanded a declaration of one's alliance either to Charcot's Salpêtrière or the Nancy School, associated with the professor of psychiatry at Nancy University, Hippolyte Bernheim. Charcot confirmed his theory of predisposition in hysteria experimentally, by artificially inducing the same symptoms with the use of his newly minted technique, hypnosis. For Charcot, only those predisposed to neurotic disaggregation were susceptible to hypnosis. Hypnosis was 'an artificially induced morbid condition – a neurosis – because there is not, so far as we know, any anatomical lesion … This neurosis discloses itself almost always on the soil predisposed by hysteria' (Charcot and Tourette 1892: 606). In contrast, the Nancy School argued that the hypnotic condition could be induced universally, regardless of predisposition, and that in this trance state everyone was highly susceptible to suggestion. Hypnotic suggestion could be used therapeutically to cure or ameliorate hysterical and other symptoms because it was an *ideodynamic* mechanism, 'an act by which an idea is introduced into the brain and accepted by it': 'The psychic centre actively intervenes to transform the impression into an idea and to elaborate it; each idea suggests other ideas, and these ideas are transformed into sensations, emotions, and various images' and finally become bodily states or acts (Bernheim 1980: 18 and 22). This replaced any physiological explanation with a 'purely psychologic' theory (Bernheim 1980: 50); indeed, Bernheim charged that Charcot's distinct physical stages of hypnosis were not objective bodily states at all but the products of the great man's own suggestion (for a history of this dispute, see Gauld 1992). By 1889, Bernheim's 'psycho-therapeutic' was being applied to describe 'all therapy which cures by the intermediary of the psychic functions of the patient' (Shamdasani 2005: 6). This method spread throughout Europe, although always as a minority practice. The first serious works on hypnosis in England produced around 1890 were all notably sympathetic toward Bernheim (Tuckey 1889, for instance).

Bernheim produced an ideational, psychical theory of mental disorders. These derived from a dysfunction of the attention: it was as if the mind narrowed itself around a particular idea, and this *idée fixe* became a dam behind which pooled a host of associated ideas that developed into unhealthy clusters that might then be converted into neurotic symptoms. Suggestion worked because Bernheim regarded hypnosis (in accord with James Braid, the man who invented the term) as a way of artificially inducing the same narrowed attention, but which instead could be targeted on unblocking *idées fixes* and allowing psychic energy to flow once more. This is clearly a nascent theory for the psychical understanding and treatment of trauma, the distressing event whose psychic imprint fixes itself in the mind in an unassimilated way, becoming the locus for a host of disorders. Yet these early psychotherapeutic writings were less interested in the cause, the precipitating trauma as it were, than in detailing the consequences, the astonishing psychical phenomena that came as sequelae.

The most sensational cases of this psychological literature were those patients who suffered *dédoublement de la personalité*. It seemed that some hysterics developed a distinct, double state where their personality was transformed more or less coherently for sustained periods of time. A central case was 'Félida X' who had been studied by the French doctor Eugène Azam for seventeen years, publishing her case history in 1875. Félida was a morbid hysteric who suffered chronic nervous pains, debility and depression. An hysterical 'crisis' (or seizure) would turn her into a relatively functional young woman again, more sociable and femininely demur, before another crisis would her return her to her primary state. Over the years, these successive personalities altered their relation, so that the second state grew more dominant – she married and became pregnant in the second state, for instance. A third state appeared irregularly: a condition of abject terror (see Binet 1977, Crabtree 1994, Hacking 1995). This case was taken up in psychotherapeutics because it was discovered that the crisis that switched personalities could be artificially induced by hypnosis and directed by suggestion. More fundamentally, double personality was regarded as an intrapsychic problem, a *disease of memory*. Félida had a complete amnesia about her second state, experiencing her life in her first state as a series of discontinuous jump cuts. Yet the second personality was not amnesiac; it knew and commented on the condition of the first. The Salpêtrière doctor Alfred Binet suggested that secondary states might be more sensitive and intelligent than normal consciousness: perceptual powers seemed enhanced, memory recall seemed to be astonishingly accurate and well beyond normal capacities. For the English writer Frederic Myers, who coined the term 'multiplex personality' for these cases, they even suggested a way in which 'moral sentiments can be improved' (Myers 1886: 657). Hysterics revealed 'the nascent art of self-modification', and hypnosis might artificially induce a national 'moral-isation' if effectively employed (Myers 1886: 656). These statements were of course a complete anathema to the dominant physicalist idea of psycho-physio-logical unity and the singular will. The case of Félida X disturbingly inverted the values ascribed to the normal and the pathological.

The historian Ian Hacking has provokingly argued that Multiple Personality Disorder (MPD) was invented on 27 July 1885 when Louis Vivet entered the health system and became the subject of intensive psychiatric experimentation (Hacking 1995). Vivet was a patchwork of as many as eight separate personalities, each with its own hysterical symptoms, and each with its own distinct memory chain. Vivet had been in and out of houses of correction, schools and prisons since the age of eight. He could veer between the respectful and modest boy to the criminal delin-quent, the paraplegic hysteric, or the atheistic radical. Most states possessed no consciousness or memory of the others. Two doctors began to experiment with hypnotic suggestion, drawing out different personalities from the boy. Their methods (an old Mesmeric one, using magnets) became the subject of a book and a controversy, drawing more doctors to the study, more experimentation, and the discovery of yet more personalities. Hundreds of pages, written by over twenty experts, were devoted to Louis in the late 1880s. Intriguingly, there are glimpses of the origin of these successive crises and personality transformations. According to Myers, at the age of fourteen a fright at seeing a viper began his serious hystero-epileptic 'oscillations'. Yet any interest in the traumatic origin is quickly displaced by a concern to trace its hysterical effects: 'A sudden shock, falling on an unstable organisation, has effected in this boy a profounder severance between the functions of the right and left hemispheres of the brain' (Myers 1886: 651). The fascination lay in the way the boy became literally sinister, left-handed and morally dissolute. He switched sides like the great alternating personality that Myers had written on earlier in 1886: Dr Jekyll and Mr Hyde (see Luckhurst 2006b). In what Adam Crabtree calls the 'alternate-consciousness paradigm', it is the bizarre state of split-ting and not the traumatic trigger that is the focus.

In contrast, contemporary theories of MPD centre specifically on the inaugu-ral trauma, and overwhelmingly (in 97 per cent of cases) identify that trauma as child sexual abuse. Abuse acts as the shattering event that lies buried and forgot-ten, yet pristinely preserved, somewhere in a fragmentary 'alter' personality. The event is teased out with recovered memory techniques, including hypnotic recov-ery, from the shards of isolated and amnesiac selves (the average number of alter personalities reached twenty-four by the end of the 1980s). For Ian Hacking, 'memory has always had political or ideological overtones, but each epoch has found its own meaning in memory' (Hacking 1995: 200). MPD presents 'a poli-tics of the secret, of the forgotten event that can be turned, if only by strange flashbacks, into something monumental' (Hacking 1995: 214).

The case of Louis Vivet displays how suggestion works not just on the hysteri-cal patient but on their doctors too. Louis learnt fast that psychiatric attention intensified with the dramatic performance of splitting. This is not at all to judge that the boy faked his personalities, but that the new label of 'double personality' actively guided his symptom formation: it was iatrogenic. This mutual act of invention between doctor and patient is typical of anything involving hypnosis, for any trance state not only abolishes will it also 'overturns the ordinarily accepted borders between "self" and "other"' (Borch-Jacobsen 1993: 100). In this interstitial space, where suggestibility uncannily bridges between doctor and patient, the therapeutic conviction of the former can be communicated to the latter, and mirrored back, as if in objective confirmation but in fact as a form of 'dynamic nominalism', where 'a kind of person … came into being at the same time as the kind itself was being invented' (Hacking 1986: 228). Many significant psychodynamic theorists before the Great War had their own Louis, a case of 'double personality' that bewildered and entranced them. Pierre Janet began experiments with Léonie, who soon became Léonie I, II and III. There were various attempts to hypnotize her at a distance, including across the English Channel. Richard von Krafft-Ebing studied Ilma S. an hystero-epileptic woman who exhibited 'three different spheres of consciousness [that] never intersect' and who had been rendered profoundly suggestible by over-hypnosis (Krafft-Ebing 1889: 125). Krafft-Ebing was persuaded her criminal acts had been committed under the suggestion of an unknown hypnotist. William James spent years investigating Mrs Piper, a Boston medium who had developed psychic sensitivity after a traffic accident affected her nerves. He was forever unable to decide if her spirit guides and trance selves were psychological or supernatural phenomena. Morton Prince's *The Dissociation of a Personality* (1919) was the product of six years researching Sally Beauchamp, whose multiple personalities presented 'a virtual typology of early-twentieth-century concepts of the feminine' that Prince believed began to emerge after the traumatic death of her mother in 1893 (Leys 1992: 182).

The brief life-story of modern MPD shows an accelerated form of this dynamic nominalism. Considered an extremely rare disorder, with perhaps only two hundred extant cases, it was nevertheless included in DSM-III in 1980. A diagnostic explosion followed, and by 1989 it was regularly claimed that one in twenty of the American population had some form of multiplicity. By 1994, MPD sufferers numbered exactly zero: it was replaced in DSM-IV with a newly named disorder, meant to carry less emphasis on discrete alter personalities: Dissociative Identity Disorder. The sceptical commentator Mikkel Borch-Jacobsen commented that year

> their hypnotic technique is extremely directive or manipulative, and it is difficult to avoid the comparison with modern technology: patients are "switched" like television channels; elements of trauma are decomposed and recomposed as easily as "processing" words on a computer … . Multiple personality is an epidemic, and psychiatrists are its vectors.
>
> (Borch-Jacobsen 1994: 52)

This passage in the vagaries of the contemporary trauma paradigm was a direct repetition of the 'diseases of memory' explored before 1914.

In MPD the trigger is a traumatic event, but the mechanism of psychic defence, the agency that creates the 'splitting' of personality, is *dissociation*. This derives from

Pierre Janet's work on psychological automatism which he conducted in the 1880s and 1890s. Janet's work had largely been forgotten, yet Henri Ellenberger's monumental history of psychodynamic psychiatry recovered Janet in 1969, arguing that 'Janet stands at the threshold of all modern dynamic psychiatry. His ideas have become so widely known that their true origin is often unrecognised' (Ellenberger 1994: 406). Ellenberger's essay prompted a full-scale revival in the 1980s when Janet became central to psychological trauma theories. In a formative paper, Frank Putnam declared that it was Janet that 'made the connection between dissociative psychopathology and traumatic experiences' and was one of the first to 'conceptualize dissociative reactions occurring in the context of acute trauma as an adaptive process that protects the individual and allows him to continue to function, though often in an automaton-like state' (Putnam 1999: 116 and 120).

Although Janet was appointed to the Salpêtrière by Charcot in 1890 after the publication of *Psychological Automatism*, Janet emphasized the psychological elements of hysteria, which he described as 'an ensemble of maladies through representation' (Janet 1901: 488). Part of Janet's later marginalisation came from the aggressive stance he took against 'the current physiological hypothesis': 'I consider the pretended physiological conditions as mere translations of the psychological ideas' (Janet 1907: 322–3). His preferred general term, psychasthenia, deliberately displaced any traces of the nervous physiology that survived in the more familiar usage neurasthenia. Nevertheless, a disease of memory had to combine with affect: 'Hystericals have not only fixed ideas; they have also persistent emotions, and emotions are complex states of the whole organism in which both the physiological and psychological phenomena are intimately blended' (Janet 1901: 513). He was enough of a student of Charcot to affirm that in psychasthenia heredity would still play 'a role absolutely preponderant' (Janet 1901: 516). Despite this, his emphasis on the non-organic mental realm guaranteed his exclusion from serious consideration by the physiologists who dominated the Salpêtrière hospital after Charcot's death in 1893, where even Charcot was considered dangerously 'psychological' in his view of hysteria. Janet moved from the medical environment to the elite academic College de France in 1902.

Janet's model worked like this: a particularly shocking moment or event might produce a defensive response of a narrowing of the field of consciousness. This would become an *idée fixe*, held outside the recall memory of the conscious mind. It would accrue its own memory chain and associations, becoming a 'new system, a personality independent of the first' (Janet 1901: 492). It was this act of splitting that created a double self, something that coalesced around the subconscious fixed idea. The subconscious (Janet's coinage) was not structural, then, but a specific product of traumatic hysteria: 'It is a special moral weakness consisting in the lack of power on the part of the feeble subject to gather, to condense, his psychological phenomena, and assimilate them to his personality' (Janet 1901: 502). Something of this lies behind current theories of traumatic dissociation, although Janet dropped the term quite early in his career. One contemporary survey has confessed that the usage of dissociation now 'lacks a single, coherent referent or conceptualisation' (Cardena 1994: 15).

Janet's case histories detail a range of 'mental accidents' or 'traumatic shocks' that produce diseases of memory. 'The most common accidents of hysteria', he argued, 'should be interpreted in the same way as the accidents of traumatic hysteria' (Janet 1901: 496). Intense emotions direct the routes of organic and nervous manifestations, but Janet was strikingly uninterested in thinking about the *types* of event that might result in such exorbitant reactions, presumably because it was predisposition rather than the nature of the trauma that resulted in dissociative sequelae. Justine developed hysterical symptoms after glimpsing the corpse of a cholera victim in China; Irène's amnesia blocked out any knowledge of her mother's death. Mrs D. was jokingly told that her husband had been killed, prompting a hysterical crisis, retrograde amnesia and anterograde memory loss, in which 'every impression skated over her without leaving the smallest trace' (Janet 2001: 487). The woman bore no apparent memory of her incarceration in the Salpêtrière for many months, nor her star turn for Charcot's lecture-demonstrations of 1891, nor of a subsequent traumatic event, an attack by a dog. Yet her phobic reactions to dogs suggested the memory was registered subconsciously, and this indeed proved recoverable by hypnosis. These diseases of memory were rarely of organic origin, since a subconscious intelligence clearly worked to 'determine the choice of things forgotten' (Janet 1901: 91).

Janet's most well-known case (undoubtedly because Ellenberger translates it fully in his history) is the treatment of Marie, a nineteen-year-old girl who suffered from hysterical seizures with every menstruation, entering severe delirium, wracked with tremors, imaginary terrors and vomiting blood for 48 hours, before returning to normal. Janet

> put her into a deep somnambulic condition, a state where … it is possible to bring back seemingly forgotten memories, and thus I was able to find out the exact memory of an incident which had hitherto been only very incompletely known.
>
> (cited Ellenberger 1994: 362–3)

The buried traumatic scene was her first experience of menstruation. Overcome with shame, she plunged herself into a bucket of icy water, shocking her body into stopping bleeding, at the cost of a fever and delirium. Janet concluded,

> Every month the scene of the cold bath repeats itself, brings forth the same stopping of the menstruation and a delirium … But in her normal state of consciousness, she knows nothing at all about this, not even that the shivering is brought forth by the hallucination of cold. It is therefore probable that this scene takes place below consciousness.
>
> (cited Ellenberger 1994: 363)

This case has a very contemporary shape: an inaugural traumatic event of sexual shame in childhood, followed by dissociation, amnesia and compulsive re-experiencing of the trauma, the original scene being recovered under hypnosis.

It matches contemporary definitions of dissociation: 'a defensive process in which experiences are split off and kept unintegrated through alterations in memory and consciousness, with a resulting impairment of the self' (Tillman *et al.* 1994: 398). Yet Janet's psychotherapeutic cure is disarmingly non-modern:

> I tried to take away from somnambulistic consciousness this fixed and absurd idea that the menstruation was stopped by a cold bath. At first, I could not manage to do it; the fixed idea persisted ... I tried again: I was able to succeed only thanks to a singular means. It was necessary to bring her back, through suggestion, to the age of thirteen, put her back into the initial circumstances of the delirium, convince her that the menstruation had lasted for three days and was not interrupted through any regrettable incident. Now once this was done, the following menstruation came at the due point, lasted for three days, without any pain, convulsion or delirium.
>
> (Cited Ellenberger 1994: 363)

Delighted by the result, Janet then addressed Marie's hysterical blindness, recovering a scene when Marie was six and had to share a bed with a child with impetigo: 'I put her back with the child who had so horrified her; I make her believe that the child is very nice and does not have impetigo ...; the sensitivity of the left eye reappears without difficulty' (cited Ellenberger 1994: 364). Cure by this active reinvention was typical: Justine's traumatic Chinese cholera corpse was replaced with a positive memory of a Chinese general seen at the Paris Universal Exposition in 1889; the associations of the very word cholera were attacked and decomposed. 'Fixed ideas must be destroyed by means of dissociation or trans-formation' (Ellenberger 1994: 373). Trauma was not to be recovered, affirmed, respected, abreacted, mourned, assimilated, brought to closure – the familiar language and trajectory of contemporary psychotherapy. Instead, a traumatic memory was to be manipulated, recomposed or replaced with another sometimes falsified memory, or else entirely erased. Given the controversies surrounding false memory and the dangers of therapeutic suggestion, Janet's defenders tend to downplay this aspect of his treatment. Yet, for the purposes of healing psycho-logical distress, Janet had, as Ian Hacking observes, 'no compunction about lying to his patients, and creating false memories through which they could deal with their distress': his 'doctrine of psychological trauma, recovered memory, and abreaction created a crisis of truth' (Hacking 1995: 196).

It was the unsatisfactory nature of these 'forcible prohibitions' or active inter-ventions that led Freud to abandon hypnotic suggestion in 1896, which he regarded as one of the founding acts of the invention of psychoanalysis (Freud 1914: 9). Freud became concerned to always distinguish Pierre Janet's ideas of mental weakness leading to dissociation from his own model of 'psychodynamic factors – of mental conflict and of repression':

> The distinction seems to me to be far-reaching enough to put an end to the glib repetition of the view that whatever is of value in psychoanalysis is

borrowed from the ideas of Janet … [H]istorically psychoanalysis is completely independent of Janet's discoveries, just as in its content it diverges
from them.

(Freud 1914: 31)

Freud obsessively wrote and rewrote his history, in part to preserve a strong distinction of psychoanalysis from other therapeutic schools. Janet became a target
after his attack on Freud and psychoanalysis at the 1913 International Congress
of Medicine. Yet Freud's early work on traumatic hysteria was largely continuous
with the history I have been outlining. My introduction detailed Freud's important role in cultural theories of trauma, despite his intermittent writings on the
subject, so here I intend only to situate him in the context of psychodynamic theories
of trauma before 1914.

Freud, a young doctor training in neurology, visited both Charcot at the
Salpêtrière (in 1885–6) and Bernheim at Nancy (in 1889). His report on Charcot
to the medical authorities that funded his trip situated him at the heart of contemporary debates. He praised Charcot's attempt to organize hysterical symptoms scientifically, and was aware 'that the proposal to regard neuroses arising
from trauma ("railway spine") as hysteria' had been opposed by Oppenheim in
Berlin, whose clinic Freud had also visited (Freud 1886: 12). Freud confessed his
'astonishment' at the demonstrable powers of hypnosis, but his committee mainly
objected to his passing statements regarding 'the enormous practical importance
of male hysteria … and particularly of the hysteria which follows upon trauma'
(Freud 1886: 12). This resulted in Freud's presentation to the Vienna Society of
Medicine of a lecture-demonstration of 'hemi-anaesthesia in a hysterical male' –
a traumatic neurosis resultant from a childhood traffic accident. In his
Autobiographical Study Freud recalled this event as an instance of his early margin-
alization from orthodox opinion, although he was merely restaging the work of
Charcot. In an encyclopaedia entry for hysteria in 1888 Freud was an orthodox
follower of Charcot in regarding the illness as a functional disorder that 'excludes
any suspicion of a material lesion' (Freud 1888: 48). Predisposition was 'entirely
in heredity', however, in keeping with the Salpêtrière stance (Freud 1888: 49). In
the range of current treatments, Freud discusses the work of Oppenheim before
ending with an outline of Joseph Breuer's technique which aimed to 'lead the
patient under hypnosis back to the psychical prehistory of the ailment and compel him to acknowledge the psychical occasion on which the disorder in question
originated' (Freud 1888: 52). Breuer and Freud published their first collaborative
work in 1893, when, Freud later stated, 'we were completely under the spell of
Charcot's researches' (Freud 1895: 44).

The very title of their Preliminary Communication, 'On the Psychical
Mechanism of Hysterical Phenomena', nailed their colours to the mast. The
essay argued for '*an extension of the concept of traumatic hysteria*' (Freud 1895: 56) from
the well-known cases where the precipitating trauma was an accident. The same
causation, obvious in accidents, could be discovered across the range of other
merely psychical hysterias, Freud and Breuer arguing that 'any experience which

calls up distressing affects – such as those of fright, anxiety, shame, or physical pain – may operate as a trauma of this kind' (Freud 1895: 56). They all produced the same puzzling 'disproportion between the many years' duration of the hysterical symptom and the single occurrence which provoked it' (Freud 1895: 54). Hysteria was psychical because it was a disease of memory, not of the body, prompting the famous dictum, '*Hysterics suffer mainly from reminiscences*' (Freud 1895: 58). Much of what followed appeared to be in keeping with Janet's work, although Freud claimed that Breuer's private treatments anticipated Janet's published work by several years. Memories likely to become traumatic were those registered with an affective intensity that does not fade: an *idée fixe*. Traumatic memory is characterized by being '*completely absent from the patient's memory when they are in a normal psychical state*' (Freud 1895: 60). Breuer and Freud use the model of 'dissociation' or a 'second consciousness' that coalesces around ideas 'cut off from associative connection with other ideas, but can be associated themselves' (Freud 1895: 63, 67 and 66). Treatment also seems to follow Janet, subjecting traumatic memory and attendant affect '*to associative correction by introducing it to normal consciousness (under light hypnosis) or by removing it through the physician's suggestions*' (Freud 1895: 68).

Yet subtle signs of divergence are premonitions of Freud's theoretical breaks with Charcot and Janet. The symptom is rarely regarded as a simple sign that leads transparently back from hysterical effect to traumatic cause. Freud and Breuer discuss the role of 'symbolization' in symptom-formation, and the idea of complex, overlaid groups of partial traumatic memories, where the symptom is marked by the sorts of metaphoric and metonymic displacements that become central to *The Interpretation of Dreams* (1900). This means originating traumatic scenes have to be interpreted or translated from a rebus or hieroglyph of puzzling symptoms, rather than being always necessarily unearthed in pristinely preserved form.

Freud and Breuer expressed some hesitations about whether hysteria could be ascribed entirely to hereditary predisposition, with a distinction made between '*dispositional* hysteria' and '*psychically acquired* hysteria' (Freud 1895: 63). In the later case histories that make up *Studies on Hysteria*, this is formulated as an explicit rejection of Janet's view of 'abnormal restriction of the field of consciousness (due to hereditary degeneracy)' (Freud 1895: 166). To ascribe psychical splitting to some inherent inability to integrate a unitary consciousness is to mistake a psychical effect of trauma as its biological cause. This opened up the possibility of a new, purely psychical topography of the mind that was structural and universal rather than pathological, although the 'unconscious' is first used by Breuer in *Studies on Hysteria* in uncertain quotation marks in his treatment of Anna O., where the double personality paradigm is not displaced by its use (Freud 1895: 100).

As a consequence of questioning hereditary predisposition, Freud and Breuer were much more interested in the *types* of memory that possess sufficient traumatic force to produce symptoms. The scenarios seemed very different: a father's death-bed, an inappropriate sexual scene witnessed between a father and daughter; a yearning for a brother-in-law; a governess's desire for her employer obscured beneath 'the many minor traumas subsidiary to that scene' (Freud 1895: 183). The speculation that it was 'some event in childhood that sets up a more or less severe symptom which persists during the years that follow' (Freud 1895: 54) came into sharp, polemical focus three years later in 'The Aetiology of Hysteria' where Freud declared that 'at the bottom of every case of hysteria there are *one or more occurrences of premature sexual experience*' (Freud 1896: 203). Freud broke with Breuer over this insistence and also, he thought, with Charcot, Janet and the entire psychiatric community. Freud held to the conviction that he had uncovered true scenes of mainly intra-familial sexual activity for two years, before confessing to Wilhelm Fliess that 'I no longer believe in my *neurotica*', partly by realizing that

> there are no indications of reality in the unconscious, so that one cannot distinguish between truth and fiction that has been cathected with affect (Accordingly, there would remain the solution that the sexual fantasy invariably seizes upon the theme of the parents).
>
> (Freud 1985: 264)

Yet for all the polemical writing on this transition after the letters were published in 1985, Freud never simply replaced the 'real event' with fantasy, truth with falsity. Rather, he considered traumatic memories as particularly hemmed in by resistances to being brought into conscious recall, and were thus subject to multiple tricks of transformation or displacement, intertwining the real and fantasmatic. To some, it was Freud's 'terrible Will to Truth' in pursuing these originary traumatic scenes (Hacking 1995: 195) that led him into the medical wilderness by replacing his seduction theory with a more eccentric proposal: universal infantile sexuality. With this theory trauma now potentially attended every phase of the fraught journey towards adult sexuality.

Inextricably connected with Freud's theoretical shift was the decision to stop any systematic use of hypnosis, since he was concerned to ensure his findings were not products of therapeutic suggestion. Psychoanalysis announced itself by abandoning hypnotic suggestion and the attendant theory that trauma is registered in some peculiarly receptive 'hypnoid state' (light trance or daydream states), an idea that permeated *Studies on Hysteria*. In 1910, Freud remembered that he 'came to dislike hypnosis, for it was a temperamental and, one might almost say, a mystical ally' (Freud 1910: 46). He would instead engage with the patient in the normal state, wrestling with 'the force that prevented [forgotten memories] from becoming conscious' (Freud 1910: 48). The struggle of the conscious mind with what it knew but did not want to know helped Freud outline his basic psychodynamic forces:

> All these experiences had involved the emergence of a wishful impulse which was in sharp contrast to the subject's other wishes … There had been a short conflict, and the end of this internal struggle was that the idea which had appeared before consciousness as the vehicle of this irreconcilable wish fell a victim to repression, was pushed out of consciousness with all its attached memories and was forgotten.
>
> (Freud 1910: 48–9)

Hypnosis actively masked the clinical observation of this conflictual dynamic: 'It is only if you exclude hypnosis that you can observe resistances and repressions and form an adequate idea of the truly pathogenic course of events', he concluded (Freud 1910: 51). That suggestion might still operate outside hypnotic rapport and predetermine findings that matched the new theory was not something that Freud apparently contemplated. Borch-Jacobsen polemically proposes that the Oedipus complex is nothing more than a 'hypnotic myth': 'In reality, his patients did their best to confirm his theories, beyond his wildest expectations. Psychoanalysis is the product of this feedback, the magical fulfilment of its own property' (Borch-Jacobsen 1996: 43 and 33).

Most importantly, Freud's distinct concept of the systematic unconscious developed in parallel with this change in therapeutic treatment of psychical traumas. The term *unconscious* would have been jarringly nonsensical to many of his contemporaries, certainly to the predominant psycho-physiological unity of body and will. How could you ascribe psychical action to what was non-conscious? How could you suggest this was a foundational element of mental action, rather than an evidently unhealthy disaggregation? Freud not only opposed the unitary model that regarded the conscious as co-terminous with all psychical action, but also objected to the way double or 'split' personality was conceived. Janet's dissociation worked as if a traumatic impact broke a unified psyche into two or more similar parts. Dissociation was a *horizontal* model, where the self floats away from coherence into separate islands of consciousness, the subsidiary selves organized around traumatic memories. Freud's topography was a *vertical* model, in which the psyche is structurally split between conscious and unconscious systems, between manifest and latent ideas and affects. Manifest contents lay on the surface, accessible to conscious recall; latent contents were buried beneath, yet leaked from their crypts like ghosts. Hysterical symptoms, dreams, and compulsive behaviours were hauntings, the signs of something restless and unquiet that was buried but still demanded witness. In this model, the unconscious 'designates not only latent ideas in general, but especially ideas with a certain character, ideas keeping apart from consciousness in spite of their intensity and activity' (Freud 1912: 262). These ideas do not fail to become conscious because they are weak and disorganized, but because they are actively prevented from reaching the surface by *repression*. Freud figured repression either as a photographic negative that is prevented from being developed or as a watchman guarding a door: 'he examines the different mental impulses, acts as a censor, and will not admit them into the drawing-room if they displease him' (Freud 1916–17: 336). What constitutes material for repression is everything that conflicts with the restraints of social being: violent emotions, fantasies of aggression, unbounded wish-fulfilment, sexual desires. Alongside these internal conflicts, repression also manages the unbounded psychic energy that comes from an external traumatic impact, expelling painful and unpleasurable memories and affects from the conscious system.

Although deriving from discussions of traumatic neurosis consequent to accidents, Freud massively extended the potential range of the term trauma. Freud's conflictual psychodynamic was not a mark of a predisposed pathology, but the emergence of the social subject, which came into being through an *inherently* traumatic development.

Both extremes of contemporary trauma theory can no longer necessarily be expected to have read Freud in any detail, if at all. For biologists, the problem remains that the theory of repression has never gained proof outside Freud's network of metaphors for its proposed mechanism. Freud also confessed that his psychic topography had '*for the present* nothing to do with anatomy' (Freud 1915: 175) although he hoped proleptically to align his psychodynamic theory inside an overarching psycho-physiological unity. Similarly, Freud admitted that the mechanism of repression was 'a preliminary working hypothesis', 'crude and fantastic and quite impermissible in a scientific account' (Freud 1916–17: 337). Patricia Kitcher argues that in biology Freud 'is widely regarded as the paradigm of bad science, a theory so obviously false that its proponents must be deluded or devious or perhaps both' (Kitcher 1992: 153). Kitcher's own position is more subtle and engaged and therefore probably even more devastating: psychoanalysis exemplifies a historical moment where Darwinian theory provided the fleeting possibility of a complete interdisciplinary science, a nineteenth-century vision superseded long before Freud's death yet which he stubbornly pursued. Meanwhile, current psychotherapies of trauma have often been virulently anti-Freudian and revived Janet and the alternative-consciousness paradigm in place of psychoanalysis. This is partly related to the scapegoating of Freud as the patriarch who denied the traumatic realities of his women patients. It must also be partly to do with the pressure of the requirement in legal and financial settings to insist on the truth or falsity of the inaugural traumatic event and its relation to subsequent symptoms: Freud's intertwining of the real and fantasmatic can't survive in a court of law, which demands simpler models of psychical causation. The ironies of replacing Freud with Janet in both these areas are manifold, given Janet's method of cure. But in the end the rejection of Freud must be mainly due to the transformation of professional psychiatry since the 1970s by neuro-biological drug treatments and the rise of other therapies, such as cognitive-behavioural therapy. PTSD is a product of these changes in the 1970s and thus is a psychological categorization that is difficult to reconcile with psychoanalysis at all. What that psychiatric revolution displaced was the dynamic-conflictual model inaugurated by Freud, a paradigmatic model that had begun to dominate psychiatry in the 1920s and now embodied a metapsychology that needed to be superseded.

Before 1914, Freud and rival schools of psychotherapy were distinctly marginal. Psychodynamic psychotherapeutics became paradigmatic only as a consequence of treatments during the First World War. This was a strange repetition of the argument between somatic and psychical theories of trauma, restaged all over again when the conditions of modernity produced yet another novel means for escalating instances of male traumatic hysteria: shell shock.

Trauma in the war ecology: Shell shock

In February 1915, the Cambridge academic psychologist and volunteer medic Charles Myers reported in *The Lancet* on the cases of three soldiers whose injuries related to being in proximity to shell bursts. His first example was a twenty-year-old private who had been caught on barbed wire during a retreat, with several shells exploding close enough to singe his clothes but cause no apparent physical injury. His symptoms involved blurred and then severely restricted vision, involuntary shivering, crying, a loss of taste and smell (but not hearing), and retrograde and anterograde amnesia. Myers called his paper 'A Contribution to the Study of Shell Shock', and although this was the first time it was used medically, he wrote as if the term was already in wide circulation. Myers concluded that comment was 'superfluous' but in fact the cases were anomalous. Clearly selected for injuries produced by proximity to explosions (the second case was buried by a shell, the third blown off a stack of bricks), Myers nevertheless treated them unorthodoxly with hypnosis and argued that 'the close relation of these cases to those of "hysteria" appears fairly certain' (Myers 1915: 320). There, in capsule, was the whole debate about trauma played out again: shell shock was named for a violent, exterior, physical cause yet also appeared to be an interior, psychical condition which was often completely detached from any causal connection to artillery bombardments. Although this confusion of aetiology led to shell shock being at first displaced and then forbidden as a diagnostic category in 1918, the term that the official report of the War Office Enquiry termed 'a grievous misnomer' in 1922 persisted and indeed has come to embody the traumatic experience of the Great War in the collective memory (*Report* 1922: 4).

Although no reliable statistics exist, an estimated 200,000 British soldiers were discharged for suffering shell shock. This number increased after the war, peaking in 1922, although in 1939 the government was still paying £2 million a year in pensions to psychiatric veterans (see Stone 1985). The shell-shocked soldier is one of the iconic trauma victims of the twentieth century:

> After a variable period of unconsciousness following "shock" the soldier may recover. If he is not dumb it will be found that his mind is in a state of confusion; there is both anterograde and retrograde amnesia. He has little or no idea of time and place, and his powers of recognition and comprehension are greatly impaired. He may be deaf or mute or a deaf-mute; it may be difficult therefore to ascertain what his mental condition is by conversation; or, unlike simple pithiatic mutism, he may be unable to write. The condition of his mind is reflected, however, in his face, for he has a dazed, stupid, mask-like, mindless expression. He probably assumes an anergic, crouched or curled-up posture, but he may wander about in an automatic-like way.
>
> (Mott 1919: 80–1)

The first reports of medics and doctors still manage to evoke the sense of bewilderment at the grotesque symptoms displayed in such numbers. The new machineries of war appeared to be producing a race of bizarrely maladapted creatures.

Despite the sense that 1914 was a profound rupture, there were continuities. The soldier was 'an industrial worker of sorts' (Leese 2002: 4) operating in a de-skilled, Taylorized assembly line. The front line was a mechanized factory of death, like the new efficient abattoirs that could process 200,000 cattle a day (early rumours on the front included German factories said to render human bodies into food). The Prussian state had been envisaged as a 'war machine' since the 1860s, and the European imagination was also haunted by the image of mechanized war as a driverless train, a 'rudderless modernity' heading towards catastrophe (Pick 1993: 108). Shell shock was an escalation of the industrial and train accident: it brought the same problems of diagnosis, management, statistics and compensation. Soldiers had begun to experience new technologies of war and rapid transport from the American Civil War in the 1860s (see Talbott 1996), and psychological injuries, sometimes called 'nostalgia', had been noted in the Russo-Japanese war of 1904. The Great War brought mass conscript armies into vast, static environments of near perpetual bombardment. Shell shock therefore 'defines for the first time ... mass trauma', but it also quickly adapted the language of hysteria and 'made a particular idiom of traumatic neurosis' (Leese 2002: 4 and 2).

All the same, the notion of psychological trauma had to confront totally new institutional conditions, most obviously a military establishment reluctant to recognize psychological illness as anything other than simulation or cowardice. To recognize shell shock was to sanction what one lieutenant-colonel termed 'a very contagious source of trouble when it gets into a battalion' (*Report* 1922: 66). In military structures the individual psyche is irrelevant to collective discipline and the hierarchy of command. Many of those treating shell shock discovered that military psychiatry was an impossible profession, caught between contradictory imperatives of cure and fitness for return to service. It explains why, from the Great War to the Gulf Wars, 'there appears to be a recurring cycle with the war neuroses: the problem is first denied, then exaggerated, then understood, and, finally, forgotten' (Shephard 2000: xxii). War studs the history of trauma with its own passages of fugue, where everything learnt is wiped away by a reiterative institutional amnesia.

In 1914, trauma enters a new ecology of industrial and bureaucratically organized war. Shell shock develops as a dynamic construction between psychology, neurology, military bureaucracy, technology, the political imperatives of warring nations and public opinion. For Chris Feudtner, 'the history of shell shock compels us to think in terms of dynamic permeation, where different elements of the disease-system interact ... continuously recreating the disorder as both an individual and a group phenomenon' (Feudtner 1993: 406). The strongest medical dynamic, between physical and psychological explanations of shell shock, did not operate in isolation but around an entity constituted and fought over by multiple interest groups. Trauma is once more a perplexing hybrid assemblage, rendered even more fraught in war conditions, an undecided 'matter of concern' (in Latourian terms) rather than sure fact.

The name shell shock was supposed to link causally traumatic impacts on the body to the effect of bombardment. Germans termed it *Granatshock* or *Granatkontusion*, the French *vent du projectile* (sometimes translated as 'windage'), using the same logic. The physicalist aetiology is principally associated with

Sir Frederick Mott, an asylum doctor trained in neurology who had worked under the pessimistic hereditary determinist Henry Maudsley. Mott had successfully linked the brain lesions found in 'general paralysis of the insane' to the syphilis bacterium: he studied physical brain changes. Mott's early work in the war speculated that shell shock was caused by aerial compression and concussion that produced shock waves through the incompressible spinal fluid and brain which resulted in invisible lesions and consequent nervous disorders. This revived Oppenheim's aetiology of traumatic neurosis in accidents, and although soon discredited by the vast increase of shell-shock cases (sometimes in training or long before arrival at the front), it was often clung to as an explanation by soldiers since it avoided the stigma of mental weakness. A physical wound was not just more honourable, it was also legitimately compensable: it determined the receipt and level of pension. Another persistent illness initially presumed to link to the physical effects of bombardment and the extreme exertions of the trenches was 'effort syndrome' or 'disordered action of the heart', known popularly as 'soldier's heart'. Arrhythmia was an unequivocally physical symptom, but it was soon under suspicion as a psychosomatic illness.

Mott, however, soon added to this 'commotional' theory a necessary emotional component, since it became evident that most shell-shock cases manifested through functional rather than organic disorders. Psychogenic causes became the predominant theory after the campaigns that began with the Somme in 1916, when cases multiplied far beyond the limited capacities of the medical corps and were clearly a response to Haig's murderous logic of frontal assault on enemy lines. Paul Fussell (1985) has influentially argued that the lunacy of these tactics induced a kind of detached absurdism, but the flight into bodily illness was a distinctly less detached and controlled response. 'The Battle of the Somme', it has been argued, 'might also be remembered as marking the point where the moral order represented by the dichotomy of courage and cowardice had to make way for a scientific and medical order represented by the idea of neurosis' (Brown 1995: 506). Whilst Mott was sympathetic to the intense fear and mental pressures of the front, he was also clear that 'the vast majority of psycho-neurotic cases studied were among soldiers who had a neuropathic or psychopathic soil' (Mott 1919: 110). Determinism returned to outbid the random accidents of war: a weak hereditary predisposition was to blame. Mott conceded that 'a combination of factors is responsible for traumatic shock. There is a great difficulty in differentiating the symptoms of emotional from commotional shock' (Mott 1919: 22). Nevertheless, he maintained that a strict use of shell shock was legitimate if it was 'limited to cases where there is definite evidence of a shell or bomb bursting near enough to knock the man down or blow him up' (Mott 1919: 2). In 1917, he helped introduce the form W3436 which was sent to the commanding officer of any man claiming shell shock to determine the extent of the 'exposure to shell fire'. This decided whether a soldier was considered to be actually wounded or merely 'sick'. Yet the battle wound was all too often buried beneath psychogenic factors that effloresced around a superficial injury. It was just as Charcot had observed in male traumatic neurotics, in the elaborate hysterical sequelae to minor accidents. Given this psychical elaboration, it was quite understandable for the neurologist Gordon Holmes, who had been in overall charge of Army treatments, to refuse to recognize the existence of shell shock at all (*Report* 1922: 40).

However, the cultural memory of the Great War is inextricably linked to the rise of psychodynamic treatments of shell shock. It is striking that the very first *Times* reports were titled 'The Wounded Mind', pleading that soldiers with 'diseases and wounds of the mind' be considered 'wounded men in a real sense of that term' ('The Wounded Mind' 1915: 5). In support of Lord Knutsford's campaign for special hospitals for soldiers, rather than placing them in the pauper asylum system, the Medical Correspondent used a rudimentary psychodynamic model of mind, the '"wounds of consciousness"' allowing the 'primitive instincts and emotions' of the 'sub-conscious' to well up uncontrolled ('Battle Shock' 1915: 11). This public sympathy with the mentally wounded soldier, in contrast to the disciplinarian response of the army, was a marked disjunction. The pressures of home-front public opinion surely fostered a context in which shell shock was not always received as a shameful weakness. *Doxa* became a dynamic element in the formation of war neuroses just as the literature of the war helped dictate its cultural afterlife. Indeed, Tim Armstrong suggests that many of the formal innovations associated with aesthetic Modernism should be linked with the effect of the Great War, which marks 'the entry of notions of trauma as temporal dislocation and anamnesis (lost memory) into Western consciousness' (Armstrong 2005: 19).

In the 1990s, shell shock was absorbed into PTSD whilst the British government still refused to pardon retrospectively men shot for desertion and cowardice. The public sympathy towards a particular kind of victimage was consolidated by Pat Barker's best-selling *Regeneration* trilogy (1992–5). The novels are centred on the anthropologist and Army psychologist W. H. R. Rivers. Rivers treated the prominent poet Siegfried Sassoon at Craiglockhart, a hospital for officers, ostensibly for shell shock, although Sassoon's stay was largely to avoid a public confrontation at a court martial after his public declaration of pacifism and refusal to return to his regiment. Despite the best efforts of historians to convey the atypical nature of this treatment (Shephard 1996), Barker's *Regeneration* dramatizes a simple and stark opposition between the vicious physical treatment by electric shock by the neurologist Lewis Yealland and the sympathetic, analytic-interpretive method pursued by Rivers, one of the earliest, if very cautious, English readers of Freud. Thus Rivers appears as an emissary of our trauma-sensitized present. *Regeneration*, intent on 'remaking the oldest recollections of shell shock' (Leese 2002: 175), retrofits the Great War with modern trauma theory.

The actual historical situation was as complex as the overlapping and competing versions of psychodynamic theory that I outlined in the previous section might suggest. Hans Binneveld has usefully proposed three distinct psychological models for shell shock: nervous exhaustion, suggestion and psychodynamic conflict (Binneveld 1997: 90). Nervous exhaustion was an acceptable compromise formation, implying neurological routes into the body for psychical damage. The generic terms traumatic or war neuroses existed in the same space. As Charles Myers emphasized, 'a shell, then, may play no part whatever in the causation of "shell shock": excessive emotion, e.g. sudden horror or fear – indeed any "psychical trauma" or "inadjustable experience" – is sufficient' (Myers 1940: 26). Very soon, conversion reactions to the traumas of war were distinguished between hysterical and neurasthenic responses. Hysteria was a short-term reaction to the extremity of a particular situation. If treated close in time and space to the front, the soldier could be returned to his unit relatively quickly, whilst evacuation was likely to turn acute problems into chronic ones. A tang of moral weakness hung around hysteria: it was associated with new working-class conscripts, with Irish cannon-fodder by British commanders and with Jews by the Germans (see Bourke 2000). Neurasthenia, on the other hand, was the result of prolonged exposure to the perpetual anxiety of the front, causing nervous 'wear and tear'. This anxiety neurosis was typically associated with officers, who were understood to suffer acceptably under the responsibilities of command and was considered an understandable collapse, responsive to simple rest and relaxation. Neurasthenia had survived as a disease-entity without much change from its coinage by George Beard in 1869 as a problem of over-exciting modernity, and the cure for officers was the same rest cure advised by Victorian alienists for bourgeois women.

Charles Myers used these relatively conventional terms, yet his career in the Army showed the difficulty in employing this basic psychological framework. Initially refused an army post, and working as a volunteer in France, the crisis in shell-shock cases rapidly elevated him to chief army specialist in 1915 and Consultant Psychiatrist to the Army in 1916. He attempted to organize rudimentary training in the identification of functional disorders at forward treatment centres, but the Royal Army Medical Corps was a backwater, subservient to Army priorities. Physicalists like Mott and Holmes were higher up the chain of command, and any organization of psychiatric support was treated with suspicion and developed only with great reluctance. Myers also evidently used hypnosis, anathema to the neurologist Holmes who would have seen it as only fostering further mental weakness. Partly at his own request, Myers was returned to the home front. His reflections on shell shock, which he was only prompted to write by the onset of the Second World War in the hope of the same mistakes being avoided, was itself traumatic for Myers: 'the revival of these long-repressed memories ... has been extremely unpleasant' (Myers 1940: 141). His case reveals the real limits to the advance of psychodynamic theories of trauma in war conditions.

Suggestion, although a dynamic theory, was more compatible with the physicalist suspicion of the weak constitution of the conscript soldier. If shell shock was a hysteria, then just as *idées fixes* converted into myriad bodily symptoms in the individual, so one officially recognized case of shell shock could run through a whole battalion, moving from soldier to soldier through neuromimesis or simulation. Myers called it a 'contagious' term (Myers 1940: 40), and many witnesses to the War Office Enquiry emphasized that shell shock was clustered in groups and fostered by weak command. A refusal of officers to release a soldier from the front line would prevent hysterical contagion. In this discussion, trauma is once more marked by the now familiar mystery of transpersonal affective transmission.

In an early understanding of the suggestive power of the mere name of an illness, Myers was involved in abolishing the very term he had coined. By 1917, forward medical units categorized the injured with the deliberately undetermined 'NYD?N' (Not Yet Diagnosed – Nervous?) in order to restrict a solider fixing on and elaborating a version of shell shock by 'auto-suggestion' between initial diagnosis and subsequent treatment. Should a soldier reach treatment centres, the imposition of the will of the doctor by aggressive counter-suggestion was a common method of cure across the spectrum. Even the physicalist Yealland, who treated a handful of hysterical mutism cases with electrical shocks to the throat, confessed that his method worked primarily through the suggestive fear of pain rather than any neurological rationale (Yealland 1918). Shell shock as suggestion was most strongly associated with Charcot's successor at the Salpêtrière, Joseph Babinski. Babinski demolished Charcot's taxonomy of hysteria, redistributing some symptoms back to organic illnesses, but with the majority of psychogenic instances redescribed as 'pithiatic'. Pithiatism, Babinski's coinage combining the Greek for persuasion and cure, made suggestion the defining element: 'Hysteria is a pathological state manifested by disorders which it is possible to reproduce exactly by suggestion in certain subjects and can be made to disappear by the influence of persuasion (counter-suggestion) alone' (Babinksi and Fremont 1918: 17). Epidemics of hysteria arose from 'a love of imitation', and had been inadvertently cultivated in ignorance by Charcot's generation, so that a reorganization of wards and treatments had been enough to end these outbreaks. The war, however, provided new favourable conditions for suggestive contagions. Babinski gathered evidence to disprove both commotional and emotional theories: he was adamant that 'emotion alone, however intense it may be, does not produce hysterical disorders' (Babinski and Fremont 1918: 24). Instead, Babinski argued that extreme situations or violent bombardments could affect a state of mental confusion where suggestion blossomed, and this explained the interregnum between the extreme event and the appearance of symptoms. 'Emotion and traumatism only predispose to manifestations of this kind. They increase suggestibility and sometimes provide the elements of auto-suggestion' (Babinski and Fremont 1918: 45). Suggestion bound shell shock to ideas of neuromimesis and simulation: it fostered a situation in which the French government refused to issue pensions to soldiers with discharged with merely psychological illnesses.

The third psychological model of shell shock, psychodynamic conflict, was developed by Rivers through the course of the war. Rivers had been initially posted to work at Maghull, the psychiatric treatment centre outside Liverpool run by R. G. Rows under an innovative therapeutic regime, far away from military disciplinary models. It was where Elliot-Smith and Pear had worked, who publicly argued for shell-shock cases as 'emotional disturbances' and advocated 'psychological analysis and re-education' (Elliot-Smith and Pear 1917: viii and ix). Maghull latterly trained psychiatrists for front-line work. Rivers, after moving to Craiglockhart where he worked intensively with a handful of officer patients, composed an important string of essays. In 'Repression of War Experience' he investigated shell shock as the result of psychological conflict, as a *process* of active forgetting rather than a structure or *state* of mind, like dissociation. The amnesias associated with shell shock were 'due to the attempt to banish from the mind distressing memories of warfare or painful affective states which have come into being as a result of their war experience' (Rivers 1917: 173). For much of the time, this was an appropriate adaptive response, where forgetting allowed psychical survival. War neurosis, however, developed around 'the hidden working of some forgotten yet active experience ... whereby painful thoughts were pushed into hidden recesses of his mind, only to accumulate such force as to make them well up and produce attacks of depression' (Rivers 1917: 175). It kept men in a neurotic state, suffering repeated relapses, unless the specific memory was confronted (this exhausting mental dynamic was hauntingly conveyed in Sassoon's poem with the same title as his analyst's essay). Rivers' thesis owed much to his reading of Freud, although the limited extent of the influence of this psychodynamic model is symbolized by its bracketing in its original *Lancet* publication by a lecture by Frederick Mott on one side and a statistical survey on the other proving that 74 per cent of war neurotics had 'a family history of neurotic or psychotic stigmata, including insanity, epilepsy, alcoholism and nervousness' (Wolfsohn 1918: 180). In a separate assessment of Freud, Rivers disregarded much of the architecture of psychoanalysis, particularly the universal sexual aetiology of neuroses, and rescued the fundamental idea of psychic conflict mediated by the mechanism of repression, that 'active suppression of unpleasant experience' (Rivers 1920: 163).

Freud wrote little on the war and treated no shell-shock cases himself, although many in his inner circle did. A symposium on the war neuroses was held at the Fifth International Psycho-Analytical Congress in September 1918, and Freud's brief introduction to the collected papers speculated on a conflict between 'the soldier's old peaceful ego and his new war-like one' in which 'the old ego is protecting itself from a mortal danger by taking flight into a traumatic neurosis' (Freud 1919: 209). But the introduction was mainly concerned with refuting 'the opponents of psychoanalysis, whose dislike of sexuality is evidently stronger than their logic, [and who] have been in a hurry to proclaim that the investigation of the war neuroses has finally disproved this portion of psycho-analytic theory' (Freud 1919: 208). Yet this was exactly the version of psychoanalysis that began to receive attention after the war. One of Freud's closest allies, Sandor Ferenczi, began to rethink trauma outside libido theory partly in response to his own treatment of war neurotics (discussed at length in Leys 2000). In the craze for 'Freudish' talk that began in England in the early 1920s, cathartic treatments of war neuroses were cited as its notable success, but praise routinely discarded any sexual theory (see Rapp 1988 and Richards 2000). The psychoanalytically trained doctor David Eder worked on shell-shock cases in Malta. His *War-Shock: The Psychoneuroses in War* proposed that most symptoms were 'the result of mental conflicts or other mental phenomena ... understood in terms of the mind without any reference to physio-pathology. The psycho-pathology of war-shock is that of the psycho-neuroses, and the mechanisms those discovered by Freud in hysteria' (Eder 1917: 144). However, his successes came with the distinctly un-Freudian method of hypnosis, and his book, Ben Shephard suggests, had little impact and effectively ended his career.

After the war, however, psychotherapeutic treatments seemed to chime with a strand of public sympathy for the still-increasing numbers of shell-shocked men. Its very marginality in military medicine during the war now worked to its advantage. Freud was called on as a witness to judge the harsh electrical treatments of war neurotics by the Austrian War Ministry, since his treatment was evidently represented an utterly opposed method (Freud 1920b). In England, the 1922 *Report* of the War Office registered this changing context. The *Report* initially uses scare quotes around '"mental wound"', reflecting military suspicion of regarding 'the emotional variety' as a proper 'battle casualty' (*Report* 1922: 115). A few pages later, it uses the language of 'psychical dissociation' or the 'functional splitting of the personality … which, in the opinion of some witnesses, should be regarded as a mental wound' (*Report* 1922: 117). The final recommendations tentatively recommended 'the simplest forms of psycho-therapy', but rejected the dangers of hypnosis and 'psycho-analysis in the Freudian sense' (*Report* 1922: 192). In the main though, as Simon Wessely observes, the *Report* 'continued to reflect traditional Edwardian values of courage and moral fibre' and called for tougher training of recruits to prevent psychological weakness (Wessely 2006: 271). In these tensions, the *Report* carried the stresses of transformed social, political and psychological understandings of the War in the early 1920s (see Bogacz 1989).

By 1941 the idea of psychical conflict, developed by Rivers and drained of Freud's investment in libido theory, was at the heart of Abram Kardiner's *Traumatic Neuroses of War*. Kardiner's book was organized around the concept of 'trauma' in a distinct way (rather than just using it as a synonymous term amongst others). It emerged from Kardiner's observation of chronic shell-shock patients at an American veteran's hospital in the early 1920s and from his dissatisfaction with Freud's libidinal or instinctual theories to account for traumatic neurosis in war. Instead, Kardiner proposed a conflict between the ego and the environment: 'a trauma is an external influence necessitating an abrupt change in adaptation which the organism fails to meet' (Kardiner 1941: 79). Symptoms, in this theory, marked places where 'an adaptation is injured, spoiled, disorganized, or shattered' and modern war was ingenious in creating 'more difficult situations to escape and thus activates disorganization of the ego' (Kardiner 1941: 74 and 70). Whilst a psychodynamic theory (claiming psychoanalysis to provide the best account of functional neuroses), Kardiner was nevertheless reviving the nineteenth-century terminology of 'traumatic neurosis' and conceiving the maladaptations to war in the same continuum as the submission of the individual ego to modern mass industry (Kardiner 1941: 70). Although Kardiner's work did not register much in the repetition of the debates about war trauma in the Second World War, it had a big influence on the Vietnam generation. Kardiner's book is 'routinely cited as a landmark in the history of posttraumatic disorders', and it became one of the key sources of the presenting symptoms for PTSD (Leys 2000: 193).

Shell shock was only ever 'a makeshift umbrella covering a varied set of administrative, disciplinary, and medical problems' (Stone 1985: 258). Like hysteria, it morphed continually as official diagnostics tried to outfox the ingenuity of soma and psyche, the plain cunning of the frontline soldier seeking ever new ways to 'swing the lead', and the ever-shifting alliances of the military, the political classes and home-front opinion. War imperatives pushed the protean tendencies of trauma into greater mobility. By World War Two, shell shock was replaced by 'battle fatigue' or the deliberately vague 'exhaustion'. Doctors attempted new treatments, including drugs like sodium amytal or pentathol, the dramatic 'acting out' of traumatic scenes, and trials with group therapy. Military commanders expressed the same suspicion or contempt for the medical 'trick cyclists' attached to units. Montgomery humiliated them; American General Patton lost his command for slapping a traumatized soldier in a military hospital, enraged by the apparent refusal to fight.

There are other continuities that suggest a dispiriting sense of repetition when trauma enters the particular ecology of war. Gulf War Syndrome has remained a disputed entity since 1991, with some commentators regarding it as a purely psychical hysteria (for instance, Showalter 1997) whilst others insist that, beyond a small number of cases of PTSD, veterans suffer physical illnesses as a result of vaccine cocktails, pesticidal spraying of equipment, low-level exposure to nerve gas or the inhalation of depleted uranium dust. In England, disability pensions have been disbursed under the category of 'Symptoms and Signs of Ill-Defined Conditions', but the Ministry of Defence has refused to accept the existence of Gulf War Syndrome (see Lloyd 2004). In America, the Research Advisory Committee on Gulf War Veterans' Illnesses issued a report in 2004 which argued that the multisymptom conditions gathered under the name Gulf War Syndrome were extensive in veterans, could not be solely explained by war-time stress or psychiatric illness, were likely the result of exposure to neuro-toxins, and would require extensive federal research funding to determine its full extent (Research Advisory Committee 2004). In 2006, studies recorded that almost one-fifth of Gulf War II veterans suffered psychiatric illnesses, with military authorities 'not doing enough to support soldiers and their families' (Townsend and Revill 2006: 8).

Whilst this suggests the continued military refusal to accept psychosomatic sequelae to combat experience, the hawkish military historian Eric Dean has blamed the recent 'rights revolution' and liberal psychiatry for privileging the individual soldier over military command, the new language of traumatic disorders virtually putting an end to the possibility of large-scale military actions by America. Dean identifies the Vietnam War as the critical passage in the reassessment and cultural transvaluation of the war neurotic. Indeed, in the 1970s, a group of committed anti-Vietnam War psychiatrists were responsible for naming and defining the parameters of what they called Post-Traumatic Stress Disorder, initially in relation to combat veterans. Yet their model of militant advocacy soon became a strategy at the heart of the new identity politics that emerged in the 1970s, uniting war veterans, Holocaust survivors and feminists speaking out over the traumas of rape and sexual abuse. When PTSD entered official diagnostics in 1980, it gave a coherent disease-entity to diverse political programmes and ensured the wide diffusion of the trauma paradigm.

Trauma and the politics of identity: Vietnam, Holocaust and abuse survivors

In 1982, the American Congress commissioned a quantitative psychiatric assessment of Vietnam veterans, in the main an attempt by Reagan to reduce funding to the ninety veteran centres established under Carter's presidency. The report, *Trauma and the Vietnam War Generation*, was eventually published in 1990, and contained startling findings. The first study of troops medically evacuated from the front line in Vietnam, conducted in 1966, had recorded that only five per cent were due to psychiatric disorders, a much lower percentage than cases during the Second World War (W. Scott 1990: 295). This was considered a testament to lessons learnt, each battalion now staffed with its own psychiatrist. Over fifteen years after the end of the war, however, Congress was told that now more than 25 per cent of veterans, over 800,000 people, suffered from PTSD. This was nearly three times the amount of soldiers who experienced *direct* combat in Vietnam. The figure increased even further if the lifetime of the veteran was the measure: 30.6 per cent of men and 26.9 per cent of women had or would suffer from full or partial PTSD as a result of their experience in Vietnam (Kulka *et al.* 1990). By 1997, the number of veteran outreach centres had in fact doubled as PTSD diagnoses reached the one million mark, and the Veterans Administration had become one of the largest federal agencies in America. The Vietnam veteran was a trauma icon, 'the quintessential "stressed-out" American' (Dean 1997: 23). The Report gave statistical authority to what had already been fixed in the cultural imaginary. Cinematic representations in particular cemented an image of the traumatized veteran, starting soon after the war with *Taxi Driver* (Martin Scorsese 1976), *The Deer Hunter* (Michael Cimino 1979), *Apocalypse Now* (Francis Ford Coppola 1979) and *Cutter's Way* (Ivan Passer 1981). These cultural representations of the Vietnam veteran had already 'helped to create a new "consciousness of trauma" in Western society' (Shephard 2000: 355).

In book after book, veterans and their psychiatrists described persistent symptoms of insomnia, hyper-vigilance, startle reactions, alcohol and drug addiction, terror, paranoia and nightmares. 'I think I don't have long to live because I have these dreams of guys in my unit standing at the end of the sofa and blood coming down off them and up the sofa' (Shay 1994: xiv). The sheer extent and delay of post-traumatic responses has been attributed to the specific conditions of combat in Vietnam: intense guerrilla engagements on the ground, where combatants and civilians were indistinguishable, where the war aims were morally ambiguous, command was openly contested and actions were shot through with notorious instances of atrocity, where the conscript troops were mainly teenagers vulnerable to drug addiction, and where the one-year tour of duty, designed to prevent 'combat fatigue', only intensified the alienation of soldiers returning alone to a home front severely divided on the prosecution of the war (see Hendin and Haas 1984). Further, in the embarrassment of defeat, veterans were given no affirmation, but felt silenced and blamed (it took Reagan to develop a revisionist account that the military 'had been denied permission to win' by a liberal conspiracy on the home front (Dean 1997: 184)). Sympathy for young conscripted soldiers had disappeared after the My Lai massacre in March 1968, when a company entered a village and murdered over four hundred civilians, an event at first denied by the military but finally confirmed when photographic evidence surfaced, causing a severe national convulsion in America (see Oliver 2006).

For the psychiatrist Robert Jay Lifton, My Lai 'brought about an abrupt change in my own relationship to the war, and in my life in general' (Lifton 1973: 16). Susan Haley, a psychiatric nurse working with veterans in Boston, had reported in 1969 that patients revealing memories of atrocities had been dismissed by staff as delusional paranoid schizophrenics. Now, a group of committed psychiatric advocates wanted to affirm the traumatic reality of events in Vietnam. Using Haley's patient as the key testimony in *Home from the War*, Lifton argued that Vietnam was an atrocity-producing situation, an existentially Absurd war that wounded everyone it touched. Lifton testified on the damaging psychological effects of war to the Sub-Committee on Veteran Affairs in 1970 and later that year began to meet with the activist group Vietnam Veterans Against the War in its New York offices. What were called 'rap groups' were a mix of anti-war planning and group therapy. Another anti-war psychiatrist Chaim Shatan became involved when the group grew in size and in May 1972 he wrote a piece for the *New York Times* arguing that a distinct 'Post-Vietnam Syndrome' was discernable in veteran behaviour. 'The so-called Post-Vietnam Syndrome confronts us with the unconsummated grief of soldiers ... Their sorrow is unspent, the grief of their wounds untold, their guilt unexpatiated' (cited W. Scott 1990: 301). Lifton continued his group treatments into 1974, by which time John Wilson had begun treating veterans on the Cleveland University campus in informal rap groups. Wilson failed to find research money for an unrecognized psychological condition until the Disabled Army Veterans group funded his work: three volumes of *The Forgotten Warrior* appeared between 1977 and 1980. Wilson was convinced that a clear 'post-Vietnam pattern of psychological reaction' required a new conceptual framework and mode of treatment as the illness 'was a multifaceted process that cut across different dimensions of psychosocial functioning' (Wilson 2006: 253). Wilson was involved in organizing the Veterans Association outreach centres, finally given Democratic funding in 1979. Charles Figley, meanwhile, entered graduate school in psychology after serving as a marine officer in Vietnam: his study, *Delayed Combat Stress Disorders*, was written for the American Legion in 1978. Using the Consortium of Veteran Studies as an initial group, Figley helped transform this into the wider-based Society for Trauma and Stress Studies in 1985, editing the first two volumes of what became its journal under the title *Trauma and its Wake*.

It was this network that used politically inflected 'advocacy research' (Lifton's coinage) to campaign for the recognition of the syndrome that eventually became Post-Traumatic Stress Disorder. There was a shuffling of potential terminologies throughout the 1970s: Shatan's Post-Vietnam Syndrome was too specific, Gross Stress Reaction was revived from follow-up studies of Second World War veterans in the 1960s, and some favoured Catastrophic Stress Disorder before PTSD emerged as a compromise in 1978. But there was a much more important reason for this shifting language: the case for a trauma syndrome could be pressed because throughout this period the American Psychiatric Association was undertaking a revolutionary transformation of its conceptual base and psychiatric terminology. For the third edition of its *Diagnostic and Statistical Manual*, the APA announced that it would depart from psychodynamic models of unconscious conflict, and instead move to an empirical, purely descriptive model of syndromes, identifiable through replicable rule-bound diagnostic criteria that had been developed in biomedical research. The chair of the Task Force on Nomenclature, Robert Spitzer, had already developed Research Diagnostic Criteria to trial the description of fourteen psychiatric disorders, something encouraged by government agencies since diagnostic accuracy was reached more rapidly than psychotherapy and could circumscribe more precisely health and welfare benefits. This new method was intended to banish aetiological speculation, and to provide instead 'a diagnostic metalanguage: a way of talking about mental disorders that is not particular to any theoretical orientation' (Young 1995: 94). This medical model was bitterly contested by psychoanalytic associations, who refused to co-operate in the overthrow of the dynamic paradigm. This was a serious mistake, for Spitzer had set up formal and informal avenues of consultation, and a successful campaign (with 10,000 professional psychiatric signatories) had removed homosexuality as a disorder from the planned *DSM* edition by 1974. This provided a model for psychiatric advocacy. Soon, 'unsolicited input from many of the nation's psychiatrists' began to make the case for other syndromes and disorders (M. Wilson 1993: 406). Chaim Shatan approached Spitzer in 1974 once it became clear that no specific combat disorder was to be included in *DSM-III*. Shatan and Susan Haley were asked to present material on Post-Vietnam Syndrome to the 1975 APA convention, and a working group was set up to gather empirical evidence for potential criteria for a disorder. The group expanded to include Lifton, the psychiatrist and Holocaust survivor Henry Krystal, Jack Smith, head of the National Veterans Resource Project, and Mardi Horowitz, whose work on stress provided a new physiological basis for traumatic reactions, thus linking Vietnam trauma to a key moment in the theorization (and funding) of stress research in America (Viner 1999). They examined several hundred cases, using techniques that persuaded the empirical biomedics on the panel, but widened the category beyond combat scenarios and eventually agreed on PTSD. This was 'a cumbersome phrase devised by a cumbersome committee' (Shephard 2000: xx), but it bound together diverse socio-political and medical aims into one term.

Yet the arrival of PTSD in 1980 was not just the product of the long history of traumatic neuroses inside the ecology of war, latterly transformed by anti-Vietnam advocacy. The term would never have been so astoundingly successful in its cultural pervasiveness if it had retained this relatively narrow focus. Instead, the advocates were self-consciously comparative, seeking out links to studies of the psychological reactions of those who survived the Hiroshima bombing, the victims of Nazi persecution, the consequences of slavery and segregation on African–American identity, and women who had suffered incest or rape trauma, and whose experiences were only just beginning to be articulated by the feminist movement. Workers in these distinct areas mutually reinforced each other; what emerged was a general category of 'the survivor' that strongly linked trauma to identity politics.

Identity politics, the idea that 'identity itself – its elaboration, expression or affirmation – is and should be a fundamental focus of political work' (Kauffman 2001: 23), is often associated in cultural and political histories on both the left and right with this era of civil rights, anti-Vietnam student protest, feminism, gay liberation and Black Power. Many of these movements were reacting to the 'unmarked' identity and 'affective foreclosures' of what Dana Nelson regards as an embedded construct of 'national manhood' in the imagined fraternity of white men (Nelson 1998: ix). These new groupings developed forms of consciousness-raising that often used the model of the rap groups developed by Lifton. Judith Herman, student civil rights campaigner in the 1960s, pioneer in consciousness raising, feminist therapist and PTSD advocate since the 1970s, argued in *Trauma and Recovery* that 'traumatic disorders are afflictions of the powerless', reinforced by mechanisms of social denial (Herman 1992: 83). Looking across from the contemporary study of sexual abuse to the Victorian hysteric and the wounded soldier, she claimed that 'traumatic reality ... requires a social context that affirms and protects the victim' (Herman 1992: 9). This in turn meant that 'the systematic study of psychological trauma therefore depends on the support of a political movement' (Herman 1992: 9). The psychiatrist must do more than diagnose and medicate; they had to be a committed person, affirming identity from 'a position of moral solidarity with the survivor' (Herman 1992: 178). Charles Figley used what became standard terms to express the purpose of this therapeutic empowerment: 'Victims and survivors are familiar in that they both experienced a traumatic event. But while the victim has been immobilized and discouraged by the event, the survivor has overcome the traumatic memories and become mobile' (Figley 1985: 399). PTSD is therefore not just a narrow medicalizing label, although it has successfully served, as I have shown, as a category determining recognizable psychiatric illness and compensable injury. Just as much, PTSD is a socio-political category that has routed a significant strand of identity politics into the language of survivorship. This is not to accuse liberal and left political advocacy as the sole cause of the rise of 'victim culture', as conservative commentators like Christopher Lasch might. When the right complains of 'political correctness' in the sphere of modern identity and risk, it nearly always conceals the capitalist economic drivers of law, insurance and medical costs behind many of these transformations.

In terms of the identity politics of this era, one of the key figures in the transvaluation of trauma was Robert Jay Lifton. It is worth spending some time on his career because, perhaps more than any other single figure, Lifton maps out the transition of psychical trauma from medical discourse to cultural condition.

Lifton's first work had been with American prisoners of war who had been subjected to Chinese 'brainwashing' techniques during the Korean War. He then travelled to study the psychological conditions of the *hibakusha* in Hiroshima in the early 1960s. *Hibakusha* translated literally as 'explosion-affected person'; the term 'survivor' was avoided by the Japanese as a dishonour to the dead. The initial awkwardness of how to name his study group reflected something of the 'extreme historical situations characteristic of our own era' (Lifton 1968: 5). This was to inaugurate Lifton's life's work. In *Death in Life*, Lifton described Hiroshima as a profound ontological shock, 'a sudden and absolute shift from normal experience to an overwhelming encounter with death' (Lifton 1968: 21). From extensive interviews, Lifton portrayed an absurdist, post-detonation world dominated by the dead, where the still-living could survive only by psychic closing-off or numbing, yet were indelibly marked by the 'death-imprint', suffered 'survival guilt' and 'thralldom to the death encounter' (Lifton 1968: 482). Those living on could only identify with the dead, living a counterfeit or automatic life, yet secretly fearing that they were contagious, 'carriers of death' (Lifton 1968: 517). The other mark of the death-encounter was the inability to formulate the experience, a collapse of narrative possibility, leaving death stalled in the psyche, a permanent rupture in the sense of life continuity. Lifton's framework was broadly psychodynamic but did not (yet) use the language of trauma. The Freudian model was held to miss the true significance of the death-encounter, so Lifton's formative book was not bound to a single school and largely invented its own, extremely accessible, technical terms. Crucially, Lifton always wanted to generalize outwards from the mental anguish of the *hibakusha*, arguing that the globally destructive potential of nuclear weapons meant that 'we are all survivors of Hiroshima' (Lifton 1968: 479). The final chapter of *Death in Life* was titled 'The Survivor', declaring that 'the holocausts of the twentieth century have thrust the survivor ethos into special prominence, and imposed upon us all a series of immersions into death' (Lifton 1968: 479). Comparisons with concentration camp inmates proliferated, again as symbols of a universal historical condition of the post-1945 world.

In the same year as *Death in Life*, Lifton was a contributor to the proceedings of the conference, *Massive Psychic Trauma*. Edited by the psychoanalyst Henry Krystal (who had been imprisoned in Auschwitz, Buchenwald and Sachsenhausen, and was his sole family survivor of the Holocaust), the conference was avowedly comparative, incorporating natural disasters, man-made catastrophes, victims of Nazi persecution, industrial accidents and work place compensation, Hiroshima, and those suffering social oppression, such as the American Negro, whose self-identity had been 'damaged in ways not repairable by himself' (Krystal 1968: 5). The opening paper was given by William Niederland, who had coined the term 'survivor syndrome' for 'emotional disorders of survivors of Nazi persecution' (Niederland 1968b: 8). In a parallel essay in 1968, Niederland had argued that traumatic neurosis, typically used for war experiences, 'does not appear sufficient to cover the multitude and severity of the clinical manifestations', the 'all-pervasive psychological scar' of camp experience (Niederland 1968b: 314, 313). In the conference, Niederland detailed the activism of a group of New York therapists urgently trying to redefine concepts of trauma, because the delayed onset of symptoms was resulting in former concentration camp inmates being refused compensation for psychiatric injury by the German government on the basis that causation from camp to symptom could not be proved. Lifton was introduced as an openly comparative instance, and he rehearsed his work with Hiroshima *hibakusha*. It was a moment where psychiatric advocacy forged new connections, and helped establish the strategies Lifton pursued with his next group of death-in-life survivors, the Vietnam veterans. As with the *hibakusha*, the veterans soon became representative figures of a general condition: 'all Americans are survivors of the Vietnam holocaust and are faced with the task of recognizing and bring-ing significance to their death immersion' (Lifton 1973: 305). Later, Lifton worked with the survivors of the industrial accident at Buffalo Creek, and in 1979 pub-lished a theoretical work, *The Broken Connection*, which contained the essay 'Survivor Experience and Traumatic Syndrome'. The book, an argument with Freud's prioritizing of libidinal theory and consequent disinterest in adult trauma, marked Lifton's acknowledgement of the new psychiatric terminology.

It is striking how soon Lifton begins morally to elevate the survivor. The sur-vivor is explicitly regarded as a prophet or visionary because they have touched death, 'crossed over to the other side and returned' and can 'now claim an exclu-sive knowledge of all matters related to death and holocaust' (Lifton 1973: 314). This echoes a long psychoanalytic tradition of believing traumatic experience gifts the patient heightened, even supernatural powers (something Sandor Ferenczi fervently believed, as Pam Thurschwell (2001) has recorded), and the value existentialism gave to the 'limit situation', where only extremity truly con-firmed being-in-the-world. This produced a curious circularity in Lifton's work. The psychiatric injuries of a specific survivor are described in all their anguish. This becomes a representative experience of a generalized psychic numbing, but traumatic experiences then become valued as those which precisely break through this numbed state. In *The Broken Connection*, Lifton argued that for the Vietnam veterans who became anti-war activists, 'the traumatic experience, or at least elements of it, had a constructive function': 'doubts about the war began with a confrontation which broke through existing patterns of numbing' (Lifton 1979: 169). The survivor alone can reconvene the shattered fragments of the post-war world, the passage through a trauma giving the sanction of privileged perspective from that rarest of things, a coherent, if trauma-defined, identity. The fear of the *hibakusha* that they carried a deathly contagion thus also has its flip-side: the victim becomes a site for identification, the survivor subject-position developing a kind of glamour. This contagion of identification begins with the psychiatric advocate: 'If one is to grasp holocaust from a distance', Lifton warned, 'one must, at some inner level, decide to become a "survivor" of that holocaust, and take on the "survivor mission" of giving it form in a way that contributes to something beyond it' (Lifton 1973: 17). Trauma passes from analysand to analyst and, through advocacy and activism, becomes a privileged site for identity.

In 1980, Robert Jay Lifton spoke to a conference on 'the survivor syndrome' in London, held to address 'the enormous resistance in the helping professions quite as much as in the population at large, to comprehending the problem of survival' (Garland 1980b: 5). The final overview of the event, after Lifton and others had spoken, asked a rather startling question: 'This Workshop ... found itself talking and thinking almost solely about the Holocaust and its survivors. How and why did it happen that all possible catastrophes, past, present, or future, were virtually ignored in favour of this one?' (Garland 1980a: 93). It is difficult to imagine this question being asked now, yet it suggests that the 'Holocaust survivor' is a relatively late construction in the psychiatric discourse of trauma, emerging alongside, or even slightly later than, the Vietnam veteran. Just as striking, though, is the entire absence from the workshop of any discussion of incest or sexual abuse survivors; these seem simply inconceivable to the participants. It is only after 1980, then, that these poles of survivorship properly enter the language of trauma studies and come to dominate the terrain. The spectrum of trauma is redrawn, with the Holocaust the worst imaginable collective trauma, sexual abuse the worst individual trauma. PTSD, initially conceived for combat veterans, was recruited to very different politics of identity at these poles, Lifton providing the model of psychiatric advocacy. These two areas of survival are the final elements that need to be included in this genealogy of trauma.

Recent discussions of the Holocaust have been fenced around with claims about the unique and unprecedented nature of the atrocity that make the kind of historicization I propose here deeply offensive to some. To historicize is to 'normalize' events, where much cultural trauma theory (as we've seen in my Introduction) wants to consider the Holocaust an aporia, traumatic enough to shatter the frame of historiography or representation itself. For Lawrence Langer, narrative possibility, coherence and normalization belong to *mémoire ordinaire*, whilst Holocaust accounts must always touch on the irresolvable and incomprehensible traumas of the *mémoire profonde* (this opposition derives from Delbo 1995). The Holocaust is, for Dori Laub, a 'massive trauma' that 'precludes its registration' in the normal way (Felman and Laub 1992: 57). Nazism and the Final Solution 'need to be theorised under the sign of massive psychic trauma', Eric Santner concurs, 'meaning that these events must be confronted and analysed in their capacity to endanger and overwhelm the composition and coherence of individual and collective identities' (Santner 1992: 151). Yet to use the notion of trauma might also itself be normalizing since, according to Robert Eaglestone, in holding out a promise of cure, 'trauma theory offers ... an illusory redemption' (Eaglestone 2004: 32). The risk for Eaglestone is that trauma

> will overcode accounts of the Holocaust with a discourse of healing analysis or therapy, and so pass over both the epistemological and ethical impossibility of comprehending the survivors' testimony by seeming to grasp and resolve it, and "work through" or finish with the ethical obligation to recall the events.
>
> (Eaglestone 2004: 33)

These positions, that virtually any framework is unethical or normalizing (including the word 'holocaust' itself, a Christian term often replaced by the

Hebrew Sho'ah), were consolidated in cultural trauma theory in the 1980s and 1990s at the same time that a very different group of Jewish–American scholars were insisting on the uniqueness of the Holocaust as immeasurably graver a genocidal act than any possible comparative events. Steven Katz's *The Holocaust in Historical Context*, for instance, demoted all acts of mass murder in history to categories below genocide, using a definition of genocide that could be filled only by the Nazi extermination of the Jews. For Gavriel Rosenfeld, this insistence was 'best understood as part of a self-consciously *defensive* response to the perceived attempts by others to diminish the event for apologetic or revisionist purposes' (Rosenfeld 2004: 371). This references the upsurge of Holocaust denial, but also the so-called Historians' Dispute in Germany, perceived by some as trying to finish with German post-war abjection, separating off its genocidal past as an historical aberration. Rosenfeld suggests an alternative reason for this debate about uniqueness, in rather more critical terms: it is the fault of multiculturalism. This is translated as 'the tendency … of ethnic groups to justify present-day demands by citing past wrongs' (Rosenfeld 2004: 389) and Rosenfeld dismisses largely as polemic the attempts of David Stannard and Ward Churchill to call the deaths of native Americans a genocide. 'In this atmosphere of vicitimization', Rosenfeld says damningly of the politics of identity in multicultural America, 'a genocidal past is an obvious political asset' (Rosenfeld 2004: 389). These are self-evidently contentious and heavily invested areas of dispute.

The view that an authentic Jewish genocide has been borrowed and diluted by other interest groups occasionally becomes explicit (E. Alexander 1980). Yet the psychiatric construct of the 'Holocaust survivor' is not the original of which others are lesser copies. Rather, the 'Holocaust survivor' developed alongside other trauma subjects in the 1960s and 1970s, explicitly so in the work of Henry Krystal and William Niederland. In that sense, Holocaust 'survival' – as a specific way of theorizing post-traumatic existence – is an intrinsically time-specific and comparative construction.

In the immediate aftermath of the war, the Displaced Persons (DPs) gradually dispersed from the camps were not necessarily identified ethnically. It has been well established by historians that there was little public discussion of the liberated prisoners of the concentration camps until Adolf Eichmann's trial in 1961 exposed the world to the bureaucracy of mass murder. Jewish organizations in America had hoped for 'a reduction of horror stories of victimized Jewry' at the end of the war (cited Novick 1999: 121). The founders of the state of Israel in 1948 similarly wished to promote an imagined national community based on heroism rather than victimage, the new political leaders being privately dismissive of camp survivors. Peter Novick has controversially suggested that it was the period of the Six Day War in 1967 and the Yom Kippur attacks of 1973 that turned Holocaust remembrance into a political means to bolster support for the state of Israel. In America, the Holocaust education programmes that began to be funded by the Anti-Defamation League in 1973 culminated in the opening of the National Holocaust Museum in Washington twenty years later, placing Holocaust remembrance at the centre of American national culture. Both Novick and the polemicist Norman Finkelstein have explored the lobbying of the writer and survivor Elie Wiesel to ensure that the Museum focused solely on the Jewish victims of Nazi persecution. Less polemically, James Young has tracked how the Israeli state has reorganized itself around a calendar of national remembrance (Young 1993). These are inevitably controversial stances, since they politicize and give a history to a rhetoric of remembrance that is saturated with the transcendent language of the sacred.

Whatever one makes of these lines of argument, the narrower discourse around the psychological effects of concentration camp internment seems to confirm that the category of 'Holocaust survivor' was relatively late to develop. There are only a handful of studies before the 1960s, and these repeat the familiar physical/psychical oscillation found throughout the history of trauma. In 1951, V. A. Kral wrote a short study of 'severe chronic stress' within the Terezin (Theresienstadt) internment camp, using psychodynamic models of adaptation to detail how the camp conditions arrested prior neurotic conditions, but produced long-term 'reactive depression' and unfinished mourning in those that survived. Internees are called DPs and not identified as predominantly Jewish. The report has a strangled objective tone, and only in the last paragraph refers to the data being collected through personal experience. 'Repatriation neurosis', an illness assumed to result from the uprooted life of DPs, was renamed 'Concentration Camp Syndrome' in 1954, when symptoms persisted for unusual lengths of time. The new term emphasized problems of physical deprivation and semi-starvation in the camps, rather than factoring in the experience of witnessing systematic, ethnically based mass murder, perhaps a product of the order in which the camps were liberated (Bloxham 2004). In 1961, Leo Eitinger reported on a study of one hundred former camp inmates (again, without any interest in what percentage were Jewish), and concluded 'that organic brain changes produced by the various traumatic situations ... form the basis of the concentration camp syndrome' (Eitinger 1961: 378). Typically, this physicalist theory failed to find much support, and psychodynamic models predominated. In the late 1960s, it was William Niederland who argued that 'traumatization of such magnitude' occurred in the camps that this burst the bounds of conventional traumatic neurosis, and so he coined the term 'survivor syndrome' (Niederland 1968a: 313). Niederland's involvement with the conference 'Massive Psychic Trauma' in 1968 brought his studies into contact with Lifton's work on Hiroshima survivors. Psychiatric advocacy from this point could remodel concentration camp experience through narratives of trauma and the identitarianism of survival.

An important figure linking professional psychiatric discussion to wider public discourse about Holocaust survival was the prominent child psychiatrist and public intellectual Bruno Bettelheim. Bettelheim, part of Vienna's pre-war intellectual scene, had been interned in 1938–9 in Dachau and Buchenwald, punitive labour camps that then held political prisoners and Jewish 'race offenders'. After a year's internment, Bettelheim was released and went into exile in America. He eventually published, after several rejections, his report on the psychology of the camps, 'Individual and Mass Behaviour in Extreme Situations', in 1943. He regarded the camps as brutal machineries of massification and infantilization, designed to produce passive subjects of the paternal Reich on a loosely psycho-analytic model. Survival involved retention of private behaviours and beliefs, to fend off the destruction of individuality. The year in the camp became the basis for Bettelheim's wider critiques of 'modern mass society' in the post-war era. Rather like Zygmunt Bauman's (1989) later claim that the Final Solution was a result of bureaucratic rationalization rather than a deviation from it, Bettelheim argued in *The Informed Heart* that the concentration camp was 'an example of the very nature of the coercive mass state' (Bettelheim 1960: 108). The book repeated material from his first study of the camps, now under the title 'Traumatization', but with little evidence of integrating the psychology of trauma into his work. Later, infantilizing defence mechanisms derived from the camps became the explicit basis for his understanding of the autistic child in *The Empty Fortress* in 1967, an influential study. He also reinterpreted his studies of schizophrenia in the 1950s as 'in some vicarious manner a compensatory experience for having suffered disintegration while in the concentration camps' (Bettelheim 1979: 113). This spiralling out from camp experience into wider cultural phenomena using the same basic psychic structure is perhaps what prompted Primo Levi's objection to Bettelheim's 'approximate and simplified' models (Levi 1989: 65). Levi was dis-missive that any psychiatric language of neurosis could begin to capture the 'atavistic anguish' of the camps (Levi 1989: 65).

In 1976, Bettelheim's essay in *The New Yorker* called 'Surviving' prompted a wide public debate. It is striking, given the situation now, to read Bettelheim's accusation that in America 'the millions who were murdered no longer arouse much interest; they seem to have been forgotten; they no longer count' (Bettelheim 1979: 284). Ostensibly an uneasy response to *The Seven Beauties* (Lina Wertmüller 1975), a film comedy partly set in a concentration camp which struck Bettelheim as marking a generational shift in attitudes to the war, the essay was really a riposte to Terence des Pres's book, *The Survivor: An Anatomy of Life in the Death Camps*. Des Pres wanted to reconfigure the Holocaust survivor as a heroic, visionary figure, in much the same idealizing terms found in Lifton: 'We require a heroism commensurate with the sweep of ruin in our time', des Pres declaimed (Des Pres 1980: 6). The camp survivor affirmed life and the biological imperative to survive, and this meant dismissing Bettelheim's pessimistic account of infan-tilization and disintegration. Elie Wiesel's determination to survive, witness, remember and campaign was the better model. Des Pres's remodelling of the concentration camp internee into the heroic Holocaust survivor is a significant moment of transfiguration. As in Lifton, the survivor approaches a messianic function:

> The survivor is a man or woman who has passed through the 'crisis of civilisation' we talk so much about …. He is the first of civilised men to live beyond the compulsions of culture; beyond a fear of death which can only be assuaged by insisting that life is worthless.
>
> (Des Pres 1980: 207)

In stark contrast, Bettelheim's late essay 'Trauma and Reintegration' regarded survivorship as a perpetual struggle to maintain 'integration in the face of the effects of past disintegration' (Bettelheim 1979: 25). Primo Levi could not have objected to this formulation, since he latterly used the language of unresolved trauma himself: 'The memory of a trauma suffered or inflicted is itself traumatic because recalling it is painful or disturbing: a person who was wounded tends to block out the memory so as not to renew the pain ... The injury cannot be healed: it extends through time' (Levi 1989: 12). After the mid-1970s, then, the psychological burdens of the 'Holocaust survivor' were the subject of general debate rather than specialist syndrome.

'I cannot believe', Elie Wiesel said in *Legends of Our Time*, 'that an entire generation of fathers and sons could vanish into the abyss without creating, by their very disappearance, a mystery which exceeds and overwhelms us' (Wiesel 1968: 182). These incomprehensible events would defy 'all the words in all the mouths of the philosophers and psychologists' who presumed to understand them (Wiesel 1968: 182). 'By its uniqueness', he proclaimed elsewhere, 'the holocaust defies literature' (Wiesel 1970: 10). This august insistence clearly infuses the cultural theory, by Felman and Caruth, Lyotard and Agamben, which places the Holocaust at the aporetic core of any discussion of trauma.

And yet it is also important to recognize that, as with other modes of trauma, Holocaust affect is unbounded and therefore extremely transmissible. It works its way across generations, to the extent that the notion of 'transgenerational haunting' has now become its own specialism (see Abraham and Torok 1994). Psychologists have tracked the 'sharing of unconscious material between progenitors and offspring which seems to be transmitted in an uncanny and unspecified fashion' (Herzog 1982: 104). This is due, Ilse Grubrich-Simitis suggests, to 'the permeability of the ego boundaries in those areas connected with the trauma' so that traumatic affect infuses interpersonal relations (Grubrich-Simitis 1984: 308). 'Some patients', she continues, 'without understanding what they are doing, concretistically act out the traumatic aspect of their parents' lives as if it were their own story' (Grubrich-Simitis 1984: 308). This transmission has been explored in memoirs like Lisa Appignanesi's *Losing the Dead* (2000).

Familial and cultural transmission within the Jewish heritage is understandable, yet these processes merely point the way to wider forms of transmission. For the more the Holocaust is proclaimed a 'unique' and incomparable trauma, the more it in fact becomes a comparative measure and metaphor for all atrocity. 'Rather than looking for the Holocaust outside of metaphor', James Young suggests in his study of the cultural circulation of Holocaust iconography, he proposes 'that we find it in metaphor, in the countless ways it has been figured, coloured, distorted, and ultimately cast as a figure for other events' (Young 1988: 89). In particular as soon as The Survivor becomes heroic, touched with the shamanistic powers of cheating death (despite the best efforts of Levi, Wiesel and others to debunk this mythic hero), the figure becomes a locus for a host of identifications. James Young's early example is the Holocaust identification in Sylvia Plath's last poems, written just before her suicide during the Eichmann trial and judgement in 1962. The poet 'moves from *seeing*, to figuring what she sees, to entering the metaphor, as agent and victim' (Young 1988: 121), depicting herself as both Nazi and Jewish victim most famously in her poem 'Daddy' (early drafts of which also included identification with Hiroshima victims). Whilst Young suspects this attempt to master personal pain through the figurations of public history only ended up introjecting Holocaust horrors and amplifying her misery, he refuses to judge this process of metaphorical transmission. After Auschwitz, one might say, there is a sort of historical inevitability about this traumatic transfer. 'Rather than disputing the authenticity of her figures', Young concludes, 'we might look to her poetry for the ways the Holocaust has entered public consciousness as a trope' (Young 1988: 132).

The potential for this kind of identification has, if anything, intensified in recent years. Binjamin Wilkomirski's harrowing memoir *Fragments* was published in 1995 to great acclaim. It was translated into twelve languages and won Jewish literary prizes in England, France and America. In shattered, hallucinatory prose, all told through the eyes of a young child without any other mediating perspective, the book detailed traumatic scenes of violence and cruelty in Majdanek and another concentration camp, later identified as Auschwitz. Philip Gourevitch suggests that book was such an international success because 'Wilkomirski was the embodiment of the purest form of victim: a child whose identity had been erased in the Holocaust, but who was condemned to stay alive' (Gourevitch 1999: 50). In 1999, Wilkomirski was publicly revealed as Bruno Grosjean, an illegitimate child born in Switzerland in 1941, later adopted by a Protestant Swiss couple: this Bruno Dössekker had no experience of the camps. Dössekker claimed that this Swiss 'pseudo-identity' had been imposed by his adoptive parents and a culture intent on suppressing his traumatic Jewish origins, as with other Holocaust 'children without identity' (Wilkomirski 1996: 154). His memories had been written as part of a therapeutic process but he angrily denied they were 'recovered memories', the technique tainted with confabulation of traumatic memories.

There have been outright denunciations of Wilkomirski, but the more interesting responses focus on the empathic conviction of *Fragments*, whether true or false. Israel Gutman, a Holocaust scholar and survivor, told the investigative reporter Elena Lappin: 'even if he is not Jewish, the fact that he was deeply affected by the Holocaust is of huge importance … He is not a fake. He is someone who lives this story very deeply in his soul. This pain is authentic' (Lappin 1999: 46). Wilkomirski is understood in this way as exploring his own traumatic childhood (an illegitimate child, an adoptive ward of state), through the matrix of Holocaust iconography. 'Swiss history has nothing remotely similar to offer, nothing so drastic to survive' (Lappin 1999: 65). Overwhelming empathy with the fate of children in the Holocaust has lost any distance and become 'identification with the experience of others and the possibility of being traumatized by it' (LaCapra 2001: 40). Transferential trauma therefore becomes *psychologically* true, outside objective history. It demonstrates, as Peter Middleton and Tim Woods observe, that 'memory can only only sustain identity because it is communicable, and this textual transmission opens it to the effects of textuality' (Middleton and Woods 2000: 94). The proliferation of *faux mémoires* in recent years suggests that Wilkomirski is only one of the more extreme indicators of the heroic allure our culture now gives to the Holocaust survivor (see Vice 2005).

This excavation of the construction of the Holocaust survivor indicates a certain misfit between the rhetoric of unprecedented trauma or aporetic representation and the way in which camp survival has entered general currency as a model for trauma, identity and community. This is perhaps because the Holocaust survivor is now one of the privileged figures for the traumatic ruptures of the post-1945 era, the survivor of unimaginable, incomparable atrocity. However, by the end of the 1980s, to be called 'a survivor' would not necessarily automatically invoke the Holocaust. In a very short period of time, cultural awareness of incest survival and sexual abuse added another aspect to contemporary traumatic experience, and another arena where transmissibility and identification prompted all kinds of public controversy.

The term 'survivor', one recent discussion confidently asserts, was 'coined by feminists' (Worrell 2003: 210). Although completely incorrect, this demonstrates how survivor identity has become closely linked to gender politics over the last thirty years. Feminism was the most successful form of identity politics to emerge in the late 1960s, developing from an internal critique of the civil rights movement. An essential early part of this phase of the women's movement was to articulate the suppressed or silenced parts of women's experience, often by sharing them in group sessions. Pioneer feminist Robin Morgan recalls that 'consciousness raising' developed in 1967, when women-only cadres would split away from Vietnam marches and other civil rights meetings to discuss their own alienation (Morgan 1970). There was clearly cross-fertilization between consciousness raising and Robert Lifton's Vietnam veteran 'rap groups'. In 1971, at a conference of the New York Radical Feminists, Florence Rush spoke out about her childhood experience of repeated rape by her father, and denounced the prevailing sexology and psychiatry that minimized the impact of such contacts (like Kinsey), or regarded them as fantasy (like Freud), or blamed the 'seductive child' who lured men into inappropriate sexual behaviour. Susan Brownmiller was in the audience, and within two days had sketched out the book proposal that would eventually become the groundbreaking *Against Our Will: Men, Women and Rape* published in 1975, by which time Rape Speak Out sessions had become a model for collective public utterance of what had been suppressed as private shame. In 1972, Ann Burgess and Lynda Holmstrom, an assistant professor of nursing and a sociologist radicalized by feminism, undertook a year-long study of women arriving at a Boston hospital with injuries from sexual violence. Two years later they published an account of what they called Rape Trauma Syndrome, defined as 'the acute phase and long-term reorganisation process that occurs as the result of forcible rape or attempted forcible rape' (Burgess and Holmstrom 1974: 982). Rape, they concluded, was far more extensive than reporting to police or criminal trials suggested, and the syndrome explained why women might delay reporting cases or suffer traumatic sequelae. Twenty years after her first report, Burgess fully integrated Rape Trauma with PTSD, and the life of the American woman was now divided into pretrauma history, the traumatic event phase and post-trauma response (Hartman and Burgess 1993: 507).

In 1977 the specific act of rape began to be incorporated into a wider, more inclusive category. Ellen Weber published an explosive essay in *Ms.* magazine, titled 'Incest: Sexual Abuse Begins at Home'. Its opening sentence proclaimed: 'One girl out of every four in the United States will be sexually abused in some way before she reaches the age of eighteen' (cited Davis 2005: 55). An academic statistical extrapolation of incest figures, conducted by Diana Russell for the then newly formed National Center for Child Abuse and Neglect, concluded that the figure was likely to be a minimum of one in six (16 per cent of American women, with 4.5 per cent abused by fathers, the rest by other male relatives). Russell's *The Secret Trauma* was published in 1986, but did not adopt PTSD as the means to organize its symptomatology (the 'trauma' of this title was a largely untheorized descriptor). This fusion began when the model of dissociated memory was used for the core of 'Sexual Abuse Accommodation Syndrome,' proposed in 1983. The trauma model was at the centre of Judith Herman's *Trauma and Recovery* in 1992 (reworking her earlier studies of father–daughter incest), an important book that fixed the diagnostic association of sexual abuse and trauma subectivity. Herman claimed that symptoms of dissociation, self-harm, multiple and border-line personality disorders or 'somatization' (conversion hysteria) could be confi-dently traced back in 97 per cent of cases to incidents of sexual abuse of childhood. The insistence that sexual abuse was the primary aetiology prompted a challenge to the diagnostic definition of PTSD. A traumatic event had been ini-tially defined in *DSM-III* as something 'outside the range of human experience'. Feminist critique argued that these 'current notions of traumatic stressors support a social and political status quo', ignoring 'all of those everyday, repetitive, inter-personal events that are so often the sources of psychic pain for women' (L. Brown 1991: 119 and 129).

The idea that abuse might be marked by the very *absence* of any conscious memory of abuse, due to traumatic dissociation, really took off with the Recovered Memory self-help movement, which used the language of conscious-ness-raising and women's empowerment borrowed directly from feminism. This was typified by the patient/analyst collaboration between Ellen Bass and Laura Davis, *The Courage to Heal*, which sold 750,000 copies between 1988 and 1992, the peak years of the movement. The book began with the claim that one in three girls were abused (and one in seven boys), but many suffered blanket traumatic amnesia of these childhood events. 'If you remember almost nothing or very little of your childhood', another guide by Renée Fredrickson stated, 'you have repressed memories' (Fredrickson 1992: 46). 'Millions of people have blocked out frightening episodes of abuse, years of their life, or their entire childhood', the guide asserted, providing detailed symptom check lists for the reader to determine their own state of dissociation and denial (Fredrickson 1992: 15). By 1996, Kali Tal asked the question: 'Can it be that *all* feminist literature is based in trauma? Perhaps not but it is certainly a proposition to take seriously. Trauma has played a formative role in the lives of many, if not *most* American women' (Tal 1996: 155). Tal suggested that all women existed in a 'preatrocity consciousness' and that this was comparatively worse than combat veterans or Holocaust survivors because 'the women who bear witness to these atrocities are still at risk, as all women are at risk, in contemporary America' (Tal 1996: 127 and 155). All women were either pre- or post-survivors, defined on the pivot of the inevitable traumatic event; saturation had been reached.

This is a trajectory of escalation, a remarkable exercise of traumatic transmission, in which incest moves from being a vanishingly rare event (perhaps two cases per million) to 'the prototype of the unspeakable story' that saturates Western cultures (Haaken 2003: 78). The acceleration of these claims was the main occasion for the eruption of the so-called 'Memory Wars' in the early 1990s, in which the nature of traumatic memory was at the core of the dispute. Recovered Memory advocates argue that traumatic events are registered outside conscious recall but in pristine, undegraded form in imagistic 'flashbulb' memories or in what Fredrickson calls 'body memory' since 'our physical bodies always remember sexual abuse' (Fredrickson 1992: 93). Therapeutic techniques, including hypnosis, could retrieve these memories in their pure, objective form. Yet other research findings argue that traumatic events are likely to be the most malleable memories, subject to continual retrospective transformation and particularly open to therapeutic suggestion. This psychological debate hardened into bitter adversarial dispute when criminal proceedings began on the basis of recovered memories of sexual abuse. Psychologists who worked as legal expert witnesses spoke up in favour of the retrieval of traumatic memory from blanket amnesia (Terr) or instead emphasized the malleability of reconstructive memory (Loftus). Accusations hardened against Recovered Memory Therapy when the False Memory Syndrome Foundation was formed in 1994, an alliance of sceptical psychologists and fathers accused of abuse. The legalistic framework forced the discussion of trauma into unproductively Manichean positions. The most vehement attacks on Recovered Memory suggested a conspiracy of twisted feminists: '*The Courage to Heal* and its fellow manuals are not about surmounting one's tragic girlhood, but about keeping the psychic wounds open, refusing forgiveness and reconciliation, and joining the permanently embittered corps of "survivors"' (Crews 1997: 194).

There can be a more nuanced analysis of this moment of escalation, analysing how recovered memory provides a compelling script of self-revelation that can renarrate a life at a stroke, crystallizing vague and disturbing symptoms or general dissatisfactions as now retrospectively meaningful after-effects of a childhood trauma. That the trauma is all the more powerful for likely being entirely absent from conscious memory is a logic that encourages self-suggestion. Auto-suggestion was strongly advocated in self-help manuals: Fredrickson told her readers 'whether what is remembered around that focal point is made up or real is of no concern at the beginning of the process; that can be decided at a later date', and later suggests that 'you will find it helpful to decide that your memories are real for at least a year' (Fredrickson 1992: 109 and 173). For Herman, these were affirmations that had to be both actively supported without question by the analyst-advocate and reinforced by the survivor-group: 'As each survivor shares her unique story, the group provides a profound experience of universality. The group bears witness to the survivor's testimony, giving it social as well as personal mean-ing' (Herman 1992: 197). The story of the 'adult survivor', Joseph Davis argues, is a transformative technology of the self, a machinery for an ultimately affirma-tive redescription that places a reconstructed individual into a new, communitar-ian identity (Davis 2005: 145). The inspirational narrative of transforming oneself from victim to survivor works to 'persuade other women of the personal benefits of mapping their experience in light of this general narrative framework' (Davis 2005: 106). There is an uncomplicated 'moral authority' that comes with survivorship (Davis 2005: 105), and this Janice Haaken sees as central to the role of the survivor within feminism: 'trauma legends may … renew collective identity by re-establish-ing the group's entitlement – the rewards of suffering and righteousness – as well as the group's mourned losses' (Haaken 1999: 23). And crucially, this is trauma no longer bounded by the specific experience of war combat or camp imprisonment: adult survivorship of unremembered childhood abuse holds out the greatest pos-sibility of universal ascription. This allure is what gives the impetus to what Ian Hacking has called the 'semantic contagion' of this particular form of dynamic nominalism (Hacking 1995: 256).

The rapidity of this trauma transmission by the late 1980s has had the unfor-tunate effect of diminishing the extraordinary achievement of second-wave fem-inism in forcing the acknowledgement of incest and familial sexual abuse, in the face of professional and general cultural denial, and its success in forcing concrete cultural and institutional change. Women who had suffered implicitly condoned violence now have supportive contexts in which to address physical and psycho-logical damage. It is important not to blame feminism for this escalation in trauma. Indeed, Joseph Davis' history of the construction of the adult abuse sur-vivor outlines numerous overlapping contexts: the family therapy movement, the development of child protection agencies, and the arrival of PTSD in official diagnostics, all of which interacted with the anti-rape movement and helped shape and reshape the contours of the adult abuse survivor in unpredictable ways. There is a convincing case to be made, for example, that sexual abuse only became conceivable in child protection discourse in the late 1970s; doctors had only really begun to acknowledge the possibility of physical abuse within the fam-ily after Battered-Child Syndrome had been proposed in 1962 (Davis 2005; see also Hacking 1991). Health and welfare institutions hybridized their developing systems for detecting physical and mental abuse with the experience being artic-ulated from within the contemporaneous feminist movement. From the mid-1970s, it was a welfarist multi-agency conjuncture that did as much to shift trauma out of a marginal identity politics and into a culturally pervasive structure of subjectivity. This in turn brought in the vast machineries of law and insurance.

Recent feminist commentary on this transformation has in fact been critical of the 'success' of this trauma subject. A common lament targets 'the widespread degeneration of the feminist practice of consciousness raising over the course of the 1970s from a radical tactic to a form of group therapy' (Kauffman 2001: 31). What had been an exercise in situating women's utterances within social and polit-ical problematics in order to expose patriarchal logic now risked being reduced to private therapeutic acts of self-improvement. The fusion with the medicalized language of trauma was also regarded as problematic: women might now be positioned as 'naïve transmitters of raw experience' (Alcoff and Gray 1993: 264) which was then translated into official diagnostic terms by experts, who obscured social oppression with the language of psychical trauma and personality disorders requiring individual management and cure. Alcoff and Gray tracked how the Speak Out had become an incitement to testify on confessional TV chat shows (led by Oprah Winfrey, who declared herself an abuse survivor in 1991), a context that frequently infantilized women, displaying them as 'pitiable instantiations of the universal truths the experts reveal' (Alcoff and Gray 1993: 277).

Other lines of critique point to the passivity with which the abuse survivor is constructed. The model is of an external traumatic impact which shatters an Edenic childhood innocence. Janice Haaken suspects that *The Courage to Heal* infantilizes female sexuality, as any complex adult sexual act or fantasy (too much or too little, too dominant or submissive) is reinterpreted as a probable restaging of childhood abuse. It implies that female sexuality has been traumatically injected into women by abusive men, that they have little or no sexual agency (Haaken 1999). A similar concern is presented by Susan Stefan's study of the use of Rape Trauma Syndrome in the law courts. The syndrome gave the authority of a medical diagnosis, yet also turned the woman into 'disordered victims' whose normal reactions of fear and anger at sexual violence became pathologies traded between experts, such that 'women win in court only by being represented as pathological and pathetic victims' (Stefan 1993–4: 1275). In fact, the feminist act of naming of Rape Trauma Syndrome in 1974 had ten years later run into legal trouble: a rape prosecution was overturned on the basis that the jury had been prejudiced by an expert witness using the syndrome to describe the psychological condition of the alleged victim. Rape Trauma Syndrome was owned to have psychotherapeutic value, but it was denied legal evidentiary weight and also did not appear in the *DSM* (see Iles 1985 and Gaffney 2003–4). This is a reminder that through all the modulations from the 1860s to the 1990s, from railway spine to abuse survival, psychical trauma still remains a fundamentally medico-legal concept.

There is a certain irony in the feminist engagement with the trauma paradigm. On the one hand, the morally authoritative discourse of the adult survivor developed from feminist consciousness-raising became one of the most influential articulations of the trauma subject, building on the cross-fertilizations of identity politics and therapeutic advocacy in the 1970s to shift welfare agencies and the general perception in favour of protecting women and children from all forms of domestic violence. On the other hand, this compelling survivor identity became the model for an uncontainable transmission of trauma subjectivity far beyond the political aims of the women's movement, and soon feminism was scapegoated for originating a universalized 'culture of survivors'. This was all the harsher, because the feminist politics behind speaking out on sexual abuse had lost much of its force as soon as it tied its analysis to the language of PTSD and the professional discourses of law and medicine. This reinforces the view that any survivor syndrome always ends up transmitting the trauma subject beyond the bounds of its own identitarian agenda.

'The history of the traumatic memory is a chain of analogies … But analogy does a better job at proliferating meanings than containing them' (A. Young 1995: 128). This genealogy has been an attempt to construct a roughly chronological narrative about the emergence and diffusion of the concept of psychical trauma from the 1860s until the coining of PTSD in 1980. It has also been a self-conscious act of multi-disciplinary synthesis that brings into contact fields that rarely acknowledge each other. By the late 1980s, I would suggest, the concept of trauma was a tightly bound knot that linked together diverse threads of knowledge. It also began to escape narrow professional discourses and diffuse into the wider culture. Now that we have the genealogy in place, we can begin to read how this complex history resonated through many aspects of culture.

Part II

Cultural symptoms

Introduction

Trauma and narrative knowledge

The second part of this book moves from an attempt to write a multi-disciplinary history of trauma to the study of paired cultural forms: the differing claims of written narrative in novels and memoirs (Chapters 2 and 3) and the static and dynamic visual representations of trauma in photography and film (Chapters 4 and 5). Given the range of disciplinary knowledges compressed into the term trauma, however, it is reasonable to address first why culture has been privileged as the means to track the trauma paradigm.

The contemporary public sphere is saturated with specialist knowledges, general accounts and stark images of traumatic experience. A traumatic event was initially defined as 'outside the range of normal human experience', something that might also be grasped as a gap between impact and understanding, influx and assimilation. Anyone who has watched rolling news services in the immediate wake of a disaster will have seen a disarray of competing and contradictory accounts, obsessive repetition of the same, unedited footage, and a collapse of distinctions between knowledge, rumour and speculation. This chaos is only gradually corralled into a meaningful, strongly shaped media story, slowly edited back into conformity with News discourse as the initial crisis recedes. The relationship between trauma as a devastating disruption and the subsequent attempts to translate or assimilate this disturbance is a fundamental tension between interruption and flow, blockage and movement. Trauma, in effect, issues a challenge to the capacities of narrative knowledge. In its shock impact trauma is anti-narrative, but it also generates the manic production of retrospective narratives that seek to explicate the trauma.

For me, the work done by cultural forms inheres in this contradiction: culture rehearses or restages narratives that attempt to animate and explicate trauma that has been formulated as something that exceeds the possibility of narrative knowledge.

In a recent project to revive the category of the aesthetic, Isobel Armstrong has argued that culture provides a space of (serious) play, a transitional mode where knowledge and meaning can be constantly disarticulated and reassembled. The aesthetic is often defined as an autonomous and non-purposive sphere, but for Armstrong it is an inherently political mode that 'mediates a life-creating, culture-modifying space which is at once transgressive and communal' (I. Armstrong

2000: 40). Given the narrative/anti-narrative tension at the core of trauma, aesthetics might step into this area because its task is (like that of the cultural critic) to '*play* with contradictions' (I. Armstrong 2000: 43). This play was formulated in a different way by the philosopher Jacques Derrida, who argued that the peculiar specificity of literature was its ability to incorporate the languages of other discourses (such as history, law, philosophy and science), yet suspend their strict protocols of meaning and reference for a time. Literature's '*being-suspended*' (Derrida 1992: 49) means that it can play seriously with all forms of knowledge by temporarily bracketing their rules of discourse. In this suspension, cultural forms can explore the foundations of an array of knowledges. This is its strength, but also its limit.

It is common to insist that culture is not reflective but constitutive of social knowledge. In the case of trauma, cultural forms have been inextricably bound up with some central concepts: the traumatic 'flashback', for instance, is borrowed from cinema, multiple personality has always shadowed the literature of the double, whilst the notion of recovering pristine recovered memories, as it developed in the 1980s, was linked to cultural technologies like television and video recorders: alters were switched like channels; memories were recorded, stored, rewound, replayed. Principally, though, cultural forms have provided the genres and narrative forms in which traumatic disruption is temporalized and rendered transmissible. Trauma has become a paradigm because it has been turned into a repertoire of compelling stories about the enigmas of identity, memory and selfhood that have saturated Western cultural life.

This is perhaps the strongest claim for examining cultural articulations of trauma, for if trauma can be seen as a problem of narrative knowledge, then aesthetics foregrounds the artifices of narrative construction. Of late, an array of visual and written stories involving trauma have ostentatiously played around with narrative time, disrupting linearity, suspending logical causation, running out of temporal sequence, working backwards towards the inaugurating traumatic event, or playing with belated revelations that retrospectively rewrite narrative significance. If these help figure the disruptions of trauma, this is not an intervention *into* some imagined state of perfect narrative orderliness, but one of the defining marks of narrative discourse. As Gérard Genette observes, anachrony (disruption of sequential narrative time) is not rare or modern, 'but is one of the traditional resources of literary narration' (Genette 1980: 36). Where law, insurance, medicine and psychiatry have often been confounded by the strange suspensions of causation that attend post-traumatic sequelae, cultural narratives have developed a repertoire of plots that explore both traumatic disruption and the possibility of release into narrative.

This is somewhat at odds with some of the most influential cultural theories of trauma, where the term trauma can be defined *in opposition* to narrative. In Jean-Francois Lyotard's view, trauma freezes time, and therefore any possibility of narrative. He argues: 'Narrative organisation is constitutive of diachronic time, and the time that it constitutes has the effect of "neutralizing" an "initial" violence' (Lyotard 1990: 16). Because trauma cannot be integrated into diachrony, it is a blockage, 'a bit monstrous, unformed, confusing, confounding' (Lyotard 1990: 17), and the traumatic memory persists in a half-life, rather like a ghost, a haunting absent presence of another time in our time. This is then given an ethical turn by Lyotard: any attempt to lay this ghostly traumatic trace is a form of tyranny or totalization. Lyotard's injunction is to 'Let us wage war on totality; let us be witnesses to the unpresentable' (Lyotard 1984: 82). This is the severe task of philosophy and art: 'What art can do is bear witness ... to this aporia of art and to this pain. It does not say the unsayable, but says that it cannot say it' (Lyotard 1990: 47). Trauma can therefore only be an aporia in narrative, and any narrative temporalization is an unethical act. Severe trauma can only be conveyed by the catastrophic rupture of narrative possibility, in what Arthur Frank terms 'an anti-narrative of time without sequence, telling without mediation' (Frank 1995: 98). This underlies allied approaches to Holocaust testimony, too. Lawrence Langer insists that Holocaust accounts must 'remain disrupted narratives' and suspects virtually any form of written codification of Holocaust experience as an attempt to 'mediate atrocity' by domesticating it in narrative or generic form (Langer 1991: xi and 9). His favouring of the oral over the written is of course problematic (as if oral utterance escaped narrative conventions), but one can read a Langer-like opposition between traumatic event and narrative possibility across the work of Caruth, Laub and Felman, and into the body of cultural trauma theory.

If narrative is at all possible, then critical theory has been particularly absorbed by the temporal paradoxes of trauma's belated effects. Trauma is *Nachträglich*, meaning delayed or deferred, an enigmatic term used by Freud and developed by subsequent psychoanalysts, to suggest that ordinary causality can be thrown into reverse by a traumatic impact, whose affect is only registered long after the first shock and which can retrospectively rewrite life narrative. Discourses requiring logical causation (such as legal proofs of causes and post-traumatic effects) cannot recognize this strange temporality. Literature can, registering it in the disarticulation of linear narration, and theorists detail a *Nachträglich* body of literature 'in which anachronism is the principle feature' (Nicholls 1996: 56).

Out of these aporias, what is identified is a few works of art that can testify to the impossible possibility of an aesthetics of trauma, works that obey the injunction to bear witness to the unpresentable: Toni Morrison's novel *Beloved*, Charlotte Delbo's Holocaust memoirs, W. G. Sebald's hybrid texts documenting the forgotten underside of European history, Daniel Libeskind's memorial architecture, Claude Lanzmann's documentary film *Shoah*. The aesthetic is uncompromisingly avant-garde: experimental, fragmented, refusing the consolations of beautiful form, and suspicious of familiar representational and narrative conventions. Ultimately, fractured Modernist form mimics narrative possibility disarmed by trauma.

In a typical disciplinary disjuncture, just as this cultural theory was abandoning narrative so psychology was discovering it. In 1991, Jerome Bruner acknowledged in 'The Narrative Construction of Reality' that these ideas were likely very familiar to cultural theorists, but revelatory for academic psychology. John McLeod's later survey of the new narrative therapy argued that the coherence of 'life narrative' was under pressure in contemporary society, resulting in disorientation as traditional scripts were torn up. 'From a historical perspective', McLeod stated, 'therapy can be regarded as a rearguard action against the erosion of opportunities to tell personal stories', since 'there is little space in the dominant social narrative of progress, development, and improvement for stories of loss' (McLeod 1997: 28 and 151). What McLeod terms 'the therapeutic narration of trauma' (McLeod 1997: 151) is the underlying premise for much work done in the area, which might be summarized as: where trauma was, there narrative shall be. In Susan Brison's account (informed by her experience of violent assault and rape), narrative reanimates the fixed traumatic intrusion, reassigning agency:

> Narrative memory is not passively endured; rather, it is an act on the part of the narrator, a speech act that defuses traumatic memory, giving shape and a temporal order to the events recalled, establishing more control over their recalling, and helping the survivor to remake a self.
>
> (Brison 1999: 40)

Similarly, Arthur Frank's work on memoirs of illness (a genre now called pathography) suggests that the onset of serious sickness constitutes 'narrative wreckage' (Frank 1995: 68). Under modernity, medicine hoped to cure but did so by distributing selfhood across different medical specialisms, demanding a further '*narrative surrender*' to professional expertise (Frank 1995: 6). 'Postmodern times are when the capacity for telling one's story is reclaimed', Frank avows: 'Stories have to *repair* the damage that illness has done' (Frank 1995: 7 and 58). The idea of 'narrative repair' is also at the centre of Hilde Lindemann Nelson's theory that moral agency can be returned to the abjected or damaged identities of individuals or groups by promoting 'identity-constituting counterstories' (Nelson 2001: xii). Narrative ideas also direct some forms of Cognitive-Behavioural Therapy. Traumatic memory persists because it is poorly integrated into autobiographical memory, but 'as therapy progresses ... the narrative tends to become more coherent' (Ehlers and Clark 2000: 339).

There seems to be a flat contradiction between cultural theory that regards narrative as betraying traumatic singularity and various therapeutic discourses that see narrative as a means of productive transformation or even final resolution of trauma. This of course reflects different disciplinary imperatives: aesthetic meditations that sustain irresolution and explore narrative disjuncture are not written under the rubrics and aims of therapeutic work with traumatized people. One should not be judged by the other – it would be as perverse to demand a greater clarity of therapeutic outcomes from a Sebald text as to lecture Susan Brison that her narrativization of her experience was an unethical act that failed to respect the singularity of her rape trauma.

Yet this split over the value of narrative is somewhat artificial. The aesthetic theory that dominates this field has emerged from the work of Lyotard, Derrida and Cathy Caruth's revision of Paul de Man and reads trauma as an aporia of representation, placing emphasis on difficulty, rupture and impossibility, consistently privileging aesthetic experimentation. Meanwhile, our culture is saturated with stories that see trauma not as a blockage but a positive spur to narrative. Beyond post-structuralist trauma theory and its trauma canon, a wide diversity of high, middle and low cultural forms have provided a repertoire of compelling ways to articulate that apparently paradoxical thing, the trauma narrative. These work from a different aspect of the same problem: if trauma is a crisis in representation, then this generates narrative *possibility* just as much as *impossibility*, a compulsive outpouring of attempts to formulate narrative knowledge. The following chapters will therefore not only examine texts where trauma brings narrative to a halt, but where trauma's stalling actively provokes the production of narrative.

To do this, I want briefly to outline two alternative ways of thinking about cultural narrative in relation to trauma. The first uses some old-fashioned resources from formalism and structuralism to focus on the mechanics of trauma's narrative spur. The second offers a more phenomenological view of what shape aesthetic narrative brings to human experience.

Boris Tomashevsky's essay 'Thematics' was a central document of the Russian Formalist School, and has provided an impressive tool-kit of terms for subsequent narrative analysis. Tomashevsky distinguished *story*, the causal and chronological sequence of events, from *plot*, the actual order in which events are presented in a narrative (Tomashevsky 1965: 66). The time of the narrative can never be identical with the time of the narrated, and one of the definitions of aesthetic narrative is the foregrounding of this anachronic disjointedness. Plot coheres because the reader is always belatedly sorting and re-sorting 'motifs' (narrative units) into meaningful, sequential stories. Sometimes the reader has to revise retrospectively the whole story, because a last plot twist recasts the significance of every plot motif (like the last scene of the film, *The Usual Suspects*). These narratives with 'regressive endings' are usually the ones we want to read or see again, although this is only one of the more severe forms of narrative anachrony. Genette subsequently tried to produce a taxonomy of these time slippages: analepsis (movements backwards), prolepsis (anticipations), ellipsis (edits that accelerate narrative time), and so on, a grid of 'all forms of discordance between the two temporal orders of story and narrative' (Genette 1980: 40). At its most abstract, Tomashevsky saw narrative as beginning in a stasis which is upset by some kind of 'exciting force' that drives plot dynamically forward towards an eventual recovery of stasis.

This formalism has been recast as an explicitly traumatic theory of narrative by Peter Brooks. Brooks borrowed from the model of trauma Freud put forward in his speculative essay, *Beyond the Pleasure Principle*, in which protective filters are overwhelmed by a traumatic impact which unleashes unbound excitations into the psychic system. The compulsion to repeat, to dream or relive or relate the traumatic event over and over, is an attempt to bind this energy, to assimilate it, and return the psyche to a state of quiescence once more. Ingeniously, Brooks maps this onto Tomashevsky's abstraction of plot as an exciting force that intrudes on, disturbs, but eventually returns to stasis, making narrative foundationally a working through of traumatic disruption. Plot starts when quiescence is stimulated into a 'state of narratability' (Brooks 1977: 291); its trajectory is aimed at returning again to 'the quiescence of the non-narratable' (Brooks 1977: 296). In between, this disruption is worked into reiterative motifs that generate meaningful plot: 'Textual energy, all that is aroused into expectancy and possibility in a text ... can become usable by plot only when it has been bound or formalised' (Brooks 1977: 290). Reading is driven by the desire for the end, for it is only here that the anachronic trauma of plot can be fully assimilated and bound up in story.

These discussions of narrative form are very suggestive. They provide a language to formalize the mechanics of narrative structure that (metaphorically at least) relates the allure of storytelling to an inaugurating trauma. They do not legislate for a particular aesthetic, but proffer a matrix of possibility that encompasses a wide diversity of narrative forms in different media (fiction, memoir, historiography, cinema) and from high to low culture. Brooks' emphasis on the drive towards the end could be taken to privilege the kinds of strong narrative closure often identified with nineteenth-century Realism, but I understand his sketch of the 'masterplot' to be an ideal, against which different kinds of resolution (including deferred, suspended, or refused resolution), and thus very different kinds of trauma narrative, might be measured. Most importantly, Brooks' reformulation of formalism is premised on the view that trauma does not halt narrative but might be regarded as the motor that drives its manifold forms.

Formal and structural analyses are always inevitably limited by their need to isolate texts artificially from context, and since I want to be able to tie recent narrative formations to the rise of a trauma paradigm in the 1980s, I need another bridge to effect this historicization. Paul Ricoeur's *Time and Narrative* is an inquiry after the distinctiveness of narrative that also argues for the substantive power of narrative form to refigure our grasp of the real world. This is the last element of narrative theory I need to introduce before we can proceed.

For Ricoeur, Western philosophy has been unable to master conceptually temporal experience, which can appear in speculative thought only as an aporia (he takes as his founding text Augustine's bafflement at being unable to answer his own simple question, 'What, then, is time?'). The entirety of Ricoeur's three-volume study could be summed up in three words: 'Narrative heals aporia' (Wood 1991: 4). This is to say that where philosophy encounters time as discordance, narrative is an act of concordance, which '"grasps together" and integrates into one whole and complete story multiple and scattered events' (Ricoeur 1984: x). Narrative is 'the privileged means by which we re-configure our confused, unformed, and at the limit mute temporal experience' (Ricoeur 1984: xi). The largest claim is that humans can comprehend time only as narrative: 'time becomes human to the extent that it is articulated through a narrative mode, and narrative attains its full meaning when it becomes a condition of temporal existence' (Ricoeur 1984: 52). However, Ricoeur is at pains to complicate the idea that narrative is a simple act of exercising order over chaos: plots incorporate contradiction, reversal and complexity, and narrative comprehension always quivers on the verge of collapse. Emplotment is a high-wire act of what Ricoeur calls *discordant concordance.* The modern novel tends to appear as a limit-case through-out the study, challenging the classical unities of Aristotelian aesthetics, since the novel has acted for three centuries as 'a prodigious workshop for experiments in the … expression of time' (Ricoeur 1985: 8). The Modernist experiments with narrative time in Virginia Woolf, Thomas Mann and Marcel Proust, for instance, take us into 'uncharted modes of discordant concordance' (Ricoeur 1985: 101), but the extreme attempts to disable narrative by Samuel Beckett are still subject to the reader's active configuration of meaning, because the imperative to find narrative coherence is so embedded. Nevertheless, Ricoeur entertains the possi-bility that 'we are the witnesses – and the artisans – of a certain death, that of the art of telling stories' and concedes that 'nothing … excludes the possibility that the metamorphosis of the plot will encounter somewhere a boundary beyond which we can no longer recognise the formal principle of temporal configuration that make a story' (Ricoeur 1985: 28). Even so, 'we have no idea of what a cul-ture would be where no one any longer knew what it meant to narrate things' (Ricoeur 1985: 28).

Although Ricoeur begins from the premise that 'in the final analysis, narratives have acting and suffering as their theme' (Ricoeur 1984: 56), these elements that threaten to dis-figure the configuration of plot seem to have grown apace, distend-ing ever further the chances of narrative concordance in the modern world. Indeed, the final volume raises those 'epoch-making' events, such as Auschwitz, that stand at the limit of speculative and historical understanding. Here, however, Ricoeur finally reaffirms the role of fictional narrative against frozen horror or defeated thought: 'Fiction gives eyes to the horrified narrator. Eyes to see and weep' (Ricoeur 1988: 188). Fiction, he continues, 'permits historiography to live up to the task of memory' and speaks for 'victims whose suffering cries less for vengeance than for narration' (Ricoeur 1988: 189).

Ricoeur's terms 'discordance' and 'concordance' are easily translated into the poles of blockage and flow, trauma and narrative, but in this case traumatic dis-cordance is the constant spur to innovations in narrative concordance. Narrative heals aporia, although can never finally seal over the wounds of tem-poral existence, and that discordance will always propel further narrative appre-hensions. However, Ricoeur's study extends beyond providing merely another set of terms to examine narrative structure, because he is ultimately concerned to argue that narrative is more than a textual configuration: narrative is also a means 'to re-figure our historical condition and thereby raise it to the level of historical consciousness' (Ricoeur 1988: 102). 'Making a narrative', he proclaims, 'resignifies the world in its temporal dimension' since it activates readers to reorient their being in the world (Ricoeur 1984: 81). It is perhaps in these grand terms that the rationale for examining cultural narratives of trauma is best made. Discourses like law, medicine, psychiatry, social policy and even critical theory itself define trauma as an enigmatic discordance or aporia. Narrative is spurred to shape this disruptive anomaly into new kinds of forms, each fore-grounding, sometimes more, sometimes less, the violent tension between discor-dance and concordance. These new forms in turn become the places where we try out the re-significations of self that trauma has wrought on contemporary subjectivity.

Ricoeur defines narrative in the broadest sense, incorporating myth, folklore, fiction and history. In that spirit, the next four chapters will examine fiction, memoir, cinema and photography in the light of the dynamics of trauma and narrative that I have outlined here.

2 Trauma in narrative fiction

The attempt to identify a distinct 'trauma novel' has been a very recent literary critical task: Anne Whitehead terms it an 'emerging genre' (Whitehead 2004: 4), which suggests that we have yet to see its full extent. Exemplars of the trauma novel cluster in the late 1980s and 1990s, after the clinical elaboration of PTSD, but forming an instrinsic part of the public controversies around post-traumatic sequelae, such as recovered memory, the politics of survival, or competing kinds of public memorialization of past violence. Indeed, the anachronies of novelistic narrative make the form an important site for configuring (and therefore refiguring) traumatic impacts for the wider culture. Literary criticism has lagged behind this new literature, perhaps because the dominant critical paradigm at this time was Postmodernism, a contested term but one that often argued for a paralysis of the historical sense, the erasure of memory, and an epochal shift from the problematic of time to space (see Jameson 1991). In retrospect (with appropriate belatedness, perhaps), an explosion in historical fiction and a literature of anamnesis has become discernable in this era. All this time, literature was exploring 'new modes of memory', producing texts that 'have been particularly effective at tracing the consequences of living out the belief in, say, traumatic memory' (Middleton and Woods 2000: 85).

For such a recent literature, there is already an emergent international canon of writers and works, and even an implicit aesthetic for the trauma novel. This cluster of trauma fictions opens, I would argue, with Toni Morrison's *Beloved* (1987), a novel which has exerted a remarkably wide cultural influence. It then extends through Margaret Atwood's *Cat's Eye* (1988), Pat Barker's *Regeneration* trilogy (1991–5), Anne Michaels' *Fugitive Pieces* (1996), Binjamin Wilkomirski's memoir-belatedly-turned-novel *Fragments* (1996), and incorporates the complete works of W. G. Sebald. Sebald's last novel *Austerlitz* (2001) explicitly embraced the organizing notion of traumatic dissociaton and recovered memory to explore post-Holocaust subjectivity. New careers in trauma fiction are still being forged: Jonathan Safran Foer's tragi-comedies of the Holocaust, *Everything is Illuminated* (2002), and 9/11, *Extremely Loud and Incredibly Close* (2005), show every sign of becoming canonical. In critical discussions different patterns of texts emerge, often because trauma fictions are seen to develop from the context of specific identity politics. Vietnam fictions start earlier, and helped shape not just any putative trauma aesthetic but the formation of PTSD itself. These texts might include the innovative reportage of Michael Herr's *Dispatches* (1977), Tim O'Brien's fiction or Larry Heinemann's novel about a group of post-traumatic combat veterans, *Paco's Story* (1986). Deborah Horvitz identifies a parallel women's trauma fiction that has a long pre-history but clusters around the issue of domestic physical and sexual abuse in the early 1990s. Although the memoir has been a key vehicle for the feminist articulation of silenced traumatic violence, Horvitz's study of fiction adds Leslie Marmon Silko and Dorothy Allison to the more canonical figures of Joyce Carol Oates, Margaret Atwood and Toni Morrison. The Holocaust perspective also refracts the novelistic canon, and sometimes claims a determining priority over the trajectory of trauma fiction. Indeed, Robert Eaglestone argues that the Holocaust hovers as the 'absent content' of much fiction since Samuel Beckett, but wonders how useful it might be to consider the category of post-Holocaust fiction as virtually synonymous with *post-war* fiction. There have also been some significant attempts to do cross-cultural comparative work (between Toni Morrison and the Haitian Edwidge Danticat's *The Farming of Bones* (1999), for instance), and to set up convergences between the trauma paradigm and the nervous conditions of post-colonial literature. This begins to imply that there is a central body of trauma fictions that might be reconceived from the margins, even as identitarian trauma politics tends to argue for its own marginality and widespread cultural aversion to its concerns.

These texts are often brought together by critics as exemplary works because they are held to share a particular trauma aesthetic. This is sometimes explicitly stated in prescriptive terms, listing elements that must be included to establish membership of a proper or authentic literature of trauma. Because a traumatic event confounds narrative knowledge, the inherently narrative form of the novel must acknowledge this in different kinds of temporal disruption. 'If trauma is at all susceptible to narrative formulation', Whitehead argues, 'then it requires a literary form which departs from conventional linear sequence' (Whitehead 2004: 6). 'Trauma narratives', Vickroy concurs, 'go beyond presenting trauma as a subject matter or in characterization; they also incorporate the rhythms, processes, and uncertainties of trauma within the consciousness and structures of these works' (Vickroy 2002: xiv). Disorders of emplotment are read as mimicking the traumatic effect. In Nicola King's view, the novel is particularly suited to a hermeneutic understanding of traumatic memory as subject to 'afterwardsness' or *Nachträglichkeit*, in which the past is open to retrospective reinterpretation once occluded material has been recovered. The plots of trauma narratives can belatedly and magically reconfigure entire life stories.

The requirement for formal disturbance is often overdetermined by ethical or politcal imperatives too. Robert Eaglestone's formulation of the features of the genre of Holocaust testimony suggests it is marked by interruptions, temporal disorder, refusal of easy readerly identification, disarming play with narrative framing, disjunct movements in style, tense, focalization or discourse, and a resistance to closure that is demonstrated in compulsive telling and retelling (Eaglestone 2004: 42–65). These are elements that might serve as an outline of a general trauma aesthetic. For Eaglestone, these formal properties are all in the service of retaining a sense of the impossibility of comprehending the Holocaust, which can never be contained within narrative. In this context, other formal choices that do not find ways of figuring this aporia become unethical. Thus, the very idea of the 'Holocaust novel', shaped by narrative, characterological and other conventions, is always a fraught and compromised form. Elsewhere, where narrativization is seen as an act acquiring agency, as in feminist discussions of trauma, a political imperative is foregrounded. 'Narrative representations of trauma', Horvitz asserts, must 'expose the need for social transformation; they target for disruption such bureaucratic institutions as the legal and medical systems or ... capitalism and consumerism' (Horvitz 2000: 18). Formal radicalism is equated with political radicalism, and sets a high bar of expectations about the political utility of fiction.

The forms favoured tend to evoke the innovations associated with Modernism (a movement that has been recast by Tim Armstrong as a species of trauma literature). The contemporary trauma aesthetic shares something else with Modernism: it is defined against banal, exploitative or routinized cultural expression. Modernism has been critically constructed as defining its own search for ceaseless novelty by abjecting the conventionalized middle- and low-brow culture that surrounded it. Even if this account has now been problematized, avant-garde innovations remain motivated by opposition to mainstream or mass cultural norms. Laurie Vickroy identifies a 'serious' and 'authentic' trauma literature explicitly against a popular culture that 'has more often exploited such anxieties with tales or terror, suspense, or prurience' (Vickroy 2002: 8, 21 and 7). Kali Tal's account of trauma literature constantly asserts vigilance against 'reducing a traumatic event to a set of standardized narratives', worrying that 'traumatic events are written and rewritten until they become codified and narrative form replaces content as the focus of attention' (Tal 1996: 6). This is a familiar argument about the numbing effect of repeated exposure to mediated traumatic material and the aesthetics of shock. Susan Sontag feared overuse of these devices was producing a 'pseudo-familiarity with the horrible' in her discussion of photography (Sontag 1977: 41), whilst she regarded the mass cultural 'imagination of the disaster' as a 'naïve and largely debased commercial art', a symptom 'stripped of sophistication, of the inadequacy of most people's response to the unassimilable terrors that infect their consciousness' (Sontag 1966: 223). Aesthetic experimentation is therefore valued because it defies the habituation of trauma into numbing and domesticating cultural conventions.

There is something of a contradiction, however, in affirming the centrality of innovation whilst identifying a specific (and sometimes prescriptive) trauma aesthetic. Paradoxically, the aesthetic means to convey the singularity of a traumatic aporia has now become highly conventionalized, the narratives and tropes of traumatic fiction easily identified. This contradiction can be avoided by making two shifts. First, rather than privileging narrative rupture as the only proper mark of a trauma aesthetic, if the focus is moved to consider narrative *possibility*, the potential for the configuration and refiguration of trauma in narrative, this opens up the different kinds of cultural work that trauma narratives undertake. This necessitates a second move: regarding trauma fiction not as a narrow canon of works, but as a mass of narratives that have exploded across high, middle and low-brow fiction since the late 1980s, texts with wildly different ambitions but that frequently share the same narrative devices. To examine this diversity of fictional forms, this chapter will start with Toni Morrison and end with W. G. Sebald, the two most recognized masters of trauma fiction, but will move between them through the generic delights of Stephen King's trauma Gothic and a cluster of mainstream trauma works that crammed bookshops in the 1990s.

Beloved: A paradigmatic trauma fiction

Beloved, a novel about the murderous legacies of slavery in America, elevated Toni Morrison to major cultural pre-eminence: the book won the Pulitzer Prize and in 1993 Morrison was awarded the Nobel Prize for Literature. The novel was intended to give some inner consciousness and humanity to the historical record of atrocities inflicted against African and African–American people as a consequence of institutional slavery. The events of the book are partly based on the case of the slave Margaret Garner who escaped her Kentucky owner in 1856 to 'freedom' across the Ohio River, but who then cut the throat of her best loved daughter at the prospect of their capture and return to slavery. This was a legally enforceable act of recovery of property under the 1850 Fugitive Slave Law. At the height of abolitionist controversies, Garner's case was used to both attack slavery and to defend the institution, since the act was argued to prove the essentially savage nature of the African race. *Beloved* took this event as a metonymy for the 'sixty million and more' subjected to the murderous institution of slavery (this is *Beloved*'s dedication), but was specifically intended to voice the female experience of slavery, a violence frequently repressed by anti-slavery campaigners and subsequent historians alike as simply 'too disgusting to appear in this narrative', as one Abolitionist put it in the 1830s (cited Foster 1994: xxxi). The traumatic experience of the slave woman was until late into the twentieth century doubly silenced: 'If, in the context of colonial production, the subaltern has no history and cannot speak, the subaltern female is even more deeply in shadow' (Spivak 1988: 287). It was the identity politics of black women's experience that made *Beloved* possible at this late date; its formal and conceptual links to the trauma paradigm reinforced its influence on American culture.

The book I think helped establish some of the basic narrative and tropological conventions of trauma fiction. It was soon regarded as a formative text in literary trauma studies, which has produced a torrent of academic commentary. There are well over five hundred articles related to *Beloved* listed on periodical databases. This is an excessive and no doubt repetitive body of critical work, but it testifies to the success of Morrison's attempt to construct a 'participative' mode of writing for dealing with such intensely disturbing material. Reflecting on the novel in 'Unspeakable Things Unspoken', Morrison wrote of devising means to throw the reader into the midst of 'compelling confusion' at the opening of each chapter, a discordance that only slowly worked 'to provide the places and spaces so that the reader can participate' (Morrison 1989: 33). This was an exemplary instance of creating what Dominick LaCapra terms 'empathic unsettlement' in the reader (LaCapra 2001: 78). The vast body of commentary is not redundant; it is a testament both to the transmissibility of trauma and the acts of compulsive repetition trauma narratives can induce in their readers.

There are three aspects of *Beloved* that make it paradigmatic: its disarticulation of linear narrative, its figuration of trauma in the ghost, and its closing reflections on the transgenerational transmission and the complex accommodations communities need to make with such traumatic history. Let's take these in turn.

When Paul D. confronts Sethe and asks for an account of what she has done to leave her exiled from her community, he is bewildered by her circumambulations:

> It made him dizzy. At first he thought it was her spinning. Circling him the way she was circling the subject … Then he thought, No, it's the sound of her voice; it's too near. Each turn she made was at least three yards from where he sat, but listening to her was like having a child whisper into your ear so close you could feel its lips form the words you couldn't make out because they were too close. He caught only pieces of what she said.
>
> (Morrison 1987: 161)

There are two more pages of Paul D. listening to this 'circling, circling' (162) until the narrative focalization shifts to Sethe:

> Sethe knew that the circle she was making around the room, him, the subject, would remain one. That she could never close in, pin it down for anybody to who to ask. If they didn't get it right off – she could never explain. Because the truth was simple … She just flew. Collected every bit of life she had made, all the parts of her that were precious and fine and beautiful, and carried, pushed, dragged them through the veil, out, away, over there where no one could hurt them. Over there. Outside this place, where they would be safe.
>
> (Morrison 1987: 163)

This is the closest we get to Sethe's account of the event, one of avoidance, delay and evasion and which is played out through the agitated movements of the body as much as through language. The account makes sense only because the events have been recounted through the hard eyes of the white slave-catchers just before this exchange – a shed, a saw, and 'a nigger woman holding a blood-soaked child to her chest with one hand and an infant by the heels in another' (Morrison 1987: 149). The core event thus appears about half-way through the novel: its extremity accounts for this delay, and for the turbulence that affects every level of narrative. Linear temporal sequence is shipwrecked against the jagged fixity of this atemporal traumatic scene. And Sethe is not alone; many of the African–American characters carry a traumatic moment of violence, humiliation or subjective death, which leaves them in a similar condition of circling what they are defined by and cannot confront, unable to communicate their story. The men of

Sweet Home are unmanned in shocking, near unendurable moments. These defining scenes always come late, and crawl crabwise into the narrative, as if the events cannot really be sustained within subjective memory or linguistic representation. In later stages, the loss of any boundaries of self between Sethe and her strange young visitor in 124 disintegrates narrative possibility and even determinate grammatical relationships. Readers encounter pages of reiterations spaced in non-causal relationships, variations on the phrase 'I am Beloved and she is mine' (Morrison 1987: 214). The book is steeped in these kinds of code that bind people together in encrypted ways. Paul D. remembers the strength garnered from slave songs sung by 'garbling up words so they could not be understood; tricking the words so their syllables yielded up other meanings' (Morrison 1987: 108), but is also locked out of the dynamics of the women in Sethe's house, unable to read 'the code they used among themselves that he could not break' (Morrison 1987: 132). Encryption is a form of compromised survival, acts of defence that every act of decoding actually threatens.

The novel proceeds by this disfiguration of narrative coherence, compelling the reader to attempt to configure a meaningful sequence, which always comes after the fact and always feels anxiously provisional, open to further revision. This occurs at the very local level, where Morrison consistently uses the device of 'delayed decoding'. Objects are defamiliarized for a time, before leaping into sharp relief: the tree traced out on Sethe's back becomes the marks of a whipping; the 'tip of the thing' under Beloved's chin becomes the scar made by the saw; the ribbon that Stamp Paid fingers in his pocket is eventually revealed as a gruesome memorial, first found 'knotted around a curl of wet woolly hair, clinging still to its bit of scalp' (Morrison 1987: 180). This is Stamp Paid's metonymic aide-memoire for 'the people of the broken necks, of fire-cooked blood and black girls who had lost their ribbons' (Morrison 1987: 181). These very local jolts make every image or motif a site of unease: the 'tip of the thing' in fact has a long life as a repeated phrase that accumulates anticipatory feelings of dread long before its significance is confirmed. The presiding aim of the novel is therefore to create a feeling of *Nachträglichkeit*, of being caught out by a time signature that consistently exposes the reader too early to traumatic markers that can only be comprehended too late.

However, this severe discordance of plot is gradually brought together by the reader to compose some kind of chronological story. The time scheme stretches from the narrative present (1874) back to Sethe's murderous act thirteen years previously (1861), which ends her twenty-eight days of freedom in Cincinnati. Memories of the slave plantation Sweet Home move further back (to 1855), and are divided between the relatively benign rule under Garner, and the brutal regime of his successor, Schoolteacher, who sanctions rape and violent emasculation of his slaves, and thus provokes the desperate escape. The historical spine therefore straddles the Civil War and although the war is an oblique presence in the novel, Sethe's story unfolds against the backdrop the shift from national division over slavery to the era of Reconstruction in the 1870s. But the narrative schema of *Beloved* is constructed kaleidoscopically through constantly shifting points of view, each narrator having their own patterns of knowledge and occlusion. It is not a continuous account, being shot through with holes, and symptomatic absences. Some leave no trace; not everyone survives to have a witness or be integrated into the narrative. This is not history writing; some losses are irretrievable.

According to Wolfgang Iser, the reader of a fictional narrative strives 'to fit everything together in a consistent pattern', projecting from the 'polysemantic possibilities' of a text a *gestalt* or pattern, an 'individual, configurative meaning' (Iser 1988: 219 and 220). This projection undergoes constant revision: 'By reading, we uncover the unformulated part of the text, and this very indeterminacy is the force that drives us to work out a configurative meaning' (Iser 1988: 222). In this working out, Iser even suggests that these configurative acts help 'formulate ourselves and so discover what had previously seemed to elude our consciousness' (Iser 1988: 226). Trauma fictions work with and against this phenomenological description of reading. In Morrison, trauma takes discordance to the very limits of coherence. If concordance is possible, this grasping together of fragments into story is far from unifying. The reader is jarred by belated recognitions of events that are barely supportable in novelistic discourse. It may be that such reading presents us with what 'seemed to elude our consciousness', but this is not an act of completion or closure so much as a confrontation with a violent history that has been held outside national history or collective memory. *Beloved* aims to de-stabilize subjectivity; it disarms the reader with narrative and figurative techniques that force a confrontation with traumatic material.

Beloved gained such cultural influence because its *Nachträglich* narrative device was reinforced by the central metaphorical device of the book: the ghostly return of Beloved. The ghost embodied the idea of the persistence of traumatic memory, the anachronic intrusion of the past into the present. Although the ghost as figure of trauma has become almost a cliché, reinforced as it was throughout the 1990s by an elaborate critical discourse of spectres and 'spectrality', *Beloved* was amongst the first texts to develop this aspect of trauma culture's *Zeitgeist*.

Ghosts suffuse the book. This is not surprising, if we follow Orlando Patterson's view of slavery as a form of social death:

> The essence of slavery is that the slave, in his social death, lives on the margin between community and chaos, life and death, the sacred and the secular. Already dead, he lives outside the mana of the gods and can cross the boundaries with social and supernatural impunity.
>
> (Patterson 1982: 51)

Ghosts are the signals of atrocities, marking sites of untold violence, a traumatic past whose traces remain to attest to a lack of testimony. A haunting does not initiate a story; it is the sign of a *blockage* of story, a hurt that has not been honoured by a memorializing narrative. The geography of *Beloved* is punctured by traumas that have not been bound into story: 'Not a house in the country ain't packed to its rafters with some dead negro's grief' (Morrison 1987: 5); 'You know as well as I do that people who die bad don't stay in the ground' (Morrison 1987: 188). The supernatural is semi-naturalized: Sethe and Paul D. calmly recall 'that headless bride back behind Sweet Home' (Morrison 1987: 13), and later Paul D. hears dead Miami native Americans growl and sigh as he passes through their land (Morrison 1987: 155). Such haunted places prompt Sethe to coin the term 'rememory': 'You know. Some things you forget. Other things you never do ... Places, places are still there. If a house burns down, its gone, but the place – the picture of it – stays, and not just in my rememory, but out there, in the real world'. It is easy enough to 'bump into a rememory that belongs to somebody else' (Morrison 1987: 36). That such ghosts mark both the traces of individual histories, stories of the unnamed that remain untold and therefore hauntingly unresolved, as well as condensations of an entire community, is evidenced in *Beloved's* ambivalent representative status. 124 is the site of a specific tragic event, but also invokes a whirlwind of multiple voices, a 'roaring' that compresses the entire history of slavery.

Beloved is a weird and unconventional kind of ghost: she appears in discontinuous forms, defying folk wisdom. Where a grave and a name on a tombstone often end haunting, here Sethe recalls that 'as soon as I got the gravestone in place you made your presence known in the house' (Morrison 1987: 184). This appears to be a benign haunting for some years until Denver discovers her mother's murderous secret. What ends her hysterical deaf-muteness is a shift in the aspect of haunting: 'From then on the presence was full of spite' (Morrison 1987: 104). Paul D. enacts the first exorcism – which only ensures Beloved's *material* return. In a text so well known, it is easy to forget the disturbing gap between the appearance of a young girl, apparently without history or explanation for her arrival, and the confirmation that this is Beloved in her third mode of haunting. Sethe only 'clicks' late (and the reader mimics her belatedness). As mutual, overwhelming desire consumes Beloved and Sethe inside 124, Beloved seems to expand to contain an entire history, the ghosts of slaves from the Middle Passage speaking in panicked, fractured paragraphs. Beloved channels a cacophony of voices, 'the people of the broken necks' that forbid Stamp Paid entry to the house. The second exorcism comes from a communal act. Ella, utterly unforgiving of Sethe's act of murder thirteen years before, 'didn't mind a little communication between the two worlds, but this was an invasion' (Morrison 1987: 257). The second ritual has to move beyond any symbolic conventions: the women's voices rise to find 'the key, the code, the sound that broke the back of words' (Morrison 1987: 261) to expel the ghost. Even then, Beloved remains in the final pages, 'a loneliness that roams', 'disremembered and unaccounted for, she cannot be lost because no one is looking for her, and even if they were, how can they call her if they don't know her name?' (Morrison 1987: 274). What Beloved embodies refuses the ghost story's conventional ending: she cannot be laid to rest. She can be captured only in contradictory formulations: 'a requiem that is a resurrection' (Rushdy 1992: 571).

The spectre has come to bear a heavy theoretical freight as a figure for a critique of amnesiac modernity in the 1990s. Jean-Francois Lyotard wrote of the ghosts that haunted any totalizing system, and of the commitment of ethical thought to be 'haunted by a familiar and unknown guest which is agitating it' (Lyotard 1991: 2). Jean-Michel Rabaté concurred: 'we might say that "modern" philosophy has always attempted to bury [its] irrational Other in some neat crypt, forgetting that it would thereby lead to further ghostly reapparitions' (Rabaté 1996: xviii). Any proclamation of self-possessed modernity induces a haunting, what David Glover terms the 'spectrality effect' (Glover 2001). All of this was undersigned by Jacques Derrida's reflections in *Specters of Marx*, in which the ghost throws time out of joint, producing a 'radical untimeliness' or 'anachrony' in which self-possession suffers permanent disjointure (Derrida 1994: 27). This temporal dislocation also opens an ethical relation, for the revenant always returns with a plea or demand for witness. For Derrida, 'to be' is 'to be *haunted by*' an Other: ontology is replaced by hauntology, a pun which works better with a French accent (Derrida 1994: 51).

This Gothic programme might almost be sketched out in the margins of *Beloved*, whose ghost, as Peter Nicholls puts it, 'evokes the traumatic force of a historicity which splits the subject, compelling it to live in different times rather than in a secure, metaphysical present' (Nicholls 1996: 58). *Beloved* is at once an act of recovery and memorialization, but also a testament to the *immemorial*, the ethical impossibility of bringing to any close the mourning for 'sixty million and more' for subsequent generations.

It is these reflections on transgenerational transmission and the difficulty of accommodation with this traumatic history that also make *Beloved* a central trauma fiction. The novel follows the route of two daughters. Beloved and her consuming desire first for recognition from and then possession of the mother locks them into a form of melancholia, in which the traumatic losses of the past are erased in their ecstatic embrace. Beloved's return allows Sethe to 'Think about all I ain't got to remember no more' (Morrison 1987: 1982) because the ghost is an insistence of the past: it obliterates memory. Denver, the surviving daughter, born as her mother crossed the Ohio River into freedom, traverses the family trauma in a different way, one that comes to spurn melancholia for a process of mourning. Denver has lost her brothers, driven out by the haunting, and suffers traumatic deaf-mutism initiated by the innocent question asked of her at school (and typically delayed by Morrison to intensify its punch): 'Didn't your mother get locked away for murder?' (Morrison 1987: 103). Denver lives sealed in the melancholic world of 124, her senses returning when a malign aspect to the haunting begins. She initially takes the pleasures of recognition from Beloved's material return, but locked out of the psychotic mother–daughter dyad, she steps off the front step of 124, a sign of her re-entry into social being. It is Denver who brings a communal rescue of her mother from melancholic entrapment, and this act that allows Sethe to utter, in her final words, a fragile return of self: '"Me? Me?"' (Morrison 1987: 273). This is the first prospect of her escape from slavery's social death some thirteen years after her freedom.

Once again, *Beloved*'s metaphorical framework is shared with theoretical work done elsewhere. The generational transmission of traumatic history has been figured as a form of haunting in the work of psychoanalysts Nicolas Abraham and Maria Torok. They explain melancholia thus: 'Grief that cannot be expressed builds a secret vault within the subject. In this crypt reposes ... the objective counterpart of the loss, as a complete person with his own topography' (Abraham and Torok 1980: 8). Crypts only remain sealed for so long: they begin to leak phantoms. 'To be sure, all the departed may return, but some are destined to haunt: the dead who have been shamed during their lifetime or those who took unspeakable secrets to the grave' (Abraham 1987: 287). This is an intersubjective understanding of traumatic effects: such secrets are forms of 'transgenerational haunting': 'What haunts are not the dead, but the gaps left within us by the secrets of others' (Abraham 1987: 287). Typically, the passage of a secret is from parent to child: 'The buried speech of the parent becomes (a) dead (gap), without a burial place, in the child' (Abraham and Torok 1984: 17). *Beloved* enacts this transmission in the symptomatic history of Denver. In a text stuffed with ghosts and phantoms, another image chain develops of sealed crypts beginning to burst: Paul D. carries a rusting tobacco tin in his chest that seals his ungovernable emotions; Sethe's belated click of understanding comes in a revealing image: 'A hobnail casket of jewels found in a tree hollow should be fondled before it is opened …. No smashing with an ax head before it is decently exhumed from the grave that has hidden it all this time' (Morrison 1987: 176). These unleash phantoms that harry those living in the wake of trauma. Just as Abraham and Torok lay out two different psychic topographies of mourning and melancholy, so Sethe's two daughters embody these paths: a melancholia that perpetuates encryption or a mourning that eventually decrypts occluded violent history.

The maturity of Morrison's vision of the accommodation to this past lies in her refusal to simply choose between what the daughters signify. It is of course necessary to overcome a pathological relation to the traumatic past, to be relieved of its violent insistence, in order to recover a sense of self and the possibility of community, but this cannot be done by a simple forgetting, since such exorbitant violence will continue to haunt the polity, much like *Beloved*'s remaining in the closing pages of the book. What Morrison seems to advocate is a kind of hesitation between two possibilities, as outlined by Derrida:

> Is the most distressing, or even the most deadly infidelity that of a *possible mourning* which would interiorise within us the image, idol, or ideal of the other who is dead and lives only in us? Or is it that of the impossible mourning, which, leaving the other to his alterity, respecting thus his infinite remove, either refuses to take or is incapable of taking the other within oneself?
>
> (Derrida 1986: 6)

This quandary is caught more economically in Morrison's coinage 'to disremember', which combines contradictory imperatives: to recall and forget, to dismember and recompose. These tensions also spell out the discordant concordance Ricoeur identifies in narrative knowledge. *Beloved* ends with Paul D. asking Sethe 'to put his story next to hers' (Morrison 1987: 273), recalling one of the Sweet Home men speak of love as a species of story: 'The pieces I am, she gather them and give them back to me in all the right order' (Morrison 1987: 272). The coda, however, honours the persistence of discordant traumatic history: that there is no story, in this sphere, that will not carry shards that pierce through any claim to closure.

Beloved suggests how important the role of fictional narrative can be in the trauma paradigm, for it demonstrates the novel form's capacity to bend the rules of history, causation and representation in order to bring into presence an occluded traumatic violence. The use of the supernatural foregrounds the limits of historiography, law or medicine to convey the lived experience of traumatized subjectivity and its transgenerational consequences: this experience requires fantastical tropes, exploded time schemes and impossible causations. In an act of creative intervention into the historical record, Morrison's narrative can at once depict the wound, keep it open, and bring a measure of concordance to what violence has shattered.

Beloved brilliantly consolidated a style of narrative distension, ethical hesitation and focus on the politics of oppressed communal identity now seen as typical of trauma fiction. However, it is striking how little commentary on the novel (including my own here) takes place in relation to the discourses of the trauma subject as they were substantially reconceived by the introduction of PTSD after 1980. This is mainly because the novel is bound up with psychoanalytic formulations. Morrison is openly indebted to this tradition: at the start of *Playing in the Dark*, for instance, she asserts that 'the narrative into which life seems to cast itself surfaces most forcefully in certain kinds of psychoanalysis' (Morrison 1993: vii), and most of the dynamics between mother and daughters in *Beloved* are thought through Freudian models. The remarkable symmetry of *Beloved* with a psychoanalytic post-structuralism gone Gothic means that the text has become an easy form of exemplification for a certain kind of cultural theory. What the text doesn't do is register how the trauma paradigm explicitly transforms narrative, trope and character-formation in the contemporary novel. To begin to sketch this historical shift in fiction, I turn to the work of Stephen King.

Stephen King's trauma Gothic

Stephen King's prolific, bestselling horror writing is frequently the source of suspicion, celebrated by fans but ignored in the main by literary critics and disdained by experts in the Gothic. S. T. Joshi in *The Modern Weird Tale* lambasts King's 'cheap sentiment, naïve moral polarisations, hackneyed, implausible and ill-explained supernatural phenomena … and a subscribing to the conventional morality of common people' (Joshi 2001: 63). A problem for those who want to regard the Gothic genre as potentially subversive is King's conservatism; his novels invoke a coercive 'we' that David Punter considers 'at all points coterminous with US norms' (Punter 1996: 122). Even worse, King seems to agree, seeing horror fiction as 'above all else an agent of the norm' (King 1991: 64). Yet this is not so simple, for King's work registers exactly the pressure on those norms across a particularly turbulent span of American history. His work might be loosely defended as 'sociopolitical' in this regard (Magistrale 1988: 2), but one can be more precise. King's horrific tales are unusually sensitive to the depredations to contemporary subjectivity, and his narratives are so compulsive because they explore this discordance within narrative structures that work (for most of the time) towards fragile kinds of concord. For me, this defines the value of reading popular fiction as a form of surrogate public history. This historicity is nowhere more apparent than in King's relationship to the reconceptualization of trauma since the 1970s.

King's work might initially be regarded as trauma fiction in two ways. First, trauma psychology frequently resorts to the Gothic or supernatural to articulate post-traumatic effects. Large-scale traumatic events involve, as Robert Jay Lifton puts it, 'a permanent encounter with death' that leaves behind it a host of 'homeless dead' that cannot easily be laid to rest (Lifton in Krystal 1968: 171 and 183). Survivors are treated as liminal beings, exaggeratedly valued or feared for now possessing 'a quality of supernatural evil' (Lifton 1968: 517). In *Trauma and Recovery*, Judith Herman proposes that

> the pathological environment of childhood abuse forces the development of extraordinary capacities, both creative and destructive. It fosters the development of abnormal states of consciousness in which the ordinary relations of body and mind, reality and imagination, knowledge and memory, no longer hold .... The language of the supernatural, banished for three hundred years from scientific discourse, still intrudes into the most sober attempts to describe the psychological manifestations of chronic childhood trauma.
>
> (Herman 1994: 96)

Janice Haaken noted that as the incest story took hold it was becoming superset with all kinds of 'social symbolic loadings' by the late 1980s, including the 'clinical preoccupation with gothic scenes of sexual torture' (Haaken 2003: 90). Post-traumatic experience is intrinsically uncanny, finding cultural expression in ghostly visitations, prophetic dread, spooky coincidence or telepathic transfer: 'Traumatic anxiety *is* a ghost! It moves through the generations with the stealth and cunning of a most skilled spectre' (Terr 1985: 528).

This is not a collection of loose metaphorical analogues, but a stronger argument: genre fictions can become imbricated in the formation new psychiatric subjects. Ian Hacking comments on the important role films like *The Three Faces of Eve* (Nunnally Johnson, 1957) or *Sybil* (Daniel Petrie, 1976) had on the diagnostic construction of multiple personality disorder. Generic scripts provide narratives for what Hacking terms 'making up people', the dynamic interaction between subjects and psychiatric categories. In a different context, the apparatus of the horror and Gothic revival of the 1970s (of which King was an integral part) clearly surfaced in the descriptions of recovered memories of Satanic Ritual Abuse in the early 1990s. That the Gothic might prove appropriate to provide scripts for trauma is perhaps because, as Robert Miles argues, the genre has from its foundation been 'embroiled within ... the history of the "subject",' presenting the self as 'dispossessed in its own house, in a condition of rupture, disjunction, fragmentation' (Miles 1993: 2–3).

Second, King's trauma fiction could be read more literally as a body of work symptomatic of personal trauma. This project has been duly undertaken, and by Lenore Terr, one of the strongest proponents in the Memory Wars of the view that buried traumatic memory can be recovered in pure, unmediated form. Her suspicion that King's work has traumatic origins begins with the non-supernatural, rite-of-passage novella 'The Body' (filmed as *Stand By Me*), in which a handful of boys from variously abusive homes follow train tracks into the forest on the rumour that they will be able to see a dead body. 'The Body' is structured as a recollection of a writer on a defining incident in his adolescence, one which is suffused with death, and Terr takes the story as barely encrypted autobiography. Sure enough, King's autobiographical writings reveal an incident of which King claims to have no direct memory, only the indirect accounts of family lore: aged four, returning home from play silent and shocked, King was the possible witness to the death of his playmate on rail tracks. How apt that King's traumatic origins as a writer are staged on this amnesiac site, the origin of trauma itself, the railway! King's account in *Danse Macabre*, however, is savage about decoding his career through this event. Such psychiatric speculation is 'jumped-up astrology': 'writers are made', he says, 'not born or created out of dreams or childhood trauma' (King 1991: 103–4). Terr nevertheless traces this symptom with a dogged and literal determination. Mechanical monsters loom in King's work: possessed cars, demonic machines, zombifying mobile phones and always, always the train. King knows 'how to present posttraumatic symptoms in his plots' (Terr 1989: 379). King's well-known writing compulsion (and other addictions), his exploration of the same scenarios of menaced children, suggest rather that he is caught in cycles of traumatic repetition rather than mastery. Even the inordinate length of the novels that King produces has a traumatic origin for Terr: the over-accumulation of detail, the slowing of narrative time, all imply King is re-experiencing the timeless time of the traumatic event. Thus King's fiction is entirely the result of 'posttraumatic play': 'King is a trauma victim, struck terrified in his own childhood by a train' (Terr 1989: 389).

Terr's account is a warning about the brutal reduction of text to autobiographical symptom, read with the alarming literalism driven by the belief that eidetic traumatic memory will never be seriously deformed or subject to revision, or even undergo any aesthetic transformation, but will simply repeat itself in the grain of texts as an open secret. This is not how I want to regard King's representative status. King is not an exemplification of trauma subjectivity; instead, his books are narrative vectors for its consolidation. My approach will be to trace how King's attunement to the *Zeitgeist* very precisely shifts the locus and narrative form of subjective terror in the Gothic directly in response to the rise of the trauma paradigm, particularly in the early 1990s and most symptomatically in his novel *Gerald's Game*.

King writes self-consciously in the American Gothic tradition, in which domestic intimacy is menaced by its dialectical other, an unearthly, cosmic and always malignant force. In *The Shining* (1978), one of King's strongest books, the father is weak entry point in the family, taken over by the venomous spirits of the Overlook hotel. For all the supernatural pyrotechnics of *The Shining*, its ambitions to render the hotel a repository of the monstrous underside the American twentieth century, the book is also an impressive study of the father's psychic failings. His alcoholism, his guilty instant of physical abuse towards his son, his teaching job lost through an eruption of rage, are traced back to an abusive father, whose exorbitant violence to his mother and siblings is recovered by Jack in a dissociative trance state in the symbolic basement of the hotel, where all manner of forgotten histories accumulate. The precognitive flashes of future violence, picked up by his psychic son, are revealed to be repetitions of a traumatic scene from his father's childhood. These traumatic motifs (the roar of '*come here and take your medicine*') cut across the narrative in distinct typographic intrusions that collapse linear temporality into the insistent presence of traumatic timeless time. This scene is coming, it is what propels the narrative, but it has also already taken place. This emplotment of psychic damage suggests an early recognition, on King's part, of psychological accounts of generational cycles of violence within the abusive family. It also indicates that King will always associate supernatural capacities with traumatic origins.

In the early 1980s, 'The Body' experimented with transferring Gothic affect out of genre trappings, locating its affect in early adolescent rites of passage. It was published in *Different Seasons* alongside 'Apt Pupil', a queasy investigation into the transmissibility of trauma. An adolescent boy, apparently a model student, discovers that an aged neighbour in his small American town has been living under a pseudonym, concealing his past as a concentration camp *unterkommandant* in Belsen, Auschwitz and Patin, where the Jews named him the Blood Fiend. Dussander is blackmailed by the boy to detail every element of crimes, a narrative that corrupts the listener and transfers the murderous impulse. The tale designedly walks a dubious line between the exploitation of historical horrors and a critique of our potentially unhealthy absorption in them. Punter observes that King offers his readers 'a series of opportunities to re-experience scenarios of childhood anxiety under conditions of relative safety' (Punter 1996: 123), but I see no reassurance in 'Apt Pupil', only a grim assessment of how unimaginable horrors can become vehicles of corrupting identification.

The 1990 long story, 'The Library Policeman' in *Four Past Midnight* signalled King's first explicit engagement with the recovered memory paradigm. The supernatural element of the story connects directly to a traumatic scene that the protagonist Sam must recover if he is to defeat the spectral figure who demands his life in payment of debt, a monstrous exaggeration of every child's fear of the punitive librarian. Sam is unaware that Junction City Library had employed a woman librarian in 1956 who had first traumatized children with a perverted storytelling hour before escalating her abuses to murder. A sort of vampiric creature occupying different human bodies, this figure has returned, the library hovering between present day and 1956 incarnations, a haunted site that collapses back to the most traumatic moment in its history. This supernatural figure identifies Sam as a potential host because Sam's unacknowledged traumatic past leaves him with an exploitable psychic flaw.

Sam's recovery of his traumatic memories could almost be transcribed from a recovered memory therapy handbook. At forty years old, his functional life is thrown into doubt by his first encounter with the sinister woman librarian. Fragile defences are crushed and when he is forced to call on help, Sam recognizes that his relationships fail, his social attachments are minimal, his business is only partially successful because his clients sense something in him is missing. The visit from the spectral library policeman sends him into a critical phase. Intrusive motifs begin to proliferate, signs of an occluded memory attempting to resurface. As in *The Shining*, these narrative anachronies are typographically marked off as urgent and insidious intrusions into linear narrative and are understood by the reader as anticipations of a recovered scene that will retrospectively rewrite Sam's life narrative. The recovery is too neatly done, emerging complete in 'a watching dream' (King 1990: 685), a symptom of dissociation, as Sam slumps unconscious. As a boy, returning in dread with a late book to the library, a figure claiming to be a policeman led Sam into the bushes and raped him, compounding the violence with shame ('*You liked it, didn't you?*' (King 1990: 691)) and threats of death should he speak of the event. His dissociative strategy at the height of the attack is reinforced by an immediate forgetting. He becomes a post-traumatic automaton. Remembering the traumatic scene, however, promises the complete reintegration that follows the emergency phases of recovering memory. Self restored, Sam slays the beast and gets the girl.

If the introduction of abuse recovery does not radically shift King's narrative mode, it might be worth wondering whether that is because popular narrative forms like King's actually inform abuse accounts and their 'clinical preoccupation with gothic scenes of sexual torture' (Haaken 2003: 90) rather than simply exploit them. Even so, the supernatural elements in the story do not so much allegorize Sam's traumatic subjectivity as offer an oneiric, doubled account of it in ways that don't quite cohere. Reintegrated, Sam can cross into this other story and slay the vampire that bears the weight of other multiple traumatic histories, yet which perhaps only obscures his own story. The ambiguous function of the supernatural becomes starker in *Gerald's Game*, all the more because the text apparently shifts genre only for the horror mode to return, to problematic effect, in the final pages of the book.

Gerald's Game (1992) and the interlinked novel *Dolores Claiborne* (1993) moved King to the centre of the trauma paradigm, focusing on female terror but ultimate resilience in the face of paternal sexual abuse. Theresa Thompson has suggested that the two books were King's ripostes to charges of misogyny, but it is more I think that at the height of the impact of the feminist self-help recovery movement, King understood that these accounts had to be focalized through women. *Gerald's Game* is a narrative tour de force: in the opening pages, Jessie, handcuffed to a bed in a sex game in a remote cabin, kicks out at her husband and accidentally kills him, leaving the protagonist (and therefore the narrative focalization) tied to a bed for the majority of the novel. The clue to escape starvation and death is buried, once more, in a traumatic memory she must confront, but since her adult life has been constructed around denial, passivity and dissociation, only extreme circumstances will force the issue.

Jessie is a thoroughly historicized subject, not just in the traumatic symptoms she displays in the narrative present. Her past typifies a certain trajectory of feminism. The abusive event occurs in 1963, the year Betty Friedan's *The Feminine Mystique* tried to express the nameless malaise American women experienced. This event is dissociated, only to obtrude dangerously now and then, forced to the surface during the era of feminist consciousness raising in the early 1970s. Jessie suppresses and domesticates herself in marriage, giving up her teaching job on her husband's insistence, and by the 1980s, the era of conservatism and backlash, has become another post-traumatic automaton, with some attempts at therapy curtailed in panic at what they might disturb.

King's populism means that he constantly expresses aggressive anti-psychiatric opinions: Jessie dismisses talk of child abuse from 'whining Cult-of-Selfers, the Live-in-the-Pasts' (King 1993: 141). Yet this only echoes the anti-establishment rhetoric of the recovery movement itself, and King's tracing of the traumatic subject seems to me very precisely worked out inside the new paradigm. The subject's minimally functioning defensive tactics are sent into crisis. This induces a disintegration: soon, the novel is driven by the competing voices in Jessie's head. These are given names and identities: the Goodwife and the countermanding Ruth, her long-lost feminist friend, Daddy's Little Girl, and a host of others sometimes termed 'UFO voices'. Early on, Jessie half-recognizes that these repeat 'the voices you heard after the dark day' (King 1993: 40), voices that splinter from the inaugurating trauma. These selves are the 'multiples' or 'alters' that feature in the official diagnostic manuals – although Multiple Personality Disorder was replaced in 1994 by Dissociative Identity Disorder:

> Each personality state may be experienced as if it has a distinct personal history, self-image, and identity, including a separate name ... . Particular identities may emerge in specific circumstances and may differ in reported age and gender, vocabulary, general knowledge or predominant affect. Alternate identities are experienced as taking control in sequence, one at the expense of the other, and may deny knowledge of one another, be critical of one another, or appear in open conflict ... . Individuals with this disorder experience frequent gaps in memory for personal history, both remote and recent.
>
> (American Psychiatric Association 2000: 526)

Thirst and pain amplify these voices, but also send her into fevered states that begin to lift her mechanisms of defence: dreams, visions and hallucinations of visitors to her bedside merge with resurgent childhood memories. Here, King makes the path to recovery much more effectively crooked from resistance: screen memories from later in childhood protect the core event of 1963 from straightforward narrative reclamation. The event hovers at the margins of the text, not really a secret, and in this King also finds a narrative means to distinguish repression from dissociation, Janet's model of trauma that had become favoured by the late 1980s. King's narrator explains: 'The secret of that day had never completely sunk in her subconscious …; it had been buried in a shallow grave, at best. There had been some selective amnesia, but of a completely voluntary sort' (King 1992: 100). As this memory begins to move in from the margin, King uses his familiar tactic of increasing the anachronic intrusions of narratively dissociated phrases (*'to put out the sun'*) that hint at the content of the traumatic memory. These produce that now-familiar narrative effect of *Nachträglich* discordance. Exactly half-way through the book, the core traumatic memory emerges. It is a studiously un-Gothic scene: on the day of the 1963 eclipse, as father and daughter stare up through polarized glass at the sun, her father ejaculates against her back as he holds her on his lap. For the following two years, she later confesses, she existed 'in a kind of fugue state', 'sharing space in my head with a kind of whispering choir, dozens of voices' (King 1992: 383).

   Recovery does not prompt instant reintegration (as it had in 'The Library Policeman'), but a phase of further defensive reactions: denial and self-accusation, dramatic psychic splitting, all of which repeat childhood dissociative tactics. Yet after a passage of disintegration, where textual focalization virtually disappears, Jessie begins to pull herself into coherence. She acknowledges her father's manipulations, the shift of blame to the daughter, the complicity of her mother, and in classic trauma paradigm fashion sees the event as the determining pivot of her entire life:

> How many of the choices she had made since that day had been directly or indirectly influenced by what had happened during the final minute or so she had spent on her daddy's lap …. And was her current situation a result of what had happened during the eclipse?
>
> (King 1992: 215)

   Yet the unconscious prompts of the traumatic scene have also been grasped. The cuffs that bind her to patriarchal domination are made for male wrists, not female, and are thus looser than they should be. Her father's concern that Jessie not cut herself on the eclipse glass reminds her that blood can be a lubricant. She stabs at her wrists with broken glass in an act that, before recovery, would have been a symptom of self-mutilating masochism but is now recast as active and agential: 'I refuse to die this way' (King 1992: 292). The escape from bondage to the marriage bed is painfully effected.

   At this point, the reader might expect (as in *The Shining*) a brief coda depicting fragile recovery, the prospect of a post-post-traumatic life. Instead, *Gerald's Game* takes a very odd turn: one of Jessie's hallucinatory bedside visitors, a deformed nightmare creature, transpires to be an actual backwoods serial killer. In the closing movement of the book, Jessie must confront Joubert across a courtroom, a Gothic condensation of male violence created by gross family dysfunction: 'He was a victim of sex abuse himself, of course, his father, his stepfather, and his step-mother all apparently had a go at him' (King 1992: 378). As if to countervail the predominantly domestic realism of the novel, Joubert's crimes are grossly excessive: grave robbery, corpse mutilation, serial murder and cannibalism. At his trial,

Joubert constantly pulls Jessie back into her own traumatic moment: 'I was back in the lake house again – it happened with no lag whatsoever. Not remembering, do you understand?' (King 1992: 380). Jessie's final act of defiance, spitting in Joubert's face, completes her escape from repetition and marks the restitution of her Self.

Is this narrative move designed to make the text even more exemplary? The serial killer became, after all, another central icon of popular trauma culture. Mark Seltzer has argued that the serial killer is a subject constituted in modernity, acting out 'the form of public violence proper to a machine culture' (Seltzer 1998: 17). The killer is a product, like the concept of trauma itself, of the statistical society that emerged in the late nineteenth century, a 'statistical person', who 'experiences identity, his own and others, as a matter of numbers, kinds, types' (Seltzer 1998: 4). The blankness of empty serial actions prompts psychological profiles replete with traumatic indicators: abuse, violence, damaged attachments. King's use of an exaggerated Gothic mode for Joubert was hardly out of place in the 1990s, when Thomas Harris' Hannibal Lecter series reached cultural saturation with the film of *The Silence of the Lambs* (1991), whilst films like *Se7en* (David Fincher, 1995) offered new levels of Gothic elaboration of serial killing and generated a ceaseless stream of imitative films, trading on the clichés of the psychological abuse profile.

Sympathetic feminist critics of *Gerald's Game* consider Joubert an 'apt symbol' (Thompson 1998: 55) or a monster 'of the realistic and plausible variety' (Senf 1998: 99) that reinforces King's critique of patriarchy. I am less convinced. The introduction of Joubert means the novel veers away from confronting the everyday story of domestic paternal abuse, replacing the father – *eclipsing* him, more aptly – with exorbitant Gothic horrors. In this regard, Joubert works as a narrative fetish: 'the serial killer serves the function of a *fetish* in public culture: he is the means of the disavowal of institutionalized violence, while the "seriality" of his acts of violence marks the place of recognition in this disavowal' (Freccero 1997: 48). This device means that intra-familial violence is half-acknowledged but at once covered over by exteriorizing it in an abjected, monstrous figure defined as the very opposite of family. The clichés of the psychological profile killer as abused or damaged place him beyond ordinary social attachments, the marginal figure that defines and empties the norm of any transgressions, the exteriority that preys on the blameless model family. The serial killer therefore embodies King's sense of Gothic menace as always an external evil, what Bernard Gallagher sees in the work as 'the coercive influence of the external world on the individual psyche' (Gallagher 1987: 60). And this also matches the model of trauma as something *done to* individuals, an event that breaches the integrity of the subject from an outside, turning them from agents to victims. Joubert's deformed body and collection of body parts distracts the force of King's critique of male violence in the family. *Dolores Claiborne* corrects this mistake by revisiting the same moment of the 1963 eclipse: the passage of visceral violence in this novel erupts exactly from within the abusive family dynamic, as Dolores gruesomely clubs her husband to death. *Dolores Claiborne* is a less interesting or at least less symptomatic text than its twin, however. The contradictions of *Gerald's Game* suggest how popular fiction can at once compellingly embody a narrative form of the insights of the trauma paradigm and at the same time work furiously to disavow them. It is this tension that makes King's work always absorbing, representative of the contrary desires of recognition and displacement that pulse through the cultural transmissions of traumatic affect.

Mainstream fiction and traumatic anachrony

The prescriptive aesthetic associated with canonical trauma fiction emphasizes the 'tendency to bring conventional narrative techniques to their limit' (Whitehead 2004: 82). Yet between Morrison's austere experimentalism and King's popular Gothic there is a substantial overlap of tropes, generic conventions and narrative devices. Ultimate aims might substantially differ, but they are on the same spectrum, composed inside the same trauma paradigm. And just to underline the pervasion of these narrative conventions for the new subject of trauma, I want briefly to range across the mass of mainstream literary fiction that appeared in the 1990s. These selected English and American texts show how quickly formal conventions were established: narrative anachrony as a symptom of buried trauma; belated revelation that regressively rewrites the significance of motifs; discordance that is reintegrated to find different levels of concordant narrative coherence.

In 1991, at the peak of American awareness about recovered memory, Jane Smiley's novel *A Thousand Acres* was awarded the Pulitzer Prize. A reworking of *King Lear*, transposing the fate of a kingdom to a mid-West farm divided amongst the patriarch Larry Cook's daughters, it was the mechanism of the revisionist reading that spoke to its time. At the play's pivotal moment – Lear's abandonment to the storm – Smiley shifts the focus back to the daughters, and Rose/Regan begins to excavate Ginny/Goneril's forgotten memories. 'You don't remember how he came after us, do you? ... When we were teenagers. How he came into our rooms ... How can you not remember?' (Smiley 1992: 188). The effect of this challenge follows the pattern of recovered memory. Ginny issues a flat denial, but the story speaks to Ginny's sense of absence and disquiet. The farm is a fragile landscape, 'the filmiest net of the modern world, over layers of rock' (Smiley 1992: 47). The brittle surface is punctured with buried secrets – Ginny's bloodied clothes from her last miscarriage, her symptomatic gaps of memory, the mother's grave. Forty pages on from Rose's challenge, the forgotten trauma returns in a flash of image-memory: 'I knew that he had been in there to me, that my father had lain with me in that bed, that I had looked at the top of his head, at his balding spot in the brown grizzled hair, while feeling him suck my breasts' (Smiley 1992: 228). The emergency phase, the intrusion of occluded memories into an identity built on an excised version of the past, follows from this one memory. The abuse retrospectively explains the awkwardness of her marriage in symptomatic behaviours that become now 'obvious evidence [of] my midnight experiences with Daddy' (Smiley 1992: 279). What Renée Fredrickson terms 'feeling memory' and 'bodily memory' accompanies the imagistic flashes that have evaded the censorious conscious memory.

With one stroke Smiley rewrites the dynamics of *Lear*, giving the motivations of Lear's daughters vital depth. The horror at the derangement of natural orders is resituated from the failure of daughterly duty to paternal incestuous desire. Lear's venomous disgust of female sexuality is marked as projection from abuser to abused, and Cordelia's loving rapprochement with her father is here transformed into Caroline's complicity in refusal to confront abuse. This is more than just an ingenious exercise in revisionary intertextuality, however. Splitting open a canonical text aims at exploding the wider cultural attitudes that would instate *King Lear* as an exemplary humanist text, thus silencing its misogyny. Smiley's decryption of a subtext of paternal abuse in *Lear* acts to counter a conservatism about the family that would precisely locate female insubordination as the greatest threat – that is, take Lear's part. As Kate Chedgzoy points out, however, 'the compelling narrative pleasures of Smiley's fiction are secured by a revision of the plot which does take the woman's part and which … refuses tragic closure' (Chedgzoy 1996: 58).

Kate Atkinson's *Behind the Scenes at the Museum* (1996) was a best-selling, prize-winning British novel that went through sixteen editions in its first year. This time, the central occlusion is the forgotten trauma of a family death. It is a sprawling, comic family saga, which tracks the generations of a dissolute family for over a century, and appears at first to be an exercise in the recovery of family memory. The forward progress of the narration of Ruby's life from 1950s childhood to the present is repeatedly disrupted by footnoted scenes from the family's transgenerational history, narratives which are sparked almost involuntarily by the secret histories of objects surviving anonymously into the present. Teaspoons, buttons, a rabbit's foot become uncanny objects, their inaccessible stores of memory impossibly voiced by a narrator who hovers somewhere between Ruby and omniscience. These objectal histories seemingly act to recuperate all the lost familial lines that derive from the originating matriarch, and gradually animate an enigmatic photograph that survives in the family from 1888. The patchwork of disordered segments works to redeem individual histories of loss, disappointment and death. This is one memorial narrative, but another belatedly intersects it and demands a retrospective revision of the family narrative. Only when Ruby is seventeen is she confronted with the repressed memory of her twin sister, who drowned at the age of five.

> I could feel a dreadful, threatening pulse beating in my stomach, yet I had no recollection of this sister and could bring no image to mind. I had a strange flash of memory – as if caught in a photographer's flash … – but nothing more.
>
> (Atkinson 1996: 328)

By a carefully staged process of hypnosis, the memory is recovered. It is this device that takes the narrative *behind* the behind of the family museum. The tonal disjunction of a comic romp which nevertheless aggregates an alarming record of death and disappearance is thus revised as a symptomatic dissonance. The strange oscillation of narrative locus – Ruby, yet not – is readable as a dissociated narrator who is the product of a saga constituted around a central traumatic core. The floor drops away from the attempt to reconstruct tangled family lines, and the belated realization of the repeated clues or signals that there is a 'hole' in this history is the classic mark of a regressive narrative that joltingly resignifies its pattern of motifs.

By 1997, Nicci French's *The Memory Game* traverses the same psychological terrain only to explore the effects of the implantation of false memories using the framework of the thriller. The novel opens with a discovery that literally shakes the foundations of the Martello family. The architect daughter strikes ground for a new building in the grounds of her parents house only to uncover a body: the corpse of her sister Natalie, who disappeared in 1968. Jane's initiation into the culture of recovered memory advocates and support groups follows her work with a therapist on retrieving the 'repressed' elements of her last memory of Natalie. It seems as if the familiar structure is operating here, Jane worrying at the disquiet that hovers over her memory:

> I've been thinking about my golden, golden childhood and a black hole in the middle of it … . Somehow it's there, always on the edge of vision, but when I turn to look at it directly it's gone, gone to the edge again.
>
> (French 1997: 57)

The results, however, are different. It is the persistence of her therapist's belief that the gap *must* contain an encrypted trauma, since Jane 'fits' the schema of symptoms of repressed memory, that leads her to uncover her father in the core memory. After his imprisonment for murder, Jane returns to the real scene only to realize the image she has worked on so intensely misremembers crucial details. The condensed finale exposes the false memory at work, and it is detective logic that identifies the brother as the real perpetrator.

This is a text programmatically written from arguments that recovered memories are no more than suggestions implanted by schema-driven therapists. *The Memory Game* dramatizes the view that therapists holding a belief in the pervasion of familial abuse, and possessing a list of symptoms and a generic script, can suggest an image a patient *ought* to hold, induce it and then confabulate fantasies which are affirmed as memory. If the novel has a strangely educative air, this may be because the plot owes much to the real-life case of Eileen Lipsker, whose recovered memories which solved a sixteen-year-old murder by accusing her father have been the subject of counter-suits in the American law courts.

Trauma fictions, then, clearly engaged with the Memory Wars and could invest in the intractable positions of the recovered memory debate. In the 1990s, the dispute was severely polarized: the sceptics Richard Ofshe and Ethan Watters argued in the polemical *Making Monsters* that 'the options for taking sides in this debate are quite unambiguous: the mind either has the ability to repress vast numbers of events, as described by recovered memory therapists, or it does not' (Ofshe and Watters 1994: 5). Although investigating the possibilities of the same structure of trauma narrative and subjectivity, the sympathies behind *A Thousand Acres* and *The Memory Game* could hardly seem more incompatible. Other novelists, however, explored this terrain with considerably more ambiguity, exploiting the suspensive hesitation of aesthetic discourse and using *Nachträglich* narrative to investigate more critically the place of traumatic memory in contemporary subjectivity.

Michèle Roberts' *Daughters of the House* (1993) is heavily indebted to *Beloved*, working through a similar project of impossible mourning for abandoned souls, this time in the house of post-war Europe. Set in France, the novel concerns the reunion of two cousins, Thérèse, a nun in a contemplative order, and Léonie, married and now living in the house in which twenty years earlier, in the 1950s, the two as girls had experienced uncanny events. Thérèse's return is occasioned by a literal unearthing of that past: 'The grave newly opened and desecrated, swastikas in red daubed on the tombstone' (Roberts 1993: 7). The violated grave has revealed a gruesome secret: the epitaph that names Henri covers over 'the tangle of bones of the unknown Jews buried with him' (Roberts 1993: 7). 'There was a secret somewhere' (Roberts 1993: 132), and Thérèse and Léonie have to sift multiple, incomplete, and fragmented evidences from diverse sources – whispered parental conversations, the oblique and hastily curtailed reminiscences of the servants, the isolated phrases that leap from the mass of letters between their mothers but that remain unread before being destroyed. The daughters of the house are penetrated and to some extent ventriloquized by the encrypted secrets of their parents' generation and events from the last days of the Nazi occupation of France. In effect, they suffer transgenerational haunting, the phantom of a history illegally buried but leaking from the edges of the crypt.

This is a complex and ambitious novel, in which the overdetermined traumatic core remains in some essentials opaque. The book opens with the shards of a nightmare featuring a dismembered body in the cellar, but if it ends with the fragments of a statue unearthed and reassembled from under the house, Roberts refuses to resolve the suggestive tangle of plot motifs into some final, determining concordance. The debt to Morrison is in this maintenance of a haunting, enigmatic core. Nevertheless, the readable dynamic of the novel is a dialectic between Léonie's attempts to suppress the interruptive presences in the house and Thérèse's openness to visionary experience and the trace of historical trauma. Léonie polices the boundaries of her house by obsessively listing her property, an inventory of familial possessions that are used as chapter titles. These attempt to fix concrete objects in a neutral taxonomy, but each leaks a history. Léonie persistently denies this haunting during her childhood: 'She wouldn't be caught, trapped in the darkness. She wasn't a Jew' (Roberts 1993: 152). This finds direct echo in her adult resentment of Thérèse's return, occasioned by the desecrated grave, and the fear it will start again: 'out of the grave of the war, the unburied and the undead [were] arriving to lay hands upon them all' (Roberts 1993: 170). Yet the final movement of the book brings Léonie toward integration of these discordant voices, in the last words of the novel:

> All she had to do was go in and join them, listen to what they had to say, unravel and reravel the different languages that they used … . The voices came from somewhere just ahead, the shadowy bit she couldn't see. She stepped forward, into the darkness, to find words.
>
> (Roberts 1993: 172)

This open-ended conclusion is an uncanny echo of Lyotard's imperative issued to post-traumatic thought, that 'It is necessary to "explain" that there might (have) be(en) this stranger in the house, and to find a "reason" for his clandestine entry and unnoticed stay' (Lyotard 1990: 17).

Helen Dunmore's *Talking to the Dead* (1997), although narratively far more conventional than Roberts, also refuses to stay in polarized debates and examines the ambiguity of memorial subjectivity. The novel opens with Nina's arrival to help her elder sister Isabel through the first days following the birth of Isabel's son. Nina is assailed by memories of childhood and Isabel's authoritative hold over the story of her early years; as she says, 'I'm in the habit of believing Isabel's version' (Dunmore 1997: 13). The air of tension, it is belatedly revealed, is the unspoken absence of their younger brother, who died in infancy from cot death. This is the core event on which the novel turns. At first its absent presence implies fears of repetition with the new child, but something else is moving in the traumatic scene. It is significant that immediately after this trauma's first telling, Nina begins to interrogate the general tenor of her childhood memories: 'It's a safe story, well-worn and comforting. ... Perhaps I tell myself this story so loudly that I can't hear anything else' (Dunmore 1997: 58). The challenge becomes more urgent as the first explicit mention of the lost brother occurs between the sisters: memory surges, and begins to animate the frozen image of Colin's death. 'I want my past back', but Nina realizes there's nothing except 'Isabel's stories' (Dunmore 1997: 91). Just before the revelation, Nina is perfectly defined as the gapped subject of traumatic amnesia: 'There's something missing in you' (Dunmore 1997: 98).

As the sisters talk, Nina captures an image of Isabel pushing down on Colin's back, smothering him, but at the brink of articulation, Isabel reverses the agency in the scene and orders her sister: 'Don't, don't. Don't remember. You were only four. It wasn't your fault' (Dunmore 1997: 100). In this version, the authority of Isabel's narrative of their childhood has served to hide from Nina her act of murder. With that knowledge, Nina's fragile self is shattered: 'uncertainty runs around me like ice. ... The iceberg hits the side of my ship, and I go down' (Dunmore 1997: 102–3). Dunmore therefore builds her plot from the phases of recovered memory: conscious recall of a placid childhood, edged by disquiet; a memory-image that becomes the focus point for retrieval; the recovery of the scene and entry into the emergency phase as identity threatens to collapse; a retrospective attribution of a new cause to Nina's various dysfunctions rewrites life narrative.

But Dunmore refuses to let the traumatic event become fixed. The scene speaks of deadly sibling rivalry, but so does the context of the recovery. As the dread gathers that contemporary events will compulsively repeat the past, the primal scene is entered once more, agency reverses itself again, and Nina this time relocates her sister, too late, as the murderous figure. By the end, following Isabel's suicide, Nina's conviction seems secure: 'It must have been hard to do. ... By the time he went still she must have hated him for taking so long to be dead' (Dunmore 1997: 204). Nevertheless, the text ends on an incomplete fragment of memory as Nina stands over her sister's grave. Reaching up to take Isabel's hand, the memory and text end on a question – 'Can I ask you something?' (Dunmore

1997: 214) – which now cannot be answered. Memory, which means talking to the dead, will be without final resolution, Dunmore implies. This echoes Freud's position in his early essay 'Screen Memories', which examines the instability and malleability of the earliest childhood memories: 'It may indeed be questioned whether we have any memories at all *from* our childhood: memories *relating to* our childhood may be all that we possess' (Freud 1899: 322). It is not that the traumatic scene is either 'true' or 'false' but is dynamic, set in motion by the imbrication of actual history, memory's imperfect and interpretive relation to that history, and the competing phantasmatic investments in the retelling of the scene. As Ian Hacking argues, recovery of trauma in particular allows 'the past [to be] rewritten in memory, with new kinds of descriptions, new words, new ways of feeling', such that 'each of us becomes a different person as we redescribe the past' (Hacking 1995: 94 and 68). As the agency in the recovered scene circulates between Nina and Isabel, new subjectivities and new histories are being elaborated as the traumatic scene submits to the impress of competing investments.

There could be many further additions to these five novels; this selection is partly a serendipitous record of my reading of this trauma plot through the 1990s. Whole oeuvres can now carry the sense that traumatic subjectivity is the abiding thematic (and sometimes formal) concern: Helen Dunmore, Maggie O'Farrell, Andrew O'Hagan, Justine Picardie and Kathryn Harrison all spring to mind. What else links these books? One might be tempted to call these works less mainstream than middlebrow, were this not such a loaded term. Middlebrow is always pejorative, coined in the 1920s (long after 'highbrow' and 'lowbrow') to describe a largely feminine, middle-class, safely unexperimental, commercial, and critically ignored writing. The middlebrow, as Virginia Woolf put it, 'is the man, or woman, of middlebred intelligence who ambles and saunters now on this side of the hedge, now on that, in pursuit of no single object, neither art itself nor life itself, but both mixed indistinguishably, and rather nastily, with money, fame, power, or prestige' (Woolf 1981: 115). Even Nicola Humble's sympathetic study of the interwar women writers for whom this term was coined suggests that whilst middlebrow works negotiate transforming class identity, they finally offer 'narrative excitement without guilt, and intellectual stimulation without undue effort' (Humble 2001: 11). There must be a contradiction to identifying something like a middlebrow trauma fiction, however, or else its allegedly undemanding textual pleasures need to be rethought. The disarticulation of identity and narrative temporality may not be as extreme as those high or low fictions examined above, but they still imply serious cultural work to manage the depredations to the contemporary subject (and predominantly female subjectivity) marked by trauma. The narrative binding of these mainstream fictions suggests that a wash of ungovernable traumatic affect saturates contemporary Western culture. In these middlebrow fictions the pleasures of narrative concordance, of grasping together, are seized from the jaws of traumatic discordance.

If these works are critically ignored it may be because their narrative pleasures are too overt for a trauma aesthetic that sanctions difficulty, interruption and aporia. Yet if we turn to the contemporary apotheosis of trauma fiction, W. G. Sebald, we can begin to discern how this austere aesthetic generates its own curious form of pleasure.

W. G. Sebald: The last traumatophile?

I want to consider W. G. Sebald's last novel *Austerlitz* (2001) as a culmination of the trauma fiction genre. It is a tortured investigation of trauma subjectivity as both endured by the eponymous central character and then transmitted to the narrator, who virtually collapses under the burden of what he has been told. This traumatic affect has since been disseminated to an enthusiastic readership in Britain and America and Sebald can be regarded as the quintessential trauma fiction writer at the turn of the century. Yet his work is a late and mannerist addition to the genre: in my view it risks traumatophilia, taking a kind of perverse delight in the repetition or abject assumption of a collapsed trauma subjectivity. Unlike the complex negotiation between mourning and melancholy explored in *Beloved*, Sebald seems interested only in the psychology of melancholic entrapment.

Sebald's brief literary ascendancy lasted in effect five years, between the English translation of *The Emigrants* (1996) and his death in 2001, soon after the publication of *Austerlitz*. An academic specializing in German literature at the University of East Anglia, Sebald began to produce poetry and prose works in German in his forties. *The Emigrants* was rapturously received in England and America, and dictated the perception of Sebald as the 'poet laureate … of missing history' (Torgovnick 2006: xii), contributing a whole new narrative relation to the legacy of the Second World War and particularly the Holocaust. Sebald was born in 1944 in a remote rural area of Germany, seemingly untouched by the war. His father served in the army, returned from France as a prisoner of war in 1947, and never spoke of his experience. Sebald 'had grown up with the feeling that something was being kept from me' (Sebald 2003: 70), and claims to have learnt of the Nazi policy of genocide only at seventeen in a culture that had almost entirely suppressed discussion of the war. The eerie sense of shocking, belated discoveries suffuses his work. Whilst the narrative perambulations of *The Emigrants* and *Austerlitz* do repeatedly circle back to the Holocaust, this view of Sebald tends to downplay his two other prose works, *Vertigo* (1990, translated 1999) and *The Rings of Saturn* (1995, translated 1998), which journey through European history on very different trajectories. Attention has been shifted by the posthumous translation in 2003 of Sebald's lectures on the saturation bombing of German cities, where the same sense of lamentation, haunted memory and forgotten history is applied to the German populations massacred by the Allies. Any consideration of this era of German history is always controversial because it is feared to offer an argument of 'moral equivalence' with Holocaust victims: some worry the lectures damage Sebald's reputation (for a discussion of their reception, see Kling 2004).

Sebald has already generated a large body of critical assessment, rather like *Beloved*. This is partly because, as one collection notes, Sebald is 'clearly conversant with the discourse of trauma theory' (Long and Whitehead 2004: 9), and thus allows for instant literary exemplification of the paradigm. The work conforms to the trauma aesthetic: experimental, aporetic, foregrounding the difficulty of representing atrocity. But more than this, Sebald's austerity and melancholia, his exile status as an unhomely German in England, means that he can be presented as a saviour of the serious European novel in an era of frivolity (the view of Susan Sontag (2002)) and one of the few inheritors of the cosmopolitan Modernist project (Walkowitz 2006). This latterday high art, already imbued with *Nachträglichkeit* or doomed belatedness, like Hegel's owl of Minerva flying at dusk, could only be reinforced by Sebald's violent and untimely death in a car accident, soon after *Austerlitz* had been translated.

Sebald's works are trauma fictions not just because they explore the legacy of the Second World War and are imbued with this suave melancholia, but also because they hold to a model of history that coincides exactly with the idea of traumatic occlusion and the belated recovery of memory. This is expressed identically across Sebald's oeuvre, whether prose, poetry or lecture. 'Certain things', as Henry Selwyn says in *The Emigrants*, 'as I am increasingly becoming aware, have a way of returning unexpectedly, often after a lengthy absence' (Sebald 1996: 23). Jacques Austerlitz is another compelling textbook example of a recovered memory patient, a model of traumatic return that Sebald utilizes both for post-war Germany in *On the Natural History of Destruction* and post-colonial English historical consciousness in *Rings of Saturn*.

Sebald's prose works are innovative hybrid forms, a mix of fiction, biography, academic essay and documentary reconstruction (complete with photographic evidence). They are like a cabinet of curiosities, stuffed with eccentric details and overlooked or forgotten histories, often obscurely connected in an expansive digressive style. Although some of these elements were borrowed from the post-war German documentary fiction tradition, the real innovation is in the narrative focalization. The 'I' is teasingly both Sebald and not, a semi-fictional narrator who filters all the details through a single voice, viewpoint and prose rhythm, and yet who seems to gain little substance throughout the course of the books. If Virginia Woolf complained about the male 'I' that stabbed the page and oppressed the reader with domineering presence, Sebald's narrator is virtually effaced, becoming only an invisible repository, an archive for collected information. 'The narrator', Sebald explained, 'is only the one who brings the tale but doesn't install himself in it' (Jaggi 2001). As Amir Eshel puts it, this focalization is 'a singular concentration, if not a fixation, on what is decisively outside the "I" – the experiences of others, the fear that their story might vanish into oblivion' (Eshel 2003: 75).

The ethical purpose of this effaced narrator is most explicit in *The Emigrants*, a book that brings together four scattered biographies of displaced or exiled figures, two of whom commit suicide, the other two suffering obliterating mental collapses – and all of whom suffer the intolerable burden of history. In one key passage, the narrator, following in the footsteps of his schoolteacher who has committed suicide, stops himself: 'Such endeavour to imagine his life and death did not, as I had to admit, bring me any closer to Paul, except at best for brief emotional moments of the kind that seemed presumptuous to me. It is in order to avoid this sort of wrongful trespass that I have written down what I know of Paul Bereyter' (Sebald 1996: 29). The narrator, driven in this endeavour by a typically Sebaldian belated discovery that Paul had been barred from teaching under Nazi Aryanization laws in the 1930s, tries to control affective identification for a principled and distanced compassion, effacing himself in an 'objective' collocation of the documents of a life. Even so, by the fourth section, when the narrator is horrified again by his own historical blindness in the tardy realization that his fellow German exile Max Ferber must have suffered under the Nazis, traumatic transmission is less containable. Many years after their first meeting, the narrator reads that Ferber's parents were deported and murdered in 1941, and is aghast: 'it seemed unforgivable that I should have omitted, or failed, in those Manchester times, to ask Ferber the questions he must surely have expected from me' (Sebald 1996: 178). Sebald's device when approaching profoundly traumatic material is to distance it through layers of narrative framing: the narrator dutifully transcribes Ferber's descriptions of his post-traumatic amnesias around the recollections of his parents and the reconstruction of that vanished pre-war Jewish past is narrated entirely through Ferber's mother's memoir. If insulated from presumption by this respectful reportage, the narrator also travels to the area in Germany, wanders through the largely obliterated traces of Jewish community, documents it in photographs, and places a stone on a Jewish grave in identification with Jewish memorial practice. The book ends with an unreproduced photograph of three Jewish factory workers. 'Who the women are I do not know', the narrator confesses, yet 'I sense that all three of them are looking across at me' (Sebald 1996: 237), in that sort of imperious ethical demand for witness that Derrida ascribes to the spectre who returns. The book ends with exactly the presumption that had been so assiduously avoided: a fantasmatic projection of possible identities of the women. It signals a collapse of narrative control, moments that pepper all four prose works.

The same kind of trauma subject appears over and over in these books. In *The Emigrants*, the aged Henry Selwyn endures the overwhelming return of memories of his childhood as Hersch Seweryn in Grodno, Lithuana before the pogroms drove his family into exile in 1899: 'For years, the images of that exodus had been gone from his memory, but recently, he said, they had been returning once again and making their presence felt' (Sebald 1996: 18–19). Ferber describes an appalling physical and mental collapse as memories 'that had long been buried and which I had never dared disturb' return (Sebald 1996: 172). In the third section, the reconstruction of the life of Ambos Adelwarth's life points to memory experienced as a form of intolerable presence and unceasing grief: someone comments that he 'had an infallible memory, but that, at the same time, he scarcely allowed himself access to it' (Sebald 1996: 100). The narrator reconstructs Ambos' voluntary submission to obliterating electro-convulsive therapy to destroy his memorial self. 'Memory', Ambos comments in a journal, 'often strikes me as a kind of dumbness. It makes one's head heavy and giddy, as if one were not looking back down the receding perspectives of time but rather down on the earth from a great height' (Sebald 1996: 145). It is *Vertigo* that traces this rhythm of nausea and subjective collapse most directly in the narrator himself who repeatedly breaks down as he moves through the rubble of European history. Yet it was in *Austerlitz* that Sebald wrote most directly within the trauma paradigm.

Austerlitz recounts his crisis of subjectivity to the narrator, who records it in intense, labyrinthine sentences that make the text a single uninterrupted paragraph. The book begins with a lengthy description of a patently symbolic structure, the Breendonk fortress in Belgium, a monument to a failed system of defence. This monstrous bulwark (which housed the SS during the war) could never keep up with new military technologies, however far it was extended. It symbolizes the collapse of Austerlitz's own mechanisms of defence and the flood of traumatic material that returns to conscious recall late in life, after his retirement. The book adopts the classic trauma plot of a delayed central secret which then retrospectively recasts Austerlitz's life narrative. That life has been full of dread and suspicion: in his childhood, 'I never shook off the feeling that something very obvious, very manifest was hidden from me' (Sebald 2001: 76). He speaks of a dissociated self, riven by 'an agency greater than or superior to my own capacity for thought ... [that] has always preserved from me my own secret, systematically preventing me from drawing the obvious conclusions' (Sebald 2001: 60). When the mechanism of dissociated memory breaks down, it is on another symbolic site, Liverpool Street station in London, built on the old Bedlam asylum, and where refurbishment has uncovered an ancient graveyard. 'As for me, said Austerlitz, I felt at this time as if the dead were returning from exile and filling the twilight around me with their strangely slow but incessant to-ing and fro-ing' (Sebald 2001: 188). It also happens in an emblematic year, 1991, the height of the recovered memory controversy (Sebald in part based the character of Austerlitz on Susie Bechhofer, a recovered memory subject that had been the focus of one of a myriad television documentaries in the 1990s). When Austerlitz enters an old section of the station his childhood memory floods back: the arrival in England, from Prague, on one of the *Kindertransport*. These child transports had been an early Nazi method of depopulating German territory of Jews, before full-scale extermination. Austerlitz had been fostered with Welsh Calvinists, renamed, and his Jewish past erased.

In the emergency phase of traumatic recovery, Austerlitz recognizes 'how hard I must always have tried to recollect as little as possible' (Sebald 1996: 197). Failed relationships, frozen affect and multiple collapses are automatic post-traumatic responses. He travels to Prague, recovers his childhood language, and picks up the trail of his vanished parents. His mother was interned in Terezin, the 'model' concentration camp (and another fortress structure) that the Nazis had used to hoodwink Red Cross inspectors. She was then sent East to certain death. His father's trail fizzles out in Paris: there will be no complete return to the past. Sebald if anything overloads Austerlitz's condensation of the history of trauma – a recovered memory 'survivor' in the 1990s, with a traumatic secret from the Holocaust in the 1930s and 1940s, who breaks down in Paris and is admitted to the Salpêtrière, home to the elaboration of traumatic neurosis in the 1880s. These concordances only intensify the unrelieved agony of Austerlitz's condition: memory does not in any way cure him. Instead, history invades him, and he can exist only in traumatic temporality: 'I feel more and more as if time did not exist at all, only various spaces ... between which the living and the dead can move back and forth as they like' (Sebald 2001: 261).

Towards the end of the book we learn that Austerlitz has given the narrator the keys to his house in the East End of London and thus the run of his archive (the house almost inevitably abuts onto an abandoned Jewish graveyard, walled off and forgotten). This weirdly digressive and anachronic narrative is therefore a reconstruction that could have pulled Austerlitz's story into a more coherent or linear form, but instead chooses to shadow the traumatic temporality of recovery. The narrator has become so etiolated that his opinions merge with his subject. At the Breendonk fort, the ethical injunction is renewed in terms that could have been spoken by Austerlitz:

> My memory ... has clouded over in the course of time ... . Even now, when I try to remember ... the darkness does not lift but becomes yet heavier as I think how little we can hold in mind, how everything is constantly lapsing into oblivion with every extinguished life, how the world is, as it were, draining itself, in that history of countless places and objects which them- selves have no power of memory.
>
> (Sebald 2001: 29–31)

Yet the narrator is markedly unable to find the means of concordance that would grasp together, as Ricoeur would put it, the discordances of Austerlitz's biography. Some have traced little flickers of concordance across Sebald's work, repeated leitmotifs, figures or dates that suggest coherence at a different level (see Whitehead 2004). Yet these are symptomatically weak, never enough to pull the elements together and seem designed to express the fragility of any aesthetic con- cordance against the massive destructive forces of discordance. *Austerlitz* certainly works towards an agitated intensification of atrocity consciousness. The trail of Austerlitz's father cold in Paris, the narrator turns instead in the final pages of the book to Dan Jacobsen's memoir, *Hershel's Kingdom,* another transgenerational tale of Holocaust trauma. The narrator, by now virtually erased by the burden of Austerlitz's history, seeks further material that will crush his ego under an irresolv- able burden of responsibility. The same impulse is there in the lectures on the bombing of Germany: authors are berated for their evasions of the actual dam- age done to bodies by fire-bombing, and Sebald pushes for the atrocious detail (traumatized mothers carrying dead babies in their luggage, and so on), yet often communicating a frustration that these hide further, even more insupportable facts that must be unveiled. These later works, as Stewart Martin observes, are determined by the experience of shock, and 'exude a post-traumatic exhaustion' (Martin 2005: 26).

Some view this intensification as a form of kitsch, a sort of adolescent affective urge merely 'to set the largest, most edifying standards of despair' (Thirlwell 2003: 28). This I think misunderstands Sebald's project. Yet Andreas Huyssen's critique of this 'relentless melancholy' is sharper, arguing that Sebald 'gives us not so much an analysis as a reinscription of the trauma by means of quotation' (Huyssen 2003: 154 and 156). By *Austerlitz*, Sebald had become a traumatophile. The relation to trauma is that it must remain unrelieved. It is perhaps rather provoking to say that Sara Paretsky's hard-boiled detective novel, *Total Recall*, which also appeared in 2001 and also featured a figure recovering memories of being on a *Kindertransport*, offered a more complex array of possible relations to the traumatic past. Survivor shame, fantasmatic investment in Jewish 'survivor' identity, the politics of financial reclamation, and heated comparativist controversies between Holocaust and slavery compensation claims are entwined plot strands. Some plot lines tie up in conventional concordances, but as is the convention with the complexification of plot in the hard-boiled genre, many discordances and irresolutions remain. The novel takes no pleasure in unrelievedness, however, and in this way seems more complexly engaged in historical legacies.

In a distinctly odd passage of her book, *The War Complex*, Marianna Torgovnick confesses to investing Sebald's book-cover photograph with all manner of fantasy projections, and emotively mourns his untimely death. In a book that begins with a personal account of living in lower Manhattan on the morning of the World Trade Center attack, her 'unusual and public act of identification with an author' (Torgovnick 2006: 129) is perhaps only another element of a trauma-inspired return to what was once called 'personal criticism'. Yet Torgovnick also offers a clue to Sebald's instant popularity in Britain and America. The blurring of the boundary between fictional narrators and authorial persona, true histories and narrative invention, was a commonly adopted writing strategy in the late 1980s and early 1990s. Philip Roth wrote a sequence of true fictions and false memoirs, starting with *The Facts* in 1988, a memoir which was attacked in an appendix for its falsehoods and evasions by Roth's fictional alter-ego, Nathan Zuckerman. Roth chased down an impersonator called Philip Roth in *Operation Shylock* (1993). In the midst of these metafictional plays, Roth wrote *Patrimony: A True Story* (1991), an ostensibly 'straight' memoir about the death of his father. Similarly, J. G. Ballard's *The Kindness of Women* (1991) was a fictional autobiography in which a character called J. G. Ballard seemed to live out a mythologized version of the author's life. The book, Ballard told Will Self, 'is my life seen through the mirror of the fiction prompted by that life' (Self 1995: 360). Both Roth and Ballard explored this breach of fiction and memoir explicitly in relation to extreme traumatic experience. Ballard lured the reader with a retrospective interpretation of his extraordinary fiction as the product of a childhood spent in a Japanese internment camp during the war. Roth wrote explicitly from a sequence of catastrophic mental collapses, punctuated by the wrenching death of his father. What Sebald offered too was a sense that the artful concordances of novelistic discourse could not contain this kind of traumatic material, that the novel form was being breached by the traumatic force of the real. Sebald was the apotheosis of trauma fiction, but at the same time, in that strange authorial presence both inside and outside the frame of the work, hinted that perhaps trauma material was better suited to the autobiographical or memoir form.

It is to the new kind of trauma memoir that emerged in the 1990s that I now turn.

3 My so-called life

The memoir boom

Martin Amis began his memoir *Experience* by observing:

> It used to be said everyone had a novel in them. ... Just now, though, in 1999, you would probably be obliged to doubt the basic proposition: what everyone has in them, these days, is not a novel, but a memoir. We live in the age of mass loquacity. We are all writing it or at any rate talking it: the memoir, the apologia, the c.v., the *cri de coeur*. Nothing, for now, can compete with experience – so unanswerably authentic, and so liberally and democratically dispensed. Experience is the one thing we share equally, and everyone senses this.
>
> (Amis 1999: 6)

This passage reflects anxiously on democratic generality, somewhat disingenuously it would appear, since Amis's introduction rather builds the case for the exceptional nature of his experience. The memoir is structured around a short period in the 1990s that included the death of his famous father, his constant presence in the tabloid press over various events in his private life, the discovery of a teenage daughter of whom he had been unaware, and the discovery that a female cousin had been the victim of the gruesomely abusive serial killer Fred West some twenty years before. This would not appear to be 'liberally and democratically dispensed' experience at all, because his memoir is prompted by an extraordinary conjuncture of distressing events. Yet Amis's anxiety perhaps reveals his awareness that this exceptionality is precisely what renders his writing so generic. The success of the genre of memoir was one of the most notable publishing phenomena of the 1990s, and as Leigh Gilmore observed, 'the cultural awareness that something significant was happening around and through memoir crystallised in relation to the recognition of trauma's centrality to it' (Gilmore 2001: 2). The experiential, if it was to gain a hearing, had to pass over certain thresholds that mark out traumatic exceptionality from the everyday. Paradoxically, experience beyond the range of the normal became the new norm. 'The age of memoir and the age of trauma may have coincided', Gilmore concluded (Gilmore 2001: 16).

For post-traumatic culture, the appeal of the memoir seemed to be its ability to outstrip the narrative conventionality of fiction in responding to what might be called the pressure of the real. In 1996, the art critic Hal Foster registered a shift from discussions about '*reality as an effect of representation*', familiar enough to those well versed in Roland Barthes' critique of realism, to a new focus on '*the real as a thing of trauma*', something that burst through representation and appeared to be its ruination. This move had been decisive 'in contemporary art, let alone in contemporary theory, fiction, and film' (Foster 1996: 146). Elsewhere, Michael Rothberg argued that the playful self-reflexivity that dominated postmodern art needed to be displaced by an urgent return to questions of reference and reality. Rothberg proposed Traumatic Realism: 'a realism in which the scars that mark the relationship of discourse to the real are not fetishistically denied, but exposed; a realism in which the claims of reference live on, but so does the traumatic extremity that disable Realist representation as usual' (Rothberg 2000: 106). This was prompted by 'various new forms of testimonial and documentary art and cultural production' (Rothberg 2000: 9), of which the Holocaust memoir was his primary instance. The pressure of the real appeared in several, often completely discontinuous guises in the 1990s, from the high theory of Slavoj Žižek, who obsessively worked and reworked Lacan's very specific notion of 'the Real', to the low cultural pleasures of the new genre of confessional celebrity and Reality TV. Whether the real was invoked in a post-theoretical concern for a more ethical criticism or a pre-critical assertion of greater authenticity, the memoir boom was situated in this matrix of concerns, its value bound to its allegedly greater proximity to the traumatic real.

That the boom in memoir in the 1990s was generated by its reorganization around trauma came with a central contradiction. The grand theorists of autobiography, such as Georges Gusdorf or James Olney, tied the genre to the deepest Western traditions of self-knowledge and humanism. Autobiography offered the unity of identity across time, interpreting life in its totality, 'a second reading of experience ... truer than the first because it adds to experience itself consciousness of it' (Gusdorf 1980: 35). Autobiography, in this tradition, secured 'the much desired unity of the subject and the object of knowledge' (Marcus 1994: 5). Memoir, although an older term, had come to be regarded as a lowlier form, an incomplete and fragmentary slice of a life, a hybrid of history and personal narrative, uncertainly locating experience between self and others. The trauma memoir takes even more distance from the autobiographical ideal, for strictly speaking it must centre on precisely that moment which escapes self-apprehension. The traumatic instant cannot be experienced as such, because trauma both distends the subject and bursts the bounds of what constitutes 'experience'. In some extreme cases, then, the trauma memoir centres the life on what has been forgotten and only belatedly recovered: a life narrative in which the main interest lies in this very process of analeptic revision. Where someone like James Olney considered the autobiographical 'I' to command a pattern that brings a life into meaningful concordance (Olney 1972), the trauma memoir recounts a discordance, a circling around a shattering event, from which self-knowledge arrives late, if at all, and with an uncomfortable awareness of the frangibility of the self.

This, at least, has been the predominant critical conception of the trauma memoir, sketched out within Caruth's model of traumatized subjectivity and Felman and Laub's view of the simultaneous necessity yet impossibility of testimony as 'a crucial mode of our relation to events of our times' (Felman and Laub 1992: 5). Hence, Linda Anderson's survey of autobiographical theory ends with a discussion of those seemingly self-cancelling testimonies in which 'traumatic history cannot become integrated into the subject's narrative or history of themselves because it was not fully experienced at the time it happened' (Anderson 2004: 128). As with the novel, a small cluster of memoirs are invoked, which foreground their experimental solutions to these difficulties: Charlotte Delbo's *Auschwitz and After* and Georges Perec's *W or History of Childhood* are common choices.

Again a sole focus on this avant-garde ignores much of the work that the trauma memoir seems to undertake in the wider culture. Bestseller lists have been dominated for over a decade by a succession of high-profile trauma memoirs, from Dave Pelzer's *A Child Called 'It'* (1995) and its many sequels, written in an authenticatingly halting prose from the perspective of a physically abused child, to the post-ironic and tirelessly self-reflexive style of Dave Eggers' *A Heartbreaking Work of Staggering Genius* (2001). Between these extremes, memoirs like Frank McCourt's *Angela's Ashes* (1996), Alice Sebold's *Lucky* (1999), Constance Bristoe's *Ugly* (2006), or James Frey's *A Million Little Pieces* (2003) caused sensations, often promoted by TV talk-show book clubs in a cross-media synergy of confessionalism. The success of such books prompts periodic controversies about their authenticity and also repetitious, supposedly concerned journalism inquiring into the 'misery memoir' trend: 'Why are we so addicted to other people's agony?' one broadsheet writer angrily asked (Adams 2006: 4). The literary editor of *The Observer* confessed bewilderment at the affective contagion unleashed by his own memoir of illness: 'I've told my own survival story. Now everyone wants to tell me theirs' (McCrum 1999: 3). Whilst often dismissed as symptomatic of a mass culture of narcissism, the success of the trauma memoir is merely further evidence of the affective transmissibility of trauma I've tracked across virtually every arena of discourse, whether scientific or cultural, professional or amateur, high or low.

This is not to deny that these popular memoirs do take a different route: the passage through trauma often works here not to undermine but rather to *guarantee* subjectivity. One perspective would be to read sequences of catastrophe, survival, and supersession as trajectories that recompense the felt depredations to identity; that these works help to narratively reconvene the self. Hal Foster is exactly right to observe that '*In trauma discourse, then, the subject is evacuated and elevated at once*' (Foster 1996: 168). We need to cover both of these movements in the trauma memoir. Both, after all, can instance Ricoeur's conception of life as a story, '*an activity and a passion in search of a narrative*' (Ricoeur 1991: 29).

In fact, the trauma memoir was only one symptom of a challenge to the Romantic and post-Romantic autobiographical monolith. By the late 1980s, autobiography could be regarded as a 'field of self-representation' that normal-ized and disciplined the self, less an exercise in self-revelation than an act of coerced fashioning of selves (Quinby 1992: 298). The memoir offered more 'sub-versive and revisionary possibilities' (Buss 2001: 595) to those traditionally excluded from the grandiose act of self-authoring. Hence, the identity politics that emerged in the 1970s and established itself institutionally in the 1980s supported an explosion of memoirs and commentary on memoir in post-colonial, African-American, Latin American, feminist, gay and lesbian writing. Terms for new kinds of hybrid writing began to proliferate: biomythography, autoethnography, autofiction, autopathography, thanatography, *testimonio*. A more inclusive term 'life writing' incorporated texts that exceeded the narrow range of the autobio-graphical canon. If the contemporary autobiography was a genre in crisis, as Susanna Egan (1999) proposed, it was because the self was undergoing trans-formation, and thus demanded new forms of narrative articulation. Trauma was one crucial model for naming this pressure on the self and its modes of self-authoring.

What follows is in three parts. First, I want to discriminate very precisely the elements that came together to create conditions conducive to the success of the trauma memoir. Of course, I have already detailed the historical routes towards the arrival of PTSD in 1980 and the subsequent cultural pervasion of the trauma paradigm. Most commentators on trauma culture would point to the insistent demand of testimony (and particularly Holocaust writing) as the drive behind the memoir boom. Here, I mean more narrowly to outline five distinct arenas that transformed life writing in the late 1980s and early 1990s: feminist revisions of autobiography and the particular impact of recovered memory on the memoir form; the AIDS diary; the rise of the illness memoir, christened 'pathography' in the early 1990s; the trend for confessional journalism; the metastasis of celebrity confession across media, from the autobiography focused on revealing 'private' trauma to *The Oprah Winfrey Show*. These arenas inevitably overlap, but it's impor-tant not to subsume all these elements into an undifferentiated trauma discourse: some have distinctly more honourable ambitions than others. After this outline, I want then to observe the controversies that regularly erupt in this field over the truth status of the confession. Binjamin Wilkomirski's Holocaust memoir *Fragments* was exposed as a fiction in 1999, but the so-called 'memoir backlash' was first associated with Kathryn Harrison's *The Kiss*, which appeared in 1997, and whose account of an (adult) affair between father and daughter was openly disbelieved. Since then, other prominent memoirs have been accused of elabora-tion or outright fabrication. New theories of autobiography have tried to avoid this judicial understanding of the confession, yet the cultural work of the trauma memoir seems intrinsically bound up not just with identification but punitive abjection too. The ability to determine the truth of a memoir is surely vital, but in the third section I try to suggest that the most interesting forms of contempo-rary life-writing are those bodies of work in which trauma induces a continual working and reworking of the event in different registers, mixing truth and fiction in various forms of autofiction.

Five elements towards the trauma memoir

Lynne Segal has claimed that 'the fundamental threat, or exhilarating promise, which feminism offers those it ignites is that of transgressing the boundaries between public and private' (Segal 2004: 21). The imperative of the slogan *the personal is political* directed forms of self-examination that sought to profess publicly, rather than merely confess privately, the everyday circumstances of being or becoming a woman. Segal considers the 'traumatic turn' of the 1990s as a falling away from the collective political praxis of her 60s and 70s generation, yet concedes that this might be an ambiguous mark of success: 'Intimacy is still imagined as a feminine preserve, the popularity of memoir writing is itself a sign of women's cultural influence' (Segal 2004: 8). She has since followed this with her own memoir (Segal 2007).

At a slightly earlier moment, in the late 1980s, a number of feminist literary critics began a concerted re-evaluation of women's autobiographical writing. Shari Benstock's collection, *The Private Self*, used post-structuralism's troubling of self-identity to undermine the monolithic 'I' of the male autobiographical canon. Simultaneously, Benstock's contributors expanded the conception of autobiographical writing to include diary forms, essayistic memoirs and textual fragments. These hitherto overlooked, apparently incomplete forms were argued to match the disrupted rhythms of women's fugitive writing lives, or represent the struggle for forms appropriate to a different, feminine order of experience. Self-conscious experiment with such new forms was associated with Modernism. Virginia Woolf was a theorist of Bloomsbury's 'New Biography', but also used diverse modes of life-writing. H. D.'s strange production of palimpsests, textual fragments and constantly re-worked autobiographical fictions could now be reconceived as a singular and coherent life-writing project, and her work was consequently rescued from obscurity. These reassessments were soon traced out in the language of the trauma paradigm. Woolf famously figured subjectivity through the extended metaphor of 'sealed vessels afloat on what it is convenient to call reality: and at some moments, the sealing matter cracks; in floods reality' (Woolf 1978: 142). The epiphanies of Modernism could suggestively be rewritten through traumatic temporality. In one of her last essays, 'A Sketch of the Past', Woolf recalled a sexual assault by her half-brother, George Duckworth. Benstock considers this 'aftershock of trauma' significant (Benstock 1988: 14). Louise deSalvo, however, reinterpreted Woolf's entire writing life as determined by this event in very contemporary terms: 'Virginia Woolf was a sexually abused child; she was an incest survivor' (deSalvo 1989: 1). Sounding rather like a text-book self-help case study, Woolf's 'story, like that of so many other women, is also one of survival and achievement against all odds' (deSalvo 1989: 13). H. D.'s reiterations were similarly related to the traumas of her childhood and the Great War, which included the death of her brother, a shell-shocked husband, and a miscarriage. Her childhood traumas were recovered later in psychotherapy undertaken with, amongst others, Sigmund Freud, and worked over in memoirs, fictions, and mythic and poetic fragments. Her life-writing 'carries through the work of reinventing the shattered self as a coherent subject capable of meaningful resistance'

(Henke 1998: xix). Suzette Henke coined the term 'scriptotherapy' for the 'process of writing out and writing through traumatic experience', claiming that 'a significant pattern of repressed trauma and psychological fragmentation began to emerge, often unexpectedly, in a large number of twentieth-century feminist autobiographies' stretching from Colette to Audre Lorde and beyond (Henke 1998: xii). Like much else, the historical trajectory of women's writing could also fit the shape of the trauma narrative.

Mary Ann Caws's *Women of Bloomsbury* (1990) connected its historical subjects to the contemporary act of feminist scholarship in a directly autobiographical way, thus helping to inaugurate a movement called 'Personal Criticism'. Nancy Miller defined this as engaging in 'an explicitly autobiographical performance within the act of criticism', 'turning its authorial voice into spectacle' in order to foreground 'the stakes of its own performance' (Miller 1991: 1 and 24). The aim was to reclaim experience from the aggression directed at the category of the subject by High Theory in the 1980s, claiming to regain political agency for the enunciating 'I'. With this fusion of feminist generations around confession as profession, Liz Stanley asserted in 1992 that 'a distinct feminist autobiography is in the process of construction, characterized by its self-consciousness and increasingly self-confident traversing of conventional boundaries between different genres of writing' (cited Marcus 1994: 281). This movement reflected, at the academic level, a wider cultural shift in the value of individualized experience. It survives into trauma theory, with personalized prefaces or epilogues reflecting, for instance, on experiences of or responses to traumatic events such as 9/11 (see Kaplan 2005 or Torgovnick 2006).

One of the most formative feminist memoirs of this era was Sylvia Fraser's *My Father's House*, since it presented an entirely new sense of the 'revisionist' feminist autobiography, encapsulated in the bewildering and apparently self-cancelling opening words of the Author's Note: 'The story I have told in this book is autobiographical. As a result of amnesia, much of it was unknown to me until three years ago' (Fraser 1989: x). Fraser's book was published the year after Ellen Bass and Laura Davis's *The Courage to Heal*, the best-selling self-help manual for women survivors of sexual abuse. Fraser's memoir was therefore one of the earliest personal accounts to explore the recovered memory of traumatic events blanketed out by protective amnesia. The memoir offered a 1950s childhood of familiar banality and awkwardness, but in the corners of these consciously recalled scenes Fraser could now add italicized memories of her father's sexual abuse, recovered retrospectively. Hence:

> In the cloakroom I teach the other kids to tie their shoelaces in a double bow just like my daddy taught me. *My daddy plays with my belly button, my daddy plays with my toes as he did when I was little … . Something hard pushes up against me, then between my legs and under my belly. It bursts all over me in a sticky stream.*
>
> (Fraser 1989: 8)

Every childhood action or reaction, every attachment or phobia, can now be recast with motivations directed by a hidden history belatedly inked back in.

Fraser's record very much conforms to the model of trauma outlined by recovered memory therapy. Ventriloquizing therapeutic language, Fraser explains early on:

> When the conflict caused by my sexual relationship with my father became too acute to bear, I created a secret accomplice for my daddy by splitting my personality in two. Thus, somewhere around the age of seven, I acquired another self with memories and experiences separate from mine, whose existence was unknown to me. My loss of memory was retroactive. I did not remember my daddy ever having touched me sexually.
>
> (Fraser 1989: 15)

Fraser never uses the technical term dissociation, in accord with a grass-roots movement suspicious of psychiatric authority and that affirms absolutely the personal voice of experience instead. Implicitly though, the theory of traumatic sexual origin of multiple personality directs Fraser's autobiographical account of the construction of femininity in her teenage years and her entire sexual life. Sexuality has been perversely implanted by the father; it means, for instance, that she marries in her dissociated persona: '*I will have no memory of the wedding ceremony. It will never be written on my consciousness … . Sexual initiation is the territory of my other self*' (Fraser 1989: 141). This trauma also shadows her professional writing: the opaque elements of her novel *Pandora* fall open retrospectively as encoded autobiographical trace. These disjunct strands of self, typographically separated on the page, eventually converge in a classic account of the 'breakthrough' of traumatic memories. This final precipitation into recall comes when a childhood friend and TV interviewer is exposed as a sexually abusive father. It plunges Fraser into the emergency phase: 'I am no longer the same … I *know* my father raped me. My brain is alive with memories, with shocking insights. In seconds, my history as I have known it undergoes a drastic shift' (Fraser 1989: 221). The book ends on a series of affirmations. 'Now I understand' begin ten successive sentences (Fraser 1989: 223). 'I know that now' repeatedly punctuates her statements settling accounts with the disadjusted past (Fraser 1989: 241). Healing is marked by a reintegrated authorial voice that can assert of this reconstructed life narrative: 'I believe in my truth' (Fraser 1989: 235). The confession ultimately aims to transfigure pain in near religious terms. Trauma, as so often, becomes the occasion for transcendence:

> Yet even here I see a gift, for in place of my narrow, pragmatic world of cause and effect and matter moving to immutable laws, I have burst into an infinite world of wonder. The whole mystery of the universe has my reverence.
>
> (Fraser 1989: 253)

Ralph Savarese has proposed that 'recovered memory becomes … a figure for the genre of memoir itself, for its revelatory drive', since therapeutic recovery can be aligned directly with the aims of specific identity politics to '"recover" and then publicize some previously repressed (if only because unspoken) injury' (Savarese 2001: 94–5). Critical of the danger of fusing identity with subject positions of unrelieved trauma, Savarese nevertheless acutely observes that objections to the narcissism of the 'misery memoir' begin to appear only once so-called 'minorities' begin to use the memoir form as a political device. In Henke's trajectory of women's autobiography, Fraser's memoir represents the contemporary feminist era. Henke does begin to unpick some of the contradictions in the idea of an amnesiac autobiography, not least in Fraser's open avowal in the 'Author's Note' that whilst she asserts *My Father's House* is a true testament, she has also 'used many of the techniques of the novelist' (Fraser 1989: x). Accepting that Fraser's narrative is an artificial construction, Henke nevertheless argues that 'her narrative proves so vivid and convincing that we, as readers, do believe her' (Henke 1998: 122). Recovered memory therapists insist that to question the patient's reconstructed memory is to repeat a form of abuse and societal denial. Yet Fraser's memoir has received substantial critical commentary because its performative contradictions and narrative symmetries are often openly disbelieved. Mark Freeman, for instance, regards the book as 'downright incredible' (Freeman 1993: 151), exploring its collision of impossible tenses: a life told in the present tense, as if ignorant of the future interpolations of a hidden past that nevertheless direct the selection of every stage of the narrative, building to a moment of revelation that has already been inscribed from the opening page. Nicola King has also expertly unravelled the inconsistent blurring of roman and italicized memory strands in the book. King wants to suspend judgement on *My Father's House*, preferring instead to use it as an occasion to argue that there are no memories *of* childhood, only always shifting constructions of memories *relating to* childhood (as Freud suggests in his conclusion to his essay 'Screen Memories'). Inevitably, though, this stance questions the fundamental belief that traumatic memory can be dissociated, preserved and recovered without distortion and King ultimately regards Fraser's sequence of breakthrough revelations to be 'too tightly plotted to be convincing as truth' and her dreams too reductively symbolic, conveying 'the unfortunate impression of having been invented' (King 2000: 81 and 83). Fraser thus gives us the first instance where the trauma memoir provokes a form of readerly trial, judgement and punishment. It is not enough casually to discard the allegedly naïve truth claims of all autobiography and insist that the form simply 'cannot ... sever its links with narrative fiction' (Evans 1999: 24). For memoirs centred around trauma, judgements of truth or falsity bristle with substantive political import.

Memoir acquires its contemporary significance from being a vehicle for testimony, a witness that Felman and Laub declare 'has become a crucial mode of our relation to events of our times ... composed of bits and pieces of a memory that has been overwhelmed by occurrences that have not settled into understanding or remembrance' (Felman and Laub 1992: 5). Holocaust testimony drives much of this discussion, although Latin American *testimonio*, transcriptions of oral testimony from murderous campaigns against racial minorities, re-energized the politics of memoir in the 1980s. John Beverley influentially argued that social struggles in specific contexts had to give rise to new forms of literature; the distention of form in the *testimonio*'s hybrid of oral and written modes stripped away conventions to produce 'if not the real then certainly a sensation of *experiencing the real* that has a determinate effect on the reader' (Beverley 1992: 102). AIDS writing, which began to emerge from America and Britain from about 1986, had similar imperatives: to testify in the face of murderous indifference, to do so by reconstructing the memoir form to meet the emergency, and to spur the reader to action. In 1998, the AIDS diary was assessed to be 'an emerging genre we have yet to learn how to read' (Chambers 1998: 32), its experimental form shadowing the constantly mutating medical enigmas of the syndrome itself. AIDS writing was therefore a crucial element in the surge of trauma memoir in the 1990s.

Acquired Immune Deficiency Syndrome, as many commentators have observed, is a complex global disease entity principally managed by governments and mass media through metaphors of invasion or pollution, with exhortations to be sexually 'pure' backed by the exhibition of those abjected minorities morally blamed for their own deaths: gay men, intravenous drug users, ignorant or superstitious Africans (see Sontag 1989 or Crimp (ed.) 1989). In the West, AIDS was identified principally with gay men and until 1996, when combination drug treatments could stabilize the health of those with HIV, the syndrome inexorably tended towards rapid multiple systems failure and death. Gay activism was directed at the wilful under-funding of AIDS research by conservative governments in America and Britain. Here the role of the memoir had a contentious place. Memorial tributes, elegies, memoirs of the untimely dead, were to be an inevitable part of a highly literate gay culture. However, Douglas Crimp, at the centre of New York activism, initially premised his politics on the last words of the labour activist, Joe Hill: 'Don't mourn, organize!' (Crimp 1989: 3). Memorials individualized and dissipated collectivity. Mourning, at least as Freud theorized it, was a period of suspended activity, a process of libidinal detachment from the loved one, and an eventual return to normalcy. Militant anger was therefore more or less aligned with the deranged refusal of reality Freud ascribed to melancholia. Crimp finally sought to think mourning and militancy together, as mutually informing, and AIDS writing has been characterized by Sarah Brophy as refusing 'to become caught up in mourning as compensatory, as an aggressive action of normalizing closure', instead generating activist energy from this refusal (Brophy 2004: 21). For Brophy, the innovations of AIDS writing are found in forms that resisted 'compensation for feelings of loss' and 'make the process of reading and interpretation impossible to bring to a conclusion' (Brophy 2004: 26, 27). This queered melancholy directly approaches the problematic core of a cultural trauma theory that explicitly forbids the closure of the wound, and insists that abjected spectres are left unrelieved. The AIDS dead must remain, rather like the ghost of Beloved, 'haunting the boundaries of what is deemed proper to the self … stalling its restoration, and even, at certain moments, revoking the belief in the possibility of redemption' (Brophy 2004: 209). This is what makes AIDS testimony a key element of what Ross Chambers describes as 'aftermath society, one regulated by a culture in which collectively traumatic events are denied' (Chambers 2004: xxi). Aftermath cultures, Chambers contends, 'are melancholic in character; in them, mourning can never really be complete for the reason that trauma, although it has happened and has the status of a historical event, is *never over*' (Chambers 2004: xxix). Caught again between a possible and impossible mourning, the argument is that AIDS writing must persist in this interstice, maintaining a pressure to keep the wound open and unhealed until the scandal is resolved medically and politically.

Hundreds of testimonies and memorials now exist, but a spine of texts has emerged as significant because their political intent is worked through in formal innovation: Paul Monette's *Borrowed Time* (1988), Eric Michaels' *Unbecoming* (1990), Hervé Guibert's *To the Friend Who Did Not Save My Life* (1990), Derek Jarman's *Modern Nature* (1991), Oscar Moore's newspaper bulletins on his illness, collected after his death as *PWA* (1996), Mark Doty's *Heaven's Coast* (1996) and Harold Brodkey's *This Wild Darkness* (1996). The form of a first-person diary or chronicle of a partner's illness works because it is episodic and additive, written in a present tense that can respond both to the sudden cruel turns of opportunistic infections and the shifting rumours and realities of emerging drug trials or new treatments. These experiences had no possibility of narrative shape or concordance, in the main because in this first decade, these documents were also a record of terminal illness and death. The published diary was also therefore a deliberate transgression, making public what advanced industrial nations wanted to sequester as a private shame (Michaels' title punned on this 'unbecoming' public act). The author, as Ross Chambers put it, borrowed his authority from death: in the trace of the writing 'something is preserved from the effect of death: an occasion of survival is offered and even a mode of posthumous action' (Chambers 1998: 5). The elegy or memorial reflects on the past; the present tense of the diary, read posthumously, is tilted toward the future and readerly action.

The philosopher Alexander Düttmann noted that this dying-before-one's-time in AIDS writing initially seemed to foil 'the constitution of a coherent time and the coherence of a life,' yet suggested that these chroniclers, in facing death, had reversed the formulation: 'AIDS becomes the paradigm ... of the coherent life story that can be told or narrated' (Düttmann 1996: 3–4). If this was the case, it was only possible by distending and reinventing the form of their testimony. It is striking how AIDS writing mixes modes. Monette's chronicle of his partner's illness and death is part unremittingly explicit medical record, part document of the unofficial 'underground railway' of sympathetic doctors and fellow patients that 'would find our own way' against official indifference (Monette 1996: 103), and part testament to a lover's endurance. Yet the diary was only one vector for Monette, and in the preface to his poetry sequence, 'Love Alone: 18 Elegies for Rog', Monette wrote that 'I wanted a form that would move with breathless speed, so I could scream if I wanted and rattle on and empty my Uzi into the air ... [I]f only a fragment remained in the future, to fade in the sulphurous rain, it would say how much I loved him and how terrible was the calamity' (Monette 1994: 28). In the memoir, these same reflections prompt Monette to explore sculptural form too (Monette 1996: 146), suggesting a restless search for an appropriate mode of expression, driven by a paradoxically energetic melancholy. Derek Jarman similarly expressed himself through a proliferation of diverse forms of very public and transgressive address: films, art-works, a fugitive garden designed in defiance of the bleak landscape of Dungeness, and journals that mixed auobiobraphy, medical report, political polemic against 'heterosoc', queer theory, gardening and sex tips, and fiction. Jarman's illness, announced publicly within days of being confirmed HIV+, energized him to become an important locus of cultural resistance to Thatcherism, far wider than the limited identity as a person living with AIDS might suggest. Proliferation of modes typifies other writers: Samuel Delany was among the first to write on AIDS, but since this was embedded in his science fiction no one appeared to notice. His use of letters from the earliest rumour-filled months of the crisis (private communications published as *1984* sixteen years later) have since joined his fiction, academic criticism on queer theory, and a series of memoirs which defiantly record a promiscuous New York gay and bisexual life, as in *The Motion of Light on Water* (1988).

Perhaps most significantly, AIDS writing consistently cuts across the boundary between truth and fiction. Testimony is commonly defined as a discourse that must be uncontaminated by fiction; even the sense of artificial narrative construction can rouse suspicion of inauthenticity. Yet this breach is so consistent in gay writing that Edmund White has borrowed the French term 'autofiction' for this ambiguous mode: 'The form, which is neither purely fact nor fiction, gives the writer both the prestige of confession [...], and the total freedom of imaginative invention' (White 1995: 8). White has moved systematically across this boundary, from some of the earliest fictional engagements with AIDS in *The Darker Proof* (1987), to AIDS autofictions (*The Farewell Symphony* (1998)), elegiac essays for a lost generation (*Loss within Loss: Artists in the Age of AIDS* (2002), a collective memorial project), and recently direct memoir, in *My Lives* (2005). White nevertheless retains a fairly conventional investment in the consolations of good form (Realism is his default novelistic form). There is none of the disorientation or scandal of the experimental work in self-exposure undertaken by the French writer, Hervé Guibert, who consistently breached decorum in his several bewilderingly confessional yet fictionalized accounts that he composed at breakneck speed in the two years before his death in 1991. His death was a suicide to cheat the progress of HIV, an event he effectively filmed (and certainly rehearsed) in his documentary *Pudeur ou L'impudeur*, perhaps best translated as *Decency or Indecency*, another wilful defiance of private shaming. Guibert's persistent dramatization of self-exposure has much to say about the general place of memoir in trauma culture, and I will return to him in the last section of this chapter.

AIDS writing amongst this group exemplifies a literature of witness that is defined by the need to transgress its own limits to catch at its traumatic object: 'it is precisely as a generic anomaly that it functions, within culture, as an infringement of cultural expectations' (Chambers 2004: 25). This is a formal transgression necessitated by the attempt to contain AIDS to marginal, abjected identities: it speaks from that 'cultural periphery where it must make do, catachrestically, with genres that scarcely admit it' (Chambers 2004: 33). Whilst the prejudices that conflated gay identity and AIDS make it a distinct form, it was also the case that by the early 1990s this writing had joined a wider stream of pathography that burgeoned in this period.

Pathography, autobiographical accounts of illness or third-person memoirs by partners, children or care-givers, is a distinctly contemporary form. Ann Hawkins has observed that whilst a mere handful of examples exist before 1950, published works in America had reached their hundreds by 1990 and then, extraordinarily, doubled in number again between 1993 and 1997. Her extensive annotated bibliography was sub-divided by illness: cancer always the most extensive, followed by AIDS/HIV, then heart disease, with Alzheimer's, multiple sclerosis and autism close behind. This is, as Garry Kinnane puts it, a largely utilitarian, demotic discourse: 'they emerge from a *demos*: individual stories from a body of people with common interests and experience but with no special claims to literary expertise' (Kinnane 2000: 102). Some circulate in samizdat form, particularly where solutions to illness, such as assisted suicide, are at the boundaries of legality. Cancer memoirs helped establish the pathogaphic genre, acquiring early intellectual weight with Susan Sontag's *Illness as Metaphor* (1978) and Audre Lorde's *Cancer Journals* (1980). Indeed, cancer has become such a dominant emblem of the sickness of modernity that the sociologist Arthur Frank has spoken of a 'remission society', where illness has to be thought differently from being an exceptional and traumatic interruption into the assumed norm of health (Frank 1995: 7). Yet rare and spectacular illnesses proved popular with mainstream publishers, as if to reaffirm the idea of a norm from which it was possible to depart, grotesquely. Oliver Sacks's case histories of peculiar neurological disorders pioneered this genre; books like Jean-Dominique Bauby's *The Diving Bell and the Butterfly* (1997), an account of Locked-in Syndrome, painstakingly spelt out by letter by letter by blinking his left eye, were literary sensations. There was even a place for semi-comical accounts: Kamran Nazeer's *Send in the Idiots*, a memoir on autism, was gently self-mocking; the best title in Hawkins's bibliography is surely *Twitch and Shout*, a memoir about Tourette's Syndrome.

Two new sub-genres were particularly notable in the 1990s. First, the taboo on discussing the debilitations of mental depression was broken. William Styron's brief and devastating *Darkness Visible* (1990) appeared, initially as a comment in *The New Yorker* on Primo Levi's suicide and Styron's own suicidal depressions, a confession which provoked an outpouring of reader empathy and thus prompted a more extended account. Styron's frame of reference was soon transformed by the pervasion of new serotonin-based drug treatments, best exemplified by Elizabeth Wurtzel's *Prozac Nation* (1994) and culminating in the encyclopaedic memoir of treatments by Andrew Solomon, *The Noonday Demon* (2001). In such instances, Abigail Cheever argued, the depression memoir was merging with identity politics, conceiving of depression 'not as a hindrance to or a vehicle for realizing the self but rather as the self itself' (Cheever 2000: 350). The second strand was the parental death memoir that saturated literary culture in a few short years after Philip Roth's *Patrimony* (1991). A British version, Blake Morrison's *And When Did you Last See your Father?* (1993), helped generate other accounts (including a parent suicide sub-genre, for instance) and a notable phase of confessional journalism in the British press, which I'll examine shortly. Nancy Miller's Personal Criticism veered into this territory in her critical assessment of the form, her own 'mediated autobiography' on the death of her parents. 'Autobiography is seen as the history of a becoming', Miller argued: 'Here the autobiographical narrative, by its focus on the failing other, provides an account of an undoing, an unbecoming' (Miller 1996: 53–4). This linked it conceptually to other forms of trauma memoir.

What does this acceleration of pathography in the 1990s signify? Many memoirists suggest the wave is a result of some kind of affective revolution in which the secrecy, repression and silences of their parents' Second World War generation has been superseded by the articulate confession in the wake of the cultural revolutions of the 1960s. John Wiltshire (2000) has suggestively linked the rise of pathography to a process of 'meaning creation' in the face of both an essentially arbitrary intervention of illness into a life story and the de-humanizing treatments of a health industry dominated since the 1960s by bio-medical technology. As the medical apparatus around the ill and dying body multiplies, so one significant strand of the genre is the memoir as accusation of misdiagnosis or mistreatment, something Hawkins dates as beginning in 1980. Allied to this suspicion of medical authority is the memoir of survival through alternative therapies dismissed by orthodox science. These instances crystallize how the memoir works at 'restoring the patient's voice to the medical enterprise' (Hawkins 1999: xii).

A more abstract framing might link pathographic writing to what Anthony Giddens termed the late modern 'sequestration of experience' (Giddens 1991: 144). In advanced capitalist societies, encounters with extremity are suppressed: birth, death, insanity, even direct experience of nature are all removed from the everyday and placed under technical and institutional command. This has is evident benefits, but it is also a 'protective cocoon' that is fragile and liable to crack if routine experience is disturbed: 'The individual faces a return of the repressed but is likely to lack the psychic and social resources to cope with the issues thus posed' (Giddens 1991: 167). Sequestration can never be total; insecurity and doubt flower at key junctures of lived experience. The 'frontiers of sequestered experience', Giddens noted, 'are fault-lines, full of tensions and poorly mastered forces' (Giddens 1991: 168). Thus illness, now removed from the social fabric and placed in closed institutional settings, becomes a catastrophic disruption to an expected norm of health. Giddens argument was also of its time: without direct recourse to trauma theory, the metaphors that he used were saturated with ideas of the traumatic event: cocoons, filters, and screens are punctured or breached; the real bursts in and overflows the channels of everyday experience.

This sociological position has been worked out in terms of consequences for narrative by Arthur Frank. Frank sees illness as 'narrative wreckage', and pathography as a literal narrative salve: 'Stories have to *repair* the damage that illness has done' (Frank 1995: 55). In Frank's view the rise of patient memoirs results from an epochal shift. In what he terms 'modern times' there was confidence in medical authority that meant a willing surrender of the patient's body and self-narrative to the machineries of health care, which dealt not with selves but diseases. Postmodern times emerge in the late 1970s, Frank argues, 'when the capacity for telling one's own story is reclaimed', often in holistic accounts that run in parallel but often counter to the objectifications of medicine (Frank 1995: 7). Frank's typology of pathographic narratives is suspicious of the dominant 'restitution' narrative, since this commands the return to health as the norm and continued illness or relapse as an implicit moral failing. Instead, from out of the 'chaos' or 'anti-narrative' of illness, where 'the story traces the edges of a wound' that it cannot initially grasp, Frank favours narratives of illness as quest and self-reinvention (Frank 1995: 98). Storytelling accrues ethical responsibility as this argument develops, an element directly borrowed from cultural trauma theory. For Frank, the ill person who tells their story becomes a healer in turn, because 'testimony *implicates* others in what they witness' (Frank 1995: 143). In the remission society, then, narrative is an affective antibody to the contagion of ill-health.

A number of these theories swirled around one of the principal vectors for the growth of pathography in the 1990s: newspaper columns devoted to the progress of an illness. In England, a distinct liberal class fraction of journalists and intellectuals helped foster sympathetic conditions for the growth of this mode of trauma memoir. Oscar Moore delivered health bulletins on being a person living with AIDS in *The Guardian* Saturday colour supplement between 1994 and 1996 (unlike the more militant writers, Moore praised his hospital treatment and even the efforts of drug companies). In 1997, a young fashion journalist Ruth Picardie was given space in *The Observer* to write about her terminal cancer. Ruth Picardie's sister, Justine, was the editor who commissioned these pieces and later collected them for a best-selling book, *Before I Say Goodbye* (1998). Justine Picardie has since published an account of her stalled mourning, which included various visits to Spiritualist séances to attempt contact with her dead sibling, *If the Spirit Moves You* (2001). The prominent journalist and broadcaster John Diamond also began a cancer column in *The Times* in 1997, later collected as *C: Because Cowards Get Cancer too* (1998). The more right-wing location for these columns was reflected in Diamond's relief that his private health insurance allowed him to avoid the murderous delays of the public health service. Diamond died in 2001, having been a long-term resident of gossip-columns, TV documentaries, West End plays and best-selling books. The latter years of the 1990s prompted one of the weirdest TV genre hybrids, the trauma cookery show, where Diamond's wife Nigella Lawson made the recipes of her sister and mother (who had both died early of breast cancer) in a house haunted by the briefly glimpsed, terminally ill husband. The display of the disturbances to boundaries of public and private demonstrated by this family seemed to be one of the starkest evidences of how an injunction to perform their traumatic identities had taken over a certain element of the liberal intelligentsia, even as its press complained about the pervasion of the 'misery memoir' (Adams 2006).

One legitimation for the obsessive interest of the fourth estate in confessional narratives of illness and trauma was that it provided scripts for reactions to traumatic life-events for a somehow peculiarly 'cocooned' class. The convention established by journalists was to articulate an initial hesitation about publishing such intimate or difficult material, an uncertainty instantly dissolved by an overwhelmingly supportive public response. The virtual communities formed around the deaths of Ruth Picardie or John Diamond were displayed by reproducing e-mail messages from 'ordinary' readers, for example. Robert McCrum, the literary editor of *The Observer*, also testified to an avalanche of letters revealing a hidden world of illness and death being endured in apparent isolation, after he published his memoir of recovery from a stroke, *My Year Off*. This is a highly specific constitution of a public, and one that emerges through a kind of empathetic identification. Yet it is also worth observing that this whole process essentially vacated the political public sphere and the allegedly traditional role of the liberal press to challenge the armatures of the state, retreating instead into individualized experience. This manoeuvre often severed accounts from critical or analytic languages (of the kind that Giddens or Frank supply) to rely entirely on the languages of self-discovery and actualization. That this was taking place in largely liberal-left locations seems symptomatic of larger processes. Charles Turner suggests that there has been a 'rejection of the claims of collective belonging and obligation which a state or political community might make on individuals' (Turner 1996: 47). Such 'slow-moving institutional failure', Turner argues, 'throws individuals increasingly back upon themselves, and makes all of us more sensitive to catastrophes of every sort'(Turner 1996: 58). All that is left are unrelieved individuals without any other social or political resources than their own sequestered experience, and that experience is pierced repeatedly by the punctures of traumatic encounter because intermediate structures of communality have disappeared, but also because the critical languages that might abstract this individualized experience have been largely abandoned.

In this account, traumatized identities become privileged sites of communality, yet they need to be compulsively restaged because there are no longer any theoretical means to process trauma. Trauma needs to be re-presented, over and over. This formulation immediately evokes the final element of the trauma memoir I want to put in place: the culture of celebrity.

The obsession with celebrity has been codified as one of the privileged sites for working through the 'active construction of identity in the social world' (Marshall 1998: xi). In line with some of the commentary on sequestration and the loss of traditional markers of communal identity, the celebrity figure has become a new site for the organization and condensation of the social meanings of selfhood, but one largely limited to emotion and psychologized motivations. This emphasis has extended beyond the realms of the culture industry in recent decades and transformed the discourse of politics, journalism, academia, and many other spheres.

Intertwined with the public enactment of private experience typified by the memoir boom, celebrity is premised on a willing confession or enforced exposé. Driven by 'the will to uncover a hidden truth' (Marshall 1998: 4), celebrity intensifies around the public performance of privacy. This is why the exaggerated virtues of the celebrity are never far from a fall from grace, as sanctioned self-exposure can topple into public shaming and vilification. In this ambivalence celebrity, as Jacqueline Rose observes, is 'our guilty secret, a veiled way of putting into public circulation certain things which do not easily admit to public acknowledgement' (Rose 2004: 201). Benign adoration can quickly become 'sadistic curiosity' (Rose 2004: 214).

If celebrity does organize commodified models of contemporary identity, then I would contend that this has been a significant vector for establishing the currency, allure (and also the repulsion) of the trauma subject. In David Marshall's lucid formulation:

> The private sphere is constructed to be revelatory, the ultimate site of truth and meaning for any representation in the public sphere. In a sense, the representation of public action as manifestation of private experience exemplifies a cultural pattern of psychologisation of the public sphere ... . The celebrity is the avant-garde of this movement to vivisect public action by identifying the originary private experience.
>
> (Marshall 1998: 247)

The revelation of a hidden trauma thus organizes the autobiographical narrative, the revealed secret becoming the pivot for every public act.

It would be possible to generate a detailed typology of celebrity that established different vectors of trauma subjectivity: here are some broad strokes. Illness survived and overcome tends to promise sympathetic identification, adoration, and the self-conscious fashioning of scripts for fans to follow, usually in best-selling memoirs (or series of reiterative memoirs) – one thinks of Lance Armstrong's survival of testicular cancer to become the most successful cyclist in history, or singer Kylie Minogue's breast cancer scare and subsequent beatification for our remission society. Equal and opposite would be the vilification heaped on those who develop addictions that result directly from the alleged temptations of the celebrity life-style, although rehabilitations of all kinds are possible, and sheer addictive persistence can be rewarded (as in the case of Keith Richards). Generations of famous families 'touched by tragedy' develop a peculiar glow of overdetermined trauma that sustains an ambivalent attraction and repulsion (the Kennedys, the Jackson family, Liza Minnelli and her mother Judy Garland). The central narrative device of current celebrity, however, is the supersession of traumatic origins and the exercise of sheer will to find fame and fortune, a script of open wish-fulfilment for commodified culture. Many instances abound: celebrity Pamela Stephenson's biography of her celebrity husband, comedian Billy Connolly, sold in its millions. It begins: 'Billy's real story is an utterly triumphant one. Not a day has passed since I met him twenty years ago, without my shaking my head and marvelling at his miraculous survival of profound childhood trauma' (Stephenson 2002: 3). The text see-saws between glimpses of Billy amongst famous friends (Steve Martin, the Prince of Wales) and details of early maternal abandonment, physical abuse from his aunt and schoolmasters, sexual abuse by his father, and consequent psychological effects, including alcoholism. Stephenson provides a patina of technical psychological explanation (she is a trained clinical psychologist), but the allure really derives from this progressive public unfolding of private trauma within a celebrity marriage. One could multiply examples indefinitely: *Being Jordan*, the memoir of the grim childhood of glamour model Katie Price, shifted over a million units in the first year of release (the phenomenal success of this text precipitated a whole British trend of celebrity trauma auto/biography). The vacuity of those 'famous for being famous' can often be filled by narratives of traumatic origin, as if this legitimates their celebrity. Thus, the most success-ful product of Britain's version of the *Big Brother* reality TV show was not one of the winners but Jade Goody, ridiculed for her ignorance and exhibitionism dur-ing the show and then refashioned as a 'survivor' of difficult childhood circum-stances in the deprived inner city. A recent biography of her – one of a number already in circulation – was entitled *Jade Goody: Story of a Survivor*. A self-fashioned millionaire, vilification then returned five years later after a display of another element of her early deprivation: an outburst of unreconstructed racism on *Celebrity Big Brother*.

These are passing figures: the inaugurating figure of contemporary trauma celebrity is undoubtedly Oprah Winfrey. Her daytime TV talk-show began in 1984; she is now a billion-dollar self-help industry, influential producer, black phi-lanthropist, and through her Book Club (launched in 1995) has become a signifi-cant influence on the direction of American publishing. Winfrey's fame began with an act of TV confession: interviewing abuse survivors, she broke down and confessed that she herself had been abandoned by her parents and abused by her uncle and cousin from the age of twelve. Her career has been subsequently organ-ized around the 'relentless public telling' of her own traumatic biography (Illouz 2003: 17): teenage pregnancy and miscarriage, eating disorders, addiction, destructive symptoms of low self-esteem, relationship difficulties, and a battle with weight that became a triumph in 1989 and then a failure as the weight crept back on. This last 'struggle' was reported in episodic, sometimes weekly, updates. The TV Oprah therefore has no apparent boundary between the public and private self, one that is engineered around a flawed and vulnerable identity, subject to virtually every subjective depredation it would be possible to encounter. This sense of intimacy with her mass audience positions her as 'structured to reinforce the feeling of close proximity to the real and the familial' (Marshall 1998: 192). At the same time, her wealth, celebrity and cultural influence mark her as excep-tional, her trajectory embodying the therapeutic narrative behind all her enter-prises: that psychological disadvantage can be superseded by the exercise of the will. Breakdown becomes breakthrough, so the mantra goes. The TV show probes the vulnerabilities of its guests until it gets the 'money-shot' of emotional collapse, expertly steered by Winfrey's empathetic identification with virtually any manner of suffering. The act of confession is then rewarded and announced as the first step towards self-empowerment. The show can engineer success sto-ries before our eyes: guests like Trudi Chase, the abuse victim who developed 92 multiple personalities, appeared initially as an object of cultural and psychiatric fascination. Her memoir, published in 1992, gave her subjective experience a voice; her therapy formed part of a self-help video, her life-story became a made-for-TV film, and she returned to *The Oprah Winfrey Show* for an hour-long special, the culmination of the construction of a trauma celebrity.

As Eva Illouz argues, 'narratives of trauma' nearly always dominate the show:

> its privileged guests embody modern prototypes: they are victims and bear-
> ers of "trauma." The trauma narrative seems to best embody modern
> tragic narratives of the suffering self … . The culture of recovery has con-
> tributed to a deep narrativization of the self through suffering. The trauma
> narrative is a powerful identity narrative that provides a "centre" to the self
> by stitching together past and present in a narrative of self-knowledge.
>
> (Illouz 2003: 97)

Winfrey's reiteration of the same subjective account thus ensures that 'the temporality of the trauma narrative … is structurally standardised' (Illouz 2003: 170).

The embedding of this trauma account has had important cultural effects, not
least through the Book Club. Winfrey chose to reposition her show in 1995, in
part to gain distance from the controversies surrounding the confrontational
'shock' confessional shows presented by the likes of Jerry Springer (from 1991) or
Rikki Lake (from 1993). Winfrey asserted the cultural and even spiritual value of her
project by becoming more concrete about channels of empowerment: in promoting reading, books could also become 'a teaching tool, a means to self-discovery'
(Hall 2003: 658). Every Book Club selection has been guaranteed best-seller
status, and Hall reported that most selections sold in the region of 750,000 copies.
Books favoured are narratives of pain, suffering and/or injustice eventually overcome. The memoir is made for this narrative arc, and the Book Club has surely
driven the shifting cultural value of the confessional memoir form in the last
decade. In Britain, the copycat Book Club of talk-show couple Richard and Judy
has begun to have similar effect. Indeed, Richard and Judy held a competition for
viewers to pitch a memoir of childhood trauma and triumph, the prize being a
book contract and substantial advance. Novels do feature in these Book Clubs, but
have to conform to this narrative model of tribulation and ultimate moral uplift.
The reading mode encouraged is one of complete identification, affective connection rather than aesthetic analysis. Winfrey herself dramatizes this in often
extreme ways: she pressed copies of Alice Walker's *The Color Purple* on friends long
before acting a central role in the film version; she similarly part financed and
acted in the film version of Toni Morrison's *Beloved*.

Identification through affect produces a circuit where Oprah's choice guarantees a book's authenticity and the book reinforces Oprah's privileging of trauma
subjectivity. In this way, the Book Club can encompass all the other elements in
the rise of the trauma memoir, guaranteeing the success of abuse survival
accounts, pathographies, celebrity confessions, so confirming the centrality of
memoir to publishing. Yet the memoir boom is haunted by anxieties about
authenticity, periodically convulsed by exposé and scandal. Is this merely an
inevitable result of the cultural weight of trauma subjectivity prompting the exaggeration of traumatic impacts? Having established the elements that constitute
the emergence and development of the boom, I can now focus in on the significance of these repeated trials of authenticity.

Memoir and the judicious truth

James Frey's memoir about severe alcoholism and addiction, *A Million Little Pieces*, was chosen for Oprah's Book Club in September 2005. Already popular, this selection contributed to a further increase in sales and a fifteen-week stint as the *New York Times* best-seller; the book sold over three million copies and was translated into 22 languages. In January 2006, however, investigative journalists for The Smoking Gun web-site pointed to at least one instance of elaboration of the details of an arrest, and the authenticity of the book began to unravel. The Smoking Gun report began: 'Oprah Winfrey's been had' (Smoking Gun 2006). Winfrey demanded Frey appear on her show to apologise; Doubleday, the publishers, made the extraordinary agreement 'to provide refunds to readers who felt they were defrauded in buying a book classified as memoir' (Barton 2006: 9). The book now carries a preface by Frey clarifying its status as a somewhat enhanced memoir, appealing to sincerity not verisimilitude. In fact the influence of the Book Club on publishing was evidently part responsible, for Frey revealed that the book had been rejected as a novel by seventeen publishers but was accepted the instant it was reclassified a memoir.

This trial joined the cases of the doubts expressed about Sylvia Fraser's novelistic reconstruction of her abusive childhood, the exposé of Benjamin Wikomirski's Holocaust memoir, *Fragments*, in 1996, and the apoplectic commentary on Kathryn Harrison's incest memoir *The Kiss* a year later. Memoirs are regularly contested now, particularly if they are literary and financial successes: Constance Briscoe's account of her childhood was rejected by her family; Kathy O'Beirne's *Don't Ever Tell*, involving childhood rape, physical abuse and incarceration in a succession of punitive children's homes in Ireland, was challenged by her siblings (see Addley 2006). The truth-status of documentary has also been undermined by various kinds of hoax, pastiche, mock-documentary and Reality TV formats which have challenged the 'central tenets of classic documentary', including 'the essential integrity of the referential image' (Roscoe and Hight 2001: 8).

These trials would initially seem to function to test the authenticity of what Philippe Lejeune terms 'the autobiographical pact'. The pact guarantees the unity of author, narrator and central protagonist in a single 'I' and brooks no ambiguity: 'Autobiography does not include degrees: it is all or nothing' (Lejeune 1989: 13). Lejeune also uses the language of crime and punishment: 'Confronted with what looks like an autobiographical narrative, the reader often tends to think of himself as a detective, that is to say, to look for breaches of contract' (Lejeune 1989: 14). In this model, discoveries of transgression would work ultimately to reinforce the integrity of testimonial discourse. These trials of trauma authenticity would therefore echo the court-room disputes of expert-witness psychologists about the status of trauma. Lenore Terr insists on pristine inscription and recovery of traumatic memory, whilst Elizabeth Loftus argues that traumatic memory is particularly malleable and therefore evidentially problematic in legal settings.

Yet this idea of a trial of the memorial truth brings to mind a very different understanding of the judicial framework of confession. In Foucault's *The History of*

Sexuality, confession is a 'procedure of individualisation', 'ordered according to the infinite task of extracting from the depths of oneself … a truth which the very form of confession holds out like a shimmering mirage' (Foucault 1981: 59). It shifts from religious to medico-legal authorities in the nineteenth century, the West becoming saturated with confession: 'one confesses one's crimes, one's sins, one's thoughts and desires, one's illnesses and troubles; one goes about telling, with the greatest precision, whatever is most difficult to tell' (Foucault 1981: 59). The discipline of confession is also the shaping of a specific kind of subjectivity: what is to be confessed is not volunteered, but compelled. Confession is 'an obligatory act of speech which, under some imperious compulsion, breaks the bonds of discretion or forgetfulness' (Foucault 1981: 62). Under this model, memoirs are not simply voluntary acts of writing, inaugurated by sovereign individuals. Rather, they are part of an incitement, as Pierre Nora puts it, 'to undertake to become memory-individuals' (Nora 1989: 16). In these terms, Linda Alcoff and Laura Gray have questioned the scenarios in which abuse survivor discourse has been at once compelled and contained, whether on television, where its shock value is converted into 'a media commodity' and corralled by expertise, or even in private therapy:

> Before we speak we need to look at where the incitement to speak originates, what relations of power and domination may exist between those who incite and those who are asked to speak, as well as to whom the disclosure is directed.
>
> (Alcoff and Gray 1993: 278 and 284)

Selves are disciplined into valuing some kinds of memory rather more than others: the content of the confession has altered as the trauma paradigm reconfigures narratives of the subject. Foucault thus forces us to consider the nature of agency in the memoir: there is a disciplining of the self that partly dictates the direction of the genre.

A third way of thinking about the law of memoir is suggested by Leigh Gilmore's work. As Gilmore observes:

> Because testimonial projects require subjects to confess, to bear witness, to make public and shareable a private and intolerable pain, they enter into a legalistic frame in which their efforts can move quickly beyond their interpretation and control, and become subject to judgments about their veracity and worth.
>
> (Gilmore 2001: 7)

The aim of a memoir might be broadly therapeutic and educative, but publication transposes the story into a different terrain of author's rights and responsibilities, where claims about traumatic pasts become open to charges of defamation or libel. Therapeutic resolutions might be publicly unravelled, a story of survival becoming a retraumatization by public humiliation or denunciation. Equally, where a testimony wants to situate a personal trauma as a representative experience, perhaps of an oppressed group, then this extension from individual to representative extremity will frequently 'draw scepticism more readily than sympathy' (Gilmore 2001: 22) and be subject to intensive forms of rebuttal if they challenge predominant beliefs.

For Gilmore, this risk has fostered a deliberate confusion of factual and fictional modes in some memoirists, precisely in order to evade this potential trial and persecution. In playing along 'the borderland between autobiography and fiction', the aim is to 'establish an alternative jurisdiction for narratives in which self-representation and the representation of trauma coincide' (Gilmore 2001: 48 and 146). This argument has large implications for the notion of an 'autobiographical pact' in trauma memoirs. When the critical imperative is driven by a demand for testimony in a legalistic sense, the trauma memoir is instantly put on trial and must verify its conformity to a strict pact: verisimilitude; identity of author, narrator and character. Yet, as has been consistently observed, trauma is not necessarily a stable or straightforwardly evidential or narratable event, but might be mobile, subject to all kinds of transformation and revision. This might well be the defining element of a traumatic memory, and what makes it particularly amenable to fictional narrative instead. The new kinds of autofiction that scuff the boundaries of fictional and factual discourse work to confound the legal measure of true and false precisely in order to preserve, in a different way, in an 'alternative jurisdiction', a traumatic truth. In the main, the memoir boom is avowedly driven by unproblematic 'true stories' of trauma, valued for their proximity to the real. Yet controversial memoirs need not be those that are exposed and vilified as in some way 'false'. These are often limit-cases that play in the margins between fact and fiction and are a scandal because they will not determine the factuality of their trauma.

In a study of confession in literature and law, Peter Brooks observed that 'there is something inherently unstable and unreliable about the speech act of confession, about its meaning and its motives' (Brooks 2000: 23). Let's now turn to three contemporary authors whose autofictions have embraced this instability.

Generating autofictions: Philip Roth, Hervé Guibert, Kathryn Harrison

Between 1988 and 1993, in other words at the moment that the trauma paradigm bloomed, Philip Roth published a sequence of four books that toyed with the confessional mode. For a satirist and provocateur notorious for fabulating tales of Jewish masculinity through a vertiginous play with alter egos, this was a striking turn. *The Facts: A Novelist's Autobiography* (1988) claimed to expose the critical confrontations that helped constitute Roth as a novelist: with his father, his first wife, and with the outrage of American Jews at his early work. This searing account, however, is addressed to Roth's fictional self Nathan Zuckerman and the text concludes with Zuckerman's letter rubbishing the accuracy and value of the account. 'The truth is', Zuckerman declares, 'that the facts are much more refactory and unmanageable and inconclusive' (Roth 1988: 166). Autobiography could only be an act of '*de*-imagining' compared to novelistic mediation (Roth 1988: 166). The densely particularized Zuckerman, meanwhile, is contemptuous of the construction of Roth:

As for characterization, you, Roth, are the least completely rendered of all
your protagonists ... . My guess is that you've written metamorphoses of
yourself so many times, you no longer have any idea what *you* are or ever
were. By now what you are is a walking text.

(Roth 1988: 162)

Although elements of *The Facts* seem verifiably true, the book, as Elaine Kauvar
has observed, acts as 'a refutation of facticity' (Kauvar 1995: 421). *Deception* (1990)
is a series of pure dialogues without any supporting description between a novelist called Philip and various interlocutors – a wife, a mistress, other women. It is
wound around some known facts of Roth's life, such as his relationship with the
English actress Claire Bloom, yet is framed as fiction. Meta-textual play increases
when the wife of the writer finds these dialogues and accuses Philip of an affair
(just as Claire Bloom reports she did on reading the manuscript of the book). The
defence is that 'I have been imagining myself, outside of my novel, having a love
affair with a character inside my novel' (Roth 1990: 176) and Philip later proclaims with annoyance: 'I write fiction and I'm told it's autobiography, I write
autobiography and I'm told it's fiction, so since I'm so dim and they're so smart,
let *them* decide what it is or it isn't' (Roth 1990: 184). This flipping between fiction
and true confession fosters uncertainty: 'Readers will never know with certainty
just how much *Deception* deceives them' (Tuerk 2005: 136). The subtitle of
Patrimony: A True Story (1991) holds out the prospect of more textual confusion, but
Roth's memoir about the death of his father appears to be an unadorned account,
pushing only at the limits of what a reader might bear in terms of the intimacies
and humiliations of dying. The memoir helped consolidate a whole pathographic
sub-genre, a bewildering outcome for such a remorselessly playful writer. *Operation
Shylock: A Confession* (1993), however, is a return to metafictional play, a fantasia in
which Philip Roth offers a story of a famous American writer Philip Roth chas-
ing down a double Philip Roth who is impersonating him in order to gain pub-
licity for an absurd anti-Semitic Judaism in a paranoid and divided Israel. This
'confession' echoes the literary tradition of the persecutory double, yet is also full
of factual transcriptions: of the trial of the alleged concentration camp guard
John Demjanjuk in Israel in 1988; of Roth's interview with writer and Holocaust
survivor Aahron Appelfeld, a dialogue verifiably published elsewhere as 'true'.
Within this encounter, however, Appelfeld tells Roth why he has written fiction,
not memoir: 'I tried several times to write "the story of my life" in the woods after
I ran way from the camp ... . The result was rather meagre, an unconvincing
imaginary tale. The things that are most true are easily falsified' (Roth 1993: 86).
The status of the book is left hopelessly entangled by Roth's engagement by
Mossad, the Israeli intelligence service. He is asked to remove the final chapter for
operational security, and does so, but is then the last directive of the book, 'This
confession is false' (Roth 1993: 399), true or false, inside the text or outside it?

At the time, Roth's shuttling between fiction and fact was understood within
the paradigm of Postmodernism: a dismantling of the authority of the paratexts
that usually secure a text as truth or fiction; a demonstration of the rhetorical or

discursive equivalence of history and literature; a lesson in displaying the author as a textual construct, the putative autobiography only able to show, as Roland Barthes had done in his anti-memoir *Roland Barthes*, that 'in the field of the subject, there is no referent' (Barthes 1977b: 56). Roth thus becomes an exemplary postmodern relativist. But in retrospect it seems obvious to observe that these moments of textual uncertainty are generated by passages of trauma, which newly disturb the relationship between representation and the real and thus prompts these swerves in truth status. Roth tells Zuckerman that *The Facts* was composed in the midst of a severe breakdown in 1987: 'what was to have been minor surgery turned into a prolonged physical ordeal that led to an extreme depression that carried me right to the edge of emotional and mental dissolution' (Roth 1988: 5). The book is a 'post-crack-up meditation': 'In order to recover what I had lost I had to go back to the moment of origin. I found no one moment of origin, but a series of moments, a history of multiple origins, and that what I have written here is the effort to repossess life' (Roth 1988: 5). Zuckerman directs his venom not at truth itself, but at the impoverished version of the truth autobiography generates in comparison with the mediations of fiction. On the question of Roth's first wife, Zuckerman posits his own traumatic origin: a hidden, hereditary alcoholism. Between them, traumatic origins are not in doubt; rather, it is the textual means to uncover them that are disputed.

Patrimony is also about the insistence of the traumatic real: this is what the central scene demands. In the later stages of his illness, the patriarch Herman Roth spectacularly loses control of his bowels; the son must clean the bathroom. A detailed, clinical description confronts abjection and utterly refuses artful significance:

> So *that* was the patrimony. And not because cleaning it up was symbolic of something else but because it wasn't, because it was nothing less or more than the lived reality that it was. There was my patrimony: not the money, not the tefillin, not the shaving mug, but the shit.
>
> (Roth 1991: 176)

Nancy Miller's rather presumptuous inhabitation of this text, using it as an occasion to recall her own father's illness and death in *Bequest and Betrayal*, insists on resymbolizing this scene as if unable to bear this singularity. Yet Roth's austerity derives from understanding trauma as the unsymbolizable thing. As he says elsewhere:

> those of us who live with and by words are a bit astonished by the real thing because we are always looking for the right word to describe the thing. The words become a substitute for the thing. But the thing is something different.
>
> (Roth cited Hedin 2005: 150)

This is not, however, the final determination. Where *Patrimony* reduces itself down to one brute scene, *Operation Shylock* doubles and redoubles narrative chaos, this Philip Roth seemingly suffering the same breakdown described in *The Facts*, but unable to master narratively the multiplication of plots and conspiracies that surround him. There is no single, appropriate representation of trauma: it is conveyed in the very swerves Roth takes between factual and fictional registers. These books, then, might be termed autofictions, not because they depend upon or expose a life but because they act out Zuckerman's law that 'with autobiography, there's always another text, a countertext if you will, to the one presented' (Roth 1988: 172). Approaching the traumatic real, Roth's persona multiplies as a means to lure in but then evade the punitive judgements that have pursued his career.

Roth's project initially seems entirely counter to the autofictions of Hervé Guibert, who appeared intent on unveiling every detail of his private life and last years with AIDS. Yet this body of work also has its own way of signalling the tremors that de-stabilize the truth of trauma. Guibert's career was dedicated to self-exposure and the betrayal of secrets. In his first book, *La Mort propagande*, published when he was twenty in 1975, he spoke of a desire 'to kill myself on stage, before the cameras. To offer up in my death this extreme, excessive spectacle of my body' (Guibert 1991a: 172, my translation). Uncannily, Guibert fantasized about 'filming my body in decomposition, day after day' (Guibert 1991a: 172), anticipating by sixteen years his video diary, *Pudeur ou L'Impudeur*, shown just weeks after his suicide in December 1991. Guibert always wrote in the borderland between autobiography and fiction. His texts were developed from his continuous journal, the extent of reworking always queasily uncertain (his journal was eventually published in 2001). Guibert's notoriety was not at first linked with his shameless confession of AIDS, but with the betrayal of confidences. In 1986, he published a private letter from Roland Barthes, who had asked to sleep with the angelic Guibert in return for writing a preface. Guibert spurned the offer; Barthes died in 1980, and Ralph Sarkonak has followed the haunting trace of this betrayal through Guibert's work. The estate had been anxious to maintain a silence on Barthes' homosexuality; Guibert betrayed one of his literary masters, although Barthes' letter, 'Fragments pour H', is now included in the *Complete Works*. Similarly, the scandal of Guibert's first AIDS autofiction *To the Friend Who Did Not Save My Life* (1990) was not Guibert's illness but the alleged betrayal of Michel Foucault. Guibert and Foucault were neighbours in Paris and the younger writer was part of Foucault's inner circle. In the novel, Guibert's death is foreshadowed by the last illness of a philosopher called Muzil, whose last months are described in detail and with enough clues to guess at the true identity. Foucault had not commented on his illness, determining not to speak of AIDS publicly, and after his death in 1984 the estate maintained silence on the cause of death: once more, Guibert had betrayed and damaged a reputation.

This, however, is to read Guibert's texts as material to decode for their autobiographical trace, as if the fictional veneer was thin enough to discern the traumatic facts beneath. Guibert's suicide amplifies this temptation: as with Sylvia Plath, the fact of the death is read retrospectively everywhere into the work. Guibert actively fostered this misrecognition, speaking of a *pacte du leurre*, a pact of deceit, that toyed with this expectation. The critic Raymond Bellour first called Guibert's work autofiction in 1988 (before the AIDS texts); Jean-Pierre Boulé coined the apparently tautological term *roman faux* or false novel for them, 'a novel which does not respect the fictional pact' (Boulé 1999: 156). French critics often seem to value Guibert's texts precisely for the taxonomical difficulties they induce, situated in that 'impossible' transgression simultaneously of fictional and autobiographical pacts. Guibert then suggested that this lifetime project of blurring truth and fiction could reach its apotheosis with his illness: 'AIDS has allowed me to make even more radical certain techniques of narration, the relation to truth, the staging of myself beyond what I had thought possible' (Guibert cited Sarkonak 2000: 7). Guibert's AIDS texts are not a series of unveilings, heading towards the unvarnished truth: read in sequence, they bewilder and confound with their shifting status.

To the Friend Who Did Not Save My Life, written in one hundred short sections, but in long, breathless sentences (a style borrowed from Thomas Bernhard), is a typical AIDS account of its era, a story of medical ignorance, rumour and false promise. The tense of the book's arresting opening sentence, 'I had AIDS for three months' is written with the prospect of a miracle cure being held out by a wealthy American friend with privileged access to the latest drug trials (Guibert 1991b: 1). The Guibert of the novel is betrayed, his place in the trial taken by a more attractive young man, but in the latter half of the book the promise of treatment is overtaken by the calmative act of writing. 'AIDS will have been my paradigm in my project of self-revelation and the expression of the inexpressible' (Guibert 1991b: 228). He agrees to meet Bill a last time, overcoming his hatred for the sake of completing the novel: 'Yes, I can write it, and that's undoubtedly what my madness is – I care more for my book than for my life, I won't give up my book to save my life' (Guibert 1991b: 237). The publication of this autofiction and an appearance on TV in which he renounced writing and declared that this was to be his final book gave Guibert celebrity. The story of the outpouring of letters praising his courage and encouraging him to continue writing is told inside his next novel, *The Compassion Protocol* (1991). The book we read is not the same as the writing this public sympathy produces: he struggles with 'telling a story whose beginning I knew, as well as its development and end, because I had lived it myself' yet which had lost 'that margin of the unpredictable that is the prerogative of living writing' (Guibert 1993a: 147). That book is clearly abandoned for the far more indeterminate fiction we are now reading. This is a novel written in remission and is a story of a deceit. All drug trials require double blind protocols, the test group matched with another that takes a placebo, neither patient nor doctor knowing which is which. Unable to face this uncertainty, since to take a placebo is to be passive before imminent death, Guibert fashions his own 'compassion protocol': he is given a stash of drugs from a now dead dancer, yet conceals this from his doctors. Guibert's own double blinds and deceits renders the truth entirely unclear. One section confesses that he has actually secretly travelled to Los Angeles to receive the very injections denied him in *To the Friend Who Did Not Save My Life*. In another lengthy sequence, he travels to a faith-healer in Casablanca, maintaining a simultaneous belief and disbelief in this charlatanry. Sufficient warning lies in the comment: 'It is when what I am writing takes the form of a journal that I most strongly feel that I am writing fiction' (Guibert 1993a: 72). The journal form of the text continually belies its own status. After a gruelling description of a fibroscopy, depicted as brutal oral rape, Guibert records: 'When I got home, I opened my journal and wrote "Fibroscopy." Nothing else, nothing more, no explanation, no description of the examination and no commentary on my suffering ... I had become incapable of recounting my experience' (Guibert 1993a: 48). This contradicts itself: the trauma of the fibroscopy is at once unrepresentable and exhaustively represented.

The third AIDS autofiction, *The Man in the Red Hat*, appeared posthumously in January 1992. This opens by determining not to mention AIDS at all, a statement of intent it does not fulfil. Nevertheless, the Guibert character does announce: 'I now can't bear any talk of AIDS. I hate my AIDS. I want to have done with it' (Guibert 1993b: 42). The novel does switch focus away from urgent medical reportage. It is loosely structured as a detective fiction and concerns Guibert's obsession with art and the subterranean world of art-forgery. Typically, Guibert thinks of building a collection not of originals but of fakes and copies. He travels to Moscow on the trail of a dealer who has disappeared; he becomes obsessed with the artist Yannis, who seems to be involved in faking his own work, utterly confusing the line between original and copy, true and false. Assessment and treatment of his illness possess similar uncertainty: test results that were negative become positive, operations are started but abandoned, and the status of the illness is forever unclear. Alongside this *roman faux* that foregrounds fakery, Guibert's diary *Cytomegalovirus* was published on the same day, an exercise in releasing apparently unadorned diary transcriptions of a two-week stay in hospital when threatened with blindness. The diary is 'a way of giving rhythm to time and a way to pass it' (1996a: 8), yet the transcriptions are not straightforward, being full of performative contradictions, such as 'Wrote nothing this evening. Too shell-shocked' (Guibert 1996a: 49) and assertions that the diary record is more a kind of purgative anti-record: 'I thought I would no longer be able to write in this diary because of the trauma, but it's the only way to forget' (Guibert 1996a: 53).

Just as one might be tempted to see the diary as the exit from the confusions of the autofictions, Guibert's last book, *Paradise*, explodes this teleology. Written six months before his death, the book appears to be based on the missing manuscript pages that bring *The Man in the Red Hat* to such an abrupt end. Yet in this novel, the character Guibert is a heterosexual man mourning the accidental death of his lover Jayne, an intense affair played out across exotic locations. Even so, the fictionality of the text keeps disintegrating, as Guibert's fevers cause an 'amnesiac state' (Guibert 1996b: 78). Fiction appears to be displaced by transparent diary transcriptions, but towards the end, these reflect only on Guibert's own unstable identity: 'I have made myself the victim of a schizophrenic device installed by myself in creating dual personalities for myself, with two different addresses, one true ... and one fictive' (Guibert 1996b: 100). Guibert seems to embrace a ramshackle, patch-work form, something that traces the ravages of his illness in the structural ruin of the text. Nevertheless, Guibert ends this bewildering sequence of indeterminate texts with his most clearly fictive work.

I have already argued that AIDS texts are central to the memoir boom, but also that the urgency of AIDS witness demands new form. 'Testimonial writing', as Ross Chambers insists, 'speaks from a cultural periphery where it must make do, catachrestically, with genres that scarcely admit it' (Chambers 2004: 33). Guibert once more exemplifies how traumatic truth is traced through the perverse interplay of fact and fiction in order to evade a punitive trial and punishment.

For someone claiming pariah status, Guibert's autofictions have been received sympathetically by a community that was able to theorize this kind of textual play (even if some have been impatient with Guibert's disinterest in AIDS activism). The same cannot be said for Kathryn Harrison, whose 1997 memoir, *The Kiss*, provoked a campaign of press vilification and prompted several commentators to observe that the 1990s memoir boom had now found its shipwreck. *The Kiss* speaks in icy, detached prose of Harrison's profoundly damaged attachments to her parents. Her mother's indifference was matched by her father's forced expulsion from the family home. Lack of maternal recognition results in a variety of hysterical stigmata, acts of masochistic self-harm and a decade of anorexia. When the daughter, aged twenty, meets her father after a ten-year absence, he forces their renewed contact into a sexual relationship, which continues for four years. Her father's first kiss, 'his tongue deep into my mouth: wet, insistent, exploring', reverses *Sleeping Beauty* (Harrison 1997: 68). It sends her into a suspended, somnambulistic state, and the blank prose style, often written in a shell-shocked present tense, conveys the post-traumatic automaton that she has become. Another kiss, of farewell to her grandfather at his funeral, wakes her from the trance and the mesmeric power of the abusive father is shattered.

Even before publication, *Vanity Fair* reported an 'extraordinary buzz' around the memoir, with the proofs becoming a kind of samizdat literature in the New York publishing scene. Michael Shnayerson considered that the memoir 'may be the work of a writer who wrote it in a dreamlike state – a state that incest victims often experience' (Shnayerson 1997: 30). Shnayerson quoted a concerned trauma counsellor to the effect that Harrison's agency in writing and choosing to publish the book was surely in question: she was a trauma victim, being asked to act out in public by unscrupulous agents and publishers. Elsewhere, the only agency allowed was to accuse Harrison of cynicism. Ed Vulliamy's vitriolic account, a month before *The Kiss* was published, painted Harrison as a failed but photogenic novelist prepared to become 'Manhattan's circus freak' by taking the confession of 'one's intimate innards' to new extremes (Vulliamy 1997: 3). Upon publication, Harrison's memoir was declared 'shameful' by Jonathan Yardley, who was sufficiently provoked to attack it in three separate articles in the *Washington Post*. For him, *The Kiss* announced 'the death of literature' (Yardley 1997: B2). James Wolcott considered the book an exercise in narcissism and the 'white zombie' routine a failed attempt to shift what had been a 'consensual act between two adults' into a narrative of incest (Wolcott 1997: 34). For Elizabeth Powers (1997), Harrison was merely another instance of catastrophic American disrespect for the paternal role, the distaste at the act of disclosure apparently far outweighing the details of what had been disclosed. Several national newspapers then dedicated themselves to discovering Harrison's father, and giving him the right to reply; soon, the memoir was openly disbelieved. The final problem was that passages of *The Kiss* appeared to be direct repetitions from Harrison's first novel, *Thicker Than Water* (1991), which offered a strikingly similar family narrative. Key scenes reappeared word for word, but the novel also contained sexual details that had been occluded in the memoir. Once more, a crisis seemed to develop around a confusion of autobiographical and fictional pacts. Harrison held to the logic of the trauma paradigm, by arguing that she needed to rewrite *Thicker than Water* as non-fiction: 'I knew there was a story that was real and that needed to be owned. To novelise a story of incest is to participate in the societal imperative to always lie about it' (Harrison 2005a: 49). Many of her reviewers, however, refused this logic: instead, the prior existence of the novel pointed only to fabrication. Here was a striking instance where the cultural authority of the memoir over the novel was refused; such a story was undermined rather than reinforced by the pre-existing fiction. Now the memoir was too artful, too archly designed to convey authentic traumatic extremity.

Such inordinate responses have themselves become the subject of critical analysis. For David Parker, the details of *The Kiss* produce uncontrollable forms of either identification or sharp disinvestment and denial (Parker 2002: 503). Even those who work to expose some cultural factors for this critical eruption seemingly cannot help but call *The Kiss* 'shamelessly commercial sensationalism' (Saverese 2001: 99). It seems obvious that much of this disturbance comes from Harrison's departure from standard incest narratives, which usually demonstrate a sharp disparity of power between the guilty adult perpetrator and the innocent child victim. Although *The Kiss* seems to me constructed to demonstrate how, psychically, a twenty-year-old woman could be left perilously arrested in an infantile state, vulnerable to a predatory father, Harrison's *legal* age makes her a consenting adult and therefore complicit. As Laura Frost comments, 'punishment is a crucial element of incest paradigms' (Frost 2002: 216), with nasty fates particularly reserved for those rare and monstrous seductive daughters.

The media trial of Kathryn Harrison presumed to judge the truth or falsity of her testimony, with attacks often making her work emblematic of an entire confessional genre. Harrison's response has been no doubt provoking for her detractors: she has produced two further memoirs, *Seeking Rapture* (2003) and *The Mother Knot* (2004) and latterly the novel *Envy* (2005b) that cuts across father–daughter incest at another angle. Combined with her first two novels, *Thicker than Water* (1991) and *Exposure* (1993), both narrated by daughters recalling fragmentary memories of their sexually abusive fathers, I would argue that this body of work constitutes another kind of autofiction, although very different from the play with authorial personae in Roth or Guibert. The facts of Harrison's damaged attachments (which I see no reason to deny) seem so exorbitant that they compel repeated traversals, in different fictional and factual forms. It is through these repetitions and modulations of difficult material that Harrison conveys the insistence of trauma, and not necessarily always in ways that she controls.

There is a striking disjunction between *The Kiss* and its commentary: this abuse account is also in large part a cancer pathography, occasioned by mourning her mother's death from breast cancer. It is the perversity of the maternal attachment that is the critical focus for much of the memoir. The daughter recalls the hunger for her mother's recognition, unable to bear her mother sleeping 'because for as long as my mother refuses consciousness, she refuses consciousness of me: I do not exist' (Harrison 1997: 8). It is her disapproving look that instigates self-starvation and her absent gaze that means she will be defenceless before her father's devouring eyes, the man who 'has somehow begun to *see* me into being' (Harrison 1997: 63). It is also the mother that first effectively rapes her daughter, by insisting a gynaecologist breaks her hymen. This maternal focus was anticipated by *Thicker Than Water*, which is a melancholic novel centred on a daughter nursing a mother through her terminal illness. There, the narrator states:

> Ever since I can remember, each hurt has gotten lost in Mother-hurt. When I was yet in grammar school, any pain, physical or emotional, would lead me back, drop me into an older, more basic agony, and in privacy I would hold myself and rock myself and say MotherMotherMother over and over and over, the way you repeated your secret mantra: an acknowledgment and prayer to the central truth of my existence.
>
> (Harrison 1991: 239)

The details of paternal abuse jut through this novel craggedly, in fragmentary and disordered italicized passages as if as yet unassimilated or unassimilable. Significantly, the scenes from the novel that recur in *The Kiss* tend to concern the mother. The visit to the gynaecologist is restaged, as is the gruesome scene forcing the eyes of newborn kittens to open, tied as it is to the hunger for recognition (the memoir in fact curtails the more abject details of this scene). What is taken up in *Seeking Rapture* and *The Mother Knot* is a more explicit sense of needing to work through the relations to her mother and grandmother, as if repositioning the centre of the family romance after the storm around *The Kiss*. The significant repetition between *The Kiss* and *Seeking Rapture* is in an anecdote about a car accident. Her mother insists on treatment by a Christian Scientist healer, where

> this stranger ushered me into an experience of something I cannot help but call rapture … I learned, at six, a truth dangerous to someone so young and lovelorn. I saw that transcendence was possible: that spirit could conquer matter, and that therefore I could overcome whatever obstacles prevented my mother's loving me. I could overcome myself.
>
> (Harrison 1997: 106; repeated almost verbatim Harrison 2003: 42)

Such trance-like states, however, are first explored in detail in the novel *Exposure*, in scenes where the daughter slips into dissociations and diabetic comas as her father obsessively photographs her. The reader accumulating these repetitions has to keep tacking between factual and fictional discourse.

Harrison's cool, abstracted style is partly the product of incorporating its own analytic commentary: these are thoroughly therapied texts. *Exposure* ends with the transcript of a 'Confidential Psychological Evaluation' of the central female character; *Envy* is written from the perspective of a male analyst. The memoirs are keen to demonstrate the extent of the therapeutic insight that has now accrued to the memoirist. Anorexia is not just recounted, it is interpreted in crisp formulations that pass for analytic wisdom: 'Anorexia can be satisfied, my mother cannot; so I replace her with this disease, with a system of penances and renunciation that offers its own reward' (Harrison 1997: 39–40). This may account for the unease at the seemingly over-artful design of *The Kiss:* experience has been processed into meaningful image-chains and narrative patterns. The repetition across the memoirs, however, rather implies that this insight has its limits and that Harrison's work obeys the law observed by Laura Marcus that 'the anxious need to produce more and yet more narrative suggests that confession is indeed endless and that the "self" cannot even catch up with itself in autobiographical representation' (Marcus 1994: 280). *Seeking Rapture* has to revisit and readjust the focus of *The Kiss; The Mother Knot* has to return again. This last, slim addition strongly demonstrates the limits of insight. It is cen-tred on Harrison's decision to exhume her mother's body and convert her remains to ashes. '"I'm not so much having my mother dug out of the ground as I am exhuming from my own body," I told my analyst' (Harrison 2004: 54). The prag-matic, possibly laconic view of the Californian cemetery authorities – this happens all the time – belies the genuinely weird decision to literalize this symbolic insight. The reader keeps expecting Harrison to reflect on how a third memoir has also been scraped out of the same ground, to put the same body on display again, but the therapeutic disinterment is carried through without such commentary. The ashes scattered, the memoir hails closure ('at last I was allowing her to go' (Harrison 2004: 82)), whilst demonstrating its perpetual entanglement: the knot will outlive the attempted negation, the *not. Envy* is soon toying with a different, fictional avenue of self-exposure in which possible father–daughter incest hauntingly returns. This trajectory leaves me in doubt about how much control Harrison exerts over these repetitions. Confusingly, the more the memoirs incorporate an analytic voice that seeks to manage interpretations, the less control the books actually seem to display.

Harrison's work embodies many of the aspects of the 1990s memoir boom that I have been attempting to delineate here. The memoir form is reoriented around extreme experience and that dramatic act of unveiling a traumatic origin which retrospectively transforms a life narrative. This act of publishing a memorial record can itself generate a form of celebrity, exemplary of a new kind of trauma subject. In Harrison's case, the privileged traumatic truth of intra-familial sexual abuse is muddied by her 'consenting' age, therefore confusing the distribution of guilt and innocence, so producing a punitive media trial. Autofiction has been one means to evade the dangers of self-exposure in a culture that at once demands this confessional truth, but also punishes its articulation. Harrison's repetitions between memoir and fiction are more difficult to determine as strategies than the devices adopted by Roth or Guibert. By *The Mother Knot*, Harrison appears to be invested in the notion of reparative or redemptive narrative, Ricoeur's notion that traumatic disfiguration can be calmatively configured by narrative. Harrison, however, seems to demonstrate that the pronouncement of closure holds no force: she generates ever more acts of confession in a dynamic process of constituting the contemporary trauma subject. The trauma paradigm achieves saturation by inciting narratives that demand instant repetition by their failure to master what has been constituted as traumatic experience.

4 The intrusive image
Photography and trauma

The cultural symptoms of the novel and memoir foreground the tension between narrative and its disruption, between concordance and the discordances that trauma produces. Yet this narrative problem remains within the linguistic register, whilst a definitional element of trauma might be that it defeats precisely this form of representation. As Elaine Scarry observes, 'physical pain does not simply resist language, but actively destroys it, bringing about an immediate reversion to a state anterior to language' (Scarry 1985: 4). One of the central ways in which contemporary trauma has been conceived is around the symptom of the intrusive or recurrent image, the unbidden flashback that abolishes time and reimmerses you in the visual field of the inaugurating traumatic instant. There is a profound disjunction implied: the visual intrusion recurs because linguistic and memorial machineries completely fail to integrate or process the traumatic image. Perhaps, then, it is in the image that the psychic registration of trauma truly resides.

The place of the intrusive image, as Ruth Leys notes, has been considerably amplified in subsequent revisions to the 1980 definition of PTSD in the *Diagnostic and Statistical Manual* of the American Psychiatric Association (Leys 2006). Two papers in 1985 argued that its centrality should be recognized. 'The most unique aspect of the PTSD diagnosis appears to be the intrusive symptoms, including intrusive images and recurrent dreams and nightmares', one group of researchers suggested. 'Because this is the most distinct aspect of the disorder and potentially its hallmark, it is unfortunate that little attention has been paid to the content of these images' (Green *et al.* 1985: 409). A similar 'neglect of imagery' was observed by Brett and Ostroff, who argued for a new emphasis on 'imagic and affective re-experiencing phenomena' in PTSD (Brett and Ostroff 1985: 422). The revised criteria in 1987 thus expanded the elements of re-experiencing to include intrusive recollections, recurrent dreams, 'sudden acting or feeling as if the traumatic event were recurring (includes a sense of reliving the experience, illusions, hallucinations, and dissociative [flashback] episodes, even those that occur upon awakening or when intoxicated)' and finally a new additional category of 'intense psychological distress at exposure to events that symbolize or resemble an aspect of the traumatic event' (American Psychiatric Association 1987: 250). The fourth edition had further accretions, in that now familiar logic of progressive extension of categories of trauma.

Ostroff and Brett also sketched out a genealogy of trauma theory that recalled how recurrent images had been part of defining traumatic or war neuroses since Freud. This could be taken back further, to Pierre Janet's treatment of *idées fixes* in the 1880s that had aimed to transform stubborn memory images into benign narrative form. In Janet's practice hypnosis recovered the scene and suggestion then edited or erased its traumatic content. The critical stage of modern development, however, had begun in the 1960s. Mardi Horowitz was a psychologist researching the relationship between image and cognition and in 1969 he published a piece on re-experiencing LSD hallucinations which he called 'flashbacks' following the hippy usage in San Francisco. These were *'recurrent unbidden images'* in which 'the contents seem to be returns of traumatic perceptions, breakthroughs of repressed ideas and affects, or screen images' (Horowitz 1969: 566 and 569). Horowitz went on to provide a central plank for physiological theories of trauma in *Stress Response Syndromes* in 1976. Stressful events could leave a legacy of an oscillation between denial or evasion and sudden, unwelcome returns to the scene: '*Intrusion* labels the period of unbidden ideas and pangs of feeling which are difficult to dispel, and of direct or symbolic behavioural re-enactments of the stress event complex' (Horowitz 1976b: 57). Horowitz, although sympathetic to psychodynamic theories, instead opted to model this theory on cognitive processing. In his view, '*active memory storage has an intrinsic tendency towards repetition of contents until the contents held in active memory are actively terminated*' (Horowitz 1976b: 93). Stress events contained information difficult to 'terminate'; the images got stuck in cycles of repetition rather than fading into conventional memories. Horowitz tied his work to the cluster of research on concentration camps, Vietnam veterans and women with rape trauma, and he became one of Robert Jay Lifton's fellow advocates on the committee that formulated PTSD, as I outlined in Chapter 1. Lifton himself consistently emphasized that the death-in-life experienced by Hiroshima survivors and war veterans was a result of 'inundating the organism with death imagery' that could not be symbolically integrated or narratively formulated (Lifton 1968: 503). *The Broken Connection* began with the assertion that '*We live on images*' and concluded that 'one could define the traumatic syndrome as the state of being haunted by images that can neither be enacted nor cast aside' (Lifton 1979: 3 and 172).

A lot of this material stands behind Bessel van der Kolk's theory that traumatic memory is registered in a specific, imagistic way that stands outside normal memory creation. Trauma is engraved in the mind under distinct conditions, etched in by the heightened adrenaline of the physiological reaction to bodily stress. It is also an explicitly non-verbal, non-narrative memory: 'The experience cannot be organized on a linguistic level and this failure to arrange the memory in words and symbols leaves it to be organized on a somatosensory or iconic level: as somatic sensations, behavioural reenactments, nightmares and flashbacks' (van der Kolk and van der Hart 1991: 442–3). Hence PTSD is marked by unnerving intrusions of images that are experienced as 'context-free, fearful associations which are hard to locate in space and time' (van der Kolk and van der Hart 1991: 442). This provides the structure in which to present a theory of recovered memory. Traumatic memory is registered outside normal memory and is thus lost to conscious recall. Its presence is marked by unfathomable flashes of disturbing images or compulsive repetitions. A therapist will pull at the threads of this 'context-free' image and will eventually uncover, engraved in pristine form, the traumatic event.

Ruth Leys has sharply observed that this history has increasingly regarded the traumatic image as a literal record of the event. Horowitz had first used the metaphor of the flashback as a return to a particular state in which elaboration, transformation and displacement of imagery regularly occurred. Relatively soon, however, the traumatic memory was not seen as a representation so much as a shard of the event itself. Traumatic nightmares of veterans dispensed with the dream logic of condensation, displacement or symbolism; instead, they were 'usually exact replicas of actual combat events' (van der Kolk *et al.* 1984: 188). 'Flashbulb' memories, first theorized in 1977, preserved a snapshot in memory of particularly shocking or momentous events, such as Kennedy's assassination. Flashbulb memories were 'very like a photograph' and 'not a narrative'; they were not registered 'in verbal form' (Brown and Kulik 1977: 74 and 85). In the 1980s, some argued that PTSD diagnostics needed to be more explicit that intrusive images were 'direct recapitulation of the event' (Green *et al.* 1985: 409). Recovered abuse memories often assumed this, and Leys also found this literalizing trace in Caruth's cultural theory of trauma (Leys 2000).

This tendency towards literalization is undoubtedly because the visual image is held to be somehow closer to the event, less mediated, than the verbal record. In C. S. Peirce's semiotics, the written sign is an arbitrary *symbol*, rendered meaningful by convention, whilst the image is an *index*, still a conventional sign but one that also carries the physical trace of the object itself. According to Roland Barthes, what the photograph announces, and what astounds us about it, is '*the thing has been there*' (Barthes 2000: 76). Photography preserves a chemical trace of the object itself, presents itself as incontestable evidence, but in a way that is inherently deathly since the indexical image is also, in the instant it is taken, a monument to what has now irrevocably passed: 'Death is the *eidos* of that Photograph' (Barthes 2000: 15). This play of presence and absence invokes all those familiar traumatic notions of spectres. Thus, as Marianne Hirsch suggests: 'The referent haunts the picture like a ghost: it is a revenant, a return of the lost and dead other' (M. Hirsch 1997: 5). The photograph is the privileged medium of postmemory, 'an intersubjective transgenerational space of remembrance, linked specifically to cultural or collective trauma' (M. Hirsch 2001: 10). The index therefore dominates thinking about visual culture, even if the category of the indexical is held to be in crisis. As Laura Mulvey puts it:

> The cinema (like photography) has a privileged relation to time, preserving the moment at which the image is registered ... Both have the attributes of the indexical sign, the mark of trauma or the mark of light, and both need to be deciphered retrospectively across delayed time.
>
> (Mulvey 2006: 9)

What emerges from this commentary is an intrinsic relationship between trauma theory and visual culture that needs to be explored. Modern technologies of the image have been inextricably associated with traumatic impacts and the theorization of trauma. Walter Benjamin considered cinema's 'formal principle' to be 'perception in the form of shocks' (Benjamin 1973: 171) and in the 1960s Marshall McLuhan regarded instant global communications as an exteriorization of the human nervous system that lost 'protective buffers' and left man vulnerable to continual traumatic 'shock' (McLuhan 1987: 43). Robert Jay Lifton built on this analysis to convey an 'emerging psychological state' at the end of the 1960s, a change attributed in part to 'the *flooding of imagery* produced by the extraordinary flow of postmodern cultural influences over mass communication networks' (Lifton 1969: 37 and 43). It is now hard to think of the contemporary psychology of trauma outside an imbrication with photography and cinema, with cultural metaphors of flashbulbs and flashbacks now literalized in scientific and cultural theory. Ulrich Baer, for instance, considers that trauma 'parallels the defining structure of photography, which also traps an event during its occurrence while blocking its transformation into memory' (Baer 2002: 9). In the contemporary era, the trauma of visual technologies continues, for the 'shock' of digital technology has been to undermine the very notion of the photographic index, as the registration of the image shifted from the chemical trace to the infinitely manipulable electronic bit.

This chapter will investigate the still image as the epitome of traumatic intrusion and disfiguration. The next chapter will reanimate the concern with narrative knowledge by examining how trauma has reconfigured cinematic storytelling. Photography will be considered in two principal frames: fine art and the fate of the atrocity photograph as photojournalism has collided with art practice to produce some of the most disturbing objects of trauma culture: beautiful books of atrocity images.

The fine art of trauma

It is now conventional, Julian Stallabrass notes, to claim that contemporary art is too bewilderingly diverse to capture critically, touching as it does 'upon feminism, identity politics, mass culture, shopping, and trauma' (Stallabrass 2004: 150). If trauma appears in this list as merely one element, it is not randomly chosen and does suggest itself as a significant way of navigating a passage through the contemporary art scene. In 1998, Jill Bennett organized the *Telling Tales* exhibition, which led to her monograph on art and trauma, *Empathic Vision*. In 2001, the Hayward Gallery toured twelve international artists under the exhibition title *Trauma*, the curators arguing that artists like Felix Gonzarez-Torres, Johan Grimonprez and Tracey Moffatt regard trauma as 'one of the key sites on which collective identity is established' (Bradley *et al.* 2001: 7). Major exhibitions also included *Beautiful Suffering: Photography and the Traffic in Pain* at the Williams College Museum of Art in 2006. 'We would like to acknowledge', the curators announced at the end of the show, 'that the most objectionable aspect of this exhibition may be its very existence' (Reinhardt *et al.* 2006: np). *After Shock: Conflict, Violence and Resolution* followed at the Sainsbury Centre for Visual Arts in 2007.

Small, private gestures of confessional art flooded the art market in the 1990s, from Tracey Emin's self-exposures to Gillian Wearing's *Trauma* (2000), a curtained confessional in which one watched masked faces detail histories of violence, guilt and abuse. The mixed media installations and writings of Everlyn Nicodemus, intertwine personal losses and genocidal histories (see Cheddie 2007). This exploration of trauma subjectivity could also be extended to the 'states of depression' that Christine Ross argues is 'one of the privileged categories through which the contemporary subject is being defined and designated, made and unmade' (Ross 2006: xvii). Her formulation of an 'aesthetic of disengagement' encompasses work by Ugo Rondinone, Vanessa Beecroft, Douglas Gordon, and others.

Meanwhile, monumental public art was, as Lisa Saltzman puts it, 'preoccupied with losses', seeking a language of memorialization just as faith in the index of traumatic history was being put in question, leaving the index 'a vestige rather than a viable means of representation' (Saltzman 2006: 13). The politics of public art and memorials has become a highly disputatious discourse; stone no longer fixes a heroic national narrative in place. Marita Sturken, for instance, has exhaustively detailed the controversies that surrounded the building of Maya Lin's Vietnam War Memorial, dedicated in Washington in 1982. Its anti-monumental form (the monument is a 500-foot cut into the ground, which bears all the names of the American war dead) prompted figural counter-monuments, counter-counter-monuments, appropriations and reappropriations, self-evidently demonstrating 'a very active scripting and re-scripting of the war' (Sturken 1997: 75). Holocaust memorials have also been problematic memorial spaces, hemmed in by questions of aesthetics as much as competing political investments in the legacy of the war. The architectural grammar of trauma was established by Daniel Libeskind at the Jewish Museum in Berlin (constructed between 1993 and 1999), although Libeskind spent many years theorizing rather than building such structures. Other monuments had difficult gestations, too. In the mid-1990s the British artist Rachel Whiteread won the competition to build a Holocaust memorial for Vienna's Judenplatz. Local shopkeepers complained that the memorial would deprive their customers of parking space. Undaunted, the Viennese community, supported by Simon Wiesenthal, the famous 'Nazi-hunter', pushed the project through city planning meetings. Once the excavations began, however, the earth revealed a secret: they uncovered the smoke-blackened floor of a synagogue burnt down in a pogrom in 1421. Vienna's chief rabbi then withdrew support from Whiteread's memorial: 'For us, the excavations alone are very moving … no other monument is necessary' (MacRitchie 1996: 9). The memorial was eventually completed, but demonstrated James Young's insight that 'memorials by themselves remain inert and amnesiac', and it is the energy of dispute around them that keeps remembrance alive (J. Young 1993: xiii). This is evidenced by the competing pressures that have continually transformed the plans for the memorial site in Manhattan where the World Trade Center once stood (see Smith 2006). Such contentions inform the memorial art of Christian Boltanski, Gerhard Richter, Krzysztof Wodiczko, William Kentridge or Kara Walker.

In 1996, Hal Foster had noted contemporary art's fascination with this material: 'For many in contemporary culture truth resides in the traumatic or abject subject, in the diseased or damaged body' (Foster 1996: 166). Foster acutely observed a central contradiction in this work. Academic theories of trauma continued to 'deconstruct' the subject, an aim much associated with art theory in the 1980s. Yet wider cultural usages of trauma understood it to allow recovery of an authentic, real self, working exactly against the alleged anti-humanism of critical theory. Foster expressed concern about the return of this pre-theoretical self, but this was unsurprising given that his work (and that of the group involved in the New York art-theory journal *October*) was associated with theorizing Postmodernism through-out the 1980s. The one thing art commentary on the 1990s agreed about was the wholesale abandonment of this 'high theory' fusion of art and criticism. The decade was marked, John Welchman observed of the American scene, by 'a strand of anti-academic counter-theorizing, popularly correlated with the material profu-sions of the grunge aesthetic and the textualist disinclinations of the "slacker generation"' (Welchman 2001: 29). What replaced theorized conceptual art were 'closely confessional narratives' and 'spectacles of the excessive':

> Not until the 1990s could so many artists allow themselves so many meas-ures for facing and reproducing their selves, intimating, at the same time, that the means and materials of this self-reflection were somehow enmeshed with the most current elements of contemporary culture.
>
> (Welchman 2001: 30 and 183)

The wounded narcissism being worked over in art was plugged directly into the wider cultural obsession with the trauma subject.

Stallabrass offered a similar view in relation to the English scene. *High Art Lite*, his survey of celebrity artists of the grouping collected by Charles Saatchi and shown under the title 'Young British Artists', repeatedly returns to the aggressively anti-theoretical stance of this group and the art-criticism associated with it. The critic John Roberts has attempted to argue that what he calls the New Philistinism is a radicalizing turn from the academicism of high theory art and criticism. If many were sceptical, this was probably due to the flimsy resources provided by the art itself for such a position (see Beech and Roberts 2002). Figures like Damien Hirst, Gary Hume, Sarah Lucas and Gavin Turk presented studiedly blank, inarticulate or perhaps even post-traumatic selves. These were constructed personae, 'new artis-tic identities' that ensured 'critical theory [would] bounce off this work' (Stallabrass 1999: 18). That these resonated within the trauma paradigm is evident from the following exchange with one of the key artists of the decade, Tracey Emin.

Do you feel you had a childhood?
Although I have a really brilliant memory – my work is about memory – in my childhood I have massive blanks. I do remember waking up in the night crocheting. I remember banging my head against a brick wall. I remember putting a bamboo stick through my leg. I remember all these weird events. But I wasn't very happy as a child. I am not very happy as an adult, now I come to think about it.

Did you consciously edit out episodes?
They just disappeared.

(Gisbourne 1998: 31)

The artist whose work famously mines a traumatic childhood here emphasizes that the hypermnesic insistence of certain events in her work (sexual humiliation, rape, and abortion) is matched by equally traumatic amnesic disturbances. This persona promised a 'tear-stained and torn guarantee of authenticity', the work elided with the life to 'proffer the cut, the wound, a still suppurating incision into body and soul' (Townsend and Merck 2002: 10). The apparent instant transparency and controversial contents of her work made for rapid success, although only after it had crossed the threshold of gallery space and private ownership. Her 1999 Turner Prize installation 'My Bed' was famous largely for the cost of the piece to Saatchi and for the avant-garde pillow fight conducted in Tate Britain by protesters shouting 'I am art'. Tabloid fascination with Emin was distinctly ambivalent: at once an occasion for decrying the lunacy of the art establishment, her tactics of disclosure, its contents, and its mode of expression often coincided with that of the popular press. It was almost inevitable that she would contribute to the trauma memoir genre, publishing *Strangeland* in 2005, an episodic and dissociated trawl of childhood memories that featured damaged attachments, violence, humiliation, and sexual transgression. Her success seems strictly circumscribed to the repetitive performance of a trauma through a persona constructed to be incapable of mastering its own compulsions.

Something similar may be said about the photographic work of Nan Goldin. Goldin has catalogued the lives and deaths of her extended family of those marginalized by sexuality, drug use or illness. Her *Ballad of Sexual Dependency* was published in book form in 1986, but her work fully coincided with the times at her major retrospective at the Whitney Museum in 1996. The snap-shot aesthetic of her intimate portraits is surrounded by markers of authenticity: the images present a brutal reality of sexual encounters, bodies of friends dying of HIV-related illnesses, open coffins at funerals, or a self-portrait after physical battery. These almost command dispensing with any need for theories of representation: they seem to be purely denotative. The work is 'free from domination by abstract constructs of art', one commentator (and Goldin subject) stated. 'Critical caution is entirely unnecessary. Nan and her photographs form a single whole' (Costa 2001: 7 and 3). This was a wholly different position from the kind of critical work of intimate photography advocated, say, by Jo Spence in the theoretical 1980s. In her last years, Spence had explored 'phototherapy' as a 'form of phototheatre of the self' that aimed at 'making visible' what she called 'repressed memories' (Spence 1995: 164). Spence's project was informed by Lacanian and Althusserian theory that interrogated the constructed nature of the self and critiqued photographic 'realism'. In contrast, Goldin expresses only the self-evidence of her images: 'My work is exactly what it's about … . There's no theory behind it. I don't want to analyse it' (Garratt 2002: 15). Goldin's retrospective at the Whitechapel Gallery in 2002 was given further pathos by her communication that many of the subjects were now dead of AIDS or overdose; the global circulation of her images also involved a certain nostalgia for the spaces of a vanished New York sub-culture.

Such confessional art was sometimes difficult to separate entirely from confessional culture as 'art celebrity' turned these figures into generic icons of trauma culture. What their art confessed seemed only to reconfirm what Foucault had argued about both the compulsion to speak and the pre-determination of the contents of any confession. Others in the international circuits of the art market perhaps retain more critical ambivalence: let's discuss three artists in more detail.

Aftermath aesthetics: Christian Boltanski, Gerhard Richter, Tracey Moffatt

Initially, it might seem that the French artist Christian Boltanski has conducted the same sort of obsessive self-investigation as Emin or Goldin. One of his earliest projects was a mock-ethnographic archival piece entitled *Research and Presentation of all that remains of my childhood, 1944–50* (1969). The work developed from discovering his school class photograph from 1951 and realizing 'I don't remember any of their names, I don't remember anything more than the faces on the photograph. It could be said that they disappeared from my memory, that this period of time was dead … . This is why I felt the need to pay homage to those "dead," who, in this image, all look more or less the same, like cadavers' (cited Gumpert 1994: 80 and 83). In this curious statement, Boltanski rehearses his abiding theme – the fragility of what he terms the 'little memory' disregarded and lost from public history – but also the suspicion that photography may not preserve the historical index so much as become a monument to its destruction. Boltanski's early explorations thus tested the lure of the index. *Ten Photographic Portraits of Christian Boltanski, 1946–64* (1972) seemed self-evident, but the images reveal themselves as fabricated portraits, something set up 'to show that photography lies, that it doesn't speak the truth but rather the cultural code' (cited Perloff 1997: 42). These devices appear to place Boltanski in an alternative tradition of photographic theory, which, like Siegfried Kracauer, places the photograph in opposition to the memory-image, arguing that photography does not record experience but actively destroys it. 'It is not the person who appears in his or her photograph', Kracauer argued, 'but the sum of what can be deducted from him or her' (Kracauer 1993: 430). Boltanski later confessed: 'In my early work I pretended to speak about my childhood, yet my real childhood had disappeared. I have lied about it so often that I no longer have a real memory of this time' (Garb 1997: 8).

However, in the 1980s, Boltanski began to employ the same qualities of the photograph for very different ends. Starting with *The Children of Dijon* (1985), Boltanski used found photographic images, rephotographed them tightly cropped around the faces and blown up to a size where individual features blurred into generic patterns of light and shade. These were then installed site-specifically, sometimes resting on columns of rusting tin-boxes, suggestive of coffins or urns, and sometimes attached to archive boxes, as if they contained the documents of a forgotten life

Figure 4.1 Christian Boltanski, 'The Reserve of Dead Swiss' (1990). Tate, London 2007. Copyright © 1990 Christian Boltanski.

(see Figure 4.1). These images were either illuminated by memorial candles or almost obliterated by the harsh glare of desk lamps that were pushed into the faces, a tangle of electrical leads destroying any neat Minimalist sculptural lines. Boltanski has shuffled and reshuffled his growing archive of anonymous faces ever since, producing postindexical monuments: public memorial arts that attest to the erasure of publics and memories. These larger-scale projects came with a new element of confession: not just that Boltanski was half-Jewish, but that during the German occupation of France his father had been hidden beneath the family home to avoid deportation. His obsessive focus on documents, archives, photographic proof and faked evidence was now reinterpreted: 'At the beginning of all the work', Boltanski said, 'there is a kind of trauma: something happened' (Garb 1997: 8). Boltanski is therefore one of the paradigmatic artists of the era because his career shares the structure of belated traumatic recovery: what was empty postmodern play is latterly re-signified with real traumatic content.

In a sequence of installations from 1987, Boltanski made his first explicit references to the Holocaust. The *Chases High School* took another graduation photograph as its source, this time from a Jewish school in 1931. Each face from this found photograph was further severed from its original context by being rephotographed and monumentalized, and although Boltanski had no knowledge of their subsequent lives, the piece indirectly evoked a likely fate: if not the concentration camps, then genocide in the sense of the destruction of culture. The same evocation of an irreparably lost culture informed his use of pre-war photographs of Jewish children in *Fête de Pourim* (1987). *Canada* (1988) used second-hand clothes, piled in their thousands, a medium Boltanski has since installed in diverse, site-specific forms. He considered worn and discarded clothes, massed in now anonymous form, conceptually equivalent to photographs: 'they are simultaneously presence and absence. They are both an object and a souvenir of a subject, exactly as a cadaver is both an object and a souvenir of a subject' (cited Gumpert 1994: 110). *Canada* directed the viewer to an explicit Holocaust reference for the first time, being the Nazi euphemism for the storage depots of materials gathered from those sent into the death camps. After this phase of intensive exploration, Boltanski has worked to reuniversalize his memorials, dislodging the automatic association of Jews and death with *The Dead Swiss* (rephotographed obituary portraits), mixing victims and perpetrators in decontextualized crime scene photographs in *Detective*, and remixing his entire archive of anonymous photographs in the randomly displayed equivalences of the 1,500 faces that constituted *Menschlich* [*Humanity*] (1994).

However abstracted from specific contexts, these haunting evocations of disappeared populations produce for Ernst Van Alphen something he calls a 'Holocaust-effect'. They create echoes of a historical trauma that resonate throughout Boltanski's practice, however indirectly, thus invoking the condition of being 'after' Auschwitz. Indeed, Arthur Danto has claimed Boltanski 'the only convincing example' of Holocaust art, 'a genre I would have thought impossible' (Danto 1997: 260). At the core of his practice, Boltanski forces the viewer to reflect on the contradiction in the memorial promise of the photographic portrait or the archive, pointing as much to their de-individualizing and amnesiac potentials. This is an investigation that proceeds 'by re-enacting principles that are defining aspects of the Holocaust: a radical emptying out of subjectivity as a road leading up to a wholesale destruction of a people – genocide' (Van Alphen 2001: 49).

Another deconstructive interrogation of the possibilities of aesthetic and photographic memory has been undertaken by the German painter Gerhard Richter. Richter has constantly and bewilderingly shifted painterly style from the extremes of abstraction to photorealism, but there is a consistent thread of inquiry into what painting can do in the age of photographic pre-eminence. The death of painting was announced as early as the first Daguerrotypes and Yve-Alain Bois has argued that since Modernism 'mourning has been the activity of painting' (Bois 1992: 329). Yet Richter has turned an apparently exhausted tradition into a device for interrogating the dangerous allure of photographic verisimilitude. In a sequence of monochromatic grey paintings, source photographs are uncannily reproduced only to be damaged to various degrees, by dragging a squeegee across the surface or by feathering the paint so that the image is blurred or by aggressively overpainting images with obliterating sweeps of the brush. Richter has spoken of needing to attack his canvases, sometimes with a palette knife, invoking the slashes and wounds of Lucio Fontana's canvases. He considers aesthetic beauty as that which is *uninjured*: a strikingly post-traumatic definition (Storr 2002: 73). These formal aggressions are in direct relation to the content of the works, and once again biographical information directs the viewer towards trauma theory.

Figure 4.2 Gerhard Richter, 'Uncle Rudi' (1965). Reproduced by kind permission of
Gerhard Richter. Copyright © 1965 Gerhard Richter.

Richter was born in 1932, his father a National Socialist and soldier captured in
the latter stages of the war. Richter was enrolled in the Hitler Youth, and after the
1945 partition grew up in Communist East Germany (training as a muralist),
before defecting to the West in 1961. As an art student, Richter was at the epi-
centre of the revolt against the silence and complicity of the previous generation.
Two early paintings show the ambivalent legacies within Richter's own family:
Uncle Rudi (1965) is a queasy monochromatic painting taken from a photograph
of his uncle grinning broadly in his new Nazi uniform (see Figure 4.2). His uncle
was killed within weeks of the war starting. *Aunt Marianne* (1965), meanwhile, is
sourced from a photograph of Richter as a baby held by an aunt who became
mentally ill and was murdered under the eugenic policies of the Third Reich (in
the same year, Richter's *Doctor Heyde* used a news photograph from the trial of the
figure who pioneered exterminations by gas in the German asylum system). In
these works Richter has connected 'the bankrupt conventions of history painting
with the banality of the family photograph' (Buchloh 1996: 64). Richter has, like
his German peer Anselm Kiefer, 'found in painting and its acknowledged inca-
pacity the very possibility of figuring something of their nation's catastrophic

history' (Saltzmann 2006: 4). This hollowed-out history painting was extended to explore one of the extreme results of 1960s revolt in Germany: the Baader-Meinhof terrorist group. The fifteen monochromatic paintings under the title *18 October 1977* (1988) record the night of the unresolved deaths of the gang in their prison cells. This group suicide or state murder has been 'a horror', Richter said, 'that distressed me and has haunted me as unfinished business ever since' (cited Storr 2002: 76). The source photographs, newspaper images and evidentiary photographs taken of the bodies, are feathered into virtual abstraction, evoking the fog of mystification that has settled around the deaths. The critique of photographic transparency is conjoined with Richter's suspicion of revolutionary ideologies that obliterate the individual: the form therefore captures Richter's ambivalence about a key traumatic event in German post-war history.

As with Boltanski, Richter's work confronts 'the status of the traditional tools available for commemoration' (Buchloh 1996: 69). Just where the theory of the intrusive traumatic image might privilege the traumatic instant as the true record, their play with the indexicality of the photograph foregrounds ambiguity.

We might say that Richter and Boltanski head a group that has developed an *aftermath aesthetic*, recalling Ross Chambers' idea of aftermath cultures that are intrinsically 'melancholic in character' because they exist in states of denial about the traumas that nevertheless determine them (Chambers 2004: xxi). Doris Salcedo works with domestic objects of Colombia's 'disappeared' to produce work that memorializes those now absent from domestic space. Zarina Bhimji has produced a photographic record of the abandoned sites of Uganda's institutions of torture called *Memories Were Trapped in the Asphalt*, whilst Guy Tillim has done the same for the ruins left by imperial and post-imperial powers in the Congo. Paul Seawright's series *Sectarian Murders* (1988) photographed sites of deaths, banal spaces of playing fields or remote paths. Joel Sternfeld's photographic book, *On This Site* (1996), similarly revisits places of American violence, the bland normality of the spaces jarring with the short textual descriptions of atrocity or murder that took place there, from the Washington bus shelter where a homeless woman froze to death to the banal car park of Kent State University where the National Guard killed student demonstrators in 1970, to the bulldozed field that then had replaced the Alfred Murrah Federal Building in Oklahoma City, site of the terrorist attack that killed 168 people. 'I think of it as a question of knowability', Sternfeld stated in his Afterword. 'Experience has taught me again and again that you can never know what lies beneath a surface or behind a façade. Our sense of place, our understanding of photographs of the landscape is inevitably limited and fraught with misreading' (Sternfeld 1996: np). Sally Mann has photographed American Civil War sites, using nineteenth-century wet plate technology: 'chemically speaking colloidon is very similar to gun powder, but it was also used by surgeons during the Civil War who poured it into wounds' (Mann 2007: 23). In *What Remains*, she has photographed the decomposing bodies used for forensic research at the notorious 'Body Farm' in Knoxville, Tennessee. All of these projects associate sites of aftermath and ruination with the intrinsic afterwardsness of the photograph itself, so redoubling the traumatic effect.

In contrast, Tracey Moffatt's work engages more critically with a number of elements of the trauma paradigm. Moffatt is an aboriginal Australian, fostered to white parents in the assimilation programmes of the 1960s and 1970s and who came to the fore as an exemplary construct of Third Cinema and post-colonial theory. Her work continues to foreground the politics of identity and the interplay of fantasy and history informed by critical theory. In 1994, she produced *Scarred for Life*, a series of ten panels of captioned photographs that froze in place a moment of psychic damage, a staging of the traumatic instant at which the intrusive image would be seared into the mind. This series seemed premised on an acute grasp of the lure of trauma narratives: the text and image recover and fix down the traumatic origin on which a life narrative will subsequently hinge. One reads: '**Heart Attack, 1970**. She glimpsed her father belting the girl from down the street. That day he died of a heart attack' (Figure 4.3). Two more read: '**Birth Certificate, 1962**. During the fight, her mother threw her birth certificate at her. This is how she found out her real father's name' (Figure 4.4); '**Doll Birth, 1972**. His mother caught him giving birth to a doll. He was banned from playing with the boy next door again' (Figure 4.5). Although Régis Durand has argued that this 'text-image mix' makes for polysemous and irresolvable work, 'charged with narrative and psychic energy' (Durand 1999: 104), I would tend to see the captioning of these images instead as a comment on the brutal way that the trauma paradigm can fix identity through the singular childhood event, destining the self to reiterate this definitional moment without prospect of resolution. The image-texts fill in, as it were, the origin of the gapped subject. These are the intrusive images never found in the family album yet which are central to the very constitution of the familial narrative. For the viewer, particularly if they are aware that these are based on true stories collected by Moffatt, the wondrous photographic presence of this originating trauma provokes you to undertake a similar process. They demand what Marianne Hirsch has proposed, in a similar context, as 'an *affiliative look* through which we are sutured into the images and through which we adopt the image' (Hirsch 1997: 93). This was demonstrated by the overwhelming response of Moffatt's audience. She reported that 'over the years people have come up to me. They couldn't wait to tell me their tragic story. I thought I could make another series of this work and it could be an ongoing project' (Cathcart 2001). *Scarred for Life II* appeared in 1999, with notably more surreal moments, e.g. '**Piss Bags, 1978**. Locked in the van while their mothers continued their affair, the boys were forced to piss into their chip bags'. Always intended as a tragi-comic series, the surreality of these later capsule narratives suggests that Moffatt, whilst working through the mechanisms of the intrusive image and recovered memory is also undercutting them. These images are, of course, staged reconstructions, and their archness is evident in the studiedly neutral language of the captions and the saturated colours that make the images redolent of faded 1970s snaps or dated magazine spreads. The care of the restaging does not authenticate, but rather exaggerates falsification, dramatizing the interplay of traumatic fixity and narrative mobility that constitutes the trauma subject. In doing so, Moffatt's series plays with but also exposes the allure of that originary plenitude promised by the imprint of the intrusive traumatic image.

Tracey Moffatt

Heart Attack, 1970 She glimpsed her father belting the
girl from down the street.
That day he died of a heart attack.

Figure 4.3 Tracey Moffatt, 'Scarred for Life: Heart Attack, 1970', from 'Scarred for Life'
(1994), offset prints, series of nine images. Reproduced by courtesy of the
Victoria Miro Gallery. Copyright © 1994 Tracey Moffatt.

This suturing of the viewer into the affective economy of the image is a
repeated effect in this kind of art. Moffatt generates a supplementary series from
audience reactions; Richard Cork sees Boltanski's success in the invitation to viewers 'to project their own private bereavements into the blankness confronting
them at every turn' (Cork 2003: 416). For Jill Bennett, it is this *relational affect* that
distinguishes art practice from other cultural discourses of trauma. Bennett avoids
looking instrumentally, reading art against pre-existent diagnostic categories, and
refuses to countenance a determinate set of trauma images: 'affect is not pre-
coded by a representational system that enables us to read an image as "about
trauma"' (Bennett 2005: 35). Instead, aesthetics explores this terrain relationally
and intersubjectively, 'figuring memory in "trauma art" as lived and felt in relation to a whole series of interconnected events and political forces, rather than as
embodied in an atomised subject' (Bennett 2005: 18). After 9/11, Bennett advocates art that makes these interconnections globally, putting distinct traumatic
instants into suggestive relationships to provoke what she calls empathic encounters. Her examples include *Documenta 11* (2002), curated by Okumi Enwezor to

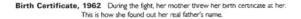

Birth Certificate, 1962 During the fight, her mother threw her birth certificate at her. This is how she found out her real father's name.

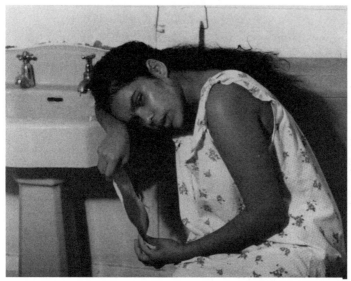

Tracey Moffatt

Figure 4.4 Tracey Moffatt, 'Scarred for Life: Birth Certificate, 1962' from 'Scarred for Life' (1994), offset prints, series of nine images. Reproduced by courtesy of the Victoria Miro Gallery. Copyright © 1994 Tracey Moffatt.

foster transnational interconnections, for instance by juxtaposing work on Palestine with images of Auschwitz and the Robben Island prison in South Africa.

To situate the fine art of trauma in this relational affect is of course highly contentious. It does not obey the frequent injunctions to respect the singularity of each specific traumatic event. Boltanski's work has been criticized for precisely this relational equivalence, as victims and perpetrators, Nazis and Jews, Jews and Swiss are all rendered interchangeable. His 'art of generic elegy', a sort of uniform wistfulness about the loss inherent in the photographic, is 'wholly inadequate to the historical, indeed to the ethical, requirements of historical commemoration' (Solomon-Godeau 1998: 7). Bennett would likely consider this command too directive, even destructive of aesthetic empathy: 'The affective image neither draws us into a narrative that simply purports to deliver us into the place of the traumatized subject nor achieves its best effects by inciting a particular kind of "moral" response' (Bennett 2005: 43–4).

This comment delivers us to the heart of the debate about photography and its relation to the intrusive, traumatic image. The area has been dominated by Susan

Tracey Moffatt

Doll Birth, 1972 His mother caught him giving birth to a doll.
He was banned from playing with the boy
next door again.

Figure 4.5 Tracey Moffatt, 'Scarred for Life: Doll Birth, 1972' from 'Scarred for Life'
(1994), offset prints, series of nine images. Reproduced by courtesy of the
Victoria Miro Gallery. Copyright © 1994 Tracey Moffatt.

Sontag's reflections on the searing impact but fatally circumscribed moral force of
trauma photography. *On Photography* narrates a primal scene:

> One's first encounter with the photographic inventory of ultimate horror is
> a kind of revelation, the prototypically modern revelation: a negative
> epiphany. For me, it was photographs of Bergen-Belsen and Dachau which
> I came across by chance in a bookstore in Santa Monica in July 1945.
> Nothing I have seen ... ever cut me as sharply, deeply, instantaneously ... .
> When I looked at those photographs, something broke. Some limit had
> been reached, and not only that of horror; I felt irrevocably grieved,
> wounded, but a part of my feelings started to tighten; something went
> dead; something is still crying.
>
> (Sontag 1978: 19–20).

Amidst this classic proto-language of trauma and overwhelming affect, hesitations are already emerging. In her very next paragraph, Sontag argues that images

can 'corrupt' conscience and compassion, transfixing with a shock that both rapidly diminishes and risks draining away the force of the real. Photographs, ultimately, are 'analgesic morally': they 'can and do distress. But the aestheticizing tendency of photography is such that the medium which conveys distress ends by neutralizing it' (Sontag 1978: 109–10). Twenty-five years later, Sontag's *Regarding the Pain of Others* views an accelerated circulation of traumatic images with the same suspicion: 'shock has become a leading stimulus of consumption and source of value' (Sontag 2003: 20).

A similar sort of suspicion lies behind one of the more extreme positions on trauma photography. Ulrich Baer suggests that 'photographs can capture the shrapnel of traumatic time' (Baer 2002: 7), conflating the camera with the specific psychological theory that trauma is registered outside normal memory systems. To remain true to the decontextualized traumatic image, not only must critics refrain from any historical explication, which would normalize the image, but photographic art must also resist the banalities of all conventional representations of trauma. Any direct images of the Holocaust, for instance, 'trivialize' the events with a 'mass-produced sublime' (Baer 2002: 77). The only possible aesthetic is abstract, anti-representational and ahistorical. Baer approves of one image from Mikael Levin's *War Story* (1997), a photo-book that retraces steps of Levin's father, who as a soldier helped liberate the concentration camps in 1945. The image, of a door at Buchenwald opening onto a black void, 'documents precisely the abolition of referential systems on which the notion of evidence depends' (Baer 2002: 117). Such voids are praised above 'referentially more stable photographs' because they challenge 'our understanding of reference itself' (Baer 2002: 77). This argument uses the familiar rhetoric that trauma can only be represented by foregrounding impossibility and aporia. Once again, the kitsch of ordinary culture is resisted by austere avant-gardism – in theory, at least.

That Baer upheld this aesthetic so forcefully, and Sontag returned to the ethics of photography two decades after her first intervention, speaks volumes about the place of the photographic image in the trauma paradigm. But these responses were dictated less by the sort of fine art practice I've outlined in this section, and more by the documentary images of the violence, wars and mass migrations that have typified the post-Cold War world. This era was in fact saturated with images of war and atrocity, in an environment of 'rolling' news and apparent instant access, from the Balkan wars and Rwandan genocide in the early 1990s to 9/11, the invasion of Iraq, and the condensation of American imperialism in the images of torture from Abu Ghraib prison, photographs that were leaked in 2004. In this very saturation, however, Barbie Zelizer has argued that the 1990s saw the emergence of a standardized atrocity aesthetic that testified only to 'atrocity's normalisation' (Zelizer 1998: 212). After a superb analysis of Holocaust photography, Zelizer presents a narrative of decline and fall. Shock registers diminishing returns, with images that 'lack the nuances and complications of earlier representations' and Zelizer bemoans 'the vacant nature of contemporary acts of bearing witness' (Zelizer 1998: 224 and 212). I would beg to differ. The 1990s were marked not just by a resurgence of photojournalism but a particular set of pressures on the traumatic documentary image. These conjunctures produced some of the most provoking forms of trauma culture, and it is to these I now turn.

Beautiful books of atrocity: Sebastião Salgado, Gilles Peress, Luc Delahaye

A major Sebastião Salgado retrospective exhibition was held at the Barbican Gallery in London in 2003. Salgado is a Brazilian photojournalist, and one of the most successful currently working. Originally a government economist, Salgado's allied photographic practice was deemed unhelpful by the military authorities and he spent a number of years in exile after 1969. He has since documented disappearing tribes in Brazil and elsewhere, worked with Medécins Sans Frontières in Ethiopia during the 1984 famine, and with land reform movements across Latin America, and runs his own environmental and humanitarian organization. Salgado then began to produce self-consciously global, monumental and unashamedly universalist series. *Workers* documented the shifting patterns of employment between North and South, First and Third Worlds over seven years. Another, *Migrants*, tracked the massive movement of displaced populations across the world – the starkest consequence of the New World Order after the end of the Cold War in 1989. In room after room at the Barbican, one looked, with increasing distress, at strikingly beautiful images of the desperate conditions of Kurds, Croatians, Serbs, Bosniaks, Albanians, Somalians, Sudanese, Hutus, Tutsis, Chechens, Chinese, Mexicans, Brazilians, Roma, and so on. The most anomalous thing about this exhibition came at the end, where, if you could afford it, you could preserve your memory of your visit by spending £65 on the book of the *Migrants* project or £70 on *Workers*. There was surely something deliberately disjunctive about the lavish production of a coffee-table art book containing so much stark imagery of suffering.

Yet Salgado was only one of many artists producing beautiful books of atrocity in the 1990s. The French photographer, Gilles Peress, attached to the famous Magnum agency, has produced a series of photo-books documenting sites of conflict, from the Iranian Revolution to Northern Ireland. In the 1990s, Peress published books documenting contemporary genocides, texts that occupied, as he put it, 'a no-man's-land, say, between "art" and "photojournalism"' (Kreisler 1997). *Farewell to Bosnia* was shot in the last months of the war before the Dayton Accord suspended hostilities in November 1995. A large-format book rapidly put together as a 'raw take, a non-edit' of his experience, there was virtually no text other than a brief set of citations from letters written by Peress in which he spoke of 'the curse of history' as taking a form of traumatic repetition in the former Yugoslavia (Peress 1994: np). This was followed by *The Silence: Rwanda*, a harrowing record of the immediate aftermath of the genocidal massacres of Tutsis by Hutus in April 1994. Black-bordered black-and-white images were accompanied by a detachable pamphlet which included a chronology of events and extracts from the preliminary report of the United Nations Commission of Experts intended to determine the international law to establish a tribunal for the prosecution of war crimes in

Rwanda. Peress then returned to Bosnia with a United Nations forensic team, publishing *The Graves: Srebrenica and Vukovar*, the images bracketing a long essay detailing the forensic analysis of illegal mass graves by Eric Stover, an activist with Physicians for Human Rights (Stover and Peress 1998). The photographs record the process of locating mass graves, their patient excavation, forensic analysis, and the occasional positive identification of remains. These images shift between aesthetic and evidential styles and collide with 'screen grabs' from media reports of the atrocities. The final book in this sequence was *A Village Destroyed, May 14, 1999: War Crimes in Kosovo*, the images once more accompanied by a text written by Fred Abrahams and Eric Stover on the forensic investigation into the massacre at Cuska (Abrahams *et al.* 2001). Peress' photographs are again mixed in with media reportage and the 'found' family photographs, now violently wrenched from their domestic contexts and sometimes violently defaced by perpetrators, as if ethnic cleansing also demanded the destruction of photographic traces too. All of Peress' books are lavishly produced by Scalo editions, and are sometimes virtually impossible to look at, the pages occupied by tangles of rotting corpses, amputee wounds, or the pathetic detritus of vanished people recovered from sites of atrocity.

Luc Delahaye, meanwhile, explicitly paralleled his photojournalism with fine art practice. Alongside his war-zone reportage for *Newsweek* and latterly for the Magnum agency, Delahaye took large-format pictures that are displayed as 4-foot-by-8-foot monumental panoramas in gallery spaces, photographs that included dead Taliban soldiers in Afghanistan, Israeli bomb damage in the Palestinian refugee camp at Jenin, or Slobodan Milosevic on trial for war crimes at the International Criminal Tribunal at The Hague. Delahaye argued that these images took time to take and time to absorb, thus resisting the illustrative, rapid scanning of press photography. The series won the Deutsche Börse Photography Prize in 2005. The limited edition artist's book of this series, *History*, initially sold for £1000.

The cluster of questions provoked by these books is: why have these images been put in circulation, why using the photo-essay form, and why in this 'no-man's-land' between art, photojournalism and near forensic documentation? Inevitably, the terms of debate about such images are whether they induce productive responses or aestheticize or neutralize pain. Sontag lambasted Salgado's *Migrants* project for its false universalism, 'inauthenticity of the beautiful', and its ultimate quietism:

> Making suffering loom larger, by globalizing it, may spur people to feel they 'care' more. It also invites them to feel that the sufferings and misfortunes are too vast, too irrevocable, too epic to be much changed by any local political intervention.
>
> (Sontag 2003: 69–70)

This echoed John Berger's short polemic about photojournalism, 'Photographs of Agony', published in response to the Vietnam images of Don McCullin. 'The truth is that any response to that photographed moment is bound to be felt as inadequate', Berger argued (Berger 2001: 280) The shutter isolates the atrocity as discontinuous from everyday experience and as soon as this happens the moment is 'effectively depoliticised. The picture becomes evidence of the general human condition' (Berger 2001: 281). Mystification rather than politicization attends the circulation of images of atrocity; this is why they continue to be 'published with impunity' in the mainstream press (Berger 2001: 281). Berger's despair was perhaps understandable. Written in 1972, American policy in Vietnam had not changed, despite a large anti-war movement. Photography had even played a part in that movement: the massacre of Vietnamese civilians at My Lai village in 1968 became a public scandal when Ron Haeberle's photographs of the bodies were released in 1969. One image, initially sold to *Life* magazine, was reproduced as an iconic anti-war poster by the Art Workers Coalition (see Schlegel 1995). Yet still the war continued. Similar arguments about the impotence of images have been rehearsed into the 1990s. Arthur and Joan Kleinman lamented image saturation:

> viewers are overwhelmed by the sheer number of atrocities … . Thus, our epoch's dominating sense that complex problems can be neither understood nor fixed works with the massive globalization of images of suffering to produce moral fatigue, exhaustion of empathy, and political despair.
>
> (A. and J. Kleinman 1996: 9)

Stephen Eisenman's book, *The Abu Ghraib Effect*, was prompted by what he felt was a notable absence of outrage or political reaction to the 'most searing and distubing' photographic record of government-sanctioned use of kidnap, torture and state murder in the images taken by American service personnel in Iraq (Eisenman 2007: 7).

To consider these curious artists' books of atrocity, I want to displace these familiar terms. Instead, I want to proceed in a different way, by putting up a series of contextual frames for these image-texts by Salgado, Peress and Delahaye, trying to establish a matrix of factors in the 1990s for which we need to account before rushing to any kind of judgement. I want to build up four frames: the alleged crisis of documentary photography, the fate of atrocity photography in recent journalistic reportage, shifts in international law about war crimes and genocide, and, finally, the rise of trauma theory itself.

The shock of the content of the atrocity photograph strips the viewer of all interpretive sophistication. You are overwhelmed by the index of violence, by what is denoted, and all the symbolic, aesthetic or ideological connotations of the image fall away: you drop the book in horror at what you have *just been shown*. As John Taylor says, 'Direct trauma makes connotation more difficult. The greater the trauma in the photograph, the greater are the denotative characteristics of directness, contingency and silence' (Taylor 1998: 53–4). 'Truly traumatic photographs are rare', Barthes observed as early as 1961, because this would mean all connotation had been destroyed. Even if this could occur 'the traumatic photograph' would be 'the photograph about which there is nothing to say; the shock-photo is by structure insignificant: no value, no knowledge, at the limit no verbal categorization can have a hold on the process instituting the signification' (Barthes 1977a: 30–1). Although Barthes would displace the banality of traumatic contents in *Camera Lucida*, preferring the eccentric search for the *punctum*, the weird or anomalous detail that pierced through the surface gloss and coherence of the image like a wound, he still relied on the idea of the photograph as deathly, an emanation of the lost referent itself. The photograph is intrinsically violent, 'not because it shows violent things but because on each occasion it *fills the sight by force*, and because nothing in it can be refused' (Barthes 2000: 91). In this sense, photojournalism could be seen to overcode an essentially violent form with atrocious content.

This sort of theorizing underwent two powerful challenges that converged at the start of the 1990s. The first was an aggressive demystification of the rhetoric of the documentary real. Documentary photography, especially in America, had honourable liberal, progressivist associations. Jacob Riis documented immigrant poverty to provoke liberal conscience in *How the Other Half Lives*. The organized documentation of farm worker poverty and displacement made by the Farm Security Agency in the 1930s was a New Deal project. Robert Capa co-founded the Magnum agency, which had many ties to the Communist left. In 1992, however, the radical photographic theorist and practitioner Martha Rosler declared such 'concerned' photography at an end, fatally compromised by both its liberal mystifications, its theoretical naïvety and the art-market commodification of such images. In direct parallel with the literary theory of the time, this new photographic theory also attacked the 'classic Realist text', estranging it into a strictly circumscribed set of representational strategies. In one of the most important photographic essays in this line, John Tagg exposed the ideological apparatus of the Realist photograph and did so by addressing the documentation of suffering. Tagg asked suspiciously: 'What is the function, *the office*, of "realistic" representations of "misery" in the bourgeois state?' (Tagg 2001: 107). The work of Salgado or Peress can be directly traced to this tradition of 'concerned' photography: their political aims, to such theorists, would be compromised from the start.

The second challenge to documentary photography was the emergence of digital technology. By replacing the chemical trace with informational bits, the very nature of the photographic sign was transformed, announcing what Fred Ritchin called 'the post-photographic age … in the sense that the fidelity of the mechanical age was being replaced by the fluidity of the digital' (Ritchin 1999: xi). Digital recording and storage displaced the negative as the anchor of authenticity, leaving the image open to endless manipulation. Caroline Brothers remarked on 'the breakdown of photography's indexical reality' and estimated that as early as 1989 ten per cent of colour photographs in American newspapers were digitally manipulated (Brothers 1997: 215). Revolutionary rhetorics often simplify the *ancien regime*, and the history of war photography has also always been one of trick photography, from the artful rearrangement of cannon balls on Crimean battlefields to the recent suspicions that Robert Capa's iconic image of the Spanish Civil War, the soldier caught at the moment the bullet hit, was a staged photograph. Even so, the theoretical 'crisis' of the documentary real was undoubtedly redoubled by the coincidence of technology change.

The second frame, the fate of the image in contemporary war journalism, was also dominated by a narrative of crisis in the 1990s. 'The age of the war correspondent as hero is clearly over', Phillip Knightley concluded in his *First Casualty* (Knightley 2000: 525). The fearless (or reckless) figure who compulsively sought out the limit-situations of war zones, where truth was wrestled from extremity, was inaugurated by William Hart Russell in the Crimean War, but fixed into stereotype by Ernest Hemingway or Robert Capa. The narrative of eclipse or decline began with Vietnam. Governments have been haunted by the prospect of losing wars through the image: the myth of Vietnam was that it was lost by an unfettered liberal anti-war press. Since the 1970s, war reportage and photography have been increasingly controlled by the new public-relations wings of the military. The model of this form of control was the Falklands War in 1982, when twenty-nine reporters were allowed to travel with the Task Force, only two of whom were photographers. Only three rolls of film came out of the war zone, two hundred images in total, and their release was managed by the Ministry of Defence during the course of the conflict (see McLaughlin 2002). The American army used this model of maximum constraint for the invasions of Grenada in 1983 and Panama in 1989 (indeed, no images *at all* were taken of the Panama invasion). Yet the apotheosis for many critics came not with this expunging of the image, but rather its entirely successful integration of the image into the military machine in the first Gulf War. Here the press pool of accredited reporters were contained in a centre hundreds of miles from the front and fed managed images from the nose-cones of allegedly smart bombs and fighter plane video cameras. Reportage was thus finally made indistinguishable from the prosthetics of optical surveillance (see de Landa 1991). Reporters outside the pool were obstructed, vilified and the integrity of their work undermined. Following Jean Baudrillard's account of the Gulf War as hyperreal, Caroline Brothers regards 'photography in the age of the simulacral' as suffering 'a dramatic narrowing in the sphere in which photography can operate as … a kind of witness'. She suggested that 'changing institutional and technological circumstances … increasingly denied it room to survive' (Brothers 1997: 202). Phillip Knightley has extended this coda of decline to the Kosovo campaign of 1999 orchestrated by NATO, and entitles his closing chapter, 'The Military's Final Victory'.

Yet the collapse of Yugoslavia seemed to renew the discourse of moral commitment or engaged journalism as international institutions failed to prevent Croatian or Serbian nationalists from acts of ethnic cleansing. Several Western intellectuals clearly regarded the siege of Sarajevo or the massacres in Bosnian 'safe areas' as traumatic events that constituted significant moral–political thresholds. This is what haunts Sontag's last book, *Regarding the Pain of Others*, which is full of symptomatic assertions about the reality of her own commitment to the abandoned people of Sarajevo as opposed to 'cynics who have never been near a war', 'war tourists' and other 'distinguished French day-trippers' (Sontag 2003: 99–100).

Western journalism itself convulsed in Yugoslavia: it prompted Martin Bell to denounce the tradition of neutrality at the BBC as producing 'bystander' journalism and instead offered a manifesto for a journalism of attachment. Bell spoke of untransmittable images and the limit of journalism: 'What you see leaves you simply speechless with grief: I actually couldn't get the words out, for, I suppose, the first time in my life' (Bell 1993: 9). He soon left the BBC for a bizarre career as a white-suited moral arbiter of British public life (being elected as a Member of Parliament in this guise). Several other journalists similarly argued for committed or partisan reportage in Yugoslavia: Ed Vulliamy of *The Guardian* considered the cleansing of Bosnia as 'the most hideous spectacle our generation will witness', and were events that demanded engagement: 'I think that if I did require myself to be neutral, I would not understand the war' (Vulliamy 1993: 6–7).

Memoirs by journalists from this era constitute another sub-set of trauma culture confessional: they are full of mildly alarming over-identifications and weird regrets. 'I didn't like what I saw in postwar Bosnia', one memoir ends:

> In a nostalgic and certainly selfish way, I preferred the spirit of the people during the siege. It would be too much to say that I missed the war, but perhaps it was the idealism of that time, that place, that I missed.
>
> (di Giovanni 2004: 257)

This sort of thing was denounced by Mick Hume as reducing 'complex conflicts to simple fairy tale confrontations between the innocent and forces of darkness' (Hume 1997: 4). In his polemic against the mainstream media coverage of the Balkan Wars, Hume related the journalism of attachment to a therapeutic or trauma culture. Journalists used foreign conflicts as a stage for 'existential angst' or 'a twisted sort of therapy,' in which they replaced the political with the personal and the sentimental' (Hume 1997: 18). 'In the world-view of the Journalism of Attachment', Hume argued, 'the war reporter emerges as an important, singularly moral figure with a sense of decency, in a world sullied by evil abroad and appeasement at home' (Hume 1997: 19).

Far from falling away, the figure of the war correspondent or photographer came to feature as a kind of moral limit, the exemplar of a Western society finally traumatized enough to be prompted to confused action. Three recent novels investigate trauma through the character of a damaged war journalist or photographer: Michael Ignatieff's *Charlie Johnson in the Flames* (2003) is set in Bosnia; Pat Barker's *Double Vision* (2003) includes a photographer with PTSD acquired after an incident in Afghanistan, and Andrew Miller's *The Optimists* (2005) involves a journalist sent off the rails by what he had witnessed in Rwanda. These novels use the familiar anachronic narratives, disfigured by a delayed traumatic event, here repeatedly presented as a photographic instant that intrudes on an unravelling post-traumatic life.

These frames give better means for understanding the appearance of books by Salgado or Peress. The revival of the photo-book provides a means both to counter the military control of the representation of war and the increasing consolidation of media outlets. Multinational ownership has severely squeezed the tradition of 'concerned' reportage and photography: one of Rupert Murdoch's first acts as new owner of *The Times* was to abolish the campaigning photo-essays associated with *The Sunday Times* magazine. Consolidation of television channels has also put severe pressure on liberal news outlets and campaigning reportage has been progressively marginalized. Yet Salgado has insisted that 'I don't believe that documentary photography is dying' (Salgado *et al.* 2002: 19), and has self-consciously set out to organize different routes of dissemination, working to build a counter-network of humanitarian organizations, circulating his images through globally touring exhibitions, publishing, disseminating through the internet, and waiving permissions for humanitarian usages of some of his photographs, as well as continuing to sell to mainstream magazines. Alternative distribution of documentary has also emerged, which accounts for the trend in limited cinematic releases for documentaries and the collaborations between independent cinemas and human rights organizations in film festivals around the world.

The artist's book is another means to evade media control: 'the idea of making the book a tool of independent, activist thought, has become one of the persistent elements of the mystique of the artist's book' (Drucker 1995: 8). Salgado and Peress in particular use the tradition of the photo-essay, a form that W. J. T. Mitchell describes as a 'strange conceptual space' that can foreground tensions between high art and low journalism, aesthetic and anti-aesthetic imperatives, and set word and image in a deliberately jarring tension to reanimate debate (Mitchell 1994: 321). The tensions between beauty and atrocity might also be read into the very *price* of these texts. Whilst Stallabrass worries that the 'highly formal, resolved, even excessive beauty' of Salgado's work risks 'sentimentality or mannerism', he argues that the cost reminds us of the economic structures the images might conceal: 'the form of these luxurious books becomes oddly appropriate for they are manifestly consumer items founded on labour which, in Salgado's realist mode, tends to disappear as the object becomes more perfect' (Stallabrass 1997: 158–9).

Luc Delahaye conceives of the gallery space as another kind of counter-point to the newspaper. Under contract to *Newsweek*, the images he took were 'vulgar, reduced to a symbolic or simplistic function'. The vast panoramas of the *History* series were therefore sized 'to make them incompatible with the economy of the press' (Sullivan 2003). It is also a different temporal economy too: the panorama of a funeral in Rwanda 'monumentalises an event that we would at best have only fleetingly encountered in the news media' (Durden 2005: 15). Delahaye argues that these monumental images have a greater truth-value than press photography, an assertion Erina Duganne interrogates by comparing his work with that of Alfredo Jaar. Jaar shares the suspicion that 'journalistic information and presentation actually discourage action' (Jaar cited Duganne 2006: 70). His solution is very different: his 'Real Images' series taken in Rwanda, *Let There Be Light* (1998) shows not the images but their metaphorical 'coffins' – the photographs are displayed closed away in archive boxes distributed around the gallery to create a 'cemetery of images' (Duganne 2006: 69). This recontextualization to the gallery might until very recently have been seen as a worrying form of aestheticization of war, if the gallery is still regarded as the 'white cube' that decoupled art from history. Brian O'Doherty influentially argued that 'the ideal gallery subtracts from the artwork all cues that interfere with that fact that it is "art." The work is isolated from everything ... . Their ungrubby surfaces are untouched by time and its vicissitudes' (O'Doherty 1986: 14–5). Yet the gallery might now be understood *relationally* to other institutions and against media consolidations and the control of the image since the 1980s. As Jacques Rancière (2004) would say, the distribution of the visible has changed and so, therefore, have the politics of aesthetics. An interest in 'the way that borders defining a practice as either artistic or political are drawn and re-drawn' (Funcke 2007: 285) means that distributions of the image might now make art spaces more conducive to the atrocity image, or stage the shock of traumatic realism with less compromise and without some inherent aesthetic dehistoricization.

Even so, there is always the risk that atrocity photography might pick up something like the 'journalism of attachment' as it enters the art book or gallery, merging with the confessional art that so marked the 1990s. Peress' work was not untouched by this confessional mode. One of the very short statements in *Farewell to Bosnia* read the whole sequence as triggered by personal trauma. Peress writes:

> The flashbacks started in a hospital room in Tuzla, filled with legless and armless men, all grimacing in pain. I remembered my father, his amputated arm and his pain, his descriptions of addiction to morphine, of World War Two, the German occupation and the concentration camps. A flow of buried images started to come back to me ... I began to think that I had come to Bosnia in part to see, almost to relive visions buried in my childhood memories ... . It pushed through to my consciousness that the Yugoslavs must also be going through the same experience. Fathers telling horror stories from the war ... . Here starts the curse of history, an illness that may not be so personal anymore.
>
> (Peress 1994: np)

Such a problematic account, which subsumes the war under an all-too-pat account of repetition compulsion (complete with amputated/castrated fathers), might well have been sanctioned by the confessional discourse also at work in art. That language was clearly dropped for the subsequent photo-books he produced, but it means that Peress took on contradictory elements from art-practice: a private language of traumatic iteration, alongside a more evidently political intent to use the less regulated space of art to evade the restrictions and compromises of contemporary photojournalism.

The language that replaces the confessional speech of the photographer in Peress' case is the discourse of human rights and international law. This is my third frame for exploring the appearance of these photo-essays. All of Peress' books after *Farewell to Bosnia* contain forms of legal documentation written for international war crimes tribunals. The investigation of the mass grave at Ovcara, documented in *The Graves*, produced the first successful prosecution at the Hague tribunal for the former Yugoslavia. It is therefore no surprise that some of Peress' work is resituated in another recent project that marries photography, literature, witness and legal documentation: *The Face of Human Rights* (2004), a collaboration between two lawyers, Walter Kälin and Judith Wyttenbach with the art-book publisher, Lars Müller. This is another strange, hybrid text which is half legal handbook, half unaffordable art object, the page layout busy with art photography, photojournalism, fold-out sections, and dense citations from United Nations documents, literature and witness testimony.

Why the convergence of photography and human rights? Human rights have been repoliticized since 1989 and the end of Cold War geopolitics. The United Nations delivered its 'Universal Declaration' in 1946, but the legal framework of those rights has been unevenly adopted, not least around questions of war crimes, crimes against humanity, and genocide. The first definition of genocide, by the Polish jurist Raphael Lemkin, was narrowed down from its original form, to include only 'national, religious or racial' groups. The Soviets ensured political persecution was not included; the Americans removed references to any 'cultural' aspects of genocide, as Ward Churchill (1997) records. There was also no court to try these crimes: a law commission started with proposals at the United Nations in 1950, but serious discussion was blocked until the end of the Cold War, beginning again in 1991. There were specific tribunals for Yugoslavia and Rwanda, established in 1993 and 1994, because there was as yet no international criminal court to try genocide. These tribunals came late, in part because many states actively wanted to avoid the naming of genocidal acts. When the images of Serb-run detention centres in Bosnia emerged in August 1992, White House officials were explicitly forbidden to use the term genocide 'so as not to trigger obligations under the 1948 Genocide Convention which imposes a duty to prevent and punish acts of genocide' (Scharf and Schabas 2002: 24). The International Criminal Court was finally agreed in the Rome Statute of 1998. Although it has no primacy over member states, only being able to act where internal national systems of justice are seen to fail, many states, led by America, refused to sign up to the treaty and have campaigned vigorously against it.

Against this background, photographic acts of witness to genocide or crimes against humanity took on a new urgency in a situation where it was possible that typical perpetrator denial was being reinforced by the evasions and delays of Security Council *Realpolitik*. The impotence of the UN was condemned in a sequence of accusatory books that examined the crises in Somalia, Bosnia and Rwanda: Linda Polman's *We Did Nothing* (2003) came from the Dutch context, a liberal state traumatized by the complicity of its UN soldiers in the massacres in Bosnian 'safe areas'. In a crucial way, too, it seemed that the indexicality of the photograph, a signification apparently readable *across* cultural difference, could reinforce the universalism of the discourse of human rights. Salgado is explicit about this: 'in the end, finally, the photograph is, for me, the universal language … . What you write in this language in Africa, we can read here with no translation. What you write in India, we can read in China' (Salgado *et al.* 2002: 13).

However, any self-evidence in the universalism of human rights is undercut by the ideological disputes that surrounded them as attempts to enforce treaties began in the 1990s. The dismissal of the internationalism of the United Nations is at the core of American neo-conservatism and the refusal to be a signatory to many key charters. For liberals, rights hold all states to account, and Adam Jones has spoken of a developing 'multidisciplinary field of comparative genocide studies' that targets the historical complicity of Western states (Jones 2004: 18). Yet there is also a leftist critique which sees humanitarian intervention as a new legitimation for war aims, veiled by transcendent appeals to an apolitical universal. This is the substance of Wendy Brown's critique of the kind of liberal justifications for humanitarian intervention. Rights claim to be 'an antipolitical politics of suffering reduction', but for Brown often act as 'tactics and vehicles of governance and domination' that 'produce and regulate the subjects to whom they are assigned' (Brown 2004: 459–60). Universalism, as Slavoj Žižek puts it, 'relies on a violent gesture of depoliticization, depriving the other of any political subjectivization' (Žižek 2005: 128). Perhaps nowhere else are the limitations of arguing on the basis of the image alone more in evidence than here, where the universalizing gesture of a humanitarian photography can be spun politically in multiple and contradictory ways.

Sontag's view was that 'The images that mobilize conscience are always linked to a given historical situation. The more general they are, the less likely they are to be effective' (Sontag 1978: 17). Commentators on Salgado suspect that 'universalizing images of global suffering are a bit problematic for they suggest an almost timeless, spaceless quality to human existence' (Scheper-Hughes 2002: 30). In Salgado's very reach for a universal pathos, 'there is a sort of humanism at work that invokes a community of casualties and victims which can obscure history and culture, socio-political circumstance, and retreats to a register of suffering' (Watts 2002: 38). T. J. Clark similarly 'will never forget the shock' Salgado can induce, but wonders whether there could be 'a photography of causes, not faces' (Clark 2002: 23 and 25), thus generating critique more than a diffuse sympathy. This seems to be where the marriage of traumatic image and legal text emerges. Peress accumulates more and more legal discourse to situate his images, to have them, as Sontag insists, 'embedded in history' (Sontag 1977: 17). From the fragments of personalized comments in *Farewell to Bosnia*, he attaches United Nations text to *The Silence: Rwanda*, yet in detachable form, as if he still wishes to preserve the separation and integrity of the image. Yet no image can profess self-sufficiency: as Clive Scott observes, photographs 'refer too pointedly and yet do not know how to name what they refer to' (Scott 1999: 55). *The Graves*, therefore, complexly interweaves text and image in the layout, constantly shifting the hierarchy between imagistic and textual testimony (Stover and Peress 1998). That legal text alone is perhaps not enough explicitly informs the project of *The Face of Human Rights*, which is intended to employ the affective immediacy of the visual image to bolster a dry legal discourse of human rights being placed under intense political pressure.

The final frame for these books must surely be trauma theory itself. On the one hand, I have shown how the intrusive visual image, the index of the traumatic event itself, moves to the centre of definitions of PTSD. On the other hand, cultural theory of trauma becomes increasingly suspicious of the direct image, fearing banality, psychic numbing, or the cheap sentiment of affective identification. Instead, an aesthetics of aporia or the sublime is invoked, 'bearing pictorial or otherwise expressive witness to the inexpressible', as Jean-Francois Lyotard put it (Lyotard 1989: 199). The aesthetic practice of Salgado and Peress would be anathema to a theorist such as Ulrich Baer, who regards all graphic images as narcissistic and suffering the delusions typical of 'restitutive or redemptive thought' (Baer 2002: 77). Similarly, Peress' images from Bosnia would be part of the slide into a generic atrocity aesthetic identified by Barbie Zelizer. Photographic practice is torn between two completely divergent notions of trauma.

It is probably quite easy to criticize recent atrocity photography for old sins, and some newly invented ones: representational naïvety, its continual risk of aestheticizing pain, its perverse reserves of pleasure, its subsumption into affective journalism or the discourse of personal trauma, and its potential complicity with universalism. Yet the contradictory form of the 'beautiful book of atrocity' is meant to dramatize some of these tensions. Within this form, one of the strongest thrusts I find in Peress' work is the registration of an urgency, an impatience with theories of aporia, hesitation or meta-critical anxiety. The aporia is the threshold on which academic discourse of trauma hovers, hesitating between the possible and the impossible, caught on the horns of a dilemma because every decision will produce a kind of ethical violence. As a result, Lyotard's sublime or Baer's trauma aesthetic always favours the aporetic or non-representational as the lesser evil, favouring the figural by abjecting the literal. The atrocity photography of Salgado, Peress and Delahaye, in both its practice and in the minimal commentary they have offered on that practice, is unapologetically literal – perhaps even embarrassingly so. But there are new reasons for this literalism that develop in the 1990s, as this section has outlined: changing conceptions of photographic realism; the pressure on outlets for campaigning photojournalism from consolidation of newspapers and television into multinational corporations; the geopolitics of international law on genocide; the trajectories of art and trauma theory. *Farewell to Bosnia* or *The Graves* transgress all the rules of an avant-garde trauma aesthetic, generating all kinds of accusations of appropriation, complicity, and representational violence. But that swirl of angry dispute is the very testament to the fact that we are far from deadened or inured by such images after all.

Perhaps every generation gets its defining traumatic image: Margaret Bourke-White's photographs of Belsen in 1945 or Ron Haeberle's images of massacre at My Lai in 1969. In the era of the trauma paradigm, footage of the World Trade Center attack and the digital snaps of American soldiers within Baghdad's Abu Ghraib prison remind us that photographs can always renew their capacity to shock. This is the simple point made by Marianne Hirsch's definition of 'postmemory': a new generation always has a new relationship to trauma images: 'Rather than desensitizing us to the "cut" of recollection they have the effect of cutting and shocking in ways that fragmented and congealed traumatic memory re-enacts the traumatic encounter' (Hirsch 2001: 29). Abu Ghraib even had the capacity to shock Sontag anew: 'The photographs are us', she acknowledged:

Figure 4.6 Abu Ghraib Prison, internet download (2004).

'That is, they are representative of distinctive policies and the fundamental corruptions of colonial rule' (Sontag 2004: 3). The limited number of images that circulated in the press was wounding enough; most news outlets could or would not carry the more gruesome records of sexually humiliated or desecrated dead bodies, now stored on web-sites like www.memoryhole.org. These less familiar images document some of the 27 confirmed homicides that occurred in Abu Ghraib prison under this occupying regime. The photograph of Abdou Hussain Saad Faleh, hooded, standing on a box and attached to electrical wires, has become a condensation of this atrocity (Figure 4.6). As Dora Apel (2005) notes, the image has been extracted from its context and *détourned* from a record of imperial triumph to be used in anti-American murals across the Middle East, on antiwar banners, on the cover of Mark Danner's investigative book, *Torture and Truth*, by artist Richard Serra in the *Artists Coming Together* exhibition, in culture jamming subversions of corporate adverts (iPod becomes iRaq), and even as part of the semiotics of recent cinema. The tableau is recreated in passing in Alfonso Cuaron's apocalyptic film *Children of Men* (2006) and also forms the basis on an art project that jabs at the Washington establishment in *The Walker* (Paul Schrader 2006). There are inevitable ideological simplifications that disembed the image from its original context in this process of circulation, but what it also does is return representation to the tortured. The tortured body is intended, as Elaine Scarry argues, to confer all power, all voice, to the torturer: the body is there 'to lend the aura of material reality to the winning construct' (Scarry 1985: 21).

The photograph, snatched from the circulation between American soldiers, defies this logic and denudes the rhetoric of 'liberation'. After Abu Ghraib, arguments that direct images of atrocity are crude, ineffective or sentimental seem problematic to me. Instead, they reinforce the sense that the photographic image is one of the privileged cultural forms of the trauma paradigm because the photographic image retains the capacity to shock us unutterably.

5 Flashbacks, mosaics and loops

Trauma and narrative cinema

The technology of cinema developed coincidentally alongside the burgeoning late Victorian discourse on industrial and military traumatic neurosis. The foundational stories of cinema themselves circle around profound physiological shock, fostered by the even greater indexicality ascribed to the moving over the still image. Apocryphally, audiences ran from the projected image in the Lumière brothers *Arrival of a Train at the Station* (1895), an account in which 'credulity overwhelms all else, the physical reflex signalling a visual trauma' (Gunning 1999: 819). By the 1920s, Sergei Eisenstein had theorized montage as a device 'that subjects the spectator to a sensual or psychological impact, experimentally regulated and mathematically calculated to produce in him certain emotional shocks' (Eisenstein 1974: 78) and Walter Benjamin isolated cinema's 'formal principle' as 'perception in the form of shocks' (Benjamin 1973: 171). This view was fostered from the very beginning by the seemingly irresistible temptation to elide conceptually the mechanics of film with the apparatus of the human psyche. Cinematographic metaphors peppered Henri Bergson's conception of memory processes and Hugo Münsterberg's *The Photoplay: A Psychological Study* (1915), regarded as one of the first pieces of film theory, argued from the premise that cinema objectified psychic processes of attention, association and memory. Freud, despite his refusal to act as a consultant on G. W. Pabst's film *Secrets of a Soul* (1926), similarly used the metaphorics of cinema for psychic mechanisms. In the era of the trauma paradigm, this elision still occurs. Laura Mulvey equates the cinema and the unconscious in these terms: 'Both have the attributes of the indexical sign, the mark of trauma or the mark of light, and both need to be deciphered retrospectively across delayed time' (Mulvey 2006: 9).

Cinema has become one of the key means for the narrative temporalization of experience in the twentieth century, and its specific stylistic devices (*mise en scène*, montage, conventions for marking point of view and temporal shifts in particular) have made it a cultural form closely attuned to representing the discordances of trauma. In this chapter, I want to pursue the stronger claim that cinema in fact helped constitute the PTSD subject in 1980, and that it has continued to interact with and help shape the psychological and general cultural discourse of trauma into the present day. For the first claim, I will investigate the history of the flashback, eventually incorporated into the official diagnostic definition of PTSD only in 1987, but which of course emerged much earlier in film practice, probably in the 1910s. For the second part, after the formulation and extension of PTSD in the 1980s, I want to suggest that the marked disruption of linear temporality in 1990s cinema – with plots presented backwards, in loops, or disarticulated into mosaics that only retrospectively cohere – is partly driven by attempts to convey the experience of traumatized subjectivity. Cinema has been particularly effective at developing formal conventions in which the disordering of narrative presages the revelation of a traumatic secret, one that retrospectively reorders the fractured elements of plot into a new kind of story.

As in previous chapters, evidence is taken from diverse sources in Western cinema, from Holocaust documentary to film noir, from the peaks of European art-house alienation in the 1950s to the low comedy of contemporary Hollywood. The trauma paradigm pervades Western culture, yet once more the cultural theory of trauma in cinema tends to privilege a specific Modernist aesthetic and a narrow canon of films. For Joshua Hirsch, a post-traumatic cinema of the Holocaust must work by 'rejecting the classical realist forms of film narration traditionally used to provide a sense of mastery over the past, and adopting instead modernist forms of narration that formally repeat the traumatic structure of experience' (J. Hirsch 2004: 3). Linda Williams' discussion of the New Documentary identified only a 'special few' that foregrounded the filmic construction of truth. This self-reflexivity was precisely *because* these works concerned 'traumatic events of the past' and used avant-garde strategies to convey an 'awareness of the final inaccessibility of a moment of crime, violence, trauma, irretrievably located in the past' (Williams 1993: 12 and 17). Janet Walker similarly defines trauma cinema as dealing 'with traumatic events in a nonrealist mode characterised by disturbance and fragmentation of the film's narrative and stylistic regimes' (Walker 2005: 19). Walker concurs with Williams that only 'a special few' films achieve this model (Walker 2005: 85). When she observes that large numbers of made-for-TV issue films focused on incest or abuse actually 'prefigure the explosion of radical subject and style' of trauma cinema in the 1980s they have to be understood to do so 'in spite of themselves' so as to preserve the automatic privilege of the avant-garde (Walker 2005: 59–60). Whilst E. Ann Kaplan and Ban Wang share a conception of trauma cinema's 'anti-*narrative* process of narration', they at least recognize that a codified Modernist aesthetic 'risks becoming a closure in its own turn' (Kaplan and Wang 2004: 10).

Often, this debate on the ethics of cinematic representation of trauma is reduced to praise for Claude Lanzmann's austere nine-hour documentary, *Shoah* (1985) and condemnation of Steven Spielberg's Holocaust melodrama *Schindler's List* (1993). Lanzmann can become splenetic at the very thought of an 'aesthetic' of trauma, as his appalled reaction to a question framed in these terms in a seminar on his documentary suggests (see Lanzmann 1991: 97). He condemned Spielberg's film as a gross moral offence, undertaken without thought. *Shoah* is an iconic instance for Shoshana Felman's trauma theory, foregrounding impossibility and aporia, a film that 'gives us to witness *a historical crisis of witnessing*' in a typically self-cancelling phrase (Felman 1991: 41). Spielberg, in Hirsch's curt dismissal, in contrast offers an offensive 'reactionary postmodernism' that co-opts and neutralizes the Modernist representational strategies exemplified by Lanzmann (J. Hirsch 2004: 140). Yet, as Miriam Hansen suggests, *Schindler's List* can be respected as being 'capable of reflecting upon the shocks and scars inflicted by modernity', but merely in a different, mass cultural register (Hansen 1997: 97). The automatic privileging of Lanzmann's apparent preservation of the 'ineffable' over the crudity of Spielberg is how Gillian Rose chooses to define 'Holocaust piety' (G. Rose 1996: 43). As Hansen further observes: 'whether we like it or not, the predominant vehicles of public memory *are* the media of technical re/production and mass consumption' (Hansen 1997: 98). I take the cast of my own inquiry from this comment: Hollywood representations are as important as those of the avant-garde in the co-constitution and diffusion of the trauma paradigm. Indeed, a significant mark of trauma in cinema is its constant movement between high and low forms. If I identify three trauma 'auteurs' of the fiction film later in this chapter, it is partly to observe how progressively difficult it is to situate their cinema of trauma as either marginal or mainstream, and I suspect that a thematic and/or formal interest in representing trauma is what prompts this mobility. Let's begin, though, with the central device of cinema's representation of trauma: the flashback.

A genealogy of the traumatic flashback

In the influential TV movie *Sybil* (Daniel Petrie, 1977), the protagonist's enslavement to a buried traumatic past is established within the opening five minutes. Sybil Dorsett is trying to manage a class of children in Central Park; the squeak of a playground swing prompts a virtually subliminal flashback to a rope and a pulley; Sybil's command of the children slips in her distraction; the continued squeak produces a second and third flashback, the remembered scene progressively accruing detail. The fourth flashback in this additive montage unfolds at greater length, strongly hinting at a bound child being hoisted on a hook in a barn. When we cut back to the narrative present, time has evidently slipped, and coming out of her dissociation Sybil finds herself ankle-deep in a lake and mocked by her children. The distress of these unprompted flashbacks causes Sybil more lost time and unnerving dissociations, suggested on screen by jump cuts between discontinuous spaces and time of day. The spectator soon learns that these flashbacks are intrusive childhood memories resisted by Sybil's defensive dissociation into separate personalities that don't share continuous memorial identity. Sally Field offers a virtuoso acting display of these multiple selves in her analyst's office, a role played by Joanne Woodward, herself famed for her performance of multiple personality in *The Three Faces of Eve* (Nunnally Johnson, 1957). Whilst this pulley image resolves itself into a form that the spectator can speculate over, it is more than half-way through the film before hypnosis opens out the frame of these flashbacks to reveal violent maternal abuse. The whole process of hypnotic recovery provides a much more conventional frame to signal a temporal shift in the narrative. Meanwhile, another flashback image chain, a lightbulb and a swinging metal shade, constantly recurs. It takes three hours of screen time to resolve this image into narrative form. As a child, her legs were tied to the kitchen lampshade as her paranoid schizophrenic mother enforced repeated vaginal douches on Sybil. With this scene finally recovered all free-floating visual motifs are corralled into narrative form and Sybil is able to move from victim to survivor in the key self-actualizing statement: 'I am Sybil and I remember and I hate her'. The analyst's controlling voice-over informs us that Sybil 'had reached the centre of the maze and come out whole … I celebrate the beginning of her emancipation'.

Recent cinema signals traumatic disturbance with the sudden flashback, unsignalled by either voice-over or transitional dissolve, and which is prompted analogically by a graphic (or auditory) match. The flashback is an intrusive, anachronic image that throws off the linear temporality of the story. It can only ever be explained belatedly, leaving the spectator in varying degrees of disorientation or suspense, depending on when or whether the flashback is reintegrated into the storyline. This brutal splicing of temporally disadjusted images is the cinema's rendition of the frozen moment of the traumatic impact: it flashes back insistently in the present because this image cannot yet or perhaps ever be narrativized as past. Experimental films tend to resist the kind of visual and narrative integration offered by *Sybil* in an attempt to foreground formally how the historicized image may not always be mastered by the spectator. This unsignalled flashback was invented by Alain Resnais in five revolutionary seconds in the severe Modernist film *Hiroshima Mon Amour* (1957), as we shall see, yet only twenty years later it was embedded in the mass cultural melodrama of *Sybil* as an instantly recognizable device to mark a traumatic return.

As early as 1915 Hugo Münsterberg declared the 'cut back' (as he termed it) 'an objectivisation of our memory function' (Münsterberg 2002: 90). Maureen Turim's history of the device details a fascinating interweaving of formal technique and psychological theory across the century: associationism in the 1910s, Freudianism in Germany in the 1920s and Hollywood in the 1940s, and eidetic visual memory in the 1950s. The link of intrusive flashbacks and post-traumatic stress, however, only appeared in the psychological literature in about 1985, after over seventy years of use in film. Turim points to scriptwriting manuals that were by 1922 already objecting to the overuse of flashback storytelling. Auteur theory has supported D. W. Griffith's claim to have invented the 'switchback' in 1911, although Turim suggests a more diffuse and probably irrecoverable origin. Nevertheless, Margaret's flashback in *The Birth of a Nation* (D. W. Griffith, 1915) to her lover killed in the Civil War is an important early indication of the analogy of photoplay and the psychology of memory, as Hugo Münsterberg had argued. The flashback was incorporated into the emerging narrative conventions of classical Hollywood in the 1910s: it 'depicts emotional states of mind' with images that 'symbolize the conditions that inform a character's emotional trauma' (Turim 1989: 39 and 40). There is a more experimental and subjective use in the European cinema of the 1920s, with German expressionism in particular influenced by Freud. This European usage was transposed to Hollywood in the émigré cinema of the 1940s, particularly film noir. Noir introduced an extraordinary period of complex, overlapping flashbacks, in which narrative authority and coherence was undermined by an endlessly malleable past and voice-overs that often failed to master their images. In *The Killers* (Richard Siodmak, 1946) or *Laura* (Otto Preminger, 1944) multiple perspective flashbacks swirled around a dead (or apparently dead) protagonist, a device borrowed from *Citizen Kane* (Orson Welles, 1941). *The Locket* (John Brahm, 1946) is an extreme instance of flashbacks placed within flashbacks, unfolding Chinese boxes designed to delay the central traumatic scene. Many critics have associated the labyrinthine disturbance of noir narrative with returning war veterans, who are commonly the anxious heroes of the genre (when Raymond Chandler made a wounded veteran the killer in *The Blue Dahlia* (George Marshall, 1946), the censor enforced rewrites). Film noir was 'about problems of what was defined as the psychological readjustment of returning veterans' these men 'in full, paranoid flight from the broken wartime dream of liberal rationalism' (Maltby 1994: 44 and 46). Hitchcock's popular Freudianism twice deployed the delayed flashback to recover the repressed origin of neurosis in *Spellbound* (1945) and *Marnie* (1964).

It was in the 1950s, however, that a distinct European 'art-house' cinema renewed experiment with flashbacks. The unnamed woman protagonist of Alain Resnais' *Hiroshima Mon Amour* (1957) spends one night with a Japanese lover. In the morning, as she stares down at him sleeping, the sight of his twitching fingers is disrupted by a jump cut to another body, another time. 'It is with one cut … that a new tendency in flashbacks emerges' (Turim 1989: 210). A revolutionary moment, the scene is captured spatially in the published screenplay as a double page spread of six stills illustrating the rhythm of viewpoint and memory. The image is focalized from the woman's point of view and works by a graphic match, but is otherwise unmotivated and only belatedly meaningful. According to Joshua Hirsh, Resnais reinvents the flashback here as 'mimicry and transmission of post-traumatic consciousness' and situates it in the foreground for the first time 'as a *pimary motivation*' (J. Hirsch 2004: 98). This new Modernist tactic under-determines the narrative significance of the disruptive image for a disorientingly lengthy period: this is the beginning of the contemporary convention, as used in *Sybil*.

Turim's history ends in 1985, just as the trauma paradigm was beginning to consolidate around PTSD. Turim's later reflections for a *Screen* 'special debate' on trauma surprisingly remains with Freud rather than following this turn (see Turim 2001). Yet if the modern flashback seems uncannily mimetic of the psychology of trauma, then it is probably because films like *Sybil* were instrumental in helping formulate the psychological symptoms of mental illnesses linked with traumatic origins. Ian Hacking observes in his history of Multiple Personality Disorder that Cornelia Wilbur's account of her patient 'Sybil' was written up as a 'dramatisation' by the journalist Flora Rheta Schreiber because orthodox medical journals rejected scientific papers about long-discredited 'multiplicity'. The best-selling novel and TV adaptation (with a shorter version also released as a film) helped in the campaign to enter Multiple Personality Disorder into the third edition of the *Diagnostic and Statistical Manual* in 1980. Schreiber's unorthodox form also resonated with a women's movement seeking to find new ways to confront a medical establishment that was accused of denying the pervasiveness of sexual abuse and its traumatic consequences. The book and film's triumphant reintegrative conclusion exemplified the aims of women's empowerment through therapeutic consciousness-raising. 'Buried in the depleted self', Schreiber said, 'had been this new woman, this whole woman, so long denied' (Schreiber 1975: 405). Janet Walker might criticize *Sybil*'s positivism and realism, yet it was precisely the drive to evidential affirmation of patient memory and the restorative closure of Sybil's case history that gave the text its cultural impact. 'Clinicians have written about the effect on some patients of reading *Sybil*', Hacking observes, in another instance of what he terms dynamic nominalism, that interaction of new psychiatric labels, self-narration and available cultural scripts. Yet Hacking is not implying that *Sybil* is the inaugural script for MPD and its abusive origins: multiples 'reflect or distort a far wider spectrum of current culture than that' (Hacking 1995: 47). The same is true of the traumatic flashback.

In Chapter 1, I detailed how the immediate pressure for the establishment of PTSD as a diagnostic category came from a coalition of advocates demanding recognition and recompense for specific identity groups in the 1970s. Comparative work encouraged an inclusive category of 'post-traumatic stress' to incorporate concentration camp survivors, Vietnam veterans, and victims of rape and sexual abuse. *Sybil* gave one visual narrative rendition of traumatic symptoms of abuse, including repressed memory, dissociation and flashbacks. The TV series *Holocaust* (1978) is often credited with transforming American memorialization of the genocide, although its melodramatic elements also prompted Elie Wiesel's insistence that the Holocaust could not and should not be contained within conventional filmic narrative or form. Sidney Lumet's *The Pawnbroker* (1965) provided an early use of the device of the unsignalled flashback in American cinema, used to convey the disturbing insistence of concentration camp memories on a survivor trying to overcome his losses in post-war New York. Split-second flashbacks, brought on by graphic matches, shock and disorient the viewer because they openly defy the conventions of continuity editing or the carefully framed and demarcated flashback sequence in classical Hollywood cinema (this perhaps explains why the film was independently financed and took three years to find a distributor). These almost subliminal insertions – what Cunningham calls 'a few instantly repressed, staccato flashes' (Cunningham 2001: 176) – work towards a more extended sequence that contains Sol's core traumatic memory of the camps: being forced to witness the rape of his wife by a Nazi officer. In Joshua Hirsch's view *The Pawnbroker* 'goes further than … any other film of which I am aware in its systematic efforts to mimic psychological flashbacks precisely, and to link these efforts to a systematic representation of PTSD at the level of content' (J. Hirsch 2004: 109). Yet in many ways this statement needs to be reversed: the film appeared fifteen years *before* the arrival of PTSD and the symptoms did not initially include the traumatic flashback as a significant diagnostic element. Psychiatric definitions of traumatic flashbacks in fact mimic the cinematic representations of memory in films like *The Pawnbroker*. This influence occurred belatedly because the notion of the flashback was only transformed following both the military experience and cultural representation of that combat in Vietnam.

Psychiatric research into the intrusive flashback was first undertaken by Mardi Horowitz in the 1960s, initially among the hippies of Haight-Ashbury who used 'flashback' to refer to the recurrence of hallucinogenic states long after LSD had left the system. A person who suffered this was known as a flashbacker. Flashback seemed to refer to general perceptual disturbances, but this was narrowed by Horowitz to 'recurrent intrusions of the same frightening image' (Horowitz 1969: 565). He developed this work on unbidden returning images of distress in his general theory, *Stress Response Syndromes* in 1976. In the same year, Horowitz showed test subjects 'stress films' of bodily injury (measuring their stress against 'positive' images derived from pornography with 'no hint of perversion'!). He theorized on the model of information-processing that after viewing stress films 'important but incompletely processed images remained in a form of active memory with an intrinsic tendency toward representations' (Horowitz 1976a: 1339): something like a recurrent cinematic flashback in other words. Horowitz allied his work with that of Robert Jay Lifton's accounts of the symptoms of returning Vietnam veterans, but the link of Vietnam combat experience and flashbacks was only made in the mid-1980s.

Mellman and Davis, in a study of twenty-five veterans suffering 'combat-related flashbacks,' suggested that it had been left out of the symptom clusters of PTSD in 1980 due to 'variations in the definition of the flashback' (Mellman and Davis 1985: 379). This was something that research could now address. Arthur Blank similarly remarked on the 'absence of study of flashbacks' suffered by Vietnam veterans, and noted: 'Even in clinical papers, the term is usually placed in quotes, notwithstanding its universal usage among veterans' (Blank 1985: 296). Blank suggested that the flashback had become significant once the use of the traumatic re-experiencing of Vietnam had been used as a legal defence for veterans committing crimes in America – another instance of trauma being formulated between law, psychiatry and culture. Assessing the entry of the traumatic flashback into the revised third edition of the *Diagnostic and Statistical Manual* in 1987, Fred Frankel pointed to an important but entirely untheorized shift. Drug flashback returned someone to a hallucinogenic state, where perceptual experience was generally heightened and liable to elaboration. The traumatic flashback, however, was assumed to be a precise return to a specific memory, and the image was taken to be eidetic and entirely veridical. Frankel was concerned, as were others weighing the clinical value of hypnotically recovered memories in the early 1990s, about the disappearance of suggestion (or fantasy) in this silent readjustment in the theory of the flashback. Frankel cited research that suggested flashbacks were heightened or exaggerated in 60 per cent of cases. 'Although the content of flashbacks might well be grounded at times in something that was once real', Frankel concluded, 'there is little mention in the literature that the reality for suggestible patients might easily be borrowed from the accounts in the media and from the reports of other patients' (Frankel 1994: 332). Susannah Radstone also argues for the importance of unconscious fantasy elaboration when considering traumatic memory (Radstone 2000)

Some ten years before psychiatric papers began to emerge on flashbacks in the Vietnam veteran, the cinema of the conflict was central in shifting the cultural representation of the veteran from violent misfit to traumatized, re-experiencing victim. Between 1965 and 1975 'the image of the veteran became the site where America's ambivalent feelings toward the conflict were made manifest' (Dittmar and Michaud 1990: 4). In films like *Welcome Home, Soldier Boys* (Richard Compton, 1972) or *The Visitors* (Elia Kazan, 1972) returning veterans were so alienated that exorbitant violence was the only relation to an indifferent American home front. This was the subtext of Travis Bickle's eruption of redemptive rage in *Taxi Driver* (Martin Scorsese, 1976), although there is only one brief, elliptical reference to his veteran status. After 1977, the disturbed veteran had another, more therapeutic trajectory. *Coming Home* (Hal Ashby, 1978) contrasts Bruce Dern's raging soldier with Jon Voight's newly politicized and reintegrated disabled veteran (nursed back to physical and social health by that iconic anti-war star, Jane Fonda). After this, Harry Haines discerns a 'therapeutic strategy' for reintegrating the veteran in cinematic representations. Veterans who resist this 'therapeutic fix are subject to marginalisation' (Haines 1990: 95). Active therapeutic revision or retrospective mastery of the Vietnam War is most famously associated with the Rambo films. Sylvester Stallone's hypermasculine, invulnerable cyborg of a veteran is hardly associated with psychic interiority. However, the beserker rage in *First Blood* (Ted Kotcheff, 1982) is initiated after his unjust treatment by bigoted small-town Americans prompts flashbacks to his Vietnam experience (four micro-second flashes back to imprisonment and torture early in the film provide all the motivation this Green Beret war hero needs to become a machinic killer again). Rambo is the newly theorized traumatized veteran whose rage state disinhibits impulse control and defaults him back into automatic combat reactions (something that was briefly called Intermittent Explosive Disorder in *DSM-III* before such rage was recategorized). Stallone might have enacted the Reaganite revision of the defeat over the course of the Rambo trilogy, but in each of the films the hardbody is pierced and torn and the audience has to endure Rambo stitching or cauterizing his own wounds, as if to emphasize that eventual triumph is premised on the traumatic wounding and narrative repair of the American male body.

Second World War films provided a historical displacement to address Vietnam, which explains why the film of Joseph Heller's novel *Catch 22* (Mike Nichols, 1970) is rarely mentioned in histories of Vietnam War cinema. Nevertheless, Yossarian's active resistance to an absurd and corrupt command structure spoke directly to the Vietnam situation (which Robert Lifton denounced as 'absurdist' throughout *Home from the War*). Nichols' adaptation also interspersed set-piece comic scenes with a recurring flashback, which accrues additional detail each time it returns. Yossarian's mania is at core driven by a profoundly traumatic scene on a bombing run, when one of his young crew dies messily and abjectly despite Yossarian's desperate ministrations. The additive montage starts this sequence as an initially unmotivated and puzzling break in linear storytelling; the formal delay in revealing its significance is designed to reinforce its shock. This cyclical return and uneasy tonal shift between comedy and abruptly violent imagery has proved highly influential. *Catch 22* appeared fifteen years before the flashback became a central element of definitions of veteran impulse control disorders and post-traumatic stress. Via the experiential language of the veterans, psychiatry incorporated popular visual culture.

The politics of identity in the 1970s was therefore in each case accompanied by and intertwined with cinematic representations of trauma marked by the experience of the intrusive flashback. It is intriguing to note that alongside Vietnam veterans and incest and Holocaust survivors, key theorists of trauma were at the same time researching the impact on communities of major accidents or disasters. Robert Lifton worked with the Buffalo Creek community and Lenore Terr with children from the Chowchilla bus kidnap. What relation might be established between this work and the sequence of over fifty Hollywood disaster movies that stretched from *Airport* (George Seaton, 1969) and the sequels that ended in 1980 via *The Poseidon Adventure* (Ronald Neame, 1972) and *The Towering Inferno* (John Guillermin, 1974)? These films spectacularized disaster, perhaps allegorizing the feared disintegration of the American polity (see Keane 2001). This imagination of disaster had a very different impact, however, from the intimate portraits of psychological trauma, because this cinema consolidated a specific formal device to transport the spectator into the heart of temporal rupture and psychic disadjustment, just as psychiatric advocates were formulating PTSD.

Experiment with the flashback has developed in the post-war era, pushing narrative anachrony in cinema to new levels of complexity. The 1990s marks a particularly intensive phase, a tendency bound up with the rise of the trauma paradigm. I want to track this development by concentrating on three exemplary directors before opening this into a wider consideration of contemporary narrative cinema.

Three trauma auteurs: Alain Resnais, Atom Egoyan, David Lynch

Alain Resnais invented the traumatic flashback in *Hiroshima Mon Amour*, the visual analogue of hands transposing one disaster upon another. In the film the site of the unspeakable catastrophe of Hiroshima is displaced from the narrative after the opening twenty minutes, the remnant of the documentary on Hiroshima Resnais had initially been commissioned to produce. The camera soon leaves behind the newsreel footage, Japanese film portrayals of the aftermath, and montages of the memorial and museum at Hiroshima. Instead, the disaster is addressed indirectly through the traumatic memories the city provokes in the visiting French actress. To her Japanese lover, the unnamed woman eventually narrates her transgressive love affair with a German soldier in the town of Nevers in 1944, his death on the eve of liberation, her discovery of his dying body (the source memory of the first enigmatic flashback), the woman's ritual punishment as a collaborator by the town, and her descent into madness as a melancholic means to keep her lover and herself alive in a suspended, living-dead state. Months later, she is spirited away from Nevers and arrives in Paris to the news of the atomic bombing of Hiroshima. This is told in innovative flashback form, the editing frequently stitching together shots of Hiroshima and Nevers to invent a phantom intermediate city of memory. The editor, Henri Colpi, referred to 'a kind of immediate transition which I like to call "leopard-linking," the reference being to a leopard's leap' – a way of introducing rapid ellipses that propelled the interwoven images and cross-cutting temporality forward (Colpi 1959–60: 15). At the end of the film, the woman insists on a permanent end to the intense affair – riven by contrary aims to at once to remain faithful to the memory of her German lover and to forget and avoid repeating the annihilating, mad intensity of that love. 'I'll forget you! I'm forgetting you already!' she tries to persuade herself in the last scene.

Controversy has always attended the explicit parallelism established between the public history of Hiroshima and a private story of transgression. 'There is Hiroshima's grotesque death imagery, and there is the intensity of two people coming together in bodily union, but the two themes merely co-exist', Robert Lifton complained in *Death in Life*, also noting the opposition to the film in Hiroshima itself 'because some *hibakusha* felt that its sensuality was an insult to the A-bomb dead' (Lifton 1968: 468). Julia Kristeva's reading of 'Durassian melancholy' suspects that political commitment is erased for 'an exclusive detailing of the rainbow of pain. We are survivors, the living dead, corpses on suspended sentence, harbouring our personal Hiroshima in the hollow of our private world' (Kristeva 1987: 144). In Cathy Caruth's reading, however, whilst the Japanese man's own history is occluded by the story of Nevers he is the only possible interlocutor of her story because of his own undisclosed traumatic past on this catastrophic site. Both are 'possessed' by the flashback narrative and he speaks as if from the impossible position of the dead soldier. 'It is indeed the enigmatic language of untold stories – of experiences not yet completely grasped – that resonates throughout the film', Caruth argues, allowing the lovers to 'communicate, across the gap, between their cultures and their experiences, precisely through what they do not comprehend' (Caruth 1996a: 56). This is Caruth's insistence on aporia, in this case reinforced by Marguerite Duras' extended comments in the screenplay, in which she proclaimed the aim 'to have done with the description of horror by horror, for that has been done by the Japanese themselves, but make this horror rise again from its ashes by incorporating it in a love that will necessarily be special' (Duras 1961: 9). Duras, for sure, inscribes the film within the familiar representational paradox beloved of trauma theory: 'Impossible to talk about Hiroshima. All one can do is talk about the impossibility of talking about Hiroshima' (Duras 1961: 9).

Hiroshima Mon Amour benefits from being grasped as a single element in a sequence of Resnais' films that constitute a systematic experiment in exploring how cinematic form can represent traumatic, temporal disturbance in the wake of violence or war. Resnais began his career as an editor and documentary filmmaker, including a piece devoted to Picasso's *Guernica* in 1950, focused on the painting that protested at a new kind of indiscriminate targeting in the tactics of air war. Resnais also made *Nuit et Bruillard* (1955), arguably the most influential Holocaust documentary of the era. Resnais worked from a script by Jean Cayrol, poet and political deportee to Mauthausen concentration camp. Cayrol's status as a 'political' has been held to be one reason why the film mentioned Jews only once, although this was a typical occlusion in discussions of the camps at the time. The film was composed under French censorship rules, meaning images of French detention centres were doctored to bury evidence of complicity. *Nuit et Bruillard* established Resnais' abiding theme of forgetfulness, tied to a montage that cut between ominous colour-saturated tracking shots of the abandoned Auschwitz camp and black-and-white footage of the camps in operation, gathered from a wide array of sources and arranged in a loosely sequential order to narrate the development of the concentration camp system. The voice-over continually draws attention to the inadequacy of the visual record: here 'memories are not mastered, but rather are experienced as involuntary, hallucinatory repetitions' (J. Hirsch 2004: 53). *Nuit et Bruillard* also established Resnais' method of working with screenplays commissioned from experimental writers. After *Hiroshima Mon Amour* with Duras, Resnais collaborated with Alain Robbe-Grillet on *Last Year at Marienbad* (1960), with Jean Cayrol on *Muriel* (1963), and with Jorge Semprun (another Holocaust survivor) on *La Guerre est Finie* (1966). These four fiction films each offered a new innovation with temporal montage and each experiment was prompted by an oblique, unrepresented trauma: after Hiroshima/Nevers, rape (perhaps) in *Marienbad*, torture in *Muriel* and violence in *La Guerre*. In this sense, Resnais offered a general indictment of post-war modernity. He exemplified, for Gilles Deleuze, an understanding of the catastrophic post-war moment as inaugurating a new rhythm of time in cinema. 'What we call temporal structure, or direct time-image, clearly goes beyond the purely empirical succession of time – past-present-future. It is, for example, a coexistence of distinct durations' (Deleuze 1989: xii). In Resnais' films, Deleuze observed, 'the present begins to float, struck with uncertainty' (Deleuze 1989: 116). This is a definitively *post-war* French cinema, marked by both the Occupation and the ghosts of the contemporaneous Algerian conflict, Naomi Greene suggests, as we watch 'numbed survivors chained to the past by remembered trauma' (Greene 1999: 32).

The structural and visual ambiguities of *Last Year in Marienbad* make it a cipher text, designed to drive its spectator into an interpretive frenzy. In a vast mansion and grounds, populated by barely animate aristocratic guests, the man X sets about persuading the woman A that they had an intense liaison a year before, recalling scenes in a remorseless, hypnotic discourse as the camera glides ceaselessly through the corridors and rooms. She at first claims to have no memory of these events, but she either begins to remember fragments of this affair or succumbs to X's hypnotic suggestion and imagines flashes of a possible affair, played out with the clichés of snatched meetings, jealous husbands, guns and threats. Any visual or narrative distinction between past and present or reality and fantasy is soon abolished; there is no story to reorganize into a linear sequence, only the plot spoken by X's circling, suffocating discourse. Labyrinths, mirrors, and *trompe l'oeil* effects visually repeat this confusion. The temporal disorientation of the spectator is complete: whilst the gliding and softly dissolving tracking shots suggest linearity and continuity, there is no definitive way to parse the temporal grammar of the film. There are no flashbacks in *Marienbad* because that requires orientation in time. Resnais thus formally abolishes *Hiroshima Mon Amour*'s innovation. Instead, narrative is frozen into hellish cycles of repetition.

Early interpretations tended to follow Robbe-Grillet's focus on male desire, a discourse that drives obsessively and sadistically at its object. Lacanian interpretations offer a neat fit (helped along by the delightful fact that Lacan delivered his lecture on 'The Mirror Stage' to the International Psychoanalytic Association when it met at Marienbad in 1936). X works to impose a fantasy on A, containing the Other's desire. When she begins to concur, however, this fantasy imposition collapses and disturbing images begin to cut into the smooth gliding discourse of male fantasy. This reading renders A the rather passive object of X's discourse, perhaps encouraged by Delphine Seyrig's extraordinary statuesque – indeed petrified – performance.

Other interpretations, however, pick out Resnais' one major departure from an otherwise meticulous faithfulness to Robbe-Grillet's screenplay. Resnais did not film this: 'A fairly quick and brutal rape scene … A struggles, but without any effect. She opens her mouth as if she is going to scream; but X, leaning over her, quickly gags her with a small piece of her underwear he had in his other hand' (Robbe-Grillet, cited E. Wilson 2006: 79). In the film, this is replaced by a repetitive jolting edit in a violently overlit corridor as the camera travels towards A's open embrace only to be continually thrown back by a jump cut repeated several times. T. Jefferson Kline reinterprets the film from A's perspective and inside the trauma paradigm: A is a post-traumatic abuse victim, frozen in affect, subject to alarming visions of violence and death the moment X is seen (or fantasized) near her bedroom. Seyrig's petrification and languor now take on a different aspect: 'all communicate the impairment of her mechanism of self-protection, coupled with a repetition compulsion with respect to abusive relationships' (Kline 1992: 77–8). X is not necessarily a rapist in this scenario, merely one of a sequence of obscurely threatening men. There is another clue for Kline in the way Resnais adds a further detail to the screenplay by naming the play that is being dully enacted in the opening scenes: *Rosmer*. Ibsen's *Rosmersholm* concerns a woman's decline from confident rule over a household, prompted by an obscure realization and debilitating guilt that Freud interpreted (in 'Some Character-Types Met with in Psycho-Analytic Work' in 1916) as a belated realization of an incestuous relation with her father. The film thus re-enacts the fractured temporal experience of the trauma victim, bleakly refusing to dramatize any resolution of occluded memories, and offering only a deadened, post-traumatic world of fragment and repetition. It is a long way from the teasing surfaces and anti-psychological thrust of Robbe-Grillet's *nouveau roman* style to this depth-model of the buried traumatic secret. As early as 1963, Peter Cowie had recognized the significance of the missing rape scene covered up by this 'traumatic sequence' (Cowie 1963: 149), yet Kline's reinterpretation becomes much more available with the consolidation of the trauma paradigm in the early 1990s.

Muriel is subtitled *The Time of a Return*, which might serve as another name for the traumatic flashback. Instead, the film remains steadfastly in the narrative present, refusing the complex time shifts of either *Hiroshima* or *Marienbad*. In its entrapment in the present, *Muriel* has been called 'an anti-memory film' (Monaco 1978: 89). Resnais advances by once more forbidding himself a signature technique: *Marienbad*'s gliding tracking shots are also abolished. The most striking element of the formal design is the rapid cutting that shreds some scenes into a disorienting clutter of isolated instants. The evocation of post-war Boulogne, for instance, splices together random takes of the old and new town, mixing up day and night scenes, ignoring temporal markers and deleting the role of the establishing shot to organize on-screen space. The narrative similarly wrong-foots expectations. At first, the 'return' appears to be the visit of Alphonse to Hélène; as in *Hiroshima*, they were involved in a passionate war-time love affair that began in 1939. Yet Alphonse brings his 'niece' (self-evidently his mistress) and his claims about his war-time and post-war life are eventually revealed as lies. Hélène seems equally indifferent to their shared past, whilst her step-son, Bernard, is actively hostile to the visitors. It is Bernard's recent return from war service in Algeria that shifts the focus of the film from one war to another. He announces early on that he is visiting Muriel, a girl who might or might not be sick, and might or might not be his fiancée. Later we are offered a rapid montage of his notebooks, photos and diaries with elliptical comments about Muriel. Exactly half-way through the film, Bernard runs footage of his time in Algeria through a projector: banal scenes of soldiers messing around in the sand. His voice-over, however, details the torture of an Algerian woman the soldiers name 'Muriel', who is kicked, punched, 'split open like a sack of potatoes' and who dies after thirty hours of torture led by Bernard's commanding officer. The visual ellipsis might have had to do with strict French government censorship of representations of the Algerian War: the film was made in 1962, although released after the war had finished. Yet the disjuncture of image and voice-over formally invokes the unrepresentable. This is not film but 'proof', Bernard insists, to his step-mother – who inadvertently burns the film in the projector. Once the sound recording of the torture is compromised too, Bernard performs an incoherent act of expiation by shooting his commanding officer, just returned from the war. In the closing scene, however, Resnais and Cayrol again slide one traumatic event over another. Comforting Bernard, Hélène recalls a moment from the boy's wartime childhood, when he was jolted awake by a direct hit from a German (?) bomb that destroyed his bedroom ceiling (and, we are left to speculate, killed his mother). Hélène gently corrects Bernard's recall of crucial details in this scene, yet this is a woman who is always distracted and disinterested in the past: 'Forgive me, I forget everything'. The uncertainty of one recalled event seems to infect another; Bernard's motivations seem at once over- and under-determined. In *Muriel* trauma inheres not in the burden of the past but in the unanchored and indeterminate present. This seemed to be Cayrol's aim: 'I am not interested in the events themselves but in what happens afterwards. Not the departure, but the return' (Cayrol cited E. Wilson 2006: 87).

La Guerre est Finie experiments with the anticipatory flash forward, splicing possible futures into the narrative present. This is a new means to unbalance spectators, leaving them in an always already belated relation to meaningful story. This device reaffirmed Resnais' Modernist commitment to constant reinvention of cinematic time. *Hiroshima Mon Amour* created the traumatic flashback, but subsequent films each formally eschewed what Deleuze dismissed as 'the false piety of the recollection-image' (Deleuze 1989: 122), exploring instead the multiple facets of the 'time-image'.

For David Bordwell, early Resnais possesses the signature style of the 'art-cinema mode' that appeared in post-war Europe and was formulated as a deliberate counter-reaction to the dominance of Hollywood classical narration. In art-cinema, plot has priority whilst story exposition is delayed or completely deferred, leaving permanent gaps in the narrative. Time signatures are manipulated, and the artifice of filmic composition is foregrounded to disrupt any spectatorial absorption (see Bordwell 1985). This is the cinema routinely described as Modernist and Resnais seems to confirm an intrinsic link of this form to the (im)possibility of narrating trauma in film. Yet there is also a sense of the intrinsic transmissibility of trauma in Resnais' work: one site (Hiroshima or Algeria) seems to invoke another (Nevers or Boulogne). This confirms, for me, the sense that trauma does not only stall narrative but *compels* narration too, becoming a site for the intensive production of story. This sense of overdetermined cinematic narrative that slides one site of trauma under another is also a device repeatedly seen in Atom Egoyan's films.

Atom Egoyan is an Armenian–Canadian director and artist whose avant-garde work in the 1980s has been succeeded by a sequence of films that explore post-traumatic conditions by combining formal experiment with the pleasures of narrative cinema. *Exotica* (1994), his breakthrough film, distributed by big Hollywood player Miramax in America, began a loose trilogy that included *The Sweet Hereafter* (1997) and *Felicia's Journey* (1999). These concerned childhood and communal traumas of complex kinds, each film touching sometimes very obliquely on incest. In *Ararat* (2002), Egoyan addressed the historical event that had always hovered at the edges of his work from the beginning: the Armenian genocide in Eastern Anatolia during the First World War, events from which his grandparents had escaped as sole survivors of large families. In these films (only a partial record of a prodigious output of work in different media), Egoyan has developed a particular device that opens out the traumatic flashback or narrative anachrony into a new kind of storytelling technique. This might be termed the *mosaic*, after Romney's use of the term in his study of Egoyan. The films open with short scenes of disparate figures that are only slowly brought together into a discernable pattern. These fragments can be disparate in time as well as space and the viewer has to work to organize them into meaningful relations and chronological sequence. It can take time to attribute recurrent sequences to particular characters; the tiles of the mosaic can float unanchored in the overall design, disturbing the building of story. The last enigmatic pieces of the mosaic are often delayed until the closing moments in regressive endings where the final pattern recasts the significance of every relation in the film. This structure of belated or retrospective narrative understanding is of course perfect for conveying the afterwardsness of post-traumatic affect. It extends beyond the capacities of the subjective traumatic flashback, the modular narrative 'offering a series of disarticulated narrative pieces, often arranged in radically achronological ways via flashforwards, overt repetition, or a destabilization of the relationship between past and present' (Cameron 2006: 65). 'You may not feel it, but you're in a state of shock', Noah Render repeatedly tells his clients in *The Adjuster* (1991), a man who believes he can value and compensate for every loss. The disarticulated mosaic of narrative puts the spectator in a similar state, struggling always belatedly to build a workable whole from a jumble of obscure elements.

Egoyan places himself in the avant-garde, auteur tradition (Resnais is a key influence alongside Bergman, Godard and Antonioni). His early films critiqued the lure of the image and disrupted narrative pleasure: the society of the spectacle, Egoyan said, had placed selves in an environment where they now were 'completely overwhelmed' (Egoyan and Virilio 1993: 107). *Family Viewing* (1987) and *Speaking Parts* (1989) explored video technology as a new prosthesis less of community and memory than of isolation and structured forgetting. These works were alienated and alienating, giving Egoyan a reputation as a cold 'strategist' (a term he preferred to director). Yet the films were valued as a counter-cinema that stood against 'easy kind of emotional investment' and 'the cacophonous static of popular entertainment' (Pevere 1995: 16 and 41). It was also part of a diasporic cinema, countering the homogenization of Hollywood by exploring post-colonial and other exilic identities, a particularly important stance in Canadian film-making. Some critics have therefore been suspicious of Egoyan's move since the 1990s to combine formal experiment with more conventional films: he now works with rather than against 'immediately cathartic emotional discharge' of popular cinema (Romney 2003: 14). Yet this is not some craven abandonment: Egoyan recognizes that narrative form and affective identification is the default from which traumatic disruptions generate their most transformative effects on the spectator.

Let's look at the quartet of films that starts with *Exotica*. *Exotica* is a mosaic of characters that are constellated around a strip-club in downtown Toronto. Structured as a striptease, the narrative gradually unveils a network of relations, leaving a last revelation about the exotic dancer, Christina, until the closing scene. The spectator at first can discern only structural parallels between short, elliptical units of narrative. Thomas, a gay man who smuggles exotic birds into the country, hits upon a ritual of picking up men by scalping ballet tickets, encounters that begin and end with the exchange of money. These scenes are intercut with Francis, a regular visitor to the Exotica club, where he pays for a private dance from Christina, always dressed as a school-girl. The ritual ends when the strip becomes too revealing and Francis escapes to the wash-room, overcome with distress. This is closely observed by the DJ, Eric, who pours a seductive discourse into the club's PA system about a school-girl's 'special innocence', playing to generic male fantasies. Eric's evident over-investment in the transaction between Christina and Francis is patrolled by the anxious Madame of the establishment, who has only recently inherited the club after her mother's death. Later, Francis pays off a young girl in his car at the end of the night. What seems to be another sexual arrangement is actually the second part of the ritual: he is paying his niece for babysitting for his nights at the club. Predatory behaviour is disarmed by his farewell: 'Say hi to your dad'. The spectator has to shuffle the relations again, speculate on another way of patterning the scenes.

Further disorientation comes with another brief and apparently wholly disconnected scene: a bright, lush field of tall grass, overlit compared to the dark interiors of Exotica, with a row of figures advancing from the horizon. It seems to be a memory – it is in fact the first flashback to a traumatic scene that will recur five times and develop with each return – yet is difficult to attribute it to a particular character, since in this first encounter we cut to it from Eric but cut away from it to Francis. Each time this scene recurs, subjective attribution is impossible to decide. The traumatic flashbacks seem to float dissociatively *between* characters: 'it is impossible to determine who "owns" them' (Romney 2003: 116).

The film's backbone is the structural repetition of ritualistic behaviour (we are taken through such a night four times), but the disparate characters are pulled into relation in intervening scenes and the resonances therefore grow with each repetition. On the penultimate night Francis, now barred from the club, has to ask Thomas to replace him for the private dance, and it is Christina who tells him the story of Francis. He is locked in a compulsive ritual since the murder of his daughter (found dead in her school uniform). Briefly suspected of the murder by the police, given motive by being taunted that his daughter is not his own but fathered by his brother in an affair with his wife, the strip-club ritual seems to stage a scenario in which Francis can test whether his desire could ever have corrupted his protective paternalism. 'How could somebody even think of doing something like that?' he has asked Christina in glassy-eyed horror over and over again. Meanwhile his niece sits in his empty home, babysitting his lost child.

The horror of this revelation gives Francis backstory: he is an auditor who has accumulated losses he can no longer calculate. But the ripples of this traumatic narrative spread wider: Eric, the DJ, found the body on the search-party to which we flash back. His menacing behaviour, his breaking-up of Francis' ritual at the club, is rewritten as an attempt to smash the post-traumatic fixation that binds them all to rehearsing the girl's death. That Christina met Eric for the first time in the search-party apparently links her to this revelation, but the film ends with an entirely different history between Francis and Christina. Years before, a caring and nurturing Francis drives the awkward adolescent Christina home from babysitting his daughter. Merely by hints and silences, her 'troubles at home' are made to seem portentous and in the final shot of the film a static camera stays at the end of the garden path and watches her become dwarfed by her house and reluctantly swallowed by her front door. Some critics call this an evocation of 'unspecified damage' (Romney 2003: 124), but others are more confident: 'Christina is a character who has been abused within a family context' (E. Wilson 2003: 32) or 'she is being sexually abused by her father' (Masterson 2002: 884). This last link finally rewrites the whole dance from her perspective: since the ritual demands that the lap-dancer cannot be touched, Francis can remain the benign father-figure she idealized as a young girl even within this degraded monetary and sexual transaction. This explains her devastation when Francis is tricked into touching her: the ideal father has fallen into traumatic history. Only at the very end of the film, then, can the viewer retrospectively navigate the multiple traumatic resonances that are condensed into the rituals of the dance.

Egoyan offers many signals for navigation between these short narrative units: explanation is only delayed, never entirely refused. Unlike the severe Modernist disruption of visual pleasure, *Exotica* rewards its viewer by finally organizing its tiles into a highly determined (even overdetermined) closure. This act of completion has been regarded as 'a commitment to the preservation of the symbolic order' that renders the film 'merely sad – and safe' (Schwartz 2003: 110–1). Yet the flashback scenes are never safely fixed in place. They hover between characters, as if the camera keeps such an intolerable event 'outside' any particular point of view or subjective memory, as if the camera, in fact, modelled dissociated traumatic memory. It is in the filmic narrative itself, then, that community is found between these disparate, post-traumatic people. This is the cinematic device Egoyan hits upon and explains how even the greater temporal and spatial disruptions of *The Sweet Hereafter* found commercial success.

The Sweet Hereafter won Egoyan prizes in Cannes and two Oscar nominations, including Best Director. It was his first adapted screenplay, taken from Russell Banks' novel. The title names a post-traumatic condition: a small town devastated by a school-bus accident that kills nearly all of the children on board. The narrative is initially focalized through Mitchell Stephens, a lawyer who travels to the town to persuade the parents to initiate a class action. Like Noah in *The Adjuster*, Stephens has his own stock phrases for comforting the bereaved, radiating professional calm. Like the adjuster or auditor in *Exotica*, Stephens is another professional who believes losses can be calculated and properly recompensed, even as his own accounts with his heroin-addicted daughter run out of control. Egoyan opens the film with the same mosaic structure, moving between initially unconnected figures. The innovation is a temporal shuffling of narrative units, too: we constantly move between events before the crash, the morning of the crash itself (built up through the points of view of different witnesses), the devastating aftermath, and a flight that Stephens takes two years after these events, where he narrates the story of the loss of his daughter to addiction. Threaded through these elements is the story of Nicole, the surviving girl from the accident, now paralysed, the potential star witness for the negligence class action.

The film heads inexorably towards the crash itself, which is staged half-way through the film and is presented from an austere distance, dwarfed by the immensity of the winter landscape, the children's screams barely audible as the bus sinks through the ice. Yet this convulsion, because of the shuffled time-scheme, is juxtaposed with two other revelations that adjust the centre of the narrative. First, the depiction of the crash and its immediate aftermath is split by moving forward two years to Stephens' extraordinary account of his daughter's near death from a spider bite when she was a baby. This binds in a free-floating set of images that have haunted the narrative from the beginning – a vision of sleeping parents and young child that seems to hover as an emblem of innocence and plenitude but which is now recast as a pre-catastrophic instant of bliss. Stephens has to carry his child to hospital prepared at any moment to perform an emergency tracheotomy with a blunt knife, a violence that would also be an act of love. This impossible conjuncture seems to corrupt his entire relationship to his daughter, shattering their slumbering idyll. The lawyer's drive to deny accident, attribute blame, recompense lost children, is prospectively laid bare. The second revelation comes before the crash and is retrospective: Nicole, who will survive the crash, is led by her father into a barn where they embrace in an incestuous act. No wonder when Nicole wakes in the hospital after the accident her father's first words to her are: 'Don't even try to remember'. From this point, the film largely shifts focalization to Nicole, leading to her decision to scupper her father's hopes of compensation by lying about the cause of the accident. Once again, one trauma slides over another: Nicole's private act of agency starts to redress the public fracture of community around the accident.

Egoyan noted that '*Exotica* ended with a young woman walking towards her house. With this film we go inside' (cited Romney 2003: 135). He has revealed in interview an interest in the effects of incest since dating someone as a teenager that he later discovered was being sexually abused. In the exotic dancer Christina, he aimed to explore how an abused person 'makes a parody of their own sexual identity as a means of trying to convince themselves that that part of themselves which has been destroyed is somehow not as vital as it is' (Egoyan 1995: 47). The brief scene of Nicole and her father in *The Sweet Hereafter* is highly stylized, even romanticized. They are surrounded by candles and soft light and the camera chastely swoops up into the rafters in a camera move repeated throughout the film, as if seeking transcendence or merely wishing to sway away from regarding disaster. Egoyan wanted to avoid the clichéd representation of abuse and to convey the blurred confusions of love felt by the child in the abusive relationship. In a short essay called 'Recovery', Egoyan argued that 'any child who is sexually abused must create some fantasy, however distorted, that will ease the pain of this violent transgressive act' (Egoyan 1997: 21). The placement of this scene in the mosaic does not allow the viewer to process its implications, as the bus crash comes hard on its heels. The spectator, in Egoyan's narrative design, therefore lives out the central thematic of the film: 'the politics of denial' (Egoyan 1997: 23). Thus public and private trauma converge in her deliberate lie at the legal pre-hearing. Nicole foregrounds how narrative itself is restorative even if untrue, as she stares her father down: 'I remember this. I do now. Now that I'm telling it'.

Egoyan overdetermines the film by the additional use of Browning's poem, 'The Pied Piper of Hamelin', read by Nicole on the night before the accident as a bed-time story told to two children who will die the next day. As a voice-over reiterated heavy-handedly over the second half of the film, it hammers home the obvious parallels of lost children and the lame sole survivor, but is presumably inserted as scaffolding in fear that in the temporal shuffling the audience will lose the pattern.

Felicia's Journey is considerably less innovative, perhaps because it was the first project Egoyan took from another production company rather than developing on his own. Nevertheless, the film layers different kinds of flashback to construct the psychology of the serial killer Hilditch. The audience soon knows that Felicia, the vulnerable Irish Catholic teenager that Hilditch befriends in her search for her boyfriend, is to be the next victim in a long line of 'lost girls', usually prostitutes, that he videotapes in his car. In his final confession to Felicia, he claims that he sends each one to sleep as they begin to struggle away from his suffocating care, although there is no violence depicted on screen. True to other serial killer conventions since *Psycho*, however, Hilditch is the product of maternal abuse: if the baroque dramas of demonic serial killers draw attention away from everyday statistics of murder, as Sarah Knox (1998) argues, they also tend to wave the fetish of the perverse mother to hide paternal abuse. Hilditch is completely stuck in time, slave to his mother's memory, actualized in the video recordings of her early 1960s television cookery programmes that he watches and acts out compulsively. Video's role as familial prosthetic memory has been central to Egoyan's work from *Next of Kin* (1984); in *Felicia's Journey* it also captures the humiliation of the boy Joey Hilditch, his mother's hapless cookery assistant. Egoyan Gothicizes this suffocating mother: the scratchy pixellation of video feeds into another order of childhood memory, represented by garish colour-saturated film-stock redolent of home movies. These passages are heightened evocations of the devouring mother: Joey attends the opera *Salomé* under his mother's tutelage, confused by the erotic kiss the dancer plants on the severed head of John the Baptist. This grand guignol mother wears her debts to Hitchcock heavily but Hilditch also fits into Egoyan's investigation of children who have been used and abused by narcissistic adults. There is a confusing kind of redemption promised in the line 'The healing will commence, the pain will wash away' that transfers from a belligerent evangelical Christian to Hilditch and finally to Felicia, each time changing meaning in the kind of modulated repetition that Egoyan favours. However, the film's relative linearity, with clearly demarcated flashbacks, contributes to a flatness of affect. *Felicia's Journey* is designed to draw the sting of Hitchcockian suspense and manipulation, but does so rather too well.

From the suffocating interiors of English suburban horror, Egoyan's *Ararat* returns to public history and the mosaic narrative. Indeed, the pressure of representing the Armenian genocide extends almost to breaking point Egoyan's signature devices of initially undetermined relations between characters, rapid time shifts and different levels of image status. This is perhaps appropriate: the film communicates a conflicted sense of urgency and over-choreographed design that reinforces the central concern with how to represent a genocidal act that continues to be aggressively denied by the Turkish state. Lisa Sirganian has convincingly displayed how Egoyan's early films, particularly *Family Viewing*, allegorize the fragility of memory in the Armenian diaspora, but *Ararat* was the first direct address.

There are three main strands to *Ararat*. In the first, the film director Edward Saroyan (played by prominent Armenian, Charles Aznavour) is finally making the film of the genocide he promised to his mother. The film-within-a-film provides a set of quotation marks around the restaged scenes of atrocity: illusion is consistently broken by panning to film crews and glimpsing the back-stories of the lead actors. The *Ararat* that is premiered inside the film is a genocide melodrama, the ghost of *Schindler's List*. There is an implicit critique of the economies of truth and pleasure in such epics, yet the status of these scenes shifts according to where they are placed in the mosaic. They can also serve as straight historical record rather than problematic reconstruction, important representations of something that has been systematically erased. In this I think the film resists the default objections to Spielberg, although critics have inevitably seen *Ararat* as a riposte to the 'dangerous passivity' of *Schindler's List* (Siraganian 2007: 148). The second strand concerns the art historian Ani, a specialist in the work of genocide-survivor Arshile Gorky, whose 'Mother and Child' memorial painting is for Ani the repository of Armenian history, a monument to a lost culture and diasporic melancholia. Her lectures prompt scenes from Gorky's studio in 1934 and within that his flashbacks to his mother in the years before the forced marches, starvation and deaths. Gorky is worked melodramatically into the film-within-a-film with evident fabrication, making it tricky to determine the exact status of these different levels of cinematic reconstruction of Armenian history. Ani has two children by different fathers, who are involved in an incestuous relationship. Celia eventually slashes at Gorky's painting in a refusal of personal and collective traumatic history. Raffi, however, travels to Turkey and shoots his own actual footage of the ruins of his civilization to reconnect with his heritage. The video diary we glimpse is self-evidently a counter-cinema to the epic on which Saroyan works. In the third strand, Raffi is interrogated about the content of his film canisters at Canadian border control, restaging at another level the question of testimony, truth and representation. If the customs officer cannot be persuaded that the cans contain film, they will be opened and the record destroyed. It is here that *Ararat* becomes less about the events of the massacres than 'how the genocide is mediated by the various reactions to later interpretations of this testimony by later generations' (Tschofen and Burwell 2007: 126).

The rapid movements across these three narrative strands ensure that multiple frames surround the worst atrocities depicted directly. Raffi reads out testimony to the customs officer; we see the oral report of this testimony staged in the film; we are allowed glimpses of the slaughter itself, witnessed by the fictional Gorky, but this scene is followed by the 'real' Gorky remembering these atrocities as he works over his unfinishable painting of his mother. Levels of the mediation of trauma are thus constantly shifting: cinema and counter-cinema, the possible and the impossible, flicker on screen in near simultaneity.

The weight of responsibility to represent and the counterweight of anxiety about cinematic representation renders *Ararat* a little airless, but overwhelming affect is here evidently kept in check by rigid structural and narrative design. There is something frozen in all of Egoyan's cinema, but this is precisely what makes it timely. His numbed or deadened characters, alienated from each other by technology and caught in compulsive repetitions, dramatize the post-traumatic subjectivity, whilst his narrative mosaics evoke post-traumatic community.

That Egoyan takes the formal cinematic experiments of Resnais beyond the confines of art-cinema and into mainstream cinema is not a betrayal of Modernist integrity: it is testament to transmissibility of trauma narrative. Whilst Egoyan remains rooted in an independent cinema and is ultimately suspicious of the allure of spectacle, David Lynch works his effects by an embrace of fascination with the cinematic image.

Lynch took several years struggling to complete his underground film *Eraserhead* (1977), yet three years later *The Elephant Man* (1980) received eight Oscar nominations and the Hollywood mainstream rushed to embrace his authentically Surrealist vision. The financial and critical catastrophe of *Dune* (1984) has meant that Lynch has subsequently worked mainly in the independent sector, yet he created a commercial network television hit with *Twin Peaks* (1990–1). Confusingly enough, the lush cinematic experimental narrative of *Mulholland Dr.* (2001) was built from the elements of a cancelled ABC television series, the same text cutting across commercial and avant-garde categories.

Lynch contributes to a cinema of trauma with his attention to overwhelming emotional display enhanced by manipulations of film form. Lynch's world is utterly polarized between light and dark: anxiety, dread and exorbitant displays of grief are juxtaposed with comedy, laughter and unembarrassed declaration of love. *Mulholland Dr.* and *Inland Empire* (2006) foreground the apparatus of Hollywood cinema itself for generating these extremes of seduction and terror. Although Lynch edges into many genres, the representation and generation of primal emotions suggests he principally uses melodrama, 'a mode of high emotionalism and stark ethical conflict' between exaggerated figures of good and evil (Brooks 1995: 12). Although associated with the alleged crudity of low culture, Peter Brooks argues that the melodramatic mode cuts across diverse forms: 'Perhaps melodrama alone is adequate to contemporary psychic affect', he suggests. 'It has the flexibility, the multifariousness, to dramatize and explicate life in imaginative forms that transgress traditional generic constraints, and the traditional demarcations of high culture from popular entertainment' (Brooks 1995: xii). In Lynch, traumatic affect travels through this melodramatic vector, far beyond the strictures of Modernist technique.

Since *The Grandmother* (1970), Lynch has focused on extreme representations of the family romance. The father barks and threatens violence, the mother veers between depressive silence, indifference and weirdly seductive manoeuvres, so that the bed-wetting boy generates a fantastical surrogate grandparent. The comfort she offers is short-lived. This primal scenario is repeated and modulated many times. *Eraserhead* roils with male dread about female reproduction. The sickly, mewling child that Henry fathers binds him to another dysfunctional family and leaves him obscurely menaced by devouringly seductive neighbours. Henry escapes into the fantasy world that opens up behind his radiator. Merrick in *The Elephant Man* has two fathers, the brutal freak show owner Bytes and his rescuer Dr Treves, who nevertheless horrifies himself by developing a middle-class freak show of his own. Merrick idealizes mothers, weeping openly at displays of normal family life and fetishizing his own absent mother's photograph (despite the obvious assumption that she must have abandoned her monstrous offspring). The fantasy of family generates extraordinary excesses of sentiment in the film, especially given its fragile proximity to the abuses Merrick undergoes at the hospital every night. Treves' tears when he first sees Merrick, a mix of pity and awe, are meant to trigger those of the audience. 'It's like a yawn', Lynch says of the tears that soak his work: 'it transfers over' (Rodley 2005: 167). *Blue Velvet* (1986) is another rendition of this family romance. The film opens with Jeffrey's father struck down by a heart attack, and with his mother passive and virtually silent throughout, the boy soon finds alluring and dangerous surrogate parents in Dorothy Vallens and Frank Booth, played in exaggerated, expressionistic mode by Isabella Rossellini and Dennis Hopper. Melodramatic polarizations structure everything in the film, condensed ultimately into the opposition between Sandy, Jeffrey's blonde girlfriend whose gauche innocence is always on the point of curdling, and Dorothy, the older femme fatale, a dark and eroticized mother-figure (as Michel Chion (2006) notes, she is another in a long line of severely depressed mothers in Lynch's work). Jeffrey plays out the Oedipal relation through these surrogates in starkly literal terms before returning, queasily, to small-town familial normality with parents and saccharine girlfriend restored in idyllic domesticity.

Using Dominick LaCapra's helpful distinction, it might appear that Lynch is interested less in specific, historical *losses* than in general, structural *absences* – that is, in the foundational trauma of what it means to be a subject rather than any locatable historical condition. Lynch sometimes seems in such close proximity to the primal conflicts described by psychoanalysis (another form of melodrama, Brooks proposes), that commentary in that vein can seem redundant. From *The Grandmother* to *Blue Velvet*, the films can easily be interpreted as exploring what Freud called 'the sexual researches of children' in his *Three Essays on Sexuality*. These researches produce different fantasies of origin – about where the child comes from (fantastical theories of reproduction), about the sexual act (misrecognized as a violent attack), and about the origins of sexual difference (misunderstood as castration). The famous scene of voyeurism in *Blue Velvet* is like a text-book navigation through the primal scene as described by the psychoanalysts Jean Laplanche and Jean-Bertrand Pontalis in 'Fantasy and the Origins of Sexuality'. Through the slats of a bedroom cupboard, Jeffrey sees his 'parents' engaged in an incomprehensible act by turns sexual and violent and mixed up with incoherent fantasies of birthing (the patch of blue velvet is at once comfort blanket, erotic tactile object and a surrogate umbilical cord). Identities are mobile, Frank and Dorothy moving between dominance and submission, adult and child, ritual and chance. Once Jeffrey is drawn into the scene, the scopic control of voyeurism collapses and he enters the mobile position of the primal scene, which Laplanche and Pontalis call 'a scenario with multiple entries'. 'The original fantasy', they suggest, 'is characterized by the absence of subjectivization, and the subject is present *in* the scene: the child, for instance, is one character amongst many' (Laplanche and Pontalis 1986: 22). Lynch's scene thus stages Jeffrey's traumatic entry into the dynamics of sexualized subjectivity, in a way that might have been scripted by cultural theory. Latterly, Lynch's work has also been the occasion for Slavoj Žižek to illustrate Lacan's theory of the subject. Lynch's polarized universe, where two worlds clash, dramatizes the discordance between everyday reality, held together in a functional coherence by fantasy, and the proximity of the traumatic Real that obtrudes through the veneer of normality in disgusting and terrifying ways (see Žižek 1994, 2000). In the same framework, Todd McGowan suggests Lynch systematically probes the compensations of fantasy: 'if we escape at all in Lynch's cinema, we escape into the trauma that remains hidden but nevertheless structures the outside world' (McGowan 2007: 24).

These readings produce varying levels of insight, since they ultimately redouble Lynch's avowed interest in primal fantasies. But if the work is held to be about the foundational trauma that brings the subject into being, it loses purchase on the historical, as LaCapra suggests, because it becomes an indifferent and generalized structure (LaCapra 1999). Lynch nonetheless had a considerable role in the consolidation of the trauma paradigm, which I would argue was historically specific and centred on the phenomenal global impact of *Twin Peaks* in 1990–1. Lynch's work develops from this point, his cinema afterwards pivoting around post-traumatic, anachronic disturbances to narrative.

Twin Peaks, created for ABC by Lynch and the TV-writer Mark Frost, ran for twenty-nine episodes over two series (five pivotal episodes were directed by Lynch himself). Lynch was interested in the way a television serial could at once slow down and open out narrative time compared to the confines of film. The mythos remained distinctly Lynchian. The traumatic murder of Laura Palmer takes place in an idyllic small-town American world, where every eccentricity is normalized. The very name, Twin Peaks, invokes maternal comfort and a world of oral satisfaction is implied by the communal obsession with doughnuts and cherry pie. Ben and Jerry Horne, named for ice cream, puff on outsized pipes and obsess about gourmet food. This plenitude is wrenched apart by the aching loss of the town's homecoming queen, Laura Palmer. The pilot was watched by one-third of the American viewing public, and the first season produced crazes in America, Britain and Japan. After the main murder plot was resolved in episode sixteen (under pressure from channel executives), audiences dramatically declined and the series was cancelled. The last episode, rewritten by Lynch, refused closure by ending on a dramatic reversal. The subsequent film, *Fire Walk with Me* (1992) confounded expectations and was therefore reviled: it did not finish things, but looped back obliquely to the start, rehearsing the last days of Laura Palmer and setting out to kill her all over again, the violence this time unconstrained by strict television guidelines.

The series was originally received as a stylish postmodern pastiche. It adopted the tropes of the detective series, but Kyle MacLachlan's pristine and preppy FBI Special Agent Dale Cooper displaced the bureaucratic rationality of police procedure for reliance on dreams, visions, and clues delivered by logs, dwarves, talkative mynah birds and giants on the basis of an intuitive method developed from Tibetan Buddhism. Surrealist juxtaposition – always intended to derange rational order – saturated the *mise en scène*. The episodes were stuffed with sly Hollywood references and replete with all the cliff-hanger endings, petty secrets and character reversals typical of soap opera. Characters periodically watched a dire soap-within-a-soap called *Invitation to Love* in the first series, presumed to act as a sort of homeopathic inoculation against the low culture it parodied.

Seeing *Twin Peaks* as pastiche seems a striking misrecognition now: what impresses is the wrenching *authenticity* of the emotional spectacle of the series. The season gripped from the start because it stopped to explore exorbitant expressions of grief in almost intolerable proximity and length. The pilot episode tracked the transmission of the news of Laura's death from the always weeping Deputy Andy, standing over the discovered body, to the first agonies of the parents, brilliantly staged, and the empty chair at school that provokes a wave of tears from Laura's best friend Donna Hayward all the way to the School Principal. In Lynch's typical yoking of opposites, heightened declarations of love were also present, multiplying the sickly sweet scene between Jeffrey and Sandy in *Blue Velvet* many times over in the different character strands of the soap opera format. Žižek is right 'to assert the absolute necessity of taking these excessive figures *absolutely seriously*' (Žižek 2000: 19). However, affective identification was always complicated by the weird or comical juxtaposition. Leland Palmer's expressions of grief have him riding up and down on his daughter's coffin lift or dancing compulsively to big band music whilst confused tourists mimic his painful gestures of unbounded loss. Screen space reinforced this continually with disjunctive tableaux: stuffed deer heads in bank deposit rooms; Sea Scouts bouncing balls around a writhing one-armed man. Again and again, extreme emotion was toppled into its opposite.

This signature device of jarring affect developed different connotations as the series moved towards its core revelation. Beneath Laura's typical teenage diary ('Asparagus for dinner again. I hate asparagus') was a secret diary that revealed a history of devastating molestation and abuse. The abuser is so monstrous he seems graspable only through supernatural visions. He is first glimpsed by Laura's mother who, touched by the 'little death' of trauma, becomes a visionary. The Gothic is openly invoked as 'Bob' crawls or creeps through the domestic clutter of the defamiliarized spaces of the Palmer household, distorted into vast planes of menace by low camera angles and wide-lenses so that Bob becomes the very instantiation of the 'unhomely' (*unheimlich*). In one memorable moment, Bob appears in the background of a wide angle shot of the Hayward living room and clambers over the furniture into the camera, engulfing it in a direct assault on the viewer's domestic comfort. Unresolved trauma compels repetition and Laura's cousin Maddy (played by the same actress, Sheryl Lee) becomes the victim of Bob in the fourteenth episode in a scene of shocking violence that rattles the very frame of the image (slow motion and inter-cutting extended the murder to four minutes of screen time). The episode reveals that Leland Palmer, inhabited by Bob, has abused and murdered many girls, including his own daughter. Two episodes later, in his dying moments, Leland recovers his memory of these events and speaks of his own abused childhood in the language of demonic possession ('I was just a boy. I saw him in my dreams. He opened me and I invited him and he came inside me. He made me do things, terrible things'). Here, at the height of the recovered memory movement and the theory of the subject driven by an occulted traumatic scene of childhood abuse, *Twin Peaks* belatedly rewrote itself into this narrative, thus becoming a significant cultural vector for post-traumatic theory. Queasy affect, genre slippage, supernatural trappings and Surrealist juxtaposition could be reinterpreted as struggles to articulate the secret of intrafamilial abuse. The series veers tonally because 'we still lack a settled language to talk about these things "realistically"', Diane Stevenson suggests, seeing the role of the fantastic elements in *Twin Peaks* as 'an expression of a genuine uncertainty about our understanding of family violence' (Stevenson 1995: 72 and 75). If melodrama loosely binds these elements together, then it may be because that overarching form allows 'a whole terrain of the "unspeakable" [to] be depicted' (Mulvey 1989: 73).

Television has been regarded by John Ellis as a forum for working through difficulties, seeking means to narrativize unprocessed or ambiguous cultural problematics through news, documentary, soap and drama (see Ellis 1999). Television's seriality and open-endedness encourages an unending cultural conversation. The dramatization of incest is hardly new – Janet Walker sees TV-movies from the 1970s onwards as important pioneers of a trauma cinema. The domestic intimacy of television redoubles this medium's particular power to confront the silencing of familial abuse. *Twin Peaks* was striking because it refused the traditional framing of the issue, disguising itself and then (arguably) working to transpose the secret it had revealed into a different register entirely.

For Diana Hume George, the series worked itself up to address father–daughter incest but then promptly looked away, seeking refuge in myth. '*Twin Peaks* lets [men] off the hook by reverting to a simplistic displacement to the supernatural', she argues (George 1995: 117). In the immediate wake of Leland Palmer's death, there is a reflective discussion between the stalwart good men of the town. The sheriff can't quite grasp that Bob is an elemental force of evil, an obtrusion into the world that leaves Leland an entirely innocent victim: 'I'm having a hard time believing'. Cooper's response is firm: 'Harry, is it easier to believe a man would rape and murder his own daughter? Any more comforting?' 'Maybe that's all Bob is', Albert concurs, 'the evil that men do'. In Sheli Ayers' view, Bob 'is a projection of suburban incest and bourgeois greed – a figure within an American mythology that mystifies violent domestic energies by displacing them onto the figure of the criminalised outsider' (Ayers 2004: 100) Does *Twin Peaks* work, like Stephen King's Gothic turn in *Gerald's Game*, to rebury a truth it had struggled so hard to uncover?

In 'The Philosophy of Composition' Edgar Allen Poe proposed that the death of a beautiful woman was 'the most poetical subject in the world' (Poe 1846). There is undoubtedly something unnerving in the way *Twin Peaks* circles back to kill Laura Palmer three times (counting Maddy's murder and the film's restaging of Laura's death). It is also surely intentionally disturbing that Lynch gave the job of writing the published version of *The Secret Diary of Laura Palmer* to his own daughter, Jennifer, compacting further levels of family romance around the primary text. Despite his professions of love for the character, Lynch seemed more enamoured of the dying fall, the evocation of unbounded sadness that wrapped up narrative, *mise en scène* and music into a total rendition of an affect that depended on Laura's repetitive murder. Melodrama can certainly articulate the oppressive contradictions faced by women, but also often punishes them for any transgressive attempt at resolution, as feminist film theory has noted (see Kaplan 2000, Mulvey 1989).

Yet there is a defence of *Twin Peaks*' turn towards the supernatural and mythic register as the series leaves behind Leland and Laura for a metaphysical struggle between White and Black Lodges deep in the mysterious, primal forest. Peter Brooks argues that the melodramatic mode emerges in a post-sacred secular world, but that its exaggerated emotions, gestures and emblems of good and evil are all attempts to push beyond the bland surface of the everyday to find a hidden yet powerful 'moral occult'. In terms that resonate powerfully with the vision of *Twin Peaks*, 'We want to believe, and yet cannot wholly credit, that we live on the brink of an abyss, the domain of occult forces which … infuse an intense meaning into the life we lead in everyday reality' (Brooks 1995: 205). Under the sign of this paradoxical secular sacred 'there is a resurrection of magic and taboo, a recognition of the diabolical forces which inhabit our world and our inner being' (Brooks 1995: 18–19). Laura and Leland's journey, followed by Cooper's trek into the Red Room of the Black Lodge, a mythical trial of the white knight, is thus part of the generic apparatus for a larger ethical inquiry into the way to manage the primal energies that bind or destroy family and community. In this way, the series does not displace the core of incest but scales up the trauma to become an act of almost cosmic disorder. The echoes, parallels and comic shadowings of the central story of *Twin Peaks* (the triangles of Shelley, Leo and Bobby or Andy, Dick and Lucy, the dalliance with incest between Audrey and her father, and so on) don't cover over the crime. Supernaturalized melodrama *suffuses* the small-town with the fact of abuse; it is drenched in this post-traumatic affect.

Twin Peaks: Fire Walk with Me begins by panning out from the snow of an untuned television, which is then axed to pieces. The confines of the box are resentfully smashed and we are returned to the cinema to violent effect. The punishment of the viewer continues: the film opens not in Twin Peaks but Deer Meadow, an anti-Twin Peaks where the police are menacing, the coffee disgusting and the diner has no specials. Some of the failings of the film might be related to this aggressive distancing from the series, but its main difficulty was the temporal paradox of the prequel. Lynch must trade on the accumulated knowledge of the series yet can depict only precursory events. Since attentive viewers know that Dale Cooper has become trapped in the timeless time of the other-dimensional Red Room, he and other denizens of this realm can appear ahead of time, in visions to a Laura who has understood in her final days that her father is her abuser. Sequential narrative logic is abandoned for a temporal loop in which the spirit of the murdered girl can be welcomed into the Red Room by the agent who has not, as yet, been dispatched to solve her death. There is some attempt at depicting Laura's redemption here (angels will guide her), but since the film precedes rather than succeeds the series, this emotional closure is cancelled. The series must end, with Cooper trapped, in order for Laura to be killed in the film and for the story to start all over again in a hellish loop. This cyclical logic suspends any narrative drive but intensifies Laura's doom and results in a film that is an almost abstract evocation of a post-traumatic mood that morphs into pre-traumatic dread.

Fire Walk with Me initiates a complex folding of linear narrative around a traumatic event that Lynch has explored in the loose trilogy, *Lost Highway* (1996), *Mulholland Dr.* (2001) and *Inland Empire* (2006). In each case, the central figure becomes so disturbed that they split into two or more personae. Near the beginning of *Lost Highway*, Fred hears a voice mutter the ominous news 'Dick Laurant is dead' through his intercom. The film sends him on a loop, through another version of himself, to the point at the end of the film where he can deliver this message to himself. The beginning requires the end: Fred can stitch himself back together, but something has been unleashed by his murderous jealousy and rage that ensures self-identity is impossible. Fred will circle this Möbius strip of a highway forever. In *Mullholland Dr.*, the Hollywood ingénue Betty disappears half-way into the film at the discovery of a rotting corpse. Betty is replaced by Diane (played by the same actress, Naomi Watts) in a joyless world of jealousy and despair and where the characters we have already encountered are shuffled into different roles. Diane's suicide is the corpse her alter-ego discovers: the film loops around this impossible self-encounter. *Inland Empire* fractures Nikki into at least three distinct identities, temporalities and criss-crossing realities – all are played by Laura Dern. Discernable narrative soon dissolves into a mosaic of parallel spaces and times in which 'Nikki' can sometimes impossibly view her alter-egos or even herself. In each of these films narrative causality is unhinged by violent death. The trauma splits apart narrative and character continuities, the temporal loop trying to master events but succeeding only in ensuring deadly repetition.

Inland Empire was shot on digital video and distributed by Lynch himself, suggesting that this particular narrative experiment has led Lynch back to his avant-garde origins and beyond the pale of mainstream cinema. *Mulholland Dr.* is Lynch's masterpiece because it brilliantly inhabits the lush fantasmatic world of 35 mm Hollywood Cinemascope and understands its every pleasure whilst simultaneously undermining audience investment and identification in it. Club Silencio is a lesson in this illusionism: no wonder Betty and Rita weep uncontrollably in their seats, mirroring back the reaction of the spectator. As the film cracks open around its central narrative rupture, it pours out a wave of traumatic affect that has become unanchored from narrative logic and thus permeates everywhere.

This section has risked solely associating the traumatic flashback with Resnais, the narrative mosaic with Egoyan and the temporal loop with Lynch. It is important, however, to see these experiments as part of a wide-scale complexification of narrative that has emerged in what is sometimes called 'post-classical' cinema. In the final section I want to illustrate briefly how extensive the temporal fracture of narrative cinema was in the 1990s, confirming its importance as a cultural vector of the trauma paradigm.

Trauma and 'post-classical' film since 1990

Classical cinema is an epithet used to describe a dominant mode of Hollywood film-making, a norm against which experiment has come to be defined. For André Bazin or Gilles Deleuze, classicism went into crisis after 1945 and the new cinema was associated with the baroque mannerisms of film noir or European experiments in neo-Realism and the New Wave. For David Bordwell, its principal theorist, classical cinema remained a stable set of structures and narratives developed by the Hollywood studio system between 1917 and 1960, although he has recently argued for its continuing dominance beyond 2000. Bordwell's *The Way Hollywood Tells It* mounts a defence of classicism against several claims that the disturbances to cinema in the 1990s at the levels of economics, technology and production as well as narrative have been decisive enough to produce a recognizable 'post-classical' cinema.

The classical mode is indicated by linear stories of coherent characters, stitched together by continuity editing and the drive towards definitive narrative and ide-ological closure. Whilst this has remained a dominant, this form was repeatedly challenged by popular and influential films inside and outside Hollywood that began to experiment with the time signatures of cinematic narrative. *Reservoir Dogs* and *Pulp Fiction* (Quentin Tarantino, 1991 and 1994) shuffled narrative sequences and used audacious flashbacks-within-flashbacks and complex narrative loops. *Groundhog Day* (Harold Ramis, 1993) looped in repetition of the same day, Hal Hartley staged the same script three times in different contexts in *Flirt* (1995), and the same event recurred successively with narratives looping around from differ-ent character perspectives in *Go* (Doug Liman, 1999) and more experimentally in *Elephant* and *Last Days* (Gus Van Sant, 2003 and 2004). Time travel and narrative loops explicitly featured in *Donnie Darko* (Richard Kelly, 2001), *Primer* (Shane Carruth, 2004), *The Jacket* (John Maybury, 2004) or *Déjà vu* (Tony Scott, 2006). The regressive ending retrospectively rewrote the narrative significance of *The Usual Suspects* (Bryan Singer, 1995) or *The Sixth Sense* (M. Night Shyamalan, 1999) and these 'trick' films spawned hosts of imitators. Narrative possibilities split into two (*Sliding Doors* (Peter Howitt, 1997)) or three (*Run Lola Run* (Tom Twyker, 1998)); whilst Lucas Belvaux's *Trilogy* (2002) offered three interconnecting films with all the plots taking place simultaneously, but which of course had to be viewed suc-cessively. *Memento* (Christopher Nolan, 2000) told its story backwards, as did *Peppermint Candy* (Lee Chang-Dong, 1999), *Irreversible* (Gaspar Noé, 2002) and *5 x 2* (François Ozon, 2004). *21 Grams* (Gonzalez Inarritu, 2003) fractured into a dis-ordered temporal mosaic of almost exactly two hundred narrative units linked by associative rather than successive logic. *Adaptation* (Spike Jonze, 2002) and *Eternal Sunshine of the Spotless Mind* (Michel Gondry, 2004), both scripted by Charlie Kauffman, made the dismantling of narrative time the subject of the narrative itself. These examples could be multiplied many times over.

The 'post-classical' epithet need not be a simplistic or decisive rupture but sim-ply something that marks a symptom of narrative complexification in contempo-rary film alongside the persistence of classical forms of narrative. Why does it happen in the 1990s? Bordwell's strictly formalist focus on narratological structure and suspicion of anything resembling interpretation leaves him only able to appeal vaguely to 'broader cultural factors' to explain this phase of experiment (Bordwell 2006: 33). Elsewhere, the impact of digital technology has been a frequent source of discussion. Narratives 'that foreground the relationship between the temporal-ity of the story and the order of its telling' are sometimes called 'database' narra-tives, on the basis that spectators have imbibed the new potentials of non-linear random access and hypertext links (Cameron 2006: 65). But Thomas Elsaesser has argued that the 'complex temporal schemes' of a post-classical cinema are more directly related to questions 'of memory and trauma, of anticipation and the *après-coup*, of dependence and interdependence' (Elsaesser 1998: 204–5). These transform the conceptual ground of film criticism, he argues, which needs to work through the matrix less of voyeurism and fetishism than ideas of bodily inscription and engulfment. Slightly earlier, Steven Shapiro argued for a cinema not of lack but of excess, an overwhelming experience that is inscribed on the body: 'cinema allows me and forces me to see what I cannot assimilate or grasp, it assaults the eye and ear, it touches and wounds' (Shapiro 1993: 259). In key ways, then, we might again link the experiments in the temporality of narrative in the 1990s to the question of trauma and post-traumatic subjectivity.

What narrative 'grasps together' and configures, in Paul Ricoeur's terms, is meant to unify a subject around a meaningful and coherent human narrative. The splintering of narrative in film often conveys the disintegration of the memorial self under traumatic impacts. It is striking, for instance, how often traumatic amnesia or memory occlusions drive characters, from action thrillers like *Total Recall* (Paul Verhoeven, 1990) and the *Bourne* trilogy (2002, 2004, 2007) to more formally adventurous films like *Memento*, where the central protagonist has a memory span of only fifteen minutes and is unable to form new memories, or *Eternal Sunshine of the Spotless Mind*, where Joel and Clementine elect to erase the memory of their catastrophic relationship only to then repeat it. The amnesiac quest of the central character of *Mysterious Skin* (Greg Araki, 2004) is constructed inside the trauma paradigm: in the final scene, an old school friend helps him uncover a dissociated memory of sexual abuse by their baseball coach. Such belated flashbacks to pivotal memories that transform narrative significance appear in the Gothic register, too. Ghosts that have failed to remember their own deaths – that misunderstand their own ontological status and therefore the relation of haunter to haunted – are at the centre of *The Sixth Sense* and *The Others* (Alejandro Amanabar, 2001). In *Identity* (James Mangold, 2003), the bewildered characters being killed off one by one are eventually revealed as the alters of a multiple personality, each with severely circumscribed memories. In *The Return* (Asif Kapadia, 2006), Joanna, played by the iconic horror actress Sarah Michelle Gellar, suffers from severe dissociations, time slips and overwhelming flashbacks. These initially point to a return of repressed memories of familial abuse. Having toyed with this familiar possibility, the returns prove to be supernatural intrusions of someone else's memory, however: Joanna is being directed by a vengeful spirit towards the murderer, who is using the conventions of traumatic subjectivity to lay down clues for the recovery of her own death.

Horror constantly stages the eruption of an undead past into the present, and this is why Adam Lowenstein suggests that in this Gothicized form of memory 'the modern horror film may well be the genre of our time that registers most brutally the legacies of historical trauma' (Lowenstein 2005: 10). In the controversies around 'torture porn' horror films such as *Saw* (James Wan, 2004), *Hostel* (Eli Roth, 2005) or *Wolf Creek* (Greg McLean, 2004), however, the opposite is played out: the lovingly detailed destruction of bodies, selves and therefore memories. Scenes of torture have filtered out of horror into relatively mainstream films too:

audiences must endure passages of intense suffering in *Syriana* (Stephen Gaghan, 2005), *The Wind that Shook the Barley* (Ken Loach, 2006) or *Pan's Labyrinth* (Guillermo Del Toro, 2006) as lessons in political tyranny. Bodies are tortured to give up truths, Elaine Scarry influentially argued, in societies where there is

> a crisis of belief – that is, when some central idea or ideology or cultural construct has ceased to elicit a population's belief either because it is man-ifestly fictitious or because it has for some reason been divested of ordinary forms of substantiation [and] the sheer material factualness of the human body will be borrowed to lend that cultural construct the aura of "realness" and "certainty".
>
> (Scarry 1985: 14)

Critics and film-makers of 'torture porn' inevitably reference 9/11 or Abu Ghraib as the traumas of their time in the American polity, although the allegor-ical transposition to film is not necessarily as obvious as it might be. What releases are found in the ecstatic cinematic demolition of body, memory and self? These might not be engagements with the trauma paradigm so much as attempts to transcend its legacies of burdened history and compromised, damaged selves.

'Post-classical' cinema registers this concern with memory dysfunction in the temporal disadjustment of narrative conventions, developing a paradoxically rec-ognizable aesthetic of trauma. The innovations around the traumatic flashback, the narrative mosaic and the temporal loop can thus be observed beyond my trio of auteurs in three important films since 2000: *Memento, 21 Grams* and *Elephant*.

Memento 'addresses the complexities of surviving trauma' (Little 2005: 67). The modular narrative presents colour segments that move backwards in time from Shelby's murder of Teddy and towards the moment where he decides he has to kill him. In between these regressing sequences, shorter black-and-white segments move forwards, acting as exposition as Shelby explains his condition in a phone call. These black-and-white inserts end where the colour segments begin, in a brief intersection of conventional causation at the end of the film. The narrative, however, innovatively inverts the usual relationship of progression and regression, making modular flashback the predominant structuring device. Shelby explains (and then explains again and again) that in the burglary where his wife was mur-dered, he picks up a head injury that leaves him with anterograde amnesia, unable to sustain any memory beyond haunting, free-floating flashback images of his dead wife. He is driven to avenge her death, but his disorder prohibits any notion of redemption through violence, because the act will be instantly forgot-ten. 'How am I supposed to heal if I can't feel time?' he asks. Shelby's subjectiv-ity thus renders him frozen in the timeless time of the post-traumatic condition, where time seems arbitrary but is in fact undergirded by a repetition compulsion that he cannot know or master. The film's slow revelation is that Shelby under-stands this precisely and is using his condition against himself to engineer an instant of false redemption anyway: Teddy will do, this time, as the fall-guy. The film culminates in Shelby's moment of self-knowledge that is also spectacular self-deceit, whose status is erased as soon as it is articulated: 'Now, where was I?' the film ends. Whilst David Bordwell argues persuasively that *Memento's* apparently radical narrative conforms perfectly well to classical structures (Bordwell 2006: 78–80), there is no undoing this profound unsettling of redemptive closure by the prospect of unending forgetful repetition.

21 Grams opens with short segments evidently presented in temporal and narrative disorder, a mosaic in which scenes switch apparently randomly between three principal characters. They are bound together in a car accident that is revealed thirty minutes into the film: the ex-con Jack kills Christina's husband Michael and her two daughters in a hit and run; Paul is the recipient of Michael's heart; Paul, overwhelmed with the gift of renewed life, leaves his partner, finds Christina and enters into a pact with her to kill Jack; Paul commits suicide rather than perpetuating a cycle of violent death. The fractured time scheme, at the simplest level, conveys the intense grief of shattered life stories. The accident itself remains off-screen, the unrepresentable central tile of the mosaic. Around it, connective narrative tissue is dissolved, there is no before and after, only a diffusion of traumatic affect that resists 'serial coherence' for 'circular, lateral, and diagonal' movements of narrative' (Hahn 2005: 56). 'The film challenges us,' Jonathan Romney observes, 'not only to reconstruct an original sequence but also to imagine a non-linear map of the action, in which any given moment appears to predetermine or ironically to pre-empt others' (Romney 2004: 148). The narrative form therefore reinforces the metaphysical speculations of the film on chance and destiny, chaos and faith.

The short, intense film *Elephant* is loosely based on the Columbine school shootings in Colorado in April 1999 and borrows its central aesthetic device from Alan Clarke's film about sectarian killings in Northern Ireland, also called *Elephant* (1989). The film is shot in long takes, often using steadicam in tight close-up to follow the complex trajectories of the students through the school buildings. The length of each sequence foregrounds the successive unfolding of time on-screen, but there is a jolt of misrecognition when the spectator realizes that these individual trajectories are not always successive but are often simultaneous. We thus loop around three times for the three perspectives of a simple encounter between John, Eli and Michelle in the school corridor, a looping that occupies the central portion of the film. Each tracking shot is thus literally its own time line, complete with subjective soundscape for each featured student. The effect of this looping is to dilate time, slowing it down (moments of these walks take place in slow motion too), and the reason becomes clear an hour into the film: this encounter is one of the last moments before the student gunmen enter the building and begin their massacre, in which Eli and Michelle will die arbitrarily. It's as if the film stutters and pulls back from starting this grim sequence, time curling in on itself to preserve the last moments of its innocent victims. Van Sant used a similar looping device to dilate time in *Last Days*, as if trying to hold off the inevitable violent act of suicide that concludes the film. In each case, form foreshadows the impending catastrophe.

Whilst the traumatic flashback has been embedded in cinema since *Hiroshima Mon Amour*, it is striking how quickly mosaics and loops can be processed into the spectator's understanding. Cinematic narratives don't just mimic but help organize popular conceptions of what trauma does to subjectivity. Some psychologists have been concerned at cinema's falsification of mental disorders: *The Psychiatric Bulletin*, for instance, suggested in an editorial that the Farrelly brothers' comedy *Me, Myself and Irene* (1999) was 'a golden opportunity' for professional psychiatrists 'to draw attention to how easy it is to mock or misrepresent mental illness' and that 'it is possible to object to a film like this without appearing to be humourless or cranky' (Byrne 2000: 365). I hope I have argued for a far more nuanced relationship between cinema and the psychology of trauma. PTSD is of course an internally consistent product of psychiatric discourse that defines some formations of the contemporary subject, but it also interacts with and is inevitably shaped by narratives that emerge in verbal and visual culture. The intrusive images and flashbacks that belatedly entered the definition of PTSD in 1987 were demonstrably cinematic before they were psychiatric. Narrative innovations, driven by new technologies, might also have similar effects. As Thomas Elsaesser has observed, 'trauma may here be ... the name of a particular contemporary subject-effect, as individual (or groups) try to reinscribe themselves into different kinds of media-memory' (Elsaesser 2001: 199).

Afterwards

My aim has been to provide a multi-disciplinary genealogy of the concept of trauma from its nineteenth-century origins and then to trace its permeation into the culture of advanced industrial nations after the arrival of PTSD in 1980. The risk of tracking the influence of the idea of the traumatic subject across psychology, medicine, law, military history, literature, autobiography, confessional TV, fine art and film is that it may end up conveying a sense of homogeneity, that societies are indifferently saturated with this model. If this were a record of inexorable advance, then the last stop might be a jeremiad against the rise of 'therapy culture'. American critics such as Philip Rieff in *The Triumph of the Therapeutic* (1966) or Eva Moskowitz in *In Therapy We Trust* (2001) have analysed the progressive psychologization of society and lamented the sanction of wounded narcissism in public life and civil society. Frank Furedi has argued that concepts like trauma have further extended these models: 'What distinguishes circumstances today from past therapeutic regimes is that the system of therapy is not confined to a distinct and functionally specific role, it has merged with wider cultural institutions and has an impact on all institutions of society' (Furedi 2004: 17). This takes us back to ideas of 'wound culture', in which the public sphere is increasingly only conceivable through communalities of trauma. Thus, for Richard Sennett, the fall of public man is announced with the rise of the Intimate Society, marked by the incivilities and evacuated politics of those 'who need others to enter the daily trauma of their own lives' (Sennett 2002: 265).

The jeremiad is never a particularly subtle or discriminating mode, however. Whilst it has been important to acknowledge the transmissibility that gives trauma its peculiar mobility across different knowledges, I have always wanted to respect the disciplinary or formal specificity of each discourse I have examined. Trauma changes shape and meaning as it crosses boundaries; it is constituted out of the controversies generated in these passages.

Every researcher inevitably overvalues their object of inquiry. Rather than proclaim the final triumph of trauma over a now thoroughly therapied West, I want to conclude by hinting at developments that might point to the limits of the trauma paradigm.

On many occasions in this study it is the post-traumatic phase, the sequelae, the weird effects of the afterwards, that has been the focus of concern. 'These are the days after. Everything is now measured by after', says Don DeLillo's narrator in *The Falling Man*, his novel about survivors of the World Trade Center attack (DeLillo 2007: 138). In Rachel Seiffert's novel, *Afterwards* (2007), two generations of men involved in British military occupations, Kenya in the 1950s and Northern Ireland in the 1970s, meet on the occluded ground of their repressed experience. These update George Steiner's proclamation about the brute persistence of the Holocaust: 'we come after, and that is the nerve of our condition' (Steiner 1967: ix). Post-Traumatic Stress Disorder has provided the clinical means to detail the symptoms of what is described in a wholly different register as 'aftermath society' (Chambers 2004: xxi). It would be easy to assume from a reading of cultural trauma theory that there is a kind of injunction to maintain the post-traumatic condition. To be in a frozen or suspended afterwards, it seems to be assumed, is the only proper ethical response to trauma, displacing any other memorial relation to the past and situating memory entirely under the sign of post-traumatic melancholia. This is worked out in the aesthetics of aporia or the sublime, a rigorously irresolute Modernism found in Sebald's writing or Lanzmann's cinema.

Psychiatric findings regarding PTSD may be enrolled to support such claims. But PTSD is not the only response to extreme events. Indeed, PTSD has a shadow condition that has been theorized in parallel with the emergence of trauma: resilience. Resilience is defined as '*positive adaptation within the context of significant adversity*' (Luthar *et al.* 2000: 543) The field was first sketched out in the 1970s in an attempt to understand the entirely healthy development of children in extreme environments such as parental mental illness, severe socioeconomic disadvantage or community violence. 'Early images of resilience', Ann Masten reports, 'implied that there was something remarkable or special about these children, often described by such words as *invulnerable* or *invincible*', but subsequent research has emphasized 'the ordinariness of the phenomena' (Masten 2001: 227). Resilience has extended to studies of grief, adaptation in war contexts, and reactions to traumatic events. This work has to counter the default assumptions of the trauma model that has 'tended to argue a unidimensional response with little variability in possible outcome trajectory among adults exposed to potentially traumatic events' (Bonnano 2004: 21). With this default, signs of resilience could even be pathologized: simply enduring mourning in an undemonstrative way, for instance, can be seen to be suffering from 'absent grief'.

There are now signs of a significant shift in psychiatric attitudes to people who have experienced events considered to be potentially traumatic. In the 1980s, the idea of 'psychological debriefing' was developed to counsel emergency services teams with the aim of preventing any post-traumatic sequelae. The automatic assumption of negative psychological impacts extended this model of debriefing to those involved in disasters, traffic accidents or bereavement. Yet studies began to emerge that early interventions might actually be inducing the very syndromes that they aimed to prevent. In a study of accident victims, for instance, 'patients who initially had high intrusion and avoidance symptoms remained symptomatic if they had received the intervention, but recovered if they did not receive the intervention' (Mayou *et al.* 2000: 589). Interventions into the ordinary process of grieving were found to have worsened the condition in nearly 40 per cent of cases (Bonnano 2004: 22). A large survey of the method issued in 1998 was similarly sceptical (Wessely *et al.* 1998). George Bonnano concluded that 'many individuals will show a genuine resilience that should not be interfered with or undermined by clinical intervention' (Bonnano 2004: 22).

One turning point in psychiatric practice may have been the July 7 bombings in London in 2005. In New York, 'during the immediate aftermath of 9/11, psychotherapists outnumbered victims and even began haggling for patients' (Linklater 2006: 35). In contrast, London services established limited support mechanisms but refrained from active early intervention, waiting instead to catch those whose ordinary resilience was unable to master their experience of the atrocity weeks or months later. Thousands of people on the tube system that day met the criteria of experiencing an extreme stressor event, yet diagnoses of PTSD fell vastly below usual statistical extrapolations. Psychiatric treatment now usually involves courses in Cognitive-Behavioural Therapy that 'directly confronts mal-adaptive belief, faulty attributions and inaccurate expectations' that have resulted from the event (Shipherd *et al.* 2006: 99). These are intensive, time-limited inter-ventions that emotionally and cognitively 'process' trauma in eight or ten sessions. If these approaches begin to predominate, it might be that the influence of the trauma model begins to wane.

This is not meant to diminish the very real existence of post-traumatic suffer-ing, but it is important to recognize the different trajectory psychiatric practice is taking from the assertions of trauma theory as it appears in the humanities. I have heard those invested in cultural trauma theory dismiss ideas of resilience and Cognitive-Behavioural Therapy as cynical new technologies of the self, designed to process suffering speedily, principally for financial reasons. One might note from history that every version of trauma, from railway spine via traumatic neurosis and shell shock to PTSD, has always been in major part a medico-legal concept bound up with economic questions of compensation, its treatment determined by medical and welfare costs. One of the principal reasons for the revolution in diag-nostics in the 1970s was the length and cost of psychodynamic therapies. The concept of trauma, including the psychoanalytic account, changes its very shape in relation to these concerns.

Of course, resilience remains just another kind of post-traumatic reaction. It does not displace the predominance of trauma so much as assume a different or parallel response to psychic depredation or collapse. Resilience is in many ways an anti-analytic category, suggesting that it is better to leave psychic mechanisms to operate in a closed and unexamined way. It is hardly a replacement for the pre-dominant trauma theory: if it were, the risk of denial of traumatic effects would be increased rather than reduced. It is not really the basis, either, for any form of cultural or political critique, in ways that have been pursued by those using notions of wounded or mournful communality, as in, for instance, the essays of Judith Butler in *Precarious Life*. Yet it is valuable to be made aware that psychiatric discourse assumes a *plurality* of possible responses to traumatic impacts. Cultural theory too often demands that the impossible, aporetic or melancholic response is the only appropriately ethical condition for individuals and communities defined by their post-traumatic afterwardsness.

Another limit began to be voiced towards the end of the 1990s, after numerous aid workers expressed concern about the export of the trauma model to war zones across the world. In 1995, the European Commission Humanitarian Office promoted psychiatric intervention in the ex-Yugoslav states, suggesting PTSD was likely to be the major health problem in the aftermath of the war. UNICEF's report, *The State of the World's Children* (1996), also estimated a new ten million children were suffering PTSD from ongoing or recent conflict zones. A critical collection, *Rethinking the Trauma of War* (Bracken and Petty 1998), took aim at the ethnocentrism of terms developed for Western models of the self in which individual psychology and intrapsychic conflict predominated over the collective or sociosomatic self often found outside the West. Survival, Derek Summerfield suggested, often depends on local traditions and embedded social networks left invisible to the diagnostic criteria parachuted into non-Western contexts with psychiatric technicians (Summerfield 1998). At the same time, a psychological intervention displaced more difficult engagements: 'By providing trauma programmes, donor agencies and NGOs have an opportunity to intervene in a way that is perceived to be useful without engaging with the broader political, economic, and human rights abuses that have characterised recent conflicts' (Bracken and Petty 1998: 2).

Since the end of the Cold War in 1989 global conflicts have accelerated. Wars are less often between state actors and more likely to be internal wars that are waged upon civilian populations. Civilians now constitute 90 per cent of casualties, compared to just five per cent in the First World War. These conflicts aim to destroy ways of life and bearers of cultural continuity, and so often target women and children. In the 1980s and 1990s, millions were killed in the civil wars in the Democratic Republic of Congo and Sudan, and systematic genocides were conducted against Mayans in Guatemala, the Dinka in Sudan, the Kurds and Shiites in Iraq under Saddam Hussein, the Tutsis in Rwanda and the civilian populations of East Timor. Ethnic cleansing by Serbs and Croats killed over 200,000 Europeans in the former Yugoslavia. Following the rise of extremist Islamic terrorism against Western targets throughout this period, the resultant American occupation of Iraq has killed an estimated 77,000 civilians, produced two million refugees and another two million internally displaced persons (current figures can be accessed at www.iraqbodycount.org).

Stephen Eisenman has professed amazement that the photographs of torture at Abu Ghraib jail in 2004 produced no political convulsion in America, and speculated that the images were embedded in a Western aesthetic tradition of representing violent triumph over colonized and therefore dehumanized peoples. There was no shock: this was imperial business as usual. But I also wonder if this relative indifference hasn't been due to the rise and rise of the trauma paradigm in the West in the same post-Cold War era. What appears superficially to be a paradigm that might address atrocity, genocide and war might shockingly fail to do so. Western eyes see the persecuted, 'feel their pain', and might even contribute to relief funds now and then, convulsing around contagions of traumatic emotion amplified by affective journalism. This is a familiar enough complaint (see, for instance, A. and J. Kleinman 1996). Yet notions of 'cultural trauma' applied to such scenarios might block pathways to practical politics. Abject theories of the ethical and empathetic response to the pain of the other pour out of academic presses, all of which find little purchase in the brutal geo-politics of the contemporary world. The testament of the multiple failures of practical politics, usually blocked by superpower *Realpolitik* at the United Nations before and since the end of the Cold War, is eloquent and shaming (see, for instance, Polman 2003). Perhaps we need to spend less time trying to rethink politics through the language of trauma, as Jenny Edkins (2003) suggests, and consider the virtues of holding these discourses apart. For all the demonstrable power trauma has in creating communalities, these identifications seem volatile and temporary alliances, weak against the merciless logic of military–industrial complexes.

Often enough, of course, communal entrapment in melancholia can be regarded as a vehicle for renewing cycles of violence – as in, for instance, the engineering of Serbian (and Croatian) extreme nationalism in the 1990s, premised on redressing the wrongs of the traumatic past. Judith Butler's trenchant comments on this subject are implicitly addressed to American neo-Conservative policy since 9/11: 'it would seem that I am as much constituted by those I do grieve for as by those whose deaths I disavow, whose nameless and faceless deaths form the melancholic background of my social world' (Butler 2004: 46). Some of the most interesting cultural work to emerge from the trauma question has involved an attempt to find a model of trauma that acknowledges yet seeks to *work through* the traumatic past, premising communality not on preserving trauma but on transforming its legacy. This is an attempt to transform Freud's distinctions between remembering, repeating and working in 1914 into a model for cultural or political critique. This is perhaps why Toni Morrison's *Beloved* remains such an important text: the melancholic ghost continues to haunt, but the other daughter, Denver, is allowed to start to refashion some other kind of community afterwards. Dominick LaCapra's insistence on the model of working through suggests that there is a mode that might renew cultural politics and replace displays of ethical abjection or the aesthetics of aporia (see LaCapra 2001, 2004)

But perhaps the last limit is that the concept of trauma is not, ultimately, abstract enough to explain its own relation to modernity. In Chapter 1 I argued that trauma emerged from nineteenth-century industrialism and a new 'accident cosmology' measured out in the accounts of the statistical society. PTSD coincides with late modernity, and it is surely significant that the success of this term has been coincident with an intensive phase of neo-liberal capitalism that has transformed economies and thus societies, cultures, narratives and selves over the last thirty years. The appeal of the language of trauma might be because it is a specialized sub-set of the discourse that dominates this intensive capitalist environment: risk. In the risk society, the process of modernization itself becomes the source of difficulty rather than the solution: over-population, technological saturation, pollution, or over-dependency on complex technological ensembles generate ever more risks. 'In the risk society', Ulrich Beck argues, 'the unknown and unintended consequences come to be a dominant force in history and society' (Beck 1992: 22). 'Risk society', he continues, 'is a *catastrophic* society. In it, the exceptional condition threatens to become the norm' (Beck 1992: 24). The progressive extension of what determines a stressor event in the diagnosis of PTSD is one sure way of delineating the widening parameters of risk in late modernity. PTSD remains the recognizable mental illness in pursuit of compensation claims, since all risks are claimed to be calculable, attributable and thus compensable. There are no accidents any more, only failures of risk management, and in 2001 a *British Medical Journal* editorial proposed abolishing 'accident' from the medical lexicon (cited Furedi 2002: 8). Even the horror films of the *Final Destination* trilogy (James Wong, 2000, David Ellis, 2003, James Wong, 2006) tell us this: you might escape a plane crash or multiple pile-up, but you cannot cheat 'Death's design', which is actually intricately charting the path of every life and deciding the proper moment of death. Trauma then works as the calculable measure of psychological risk but it is also the term invoked when the unforeseeable catastrophe strikes. It is a cusp term, both a product of modernity and a description of what occurs when modern systems fail. The need to circulate so many traumatic stories, finally, suggests that this has become a means to articulate some of the psychic costs of capitalist modernity. This translation into the abstract language of socio-political analysis does not for one moment deny the reality of post-traumatic reactions or abolish the relevance of professional psychology to manage such distress. But it does reaffirm the spirit of this investigation, to regard trauma as a complex knot that binds together multiple strands of knowledge and which can be best understood through plural, multi-disciplinary perspectives.

Bibliography

Abraham, N. (1987) 'Notes on the Phantom: A Complement to Freud's Metapsychology', trans. N. Rand, *Critical Inquiry* 13: 287–92.

Abraham, N. and M. Torok (1980) 'Introjection – Incorporation: Mourning or Melancholia', trans. N. Rand, in S. Lebovici and D. Widlocher (eds), *Psychoanalysis in France*, New York: International University Press, 3–16.

——(1984) 'A Poetics of Psychoanalysis: "The Lost Object – Me"', trans. N. Rand, *Substance* 43: 3–18.

——(1994) *The Shell and the Kernel: Renewals of Psychoanalysis*, trans. N. Rand, Chicago: University of Chicago Press.

Abrahams, F., G. Peress and E. Stover (2001) *A Village Destroyed, May 14, 1999: War Crimes in Kosovo*, Berkeley: University of California Press.

Adams, T. (2006) 'From Dave Pelzer to the Latest Women's Magazine, the Misery Memoir is a Surefire Bestseller. But Why are We so Addicted to Other People's Agony?' *The Observer*, 29 January: 4–5.

Addley, E. (2006) 'Author Accused of Literary Fraud says: "I am not a liar. And I am not running any more"', *The Guardian*, 23 September 3.

Adorno, T. (1973) *Negative Dialectics*, trans. A. B. Ashton, London: Routledge.

——(1981) *Prisms*, trans. S. and S. Weber, Cambridge: MIT Press.

Adshead, G. and Mezey, G. (1997) 'Post-traumatic Stress Reactions and the Criminal Law', in D. Black *et al.* (eds), *Psychological Trauma: A Developmental Approach*, London: Gaskell, 351–62.

Agamben, G. (1999) *Remnants of Auschwitz: The Witness and the Archive*, trans. D. Heller-Roazen, New York: Zone.

Alcoff, L. and L. Gray (1993) 'Survivor Discourse: Transgression or Recuperation?', *Signs* 18/2: 260–90.

Alexander, E. (1980) 'Stealing the Holocaust', *Midstream*, Nov: 46–50.

Alexander, J. (2004) 'Towards a Theory of Cultural Trauma', in J. Alexander *et al.* (eds), *Cultural Trauma and Collective Identity*, Berkeley: University of California Press, 1–30.

Allen, G. (1894) *Post-Prandial Philosophy*, London: Chatto and Windus.

American Psychiatric Association (1980) *Diagnostic and Statistical Manual*, 3rd edn, Washington: APA.

——(1987) *Diagnostic and Statistical Manual*, 3rd rev. edn, Washington: APA.

——(1994) *Diagnostic and Statistical Manual*, 4th edn, Washington: APA.

——(2000) *Diagnostic and Statistical Manual*, 4th rev. edn, Washington: APA.

Amis, M. (1999) *Experience*, London: Jonathan Cape.

Anderson, Linda (2004) *Autobiography*, London: Routledge.

Antze, P. and M. Lambek (1996) 'Forecasting Memory', in P. Antze and M. Lambek (eds), *Tense Past: Cultural Essays in Trauma and Memory*, London: Routledge, xi-xxxviii.

Apel, D. (2005) 'Torture Culture: Lynching Photographs and the Images of Abu Ghraib', *Art Journal* 64/2: 89–100.

Appignanesi, L. (2000) *Losing the Dead*, London: Vintage.

Armstrong, I. (2000) *The Radical Aesthetic*, Oxford: Blackwell.

Armstrong, T. (2005) *Modernism*, Cambridge: Polity.

Atkinson, K. (1996) *Behind the Scenes at the Museum*, London: Black Swan.
Ayers, S. (2004) '*Twin Peaks*, Weak Language and the Resurrection of Affect', in E. Sheen and A. Davison (eds), *The Cinema of David Lynch: American Dreams, Nightmare Visions*, London: Wallflower, 93–106.
Babinski, J. and J. Fremont (1918) *Hysteria or Pithiatism, and Reflex Nervous Disorders in the Neurology of War*, trans. J. D. Rolleston, London: University of London Press.
Baer, U. (2002) *Spectral Evidence: The Photography of Trauma*, Cambridge, MA: MIT.
Ballard, J. G. (1991) *The Kindness of Women*, London: HarperCollins.
Barker, P. (1992) *Regeneration*, London: Penguin.
——(1993) *The Eye in the Door*, London: Viking.
——(1995) *The Ghost Road*, London: Viking.
Barthes, R. (1977a) 'The Photographic Message', in *Image Music Text*, trans. S. Heath, New York: Noonday: 15–31.
——(1977b) *Roland Barthes*, trans. R. Howard, London: Macmillan.
——(2000) *Camera Lucida: Reflections on Photography*, trans. R. Howard, London: Vintage.
Barton, L. (2006) 'The Man Who Re-Wrote His Life', *The Guardian*, G2, 15 September: 6–11.
Bartrip, P. (1985) 'The Rise and Decline of Workmen's Compensation', in P. Weindling (ed.): 157–79.
Bartrip, P. W. J. and S. B. Burman (1983) *The Wounded Soldiers of Industry: Industrial Compensation Policy 1833–1897*, Oxford: Clarendon Press.
Bass, E. and L. Davis (2002) *The Courage to Heal: A Guide for Women Survivors of Sexual Abuse*, London: Vermilion. (First published New York, 1988.)
'Battle Shock. The Wounded Mind and its Cure' (1915) *The Times*, 25 May: 11.
Bauman, Z. (1989) *The Holocaust and Modernity*, Cambridge: Polity.
Beck, U. (1992) *Risk Society: Towards a New Modernity*, trans. M. Ritter, London: Sage.
Beech, D. and J. Roberts (eds) (2002) *The Philistine Controversy*, London: Verso.
Bell, M. (1993) 'Testament of an Interventionist', *British Journalism Review* 4/4: 8–11.
Benjamin, W. (1973) 'On Some Motifs in Baudelaire', *Illuminations*, trans. H. Zohn, London: Fontana: 152–96.
Bennett, J. (2005) *Empathic Vision: Affect, Trauma and Contemporary Art*, Stanford, CA: Stanford University Press.
Benstock, S. (1988) 'Authorizing the Autobiographical', in S. Benstock (ed.), *The Private Self: Theory and Practice of Women's Autobiographical Writing*, London: Routledge.
Berger, J. (2001) 'Photographs of Agony', in *Selected Essays*, London: Bloomsbury: 279–81.
Berman, M. (1983) *All That is Solid Melts into Air*, London: Verso.
Bernheim, H. (1980) *New Studies in Hypnotism*, trans. R. S. Sandor of *Hypnotisme, Suggestion, Psychothérapie* (1891), New York: International Universities Press.
Bettelheim, B. (1943) 'Individual and Mass Behaviour in Extreme Situations', *Journal of Abnormal Psychology* 38: 417–52.
——(1960) *The Informed Heart: The Human Condition in Modern Mass Society*, London: Thames & Hudson.
——(1979) *Surviving, and Other Essays*, London: Thames & Hudson.
Beverley, J. (1992) 'The Margin at the Center: On *Testimonio* (Testimonial Narrative)', in S. Smith and J. Watson (eds), *De/Colonizing the Subject: The Politics of Gender in Women's Autobiography*, Minneapolis, MN: University of Minnesota Press, 91–114.
Binet, A. (1977) *On Double Consciousness* (1890), ed. D. Robinson, Significant Contributions to the History of Psychology 1750–1920 Series, Washington, DC: University Publications of America.
Binneveld, H. (1997) *From Shell Shock to Combat Stress: A Comparative History of Military Psychiatry*, trans. John O'Kane, Amsterdam: Amsterdam University Press.
Black, S. E. (1981) 'Pseudopods and Synapses: The Amoeboid Theories of Neuronal Mobility and the Early Formulation of the Synapse 1894–1900', *Bulletin of the History of Medicine* 55: 43–58.
Blank, A. (1985) 'The Unconscious Flashback to the War in Viet Nam Veterans: Clinical Mystery, Legal Defense, and Community Problem', in S. M. Sonnenberg, A. S. Blank and J. A. Talbott (eds), *The Trauma of War: Stress and Recovery in Viet Nam Veterans*, Washington, DC: American Psychiatric Press, 293–308.
Bloxham, D. (2004) 'The Missing Camps of *Aktion Reinhard*: The Judicial Displacement of a Mass Murder', in P. Gray and K. Oliver (eds), *The Memory of Catastrophe*: 118–31.

Bogacz, T. (1989) 'War Neurosis and Cultural Change in England, 1914–22: The Work of the War Office Committee of Enquiry into "Shell-Shock"', *Journal of Contemporary History* 24: 227–56.

Bois, Y-A. (1992) 'Painting: The Task of Mourning,' in F. Frascina and J. Harris (eds), *Art in Modern Culture*, London: Phaidon: 326–9.

Bonnano, G. A. (2004) 'Loss, Trauma and Human Resilience: Have we Misunderstood the Human Capacity to Thrive after Extremely Adverse Events?', *American Psychologist* 59: 20–8.

Borch-Jacobsen, M. (1993) *The Emotional Tie: Psychoanalysis, Mimesis, Affect*, trans. Douglas Brick *et al.*, New Haven: Yale University Press.

——(1994) 'Who's Who? Introducing Multiple Personality', in J. Copjek (ed.), *Supposing the Subject*, London: Verso: 45–63.

——(1996) 'Neurotica: Freud and the Seduction Theory', *October* 76: 15–43.

Bordwell, D. (1985) *Narration in the Fiction Film*, Madison, WI: University of Wisconsin Press.

——(2006) *The Way Hollywood Tells It: Story and Style in Modern Movies*, Berkeley, CA: University of California Press.

Boulé, J-P. (1999) *Hervé Guibert: Voices of the Self*, trans. J Fletcher, Liverpool: Liverpool University Press.

Bourke, J. (2000) 'Effeminacy, Ethnicity and the End of Trauma: The Sufferings of "Shell-shocked" Men in Great Britain and Ireland, 1914–39', *Journal of Contemporary History* 35/1: 57–69.

Bracken, P. J. and C. Petty (eds) (1998) *Rethinking the Trauma of War*, London: Free Association.

Bradley, F., K. Brown and A. Nairne (2001) 'Trauma', in *Trauma*, London: Hayward Gallery: 6–9.

Brett, E. and R. Ostroff (1985) 'Imagery and Posttraumatic Stress Disorder: An Overview', *American Journal of Psychiatry* 142: 417–24.

Brison, S. J. (1999) 'Trauma Narratives and the Remaking of the Self', in M. Bal, J. Crewe, and L. Spitzer (eds), *Acts of Memory: Cultural Recall in the Present*, Hanover, NH: University of New England Press: 39–54.

Brooks, P. (1977) 'Freud's Masterplot', *Yale French Studies* 55–6: 280–99.

——(1995) *The Melodramatic Imagination: Balzac, Henry James, and the Mode of Excess*, 2nd edn, New Haven: Yale University Press.

——(2000) *Troubling Confession: Speaking Guilt in Law and Literature*, Chicago: University of Chicago Press.

Brophy, S. (2004) *Witnessing AIDS: Writing, Testimony, and the Work of Mourning*, Toronto: University of Toronto Press.

Brothers, C. (1997) *War and Photography: A Cultural History*, London: Routledge.

Brown, E. M. (1995) 'PTSD and Shell Shock: Social Section', in G. Berrios and R. Porter (eds), *A Cultural History of Psychiatry: The Origin and History of Psychiatric Disorders*, London: Athlone: 501–08.

Brown, L. S. (1991) 'Not Outside the Range: One Feminist Perspective on Psychic Trauma', *American Imago* 48/1: 119–31.

Brown, W. (2004) '"The Most We Can Hope For": Human Rights and the Politics of Fatalism', *South Atlantic Quarterly* 103/2–3: 452–63.

Brown, R. and J. Kulik (1977) 'Flashbulb Memories', *Cognition* 5: 73–99.

Bruner, J. (1991) 'The Narrative Construction of Reality', *Critical Inquiry* 18: 1–21.

Buchloh, B. H. D. (1996) 'Divided Memory and Post-Traditional Identity: Gerhard Richter's Work of Mourning', *October* 75: 61–82.

Burgess, A. W. and L. L. Holmstrom (1974) 'Rape Trauma Syndrome', *American Journal of Psychiatry* 131: 981–6.

Buss, H. (2001) 'Memoirs', in M. Jolly (ed.), *Encyclopedia of Life Writing*, 2 vols, London: Fitzroy Dearborn: II: 595–7.

Butler, J. (2004) *Precarious Life: The Powers of Mourning and Violence*, London: Verso.

Byrne, P. (2000) 'Schizophrenia in the Cinema: *Me, Myself and Irene*', *Psychiatric Bulletin* 24: 364–5.

Cameron, A. (2006) 'Contingency, Order, and the Modular Narrative: *21 Grams* and *Irreversible*', *Velvet Light Trap* 58: 65–78.

Campbell, R. (1997) 'Philosophy and the Accident', in R. Cooter and B. Luckin (eds): 17–34.

Caplan, E. M. (1995) 'Trains, Brains and Sprains: Railway Spine and the Origins of Psychoneuroses', *Bulletin of the History of Medicine* 69: 387–419.

Cardena, E. (1994) 'The Domain of Dissociation', in S. Lynne and J. W. Rhine (eds), *Dissociation: Clinical and Theoretical Perspectives*, London: Guildford Press: 15–31.

Caruth, C. (1991a) 'Introduction to Psychoanalysis, Trauma and Culture I', *American Imago* 48/1: 1–12.
——(1991b) 'Introduction to Psychoanalysis, Trauma and Culture II', *American Imago* 48/4: 417–24.
——(1996a) *Unclaimed Experience: Trauma, Narrative, and History*, Baltimore, MD: Johns Hopkins University Press.
——(1996b) 'An Interview with Geoffrey Hartman', *Studies in Romanticism* 35: 631–52.
Cathcart, M. (2001) 'Interview with Tracey Moffatt', *Arts Today*: 9 January. Transcript at www.abc.net.au/rn/arts/atoday/stories/s229128.htm
Caws, M. A. (1991) *The Women of Bloomsbury: Virginia, Vanessa and Carrington*, New York: Routledge.
Chamberlain, E. and S. Gilman (eds) (1985) *Degeneration: The Dark Side of Progress*, New York: Columbia University Press.
Chambers, R. (1998) *Facing It: AIDS Diaries and the Death of the Author*, Ann Arbor, MI: University of Michigan Press.
——(2004) *Untimely Interventions: AIDS Writing, Testimonial, and the Rhetoric of Haunting*, Ann Arbor, MI: University of Michigan Press.
Charcot, J-M. (1991) *Clinical Lectures on Diseases of the Nervous System* (1889), London: Routledge.
Charcot, J-M. and G. de la Tourette (1892) 'Hypnotism in the Hysterical', in D. H. Tuke (ed.), *A Dictionary of Psychological Medicine* I: 606–8.
'Charles Darwin. V' (1882) *Nature* 22 June: 169.
Cheddie, J. (2007) 'Listening to Trauma in the Art of Everlyn Nicodemus', *Third Text* 21/1: 79–89.
Chedgzoy, K. (1996) *Shakespeare's Queer Children*, Manchester: Manchester University Press.
Cheever, A. (2000) 'Prozac Americans: Depression, Identity, and Selfhood', *Twentieth Century Literature* 46/5: 346–68.
Chion, M. (2006) *David Lynch*, trans. Robert Julian, London: BFI Publishing.
Churchill, W. (1997) *A Little Matter of Genocide: Holocaust and Denial in the Americas 1492 to the Present*, San Francisco, CA: City Lights.
Clark, M. J. (1981) 'The Rejection of Psychological Approaches to Mental Disorder in Late Nineteenth Century British Psychiatry', in Scull A (ed.), *Madhouses, Mad-Doctors and Madmen: The Social History of Psychiatry in the Victorian Era*, London: Athlone: 271–312.
Clark, T. J. (2002) 'Commentary', in S. Salgado *et al.*: 23–6.
Colpi, H. (1959–60) 'Editing *Hiroshima Mon Amour*,' *Sight and Sound* 29/1: 14–16.
Connerton, P. (1989) *How Societies Remember*, Cambridge: Cambridge University Press.
Connor, S. (2004) *The Book of Skin*, London: Reaktion.
Conway, M. A. (ed.) (1997) *Recovered Memories and False Memories*, Oxford: Oxford University Press.
Cooter, R. (1997) 'The Moment of the Accident: Culture, Militarism and Modernity in Late-Victorian Britain', in R. Cooter and B. Luckin (eds): 107–57.
Cooter, R. and B. Luckin (eds) (1997) *Accidents in History: Injuries, Fatalities and Social Relations*, Amsterdam: Rodopi.
Cork, R. (2003) *Breaking Down the Barriers: Art in the 1990s*, New Haven, CT: Yale University Press.
Costa, G. (2001) *Nan Goldin*, London: Phaidon.
Cowie, P. (1963) *Michelangelo Antonioni, Ingmar Bergman, Alain Resnais*, London: Tantivity Press.
Crabtree, A. (1994) *From Mesmer to Freud: Magnetic Sleep and the Roots of Psychological Healing*, New Haven, CT: Yale University Press.
Crews, F. (1997) *The Memory Wars: Freud's Legacy in Dispute*, London: Granta.
Crimp, D. (1989) 'Mourning and Miltancy', *October* 51: 3–18.
Crimp, D. (ed.) (1989) *AIDS: Cultral Analysis/Cultural Activism*, Cambridge, MA: MIT Press.
Cunningham, F. R. (2001) *Sidney Lumet: Film and Literary Vision* 2nd edn, Lexington, KY: University of Kentucky Press.
Dana, C. (1900) 'The Traumatic Neuroses: Being a Description of the Chronic Nervous Disorders that Follow Shock and Injury', in A. McLane Hamilton and L. Godkin (eds) *A System of Legal Medicine*, 2 vols, 2nd edn, New York: E B Treat: II: 297–361.
Danto, A. C. (1997) *Encounters and Reflections: Art in the Historical Present*, Berkeley, CA: University of California Press.
Davis, J. E. (2005) *Accounts of Innocence: Sexual Abuse, Trauma and the Self*, Chicago: University of Chicago Press.

Dean Jr., E. T. (1997) *Shook over Hell: Post-Traumatic Stress, Vietnam and the Civil War*, Cambridge, MA: Harvard University Press.

de Landa, M. (1991) *War in the Age of Intelligent Machines*, New York: Zone.

Delbo, C. (1995) *Auschwtiz and After*, trans. Rosette C. Lamont, New Haven, CT: Yale University Press.

Deleuze, G. (1986) *Cinema 1: The Movement-Image*, trans. H. Tomlinson and B. Habberjam, London: Athlone.

——(1989) *Cinema 2: The Time-Image*, trans. H. Tomlinson and R. Galeta, London: Athlone.

DeLillo, D. (2007) *The Falling Man*, London: Picador.

de Man, P. (1979) *Allegories of Reading: Figural Language in Rousseau, Nietzsche, Rilke and Proust*, New Haven, CT: Yale University Press.

Derrida, J. (1986) *Mémoires for Paul de Man*, trans. C. Lindsay, J. Culler and E. Cadava, New York: Columbia University Press.

——(1991) *Cinders*, trans. N. Lukacher, Lincoln: University of Nebraska Press.

——(1992) '"This Strange Institution Called Literature": An Interview with Jacques Derrida', in D. Attridge (ed.), *Acts of Literature* (1993): 33–75.

——(1993) *Aporias*, trans. T. Dutoit, Stanford, CA: Stanford University Press.

——(1994) *Specters of Marx: The State of the Debt, the Work of Mourning, and the New International*, trans. P. Kamuf, New York: Routledge.

——(2001) *The Work of Mourning*, P-A. Brault and M. Naas (eds), New York: Columbia University Press.

——(2005) *Sovereignties in Question: The Poetics of Paul Celan*, trans. T. Dutoit and O. Pasanen, New York: Fordham University Press.

deSalvo, L. (1989) *Virginia Woolf: The Impact of Child Sexual Abuse on Her Life and Work*, London: The Women's Press.

Des Pres, T. (1980) *The Survivor: An Anatomy of Life in the Death Camps*, Oxford: Oxford University Press.

Dickens, C. ([1865]1997) *Our Mutual Friend*, ed. A. Poole, Harmondsworth: Penguin.

Didi-Huberman, G. (2003) *Invention of Hysteria: Charcot and the Photographic Iconography of the Salpêtrière*, trans. A. Hartz, Cambridge, MA: MIT Press.

Di Giovanni, J. (2004) *Madness Visible: A Memoir of War*, London: Bloomsbury.

Dittmar, L. and G. Michaud (1990) 'America's Vietnam War Films: Marching Towards Denial', in Dittmar and Michaud (eds), *From Hanoi to Hollywood: The Vietnam War in American Film*, New Brunswick, NJ: Rutgers University Press: 1–15.

Drucker, J. (1995) *The Century of Artists' Books*, New York: Granary Books.

Duganne, E. (2006) 'Photography after the Fact', in Reinhardt *et al.* (eds): 57–74.

Dunmore, H. (1997) *Talking to the Dead*, Harmondsworth: Penguin.

Durand, R. (1999) 'Specific Climates', in L. Monreal (ed.), *Tracey Moffatt*, Barcelona: Fondacion 'la Caixa': 103–5.

Duras, M. (1961) *Hiroshima Mon Amour: A Screenplay*, trans. R. Seaver, New York: Grove Press.

Durden, M. (2005) 'Luc Delahaye: Global Documentary', *Deutsche Börse Photography Prize 2005*, London: Photographer's Gallery: 13–15.

Düttmann, A. G. (1996) *At Odds with AIDS: Thinking and Talking about a Virus*, trans. P. Gilger and C. Scott-Curtis, Stanford, CA: Stanford University Press.

Eaglestone, R. (2004) *The Holocaust and the Postmodern*, Oxford: Oxford University Press.

Eder, M. D. (1917) *War-Shock: The Psychoneuroses in War*, London: Heinemann.

Edkins, J. (2003) *Trauma and the Memory of Politics*, Cambridge: Cambridge University Press.

Egan, S. (1999) *Mirror Talk: Genres of Crisis in Contemporary Autobiography*, Chapel Hill, NC: University of North Carolina Press.

Egoyan, A. (1995) *Exotica: The Screenplay*, Toronto: Coach House Press.

——(1997) 'Recovery', *Sight and Sound*, October: 20–3.

Egoyan, Atom and Paul Virilio (1993) 'Video Letters', in Carole Desbarats, Daniele Riviere, Jacinto Lageira and Paul Virilio, *Atom Egoyan*, trans. B. Holmes, Paris: Editions Dis Voir: 105–15.

Ehlers, A. and D. Clark (2000) 'A Cognitive Model of Posttraumatic Stress Disorder', *Behaviour Research and Therapy* 38: 319–45.

Eisenman, S. F. (2007) *The Abu Ghraib Effect*, London: Reaktion.

Eisenstein, S. (1974) 'Montage of Attractions', *Drama Review* 18: 77–84.

Eitinger, L. (1961) 'Pathology of the Concentration Camp Syndrome', *Archives of General Psychiatry* 5: 371–9.

Ellenberger, H. (1994) *The Discovery of the Unconscious*, London: Fontana.

Elliot-Smith, G. and T. H. Pear (1917) *Shell Shock and its Lessons*, London: Longman.

Ellis, J. (1999) 'Television as Working-Through', in J. Gripsrud (ed.), *Television and Common Knowledge*, London: Routledge: 55–70.

Elsaesser, T. (1998) 'Spectacularity and Engulfment: Francis Ford Coppola and *Bram Stoker's Dracula*', in S. Neale and M. Smith (eds), *Contemporary Hollywood Cinema*, London: Routledge: 191–208.

——(2001) 'Postmodernism as Mourning Work', *Screen* 42/2: 193–201.

Erichsen, J. E. (1875) *On the Concussion of the Spine, Nervous Shock, and Other Obscure Injuries of the Nervous System*, 2nd edn, London: Longman.

Erikson, K. (1991) 'Notes on Trauma and Community', *American Imago* 48/4: 455–72.

Eshel, A. (2003) 'Against the Power of Time: The Poetics of Suspension in W. G. Sebald's *Austerlitz*', *New German Critique* 88: 71–96.

Evans, M. (1999) *Missing Persons: The Impossibility of Auto/Biography*, London: Routledge.

Eyal, G. (2004) 'Identity and Trauma: Two Forms of the Will to Memory', *History and Memory* 16/1: 5–36.

Felman, S. (1977) 'Turning the Screw of Interpretation', *Yale French Studies* 55–6: 94–207.

——(1991) 'In an Era of Testimony: Claude Lanzmann's *Shoah*', *Yale French Studies* 79: 39–81.

Felman, S. and D. Laub (1992) *Testimony: Crises of Witnessing in Literature, Psychoanalysis, and History*, London: Routledge.

Ferenczi, S. (1955) *Final Contributions to the Problems and Methods of Psychoanalysis*, M. Balint (ed.), London: Hogarth Press.

Feudtner, C. (1993) '"Minds the Dead Have Ravished": Shell Shock, History, and the Ecology of Disease-Systems', *History of Science* 31: 377–420.

Figley, C. R. (1985) 'From Victim to Survivor: Social Responsibility in the Wake of Catastrophe', in C. Figley (ed.), *Trauma and its Wake, Vol. I: The Study and Treatment of Post-Traumatic Stress Disorder*, New York: Brunner: 398–415.

Figley, C. R. (ed.) (2006) *Mapping Trauma and its Wake: Autobiographical Essays by Pioneer Trauma Scholars*, London: Routledge.

Figlio, K. (1985) 'What is an Accident?', in P. Weindling (ed.): 180–206.

Finkelstein, N. (2000) *The Holocaust Industry: Reflections on the Exploitation of Jewish Suffering*, London: Verso.

Foster, F. S. (1994) *Witnessing Slavery: The Development of Ante-Bellum Slave Narratives*, 2nd edn, Madison, WI: University of Wisconsin Press.

Foster, H. (1996) *The Return of the Real: The Avant-Garde at the End of the Century*, Cambridge, MA: MIT Press.

Foucault, M. (1974) *The Archaeology of Knowledge*, trans. A. Sheridan, London: Tavistock.

——(1981) *The History of Sexuality: An Introduction*, trans. R Hurley, Harmondsworth: Pelican.

——(2003) *"Society Must Be Defended": Lectures at the Collège de France 1975–6*, M. Bertani and A. Fontuna (eds), trans. David Macey, London: Allen Lane.

Frank, A. W. (1995) *The Wounded Storyteller: Body, Illness and Ethics*, Chicago: University of Chicago Press.

Frankel, F. H. (1994) 'The Concept of Flashbacks in Historical Perspective', *International Journal of Clinical and Experimental Hypnosis*, 42/4: 321–36.

Fraser, S. (1989) *My Father's House: A Memoir of Incest and of Healing*, London: Virago.

Freccero, C. (1997) 'Historical Violence, Censorship, and the Serial Killer: The Case of *American Psycho*', *Diacritics* 27/2: 44–58.

Fredrickson, R. (1992) *Repressed Memories: A Journey to Recovery from Sexual Abuse*, New York: Fireside.

Freeman, M. (1993) *Rewriting the Self: History, Memory, Narrative*, London: Routledge.

French, N. (1997) *The Memory Game*, London: Heinemann.

Freud, S. ([1886] 1966–74) 'Report on My Studies in Paris and Berlin', *Standard Edition* vol. 1: 1–15.

——([1888] 1966–74) 'Hysteria', *Standard Edition* vol. 1: 37–59.

——([1895] 1974) *Studies on Hysteria, Standard Edition* vol. 3, reprinted in Penguin Freud Library vol. 3, Harmondsworth: Penguin.

——([1896] 1966–74) 'The Aetiology of Hysteria', *Standard Edition* vol. 3: 187–222.

——([1899] 1966–74) 'Screen Memories', *Standard Edition* vol. 3, London: Hogarth Press: 301–22.

——([1900] 1976) *The Interpretation of Dreams,* trans. J. Strachey, Harmondsworth: Penguin.

——([1910] 1966–74) 'Five Lectures on Psychoanalysis', *Standard Edition* vol. 11: 1–55, reprinted in *Two Short Accounts of Psycho-analysis*, Harmondsworth: Penguin.

——([1912] 1966–74) 'A Note on the Unconscious', *Standard Edition* vol. 12: 255–66.

——([1914] 1966–74) 'Remembering, Repeating and Working Through', *Standard Edition* vol. 12: 145–56.

——([1915] 1966–74) 'The Unconscious', *Standard Edition* vol. 14: 159–215.

——([1916–17] 1973) *Introductory Lectures on Psychoanalysis, Standard Edition* vol. 15, reprinted in Penguin Freud Library vol. 1, Harmondsworth: Penguin.

——([1919] 1966–74) 'Introduction to *Psycho-Analysis and the War Neuroses*', *Standard Edition*, vol. 17: 203–10.

——([1920a] 1984) 'Beyond the Pleasure Principle', *Standard Edition* vol. 18: 1–65, reprinted in Penguin Freud Library vol.11, Harmondsworth: Penguin: 269–338.

——([1920b] 1966–74) 'Memorandum on the Electrical Treatment of War Neurotics', *Standard Edition* vol. 17: 211–15.

——([1924] 1966–74) 'On the History of the Psychoanalytic Movement', *Standard Edition* vol. 14: 1–66.

——([1939] 1966–74) *Moses and Monotheism, Standard Edition* vol. 23: 1–137.

——(1966–74) *The Standard Edition of the Complete Psychological Works of Sigmund Freud*, trans. and ed. J. Strachey, London, Hogarth Press, 24 volumes.

——(1985) *The Complete Letters of Sigmund Freud to Wilhelm Fliess 1887–1904*, trans. Jeffrey Moussaieff Masson, New Haven, CT: Harvard University Press.

Frey, J. (2003) *A Million Little Pieces*, London: Murray.

Frost, L. (2002) 'After Lot's Daughters: Kathryn Harrison and the Making of Memory', in N. Miller and J. Tougaw (eds), *Extremities: Trauma, Testimony and Community*, Urbana, IL: University of Illinois Press, 213–29.

Funcke, B. (2007) 'Displaced Struggles', *Artforum* March: 282–5 and 341.

Furedi, F. (2002) *Culture of Fear: Risk-Taking and the Morality of Low Expectations*, rev. edn, London: Continuum.

——(2004) *Therapy Culture: Cultivating Vulnerability in an Uncertain Age*, London: Routledge.

Fussell, P. (1985) *The Great War and Modern Memory*, Oxford: Oxford University Press.

Gaffney, D. A. (2003–4) 'PTSD, RTS and Child Abuse Accommodation Syndrome: Therapeutic Tools or Fact Finding Aids', *Pace Law Review* 24: 274–91.

Gallagher, B. J. (1987) 'Breaking Up Isn't Hard to Do: Stephen King, Christopher Lasch, and Psychic Fragmentation', *Journal of American Culture* 10/4: 59–67.

Garb, T. (1997) 'Interview with Christian Boltanski,' in Didier Semin, Tamar Garb and Donald Kuspit, *Christian Boltanski*, London: Phaidon: 6–40.

Garland, C. (1980a) 'Overview', *Group Analysis*, November: 93–7.

——(1980b) 'The Survivor Syndrome', *Group Analysis*, November: 5–8.

Garratt, S. (2002) 'The Dark Room' [interview with Nan Goldin], *The Observer* Life section, 6 January: 15.

Gauld, A. (1992) *A History of Hypnotism*, Cambridge: Cambridge University Press.

Genette, G. (1980) *Narrative Discourse: An Essay in Method*, New York: Cornell University Press.

George, D. H. (1995) 'Lynching Women: A Feminist Reading of *Twin Peaks*', in D. Lavery (ed.): 109–119.

Giddens, A. (1990) *The Consequences of Modernity*, Stanford, CA: Stanford University Press.

——(1991) *Modernity and Self-Identity: Self and Society in the Late Modern Age*, Cambridge: Polity.

Giliker, P. and S. Beckwith (2000) *Tort*, London: Sweet and Maxwell.

Gilmore, L. (2001) *The Limits of Autobiography: Trauma and Testimony*, Ithaca, NY: Cornell University Press.

Gisbourne, M. (1998) 'Life into Art' [interview with Tracey Emin], *Contemporary Visual Arts* 20: 28–34.

Glover, D. (2001) 'The "spectrality effect" in early modernism', in A. Smith and J. Wallace (eds), *Gothic Modernisms*, Basingstoke: Palgrave: 29–43.

Gourevitch, P. (1999) 'The Memory Thief', *The New Yorker*, 14 June: 48–64.

Green, B. L., Jacob, Lindy and Grace, Mary (1985) 'Posttraumatic Stress Disorder: Toward DSM-IV', *Journal of Nervous and Mental Disease* 173: 406–11.

Greene, N. (1999) *Landscapes of Loss: The National Past in Postwar French Cinema*, Princeton, NJ: Princeton University Press.

Greenslade, W. (1994) *Degeneration, Culture and the Novel 1880–1940*, Cambridge: Cambridge University Press.

Grubrich-Simitis, I. (1984) 'From Concretism to Metaphor: Thoughts on Some Theoretical and Technical Aspects of the Psychoanalytic Work with Children of Holocaust Survivors', *The Psychoanalytic Study of the Child* 39: 301–19.

Guibert, H. (1991a) *La Mort Propagande et autres textes de jeunesse* [1975], Paris: Editions Régine Deforges.

——(1991b) *To the Friend Who Did Not Save My Life*, trans. Linda Coverdale, London: Quartet. (First published Paris, 1990.)

——(1993a) *The Compassion Protocol*, trans. James Kirkup, London: Quartet.

——(1993b) *The Man in the Red Hat*, trans. James Kirkup, London: Quartet.

——(1996a) *Cytomegalovirus: A Hospitalization Diary*, trans. Clara Orban, New York: University Press of America.

——(1996b) *Paradise*, trans. James Kirkup, London: Quartet.

Gumpert, L. (1994) *Christian Boltanski*, Paris: Flammarion.

Gunning, T. (1999) 'An Aesthetic of Astonishment: Early Film and the (In)credulous Spectator', in L. Braudy and M. Cohen (eds), *Film Theory and Criticism: An Introductory Reader*, 5th edn, Oxford: Oxford University Press: 818–32.

Gusdorf, G. (1980) 'Conditions and Limits of Autobiography', trans. J. Olney in J. Olney (ed.), *Autobiography: Essays Theoretical and Critical*, Princeton, NJ: Princeton University Press: 28–48.

Haaken, J. (1999) 'Heretical Texts: *The Courage to Heal* and the Incest Survivor Movement', in S. Lamb (ed.), *New Versions of Victims: Feminists Struggle with the Concept*, New York: New York University Press: 13–41.

——(2003) 'Traumatic Revisions: Remembering Abuse and the Politics of Forgiveness,' in P. Reavey and S. Warner (eds), *New Feminist Stories of Child Sexual Abuse*, London: Routledge: 77–93.

Hacking, I. (1986) 'Making Up People', in T. Heller *et al.* (eds), *Reconstructing Individualism: Autonomy, Individuality, and the Self in Western Thought*, Stanford, CA: Stanford University Press, 222–36.

——(1991) 'The Making and Molding of Child Abuse', *Critical Inquiry* 17: 253–88.

——(1995) *Rewriting the Soul: Multiple Personality and the Sciences of Memory*, Princeton, NJ: Princeton University Press.

Hahn, R. (2005) '*21 Grams*', *Film Quarterly* 58/3: 53–8.

Haines, H. (1990) '"They Were Called and They Went": The Political Rehabilitation of the Vietnam Veteran', in L. Dittmar and G. Michaud (eds), *From Hanoi to Hollywood: The Vietnam War in American Film*, New Brunswick, NJ: Rutgers University Press, 81–97.

Halbwachs, M. (1992) *On Collective Memory*, ed. and trans. L. Coser, Chicago: University of Chicago Press.

Hall, R. M. (2003) 'The "Oprahfication" of Literacy: Reading "Oprah's Book Club"', *College English* 65: 646–67.

Hansen, M. B. (1997) '*Schindler's List* is not *Shoah*: Second Commandment, Popular Modernism, and Public Memory', in Y. Loshitzky (ed.), *Spielberg's Holocaust: Critical Perspectives on* Schindler's List, Bloomington, IN: Indiana University Press, 77–103.

Harrington, R. (1994) 'The Neuroses of the Railway', *History Today* 44: 15–21.

——(2003) 'On the Tracks of Trauma: Railway Spine Reconsidered', *Social History of Medicine* 16/2: 209–23.

Harris, R. (1985) 'Murder Under Hypnosis in the Case of Gabrielle Bompard: Psychiatry in the Courtroom in Belle Époque Paris', in W. F. Bynum, R. Porter and M. Shephard (eds), *Anatomy of Madness* vol. 2, London: Tavistock: 197–241.

——(1991) 'Introduction' to Charcot, *Clinical Lectures*, ix–lxviii.

Harrison, K. (1991) *Thicker Than Water*, New York: Random House.

——(1994) *Exposure*, London: Fourth Estate.

——(1997) *The Kiss: A Secret Life*, London: Fourth Estate.

——(2003) *Seeking Rapture: A Memoir*, London: Fourth Estate.

——(2004) *The Mother Knot: A Memoir*, New York: Random House.

——(2005a) 'Therapy, Taboo and Perdition Eternal: Kathryn Harrison Talks to *Bookforum*', *Bookforum* (Summer): 48–9.

——(2005b) *Envy*, London: Fourth Estate.

Hartman, C. R. and A. Burgess (1993) 'Treatment of Victims of Rape Trauma', in J. P. Wilson and B. Raphael (eds), *International Handbook of Traumatic Stress Syndromes*, New York: Plenum: 507–16.

Hartman, G. (1995) 'On Traumatic Knowledge and Literary Studies', *New Literary History* 26: 537–66.

Hawkins, A. H. (1999) *Reconstructing Illness: Studies in Pathography*, 2nd edn, West Lafayette, IN: Purdue University Press.

Hedin, B. (2005) 'The Measure of All Things: *Patrimony*', in D. P. Royal (ed.), *Philip Roth: New Perspectives on an American Author*, Westport: Praeger: 143–51.

Hendin, H. and A. P. Haas (1984) *Wounds of War: The Psychological Aftermath of Combat in Vietnam*, New York: Basic Books.

Henke, S. A. (1998) *Shattered Subjects: Trauma and Testimony in Women's Life-Writing*, Basingstoke: Macmillan.

Herman, J. (1992) 'Complex Trauma: A Syndrome in Survivors of Prolonged and Repeated Trauma', *Journal of Traumatic Stress* 5: 377–91.

——(1994) *Trauma and Recovery: From Domestic Abuse to Political Terror*, London: HarperCollins.

Herzog, J. (1982) 'World Beyond Metaphor: Thoughts on the Transmission of Trauma', in M. Bergmann and M. Jucovy (eds), *Generations of the Holocaust*, New York: Basic Books: 103–119.

Hirsch, J. (2004) *After Image: Film, Trauma and the Holocaust*, Philadelphia, PA: Temple University Press.

Hirsch, M. (1997) *Family Frames: Photography, Narrative and Postmemory*, Cambridge, MA: Harvard University Press.

——(2001) 'Surviving Images: Holocaust Photographs and the Work of Postmemory', *Yale Journal of Criticism* 14/1: 5–37.

Horowitz, M. (1969) 'Flashbacks: Recurrent Intrusive Images after the use of LSD', *American Journal of Psychiatry* 126: 565–9.

——(1976a) 'Stress Films, Emotion, and Cognitive Response', *Archives of General Psychiatry* 33: 1339–44.

——(1976b) *Stress Response Syndromes*, New York: Jason Aronson.

Horvitz, D. (2000) *Literary Trauma: Sadism, Memory, and Sexual Violence in American Women's Fiction*, Albany, NY: SUNY Press.

Howe, S. (2003) 'Internal Decolonization? British Politics since Thatcher as Post-colonial Trauma', *Twentieth Century British History* 14/3: 286–304.

Humble, N. (2001) *The Feminine Middlebrow Novel, 1920s to 1950s: Class, Domesticity, and Bohemianism*, Oxford: Oxford University Press.

Hume, M. (1997) *Whose War is it Anyway? The Dangers of the Journalism of Attachment*, London: BM Inform.

Huyssen, A. (2003) *Present Pasts: Urban Palimpsests and the Politics of Memory*, Stanford, CA: Stanford University Press.

Iles, C. L. (1985) 'Rape Trauma Syndrome', *Missouri Law Review* 50: 948–67.

Illouz, E. (2003) *Oprah Winfrey and the Glamor of Misery*, New York: Columbia University Press.

Iser, W. (1988) 'The Reading Process: A Phenomenological Approach', in D. Lodge (ed.), *Modern Criticism and Theory*, London: Longman: 211–228.

Jaggi, M. (2001) 'Recovered Memories' [The *Guardian* Profile: W. G. Sebald], *The Guardian*, 21 Sept, http://www.guardian.co.uk/Saturday_review/story/0,3605,555861,00.html. Accessed March 10 2006.

Jameson, F. (1991) *Postmodernism, of the Cultural Logic of Late Capitalism*, London: Verso.

Janet, P. (1901) *The Mental State of Hystericals: A Study of Mental Stigmata and Mental Accidents*, trans C. Corson, New York: Putnam.

——(1907) *The Major Symptoms of Hysteria*, New York: Macmillan.

——(2001) 'Study of Cases of Anterograde Amnesia in a Disease of Mental Disintegration' (1892), *History of Psychiatry* 12: 481–8.

Jones, A. (2004) 'Introduction: History and Complicity', in A. Jones (ed.), *Genocide, War Crimes and the West: History and Complicity*, London: Zed Books: 3–30.

Joshi, S. T. (2001) *The Modern Weird Tale*, Jefferson, NC: McFarland.

Kälin, W., L. Müller and J. Wyttenbach (2004) *The Face of Human Rights*, Baden: Lars Müller Publishers.

Kansteiner, W. (2004) 'Genealogy of a Category Mistake: A Critical, Intellectual History of the Cultural Trauma Metaphor', *Rethinking History* 8/2: 193–221.

Kaplan, E. A. (2000) 'Classical Hollywood Film and Melodrama', in J. Hill and P. Gibson (eds), *American Cinema and Hollywood: Critical Approaches*, Oxford: Oxford University Press: 46–56.

——(2005) *Trauma Culture: The Politics of Terror and Loss in Media and Literature*, New Brunswick, NJ: Rutgers University Press.

Kaplan, E. A. and B. Wang (2004) 'From Traumatic Paralysis to the Force Field of Modernity', in Kaplan and Wang (eds), *Trauma and Cinema: Cross-Cultural Explorations*, Hong Kong: Hong Kong University Press: 1–22.

Kardiner, A. (1941) *The Traumatic Neuroses of War*, New York: Paul Hoeber.

Kauffman, L. A. (2001) 'Identity Politics: The Past, the Present, and the Future', in B. Ryan (ed.), *Identity Politics in the Women's Movement*, New York: New York University Press: 23–34.

Kauvar, E. M (1995) 'This Doubly Reflected Communication: Philip Roth's "Autobiographies"', *Contemporary Literature* 36: 412–46.

Keane, S. (2001) *Disaster Movies: The Cinema of Catastrophe*, London: Wallflower.

King, N. (2000) *Memory, Narrative, Identity: Remembering the Self*, Edinburgh: Edinburgh University Press.

King, S. (1978) *The Shining*, London: New English Library.

——(1990) *Four Past Midnight*, London: Hodder.

——(1991) *Danse Macabre* [1981], London: Hodder.

——(1992) *Gerald's Game*, London: New English Library.

——(1993) *Dolores Claiborne*, London: Hodder.

——(2003) *Different Seasons* [1982], London: TimeWarner.

Kinnane, G. (2000) 'Metaphor, Pathography and Hysteria: Recent American Writing About Illness', *Critical Review* 40: 91–108.

Kitcher, P. (1992) *Freud's Dream: A Complete Interdisciplinary Science of Mind*, Cambridge: MIT Press.

Kleinman, A. and J. (1996) 'The Appeal of Experience, the Dismay of Images: Cultural Appropriations of Suffering in Our Times', *Daedalus* 125: 1–23.

Kline, T. J. (1992) *Screening the Text: Intertextuality in New Wave French Cinema*, Baltimore, MD: Johns Hopkins University Press.

Kling, V. (2004) 'The Prophetic Voice: W. G. Sebald and *On the Natural History of Destruction*', *Southern Humanities Review* 38: 347–81.

Knightley, P. (2000) *First Casualty: The War Correspondent as Hero and Myth-Maker*, rev. edn, London: Prion.

Knox, S. (1998) *Murder: A Tale of Modern American Life*, Durham, NC: Duke University Press.

Kracauer, S. (1993) 'Photography' [1927], *Critical Inquiry* 19: 421–36.

Krafft-Ebing, R. von (1889) *An Experimental Study in the Domain of Hypnotism*, trans. Charles Chaddock, New York: Putnam.

Kral, V. A. (1951) 'Psychiatric Observations under Severe Chronic Stress', *American Journal of Psychiatry* 108/3: 185–92.

Kreisler, H. (1997) 'Images, Reality, and the Curse of History: Conversation with Gilles Peress', http://globetrotter.berkeley.edu/Peress

Kristeva, J. (1987) 'The Pain of Sorrow in the Modern World: The Works of Marguerite Duras', trans. K. Jenson, *PMLA* 102/2: 138–52.

Krystal, H. (ed.) (1968) *Massive Psychic Trauma*, New York: International Universities Press.

Kulka, R. *et al.* (1990) *Trauma and the Vietnam War Generation: Report of Findings from the National Vietnam Veterans Readjustment Study*, Levittown: Brunner/Mazel.

LaCapra, D. (1999) 'Trauma, Absence, Loss', *Critical Inquiry* 25: 696–727.

——(2001) *Writing History, Writing Trauma*, Baltimore, MD: Johns Hopkins University Press.

——(2004) *History in Transit: Experience, Identity, Critical Theory*, Ithaca, NY: Cornell University Press.

Langer, L. L. (1991) *Holocaust Testimonies: The Ruins of Memory*, New Haven, CT: Yale University Press.

Lant, K. M. and T. Thomoson (eds) (1998) *Imagining the Worst: Stephen King and the Representation of Women*, Westport, CT: Greenwood.

Lanzmann, C. (1991) 'Seminar with Claude Lanzmann 11 April 1990', *Yale French Studies* 79: 82–99.

Laplanche, J. (1999) 'Notes on Afterwardsness', in *Essays on Otherness*, trans. J. Fletcher, London: Routledge: 260–5.

Laplanche, J. and J-B. Pontalis (1986) 'Fantasy and the Origins of Sexuality', in V. Burgin, J. Donald and C. Kaplan (eds), *Formations of Fantasy*, London: Methuen: 5–34.

Lappin, E. (1999) 'The Man with Two Heads', *Granta* 66: 7–65.

Latour, B. (1987) *Science in Action: How to Follow Scientists and Engineers through Society*, Cambridge, MA: Harvard University Press.

——(1999) *Pandora's Hope: Essays on the Reality of Science Studies*, Cambridge, MA: Harvard University Press.

——(2004) *Politics of Nature: How to Bring the Sciences into Democracy*, trans. C. Porter, Cambridge, MA: Harvard University Press.

Laureance, J. R. and C. Perry (1998) *Hypnosis, Will and Memory: A Psycho-Legal History*, New York: Guilford Press.

Lavery, D. (ed.) (1995) *Full of Secrets: Critical Approaches to* Twin Peaks, Detroit, MI: Wayne State University Press.

Law Commission (1998) *Liability for Psychiatric Illness*. Available at www.open.gov.uk/lawcomm/ (accessed 8 March 2006).

Leese, P. (2002) *Shell Shock: Traumatic Neurosis and the British Soldiers of the First World War*, Basingstoke: Palgrave.

Lejeune, P. (1989) *On Autobiography*, trans. K. Leary, Minneapolis, MN: University of Minnesota Press.

Lerner, P. (2001) 'From Traumatic Neurosis to Male Hysteria: The Decline and Fall of Hermann Oppenheim 1889–1919', in M. Micale and P. Lerner (eds): 141–71.

Levi, P. (1989) *The Drowned and the Saved*, trans. R. Rosenthal, London: Abacus.

Leys, R. (1992) 'The Real Miss Beauchamp: Gender and the Subject of Imitation', in J. Butler and J. Scott (eds), *Feminists Theorize the Political*, London: Routledge: 167–214.

——(2000) *Trauma: A Genealogy*, Chicago: University of Chicago Press.

——(2006) 'Image and Trauma', *Science in Context* 19/1: 137–49.

Lifton, R. J. (1968) *Death in Life: The Survivors of Hiroshima*, London: Weidenfeld and Nicolson.

——(1969) *Boundaries: Psychological Man in Revolution*, New York: Random House.

——(1973) *Home from the War: Vietnam Veterans: Neither Victims nor Executioners*, New York: Simon & Schuster.

——(1979) *The Broken Connection: On Death and the Continuity of Life*, New York: Simon & Schuster.

Lindsay, R. (2004) 'Remembering Vukovar, Forgetting Vukovar: Constructing National Identity through the Memory of Catastrophe in Croatia', in P. Gray and K. Oliver (eds), *The Memory of Castrophe*, Manchester: Manchester University Press: 190–204.

Linklater, A (2006) 'After Shock', *The Guardian* Weekend, 17 June: 32–7.

Little, W. G. (2005) 'Surviving *Memento*', *Narrative* 31/1: 67–83.

Lloyd, A. (2004) *Independent Public Inquiry on Gulf War Illnesses* (the 'Lloyd Report'), available at www.lloyd-gwii.com/admin/ManagedFiles/4/ReportResume.doc (accessed 27 January 2005).

Loftus, E. and D. Davis (2002) 'Dispatch from the Repressed-Memory Legal Front', *Psychiatric Times* 19/4. Available at www.psychiatric time.com/p020444.html (accessed 13 March 2006).

Loftus, E. and K. Ketcham (1996) *The Myth of Repressed Memories: False Memories and Allegations of Sexual Abuse*, New York: St. Martin's Griffin.

Long, J. J. and A. Whitehead (eds) (2004) *W. G. Sebald: A Critical Companion*, Edinburgh: Edinburgh University Press.

Lowenstein, A. (2005) *Shocking Representation: Historical Trauma, National Cinema, and the Modern Horror Film*, New York: Columbia University Press.

Luckhurst, R. (1996) '"Impossible Mourning" in Toni Morrison's *Beloved* and Michèle Roberts's *Daughters of the House*', *Critique* 37/4: 243–260.

——(1998) 'The Science-fictionalization of Trauma: Remarks on Narratives of Alien Abduction', *Science Fiction Studies* 25/1: 29–52.

——(1999) 'Memory Recovered/Recovered Memory', in R. Luckhurst and P. Marks (eds), *Literature and the Contemporary*, Harlow: Pearson: 80–93.

——(2002) *The Invention of Telepathy*, Oxford: Oxford University Press.

——(2003) 'Traumaculture', *New Formations* 50: 28–47.

——(2006a) 'Bruno Latour's Scientifiction: Networks, Assemblages, and Tangled Objects', *Science Fiction Studies* 33/1: 4–17.

——(2006b) 'Introduction' to Robert Louis Stevenson, *Strange Case of Doctor Jekyll and Mr Hyde*, Oxford: World's Classics: vii–xxxii.

Luthar, S., D. Cicchetti and B. Becker (2000) 'The Construct of Resilience: A Critical Evaluation and Guidelines for Future Work', *Child Development* 71/3: 543–62.

Lynch, J. (1990) *The Secret Diary of Laura Palmer*, Harmondsworth: Penguin.

Lyotard, J-F. (1984) *The Postmodern Condition: A Report on Knowledge*, trans. G. Bennington, Manchester: Manchester University Press.

——(1988) *The Differend: Phrases in Dispute*, trans. G. Van Den Abbeele, Minneapolis, MN: University of Minnesota Press.

——(1989) 'The Sublime and the Avant-Garde', in A. Benjamin (ed.), *The Lyotard Reader*, Oxford: Basil Blackwell: 196–211.

——(1990) *Heidegger and 'the Jews'*, trans. A. Michel and M. Roberts, Minneapolis: University of Minnesota Press.

——(1991) *The Inhuman: Reflections on Time*, trans. G. Bennington and R. Bowlby, Cambridge: Polity.

McCrum, R. (1999) 'The Suffering of Strangers: I've Told My Own Survival Story. Now Everyone Wants to Tell Me Theirs', *The Observer*, 7 February: 3.

McGowan, T. (2007) *The Impossible David Lynch*, New York: Columbia University Press.

McLaughlin, G. (2002) *The War Correspondent*, London: Pluto.

McLeod, J. (1997) *Narrative and Psychotherapy*, London: Sage.

McLuhan, M. (1987) *Understanding Media: The Extensions of Man*, London: Routledge.

McNally, R. J. (2003) *Remembering Trauma*, Cambridge, MA: Harvard University Press.

MacRitchie, L. (1996) 'The War over Rachel', *The Guardian*, 5 November: 9.

Magistrale, T. (1988) *Landscape of Fear: Stephen King's American Gothic*, Bowling Green, OH: Bowling Green University Press.

Malcolm, J. (1997) *In the Freud Archives*, London: Papermac.

Maltby, R. (1994) 'The Politics of the Maladjusted Text', in I. Cameron (ed.), *The Movie Book of Film Noir*, London: Studio Vista: 39–48.

Mann, S. (2007) 'The Darkness of Light', *Hotshoe* 147: 18–29.

Marcus, L. (1994) *Auto/Biographical Discourses: Theory, Criticism, Practice*, Manchester: Manchester University Press.

Marshall, P. D. (1998) *Celebrity and Power: Fame in Contemporary Culture*, Minneapolis, MN: University of Minnesota Press.

Martin, S. (2005) 'W. G. Sebald and the Modern Art of Memory', *Radical Philosophy* 132: 18–30.

Marx, K. (1980) *Marx's Grundrisse*, ed. D. McLellan, 2nd edn, Basingstoke: Macmillan.

Masson, J. (1992) *The Assault on Truth: Freud and Child Sexual Abuse*, London: Fontana. (First published 1984.)

Masten, A. S. (2001) 'Ordinary Magic: Resilience Processes in Development', *American Psychologist* 56: 227–38.

Masterson, D. (2002) 'Family Romances: Memory, Obsession, Loss and Redemption in the Films of Atom Egoyan', *University of Toronto Quarterly* 71/4: 881–91.

Matus, J. L. (2001) 'Trauma, Memory, and Railway Disaster: The Dickensian Connection', *Victorian Studies* 43/3: 413–36.

Maudsley, H. (1883) *Body and Will, Being an Essay Concerning Will in its Metaphysical, Physiological and Pathological Aspects*, London: Kegan Paul.

Mayou, R. (1996) 'Accident Neurosis Revisited', *British Journal of Psychiatry* 168: 399–403.

Mayou R., A. Ehlers and M. Hobbs (2000) 'Psychological Debriefing for Road Traffic Accident Victims: Three-Year Follow-up of a Randomised Control Trial', *British Journal of Psychiatry* 176: 589–93.

Mellman, T. A. and G. C. Davis (1985) 'Combat-Related Flashbacks in Post-Traumatic Stress Disorder: Phenomenology and Similarity to Panic Attacks', *Journal of Clinical Psychology* 46/9: 379–82.

Memon, A. and M. Young (1997) 'Desperately Seeking Evidence: The Recovered Memory Debate', *Legal and Criminological Psychology* 2/2: 131–54.

Mendelson, D. (1997) 'The History of Damages for Psychiatric Injury', *Psychiatry, Psychology and Law* 4: 169–75.

Micale, M. (2001) 'Jean-Martin Charcot and *les névroses traumatiques*: from Medicine to Culture in French Trauma Theory of the Late Nineteenth Century', in Micale and Lerner (eds): 115–39.

Micale, M. and P. Lerner (2001) 'Trauma, Psychiatry and History: A Conceptual and Historiographical Introduction', in Micale and Lerner (eds): 1–27.

Micale, M. and P. Lerner (eds) (2001) *Traumatic Pasts: History, Psychiatry and Trauma in the Modern Age 1870–1930*, Cambridge: Cambridge University Press.

Middleton, P. and T. Woods (2000) *Literatures of Memory: History, Time and Space in Post-war Writing*, Manchester: Manchester University Press.

Miles, R. (1993) *Gothic Writing 1750–1820: A Genealogy*, London: Routledge.

Miller, N. K. (1991) *Getting Personal: Feminist Occasions and other Autobiographical Acts*, London: Routledge.

——(1996) *Bequest and Betrayal: Memoirs of a Parent's Death*, Bloomington, IN: Indiana University Press.

Mitchell, W. J. T. (1994) *Picture Theory: Essays on Verbal and Visual Representation*, Chicago: University of Chicago Press.

Monaco, J. (1978) *Alain Resnais: The Role of Imagination*, London: Secker and Warburg.

Monette, P. (1994) *West of Yesterday, East of Summer: New and Selected Poems*, New York: St. Martin's Press.

——(1996) *Borrowed Time: An AIDS Memoir*, London: Abacus. (First published New York, 1988.)

Morgan, R. (1970) 'Introduction: The Women's Revolution', in R. Morgan (ed.), *Sisterhood is Powerful: An Anthology of Writings from the Women's Liberation Movement*, New York: Random House, xiii–xli.

Morrison, T. (1987) *Beloved*, London: Chatto and Windus.

——(1989) 'Unspeakable Things Unspoken', *Michigan Quarterly Review* 28: 1–34.

——(1993) *Playing in the Dark: Whiteness and the Literary Imagination*, London: Picador.

Mott, F. W. (1919) *War Neuroses and Shell Shock*, London: Hodder & Stoughton.

Mullany, N. and P. Handford (1997) 'Hillsborough Replayed', *Law Quarterly Review* 113: 410–7.

Mulvey, L. (1989) 'Melodrama Inside and Outside the Home' in *Visual and Other Pleasures*, Bloomington, IN: Indiana University Press: 63–77.

——(2006) *Death 24× A Second: Stillness and the Moving Image*, London: Reaktion.

Münsterberg, H. ([1915] 2002) *The Photoplay: A Psychological Study, and Other Writings*, ed. A. Lanydale, New York: Routledge.

Myers, C. S. (1915) 'A Contribution to the Study of Shell Shock', *The Lancet* 13 February: 316–20.

——(1940) *Shell Shock in France 1914–18*, Cambridge: Cambridge University Press.

Myers, F. (1886) 'Multiplex Personality', *Nineteenth Century* 68: 648–666.

Nelson, D. D. (1998) *National Manhood: Capitalist Citizenship and the Imagined Fraternity of White Men*, Durham, NC: Duke University Press.

Nelson, L. H. (2001) *Damaged Identities, Narrative Repair*, Ithaca, NY: Cornell University Press.

Nicholls, P. (1996) 'The Belated Postmodern: History, Phantoms, and Toni Morrison', in S. Vice (ed.), *Psychoanalytic Criticism: A Reader*, Cambridge: Polity: 50–67.

Niederland, W. (1968a) 'Clinical Observations on the "Survivor Syndrome"', *International Journal of Psychoanalysis* 49: 313–15.

——(1968b) 'The Psychiatric Evaluation of Emotional Disorders in Survivors of Nazi Persecution', in Krystal (ed.), *Massive Psychic Trauma*: 8–22.

Nolan, D. (2005) 'Reforming Liability for Psychiatric Injury in Scotland: A Recipe for Uncertainty?', *Modern Law Review* 68: 983–95.

Nora, P. (1989) 'Between Memory and History: *Les Lieux de Mémoire*', *Representations* 26: 7–25.

Nordau, M. (1895) *Degeneration*, London: Heinemann.

Novick, P. (1999) *The Holocaust and Collective Memory: The American Experience*, London: Bloomsbury.

O'Doherty, B. (1986) *Inside the White Cube: The Ideology of the Gallery Space*, Berkeley, CA: University of California Press.

Ofshe, R. and E. Watters (1994) *Making Monsters: False Memories, Psychotherapy, and Sexual Hysteria*, New York: Scribner.

Oliver, K. (2006) *The My Lai Massacre in American History and Memory*, Manchester: Manchester University Press.

Olney, J. (1972) *Metaphors of the Self: The Meaning of Autobiography*, Princeton, NJ: Princeton University Press.

Oppenheim, H. (1911) *Text-book of Nervous Diseases, for Physicians and Students*, trans. A. Bruce 2 vols, Edinburgh: Otto Schulze.

Oppenheim, J. (1991) *'Shattered Nerves': Doctors, Patients and Depression in Victorian England*, Oxford: Oxford University Press.

Page, H. W. (1883) *Injuries of the Spine and Spinal Cord without Apparent Mechanical Lesion, and Nervous Shock in their Surgical and Medico-Legal Aspects*, London: J & A. Churchill.

Parker, D. (2002) 'Counter-Transference in Reading Autobiography: The Case of Kathryn Harrison's *The Kiss*', *Biography* 25: 493–504.

Patterson, O. (1982) *Slavery and Social Death: A Comparative Study*, Cambridge, MA: Harvard University Press.

Peress, G. (1994) *Farewell to Bosnia*, New York: Scalo.

——(1995) *The Silence: Rwanda*, New York: Scalo.

Perloff, M. (1997) '"What has occurred only once": Barthes's Winter Garden/Boltanski's Archives of the Dead', in J-M. Rabaté (ed.), *Writing the Image After Roland Barthes*, Philadelphia, PA: University of Pennsylvania Press: 32–58.

Pevere, G. (1995) 'No Place Like Home: The Films of Atom Egoyan', in Egoyan, *Exotica: The Screenplay*: 9–41.

Pick, D. (1993) *War Machine: The Rationalisation of Slaughter in the Modern Age*, New Haven, CT: Yale University Press.

Poe, E. A. (1846) 'The Philosophy of Composition', reprinted at http://xroads.virginia.edu/ ~HYPER/ poe/composition.html

Polman, L. (2003) *We Did Nothing: Why the Truth Doesn't Always Come Out when the UN Goes In*, trans R. Bland, London: Penguin.

Porter, T. (1986) *The Rise of Statistical Thinking 1820–1900*, Princeton, NJ: Princeton University Press.

Powers, E. (1997) 'Doing Daddy Down', *Commentary* June: 38–41.

Prince, M. (1919) *The Dissociation of a personality: A Biographical Study in Abnormal Psychology*, New York: Longman, Green.

Pugh, C. and M. Trimble (1993) 'Psychiatric Injury After Hillsborough', *British Journal of Psychiatry* 163: 425–9.

Punter, D. (1996) 'Problems of Recollection and Construction: Stephen King', in V. Sage and A. Smith (eds), *Modern Gothic: A Reader*, Manchester: Manchester University Press: 121–40.

Putnam, F. (1999) 'Pierre Janet and Modern Views of Dissociation' (1989), reprinted in M. Horowitz (ed.), *Essential Papers on Posttraumatic Stress Disorder*, New York: New York University Press: 116–35.

Quinby, L. (1992) 'The Subject of Memoirs: *The Woman Warrior*'s Technology of Ideographic Selfhood', in S. Smith and J. Watson (eds), *De/Colonizing the Subject: The Politics of Gender in Women's Autobiography*, Minneapolis, MN: University of Minnesota Press: 297–320.

Rabaté, J-M. (1996) *The Ghosts of Modernity*, Gainesville, FL: Florida University Press.

Rabinbach, A. (1996) 'Social Knowledge, Social Risk, and the Politics of Industrial Accidents in Germany and France', in D. Rueschmeyer and T. Skocpol (eds), *States, Social Knowledge and the Origins of Modern Social Policies*, Princeton, NJ: Princeton University Press: 48–89.

Radstone, S. (2000) 'Screening Trauma: *Forrest Gump*, Film and Memory', in S. Radstone (ed.), *Memory and Methodology*, New York: Berg: 79–107.

Rancière, J. (2004) *The Politics of Aesthetics*, trans. G. Rockhill, London: Continuum.

Rapp, D. (1988) 'The Reception of Freud by the British Press: General Interest and Literary Magazines, 1920–5', *Journal of the History of the Behavioural Sciences* 24: 191–201.

Reinhardt, M., H. Edwards and E. Duganne (eds) (2006) *Beautiful Suffering: Photography and the Traffic in Pain*, Chicago: University of Chicago Press.

Report of the War Office Committee of Enquiry into 'Shell-Shock' (1922) London: HMSO.

Research Advisory Committee on Gulf War Veterans' Illnesses (2004) *Scientific Progress in Understanding Gulf War Veterans' Illnesses: Report and Recommendations*, available at www.va-gov/rac-gwi/docs/ReportandRecommendations_2004.pdf. (accessed 16 May 2006).

Ribot, T. (1892) 'Will, Disorders of', in D. H. Tuke (ed.), *A Dictionary of Psychological Medicine*, London, J. & A. Churchill, 2 vols, II: 1366–8.

Richards, G. (2000) 'Britain on the Couch: The Popularization of Psychoanalysis in Britain 1915–40', *Science in Context* 13/2: 183–230.

Ricoeur, P. (1984) *Time and Narrative*, Vol. I, trans. K. McLaughlin and D. Pellauer, Chicago: University of Chicago Press.

——(1985) *Time and Narrative*, Vol. II, trans. K. McLaughlin and D. Pellauer, Chicago: University of Chicago Press.

——(1988) *Time and Narrative*, Vol. III, trans. K. McLaughlin and D. Pellauer, Chicago: University of Chicago Press.

——(1991) 'Life in Quest of Narrative', in D. Wood (ed.), *On Paul Ricoeur: Narrative and Interpretation*, London: Routledge: 20–33.

Ritchin, F. (1999) *In Our Own Image: The Coming Revolution in Photography*, New York: Aperture.

Rivers, W. H. R. (1917) 'Repression of War Experience', *The Lancet*, 2 February: 173–7.

——(1920) *Instinct and the Unconscious*, Cambridge: Cambridge University Press.

Roberts, M. (1993) *Daughters of the House*, London: Virago.

Rodley, C. (2005) *Lynch on Lynch*, rev. edn, London: Faber.

Romney, J. (2003) *Atom Egoyan*, London: BFI.

——(2004) 'Middle, End, Beginning', *Frieze* 86: 147–8.

Roscoe, J. and C. Hight (2001) *Faking It: Mock-Documentary and the Subversion of Factuality*, Manchester: Manchester University Press.

Rose, G. (1996) *Mourning Becomes the Law: Philosophy and Representation*, Cambridge: Cambridge University Press.

Rose, J. (2004) 'The Cult of Celebrity', in *On Not Being Able to Sleep: Psychoanalysis and the Modern World*, London: Vintage: 201–15.

Rosenfeld, G. D. (2004) 'The Politics of Uniqueness: Reflections on the Recent Polemical Turn in Holocaust and Genocidal Scholarship', in D. Ceserani (ed.), *Holocaust: Critical Concepts in Historical Studies, Vol. VI: The End of the 'Final Solution' and its Aftermath*, London: Routledge: 369–404.

Rosler, M. (1992) 'in, around, and afterthoughts (on documentary photography)', in R. Bolton (ed.), *The Contest of Meaning: Critical Histories of Photography*, Cambridge, MA: MIT: 303–40.

Ross, C. (2006) *The Aesthetics of Disengagement: Contemporary Art and Depression*, Minneapolis, MN: University of Minnesota Press.

Roth, P. (1988) *The Facts: A Novelist's Autobiography*, New York: Vintage.

——(1990) *Deception*, London: Vintage.

——(1991) *Patrimony: A True Story*, London: Vintage.

——(1993) *Operation Shylock: A Confession*, London: Vintage.

Rothberg, M. (2000) *Traumatic Realism: The Demands of Holocaust Representation*, Minneapolis, MN: University of Minnesota Press.

Rushdy, A. H. A. (1992) 'Daughters Signifyin(g) History: The Example of Toni Morrison's *Beloved*', *American Literature* 64/3: 567–97.

Russell, D. H. (1986) *The Secret Trauma: Incest in the Lives of Girls and Women*, New York: Basic Books.

Salgado, S. with T. J. Clark, O. Schell, N. Scheper-Hughes C. Slater and M. Watts (2002) *Migrations: The Work of Sebastião Salgado*, Berkeley, CA: Doreen B. Townsend Center Occasional Papers: 26.

Saltzman, L. (2006) *Making Memory Matter: Strategies of Remembrance in Contemporary Art*, Chicago: University of Chicago Press.

Santner, E. L. (1990) *Stranded Objects: Mourning, Memory and Film in Postwar Germany*, Ithaca, NY: Cornell University Press.

——(1992) 'History Beyond the Pleasure Principle: Some Thoughts on the Representation of Trauma', in S. Friedlander (ed.), *Probing the Limits of Representation: Nazism and the "Final Solution"*, Cambridge, MA: Harvard University Press: 143–54.

Sarkonak, R. (2000) *Angelic Echoes: Hervé Guibert and Company*, Toronto: University of Toronto Press.

Savarese, R. J. (2001) 'The Memoir Wars: Identity Politics, Recovered Memory, and Kenny Fries' *Body, Remember*', *Prose Studies* 24/1: 93–124.

Scarry, E. (1985) *The Body in Pain: The Making and Unmaking of the World*, Oxford: Oxford University Press.

Scharf, M. P. and W. A. Schabas (2002) *Slobodan Milosevic on Trial: A Companion*, New York: Continuum.

Scheper-Hughes, N. (2002) 'Commentary', in S. Salgado *et al.*: 27–34.

Schivelbusch, W. (1986) *The Railway Journey: The Industrialization of Time and Space in the Nineteenth Century*, New York: Berg.

Schlegel, A. (1995) 'My Lai: "We Lie, They Die": Or, a Small History of an "Atrocious" Photograph', *Third Text* 31: 47–61.

Schreiber, F. R. (1975) *Sybil: The True Story of a Woman Possessed by Sixteen Separate Personalities*, Harmondsworth: Penguin.

Schwartz, N. (2003) 'Exotic Rituals and Family Values in *Exotica*', in M. A. Rothenberg, D. Foster and S. Zizek (eds), *Perversion and the Social Relation*, Durham, NC: Duke University Press: 93–111.

Scott, A. (1996) *Real Events Revisited: Fantasy, Memory, Psychoanalysis*, London: Virago.

Scott, C. (1999) *The Spoken Image: Photography and Language*, London: Reaktion.

Scott, W. J. (1990) 'PTSD in DSM-III: A Case in the Politics of Diagnosis and Disease', *Social Problems* 37/3: 294–310.

Sebald, W. G. (1996) *The Emigrants*, trans M. Hulse, London: Harvill.

——(1998) *The Rings of Saturn*, trans. M. Hulse, London: Harvill.

——(1999) *Vertigo*, trans. M.Hulse, London: Harvill.

——(2001) *Austerlitz*, trans. A. Bell, London: Hamish Hamilton.

——(2003) *On the Natural History of Destruction*, trans. A. Bell, London: Hamish Hamilton.

Segal, L. (2004) 'Formations of Feminism: Political Memoirs of the Left (II)', *Radical Philosophy* 123: 8–21.

——(2007) *Making Trouble: Life and Politics*, London: Serpent's Tail.

Seiffert, R. (2007) *Afterwards*, London: Heinemann.

Self, W. (1995) 'Conversations: J. G. Ballard', *Junk Mail*, London: Penguin: 329–71.

Seltzer, M. (1997) 'Wound Culture: Trauma in the Pathological Public Sphere', *October* 80: 3–26.

——(1998) *Serial Killers*, London: Routledge.

Senf, C. A. (1998) '*Gerald's Game* and *Dolores Claiborne*: Stephen King and the Evolution of an Authentic Female Narrative Voice', in K. Lant and T. Thompson (eds): 91–107.

Sennett, R. (2002) *The Fall of Public Man* (1977), Harmondsworth: Penguin.

Shamdasani, S. (2005) '"Psychotherapy": The Invention of a Word', *History of the Human Sciences* 18: 1–22.

Shapiro, S. (1993) *The Cinematic Body*, Minneapolis, MN: University of Minnesota Press.

Shay, J. (1994) *Achilles in Vietnam: Combat Trauma and the Undoing of Character*, New York: Atheneum.

Shephard, B. (1996) 'Digging up the Past', *Times Literary Supplement* 22 March: 12–13.

——(2000) *A War of Nerves*, London: Jonathan Cape.

Shipherd, J. C., A. E. Street and P. A. Resick (2006) 'Cognitive Therapy for Post-Traumatic Stress Disorder', in V. M. Follette and J. I. Rusek (eds), *Cognitive-Behavioral Therapies for Trauma*, 2nd edn, New York: Guilford Press: 96–116.

Shnayerson, M. (1997) 'Women Behaving Badly', *Vanity Fair* (February): 26–31.

Showalter, E. (1997) *Hystories: Hysterical Epidemics and Modern Culture*, London: Picador.

Shuman, D. (2003) 'Persistent Re-experiences in Psychiatry and Law: Current and Future Trends for the Role of PTSD in Litigation', in R. I. Simon (ed.): 1–17.

Simon, R. I. (ed.) (2003) *Post-traumatic Stress Disorder in Litigation*, 2nd edn, Washington: American Psychiatric Publishing.

Siraganian, L. (2007) 'Telling a Horror Story, Conscientiously: Representing the Armenian Genocide from *Open House* to *Ararat*', in M. Tschofen and J. Burwell (eds): 133–56.

Smiley, J. (1992) *A Thousand Acres*, London: Flamingo.

Smith, T. (2006) *The Architecture of Aftermath*, Chicago: University of Chicago Press.

Smoking Gun (2006) 'A Million Little Lies: Exposing James Frey's Fiction Addiction': 8 January. http://www.thesmokinggun.com/archive/ 0104061jamesfrey1.html

Solomon-Godeau, A. (1998) 'Mourning or Melancholia: Christian Boltanski's *Missing House*', *Oxford Art Journal* 21/2: 1–20.

Sontag, S. (1966) 'The Imagination of Disaster', in *Against Interpretation*, New York: Farrar, Strauss and Giroux: 209–25.

——(1977) *On Photography*, Harmondsworth: Penguin.

——(1989) *AIDS and its Metaphors*, London: Allen Lane.

——(2002) 'A Mind in Mourning', *Where the Stress Falls*, London: Cape: 41–8.

——(2003) *Regarding the Pain of Others*, London: Hamish Hamilton.

——(2004) 'What Have We Done?', *The Guardian*, 26 May, G2: 2–5.

Spence, J. (1995) *Cultural Sniping: The Art of Transgression*, London: Routledge.

Spivak, G. C. (1988) 'Can the Subaltern Speak?', in C. Nelson and L. Grossberg (eds), *Marxism and the Interpretation of Culture*, Urbana, IL: University of Illinois Press: 271–313.

Stallabrass, J. (1997) 'Sebastião Salgado and Fine Art Photojournalism', *New Left Review* 223: 131–60.

——(1999) *High Art Lite: British Art in the 1990s*, London: Verso.

——(2004) *Art Incorporated: The Story of Contemporary Art*, Oxford: Oxford University Press.

Stefan, S. (1993–4) 'The Protection Racket: Rape Trauma Syndrome, Psychiatric Labeling, and Law', *Northwestern University Law Review* 88: 1271–1344.

Steiner, G. (1967) *Language and Silence: Essays on Language, Literature and the Inhuman*, New York: Atheneum.

Stephenson, P. (2002) *Billy: The Complete Life Story of a Comic Genius*, London: HarperCollins.

Sternfeld, J. (1996) *On this Site: Landscape in Memoriam*, San Francisco, CA: Chronicle Books.

Stevenson, D. (1995) 'Family Romance, Family Violence, and the Fantastic in *Twin Peaks*', in D. Lavery (ed.): 70–81.

Stone, M. (1985) 'Shellshock and the Psychologists', in W. F. Bynum, R. Porter and M. Shepherd (eds), *The Anatomy of Madness: Essays in the History of Psychiatry, vol II: Institutions and Society*, London: Tavistock: 242–71.

Storr, R. (2002) *Gerhard Richter: Forty Years of Painting*, New York: Museum of Modern Art.

Stover, E. and G. Peress (1998) *The Graves: Srebrenica and Vukovar*, New York: Scalo.

Sturken, M. (1997) *Tangled Memories: The Vietnam War, the AIDS Epidemic, and the Politics of Remembering*, Berkeley, CA: University of California Press.

Sullivan, B. (2003) 'The Real Thing: Photographer Luc Delahaye', *Artnet*, http://www.artnet.com/magazine/features/sullivan/sullivan4-10-03.asp

Sulloway, F. J. (1992) *Freud, Biologist of the Mind: Beyond the Psychiatric Legend*, Harvard, MA: Harvard University Press.

Sully, J. (1892) *The Human Mind: A Text-Book of Psychology*, 2 vols, London: Longmans.

Summerfield, D. (1998) 'The Social Experience of War and Some Issues for the Humanitarian Field', in P. Bracken and C. Petty (eds): 9–37.

Tagg, J. (2001) 'The Currency of Photography' [1978], in M. Alvarado, E. Buscombe and R. Collins (eds), *Representation and Photography*, London: Palgrave: 87–118.

Tal, K. (1996) *Worlds of Hurt: Reading the Literatures of Trauma*, Cambridge: Cambridge University Press.

Talbott, J. (1996) 'Combat Trauma in the American Civil War', *History Today* (March): 41–7.

Taylor, J. (1998) *Body Horror: Photojournalism, Catastrophe and War*, Manchester: Manchester University Press.

Terdiman, R. (1993) *Present Past: Modernity and the Memory Crisis*, Ithaca, NY: Cornell University Press.

Terr, L. (1985) 'Remembered Images and Trauma: A Psychology of the Supernatural', *Psychoanalytic Study of the Child* 40: 493–533.

——(1989) 'Terror Writing by the Formerly Terrified: A Look at Stephen King', *Psychoanalytic Study of the Child* 44: 369–90.

——(1994) *Unchained Memories: True Stories of Traumatic Memories, Lost and Found*, New York: Basic.

Thirlwell, A. (2003) 'Kitsch and W. G. Sebald', *Areté* 12: 27–54.

Thompson, T. (1998) 'Rituals of Male Violence: Unlocking the (Fe)Male Self in *Gerald's Game* and *Dolores Claiborne*', in K. Lant and T. Thompson (eds): 47–58.

Thurschwell, P. (2001) *Literature, Technology and Magical Thinking, 1880–1920*, Cambridge: Cambridge University Press.

Tillman, J., M. Nash and P. Lerner (1994) 'Does Trauma Cause Dissociative Pathology?', in S. Lynn and J. Rhine (eds), *Dissociation: Clinical and Theoretical Perspectives*, London: Guildford Press: 395–414.

Tomashevsky, B. (1965) 'Thematics', in L. T. Lemon and M. J. Reis (eds), *Russian Formalist Criticism: Four Essays*, Lincoln, NE: University of Nebraska Press.

Torgovnick, M. (2006) *The War Complex: World War II in our Time*, Chicago: University of Chicago Press.

Townsend, C. and M. Merck (2002) 'Eminent Domain: The Cultural Location of Tracey Emin', in M. Merck and C. Townsend (eds), *The Art of Tracey Emin*, London: Thames & Hudson: 6–20.

Townsend, M. and J. Revill (2006) 'Mental Health Crisis Hits UK Troops', *The Observer* 14 May: 8.

Trimble, M. (1981) *Post-Traumatic Neurosis: From Railway Spine to the Whiplash*, Chichester: John Wiley.

Tschofen, M. and J. Burwell (eds) (2007) *Image and Territory: Essays on Atom Egoyan*, Waterloo, Ontario: Laurier University Press.

Tschofen, M. and J. Burwell (2007) 'Mobile Subjectivity and Micro-Territories: Placing the Diaspora', in Tschofen and Burwell (eds): 125–31.

Tuckey, C. L. (1889) *Psycho-Therapeutics; or, Treatment by Sleep and Suggestion*, London: Balliere, Tindall, & Cox.

Tuerk, R. (2005) 'Caught Between *The Facts* and *Deception*', in D. P. Royal (ed.), *Philip Roth: New Perspectives on an American Author*, Westport, CT: Praegar: 129–42.

Tuke, D. H. (ed.) (1892) *A Dictionary of Psychological Medicine, giving the definition, etymology, and synonyms of the terms used in medical psychology with the symptoms, treatment, and pathology of insanity and the law of lunacy and Great Britain and Ireland*, 2 vols, London: J. & A. Churchill.

Turim, M. (1989) *Flashbacks in Film: Memory and History*, London: Routledge.

——(2001) 'The Trauma of History: Flashbacks upon Flashbacks', *Screen* 42/2: 205–10.

Turner, C. (1996) 'Holocaust Memories and History', *Journal of the History of the Human Sciences* 9/4: 45–63.

Van Alphen, E. (2001) 'Deadly Historians: Boltanski's Intervention in Holocaust Historiography', in B. Zelizer (ed.), *Visual Culture and the Holocaust*, London: Althlone: 45–73.

Van der Kolk, B. and O. van der Hart (1991) 'The Intrusive Past: The Flexibility of Memory and the Engraving of Trauma', *American Imago* 48/4: 425–54.

Van der Kolk, B. and R. Blitz, W. Burr, S. Sherry and E. Hartmann (1984) 'Nightmares and Trauma: A Comparison of Nightmares After Combat with Lifelong Nightmares in Veterans,' *American Journal of Psychiatry* 141: 187–90.

Vice, S. (2005) 'False Testimony', paper at 'The Future of Memory' conference, University of Manchester.

Vickroy, L. (2002) *Trauma and Survival in Contemporary Fiction*, Charlottesville, VA: University of Virginia Press.

Vulliamy, E. (1993) 'This War has Changed My Life', *British Journalism Review* 4/2: 5–11.

——(1997) 'Pen and Shrink', *The Guardian*, 13 February: 2–3.

Viner, R. (1999) 'Putting Stress in Life: Hans Selye and the Making of Stress Theory', *Social Studies of Science* 29/3: 391–410.

Walker, J. (2005) *Trauma Cinema: Documenting Incest and the Holocaust*, Berkeley, CA: University of California Press.

Walkowitz, R. L. (2006) *Cosmopolitan Style: Modernism Beyond the Nation*, New York: Columbia University Press.

Watts, M. (2002) 'Commentary', in S. Salgado *et al.*, 35–42.

Webster, R. (1995) *Why Freud was Wrong: Sin, Science and Psychoanalysis*, London: HarperCollins.

Weindling, P. (ed.) (1985) *The Social History of Occupational Health*, London: Croom Helm.

Weir, T. (2000) *A Casebook on Tort*, 9th edn, London: Sweet & Maxwell.

Welchman, J. C (2001) *Art After Appropriation: Essays on Art in the 1990s*, Amsterdam: G+B International.

Wells, C., D. Morgan and O. Quick (2000) 'Disasters: A Challenge for the Law', *Washburn Law Journal* 39: 496–525.

Wessely, S. (2006) 'Twentieth-Century Theories on Combat Motivation and Breakdown', *Journal of Contemporary History* 41: 269–86.

Wessely, S., S. Rose and J. Bisson (1998) 'A Systematic Review of Brief Psychological Interventions ("Debriefing") for the Treatment of Immediate Trauma-Related Symptoms and the Prevention of Post-Traumatic Stress Disorder', *Cochrane Library* 4, Oxford: Update Software.

White, E. (1995) '"Today the artist is a saint who writes his own life" – Edmund White on the Genre of Gay Autofiction', *London Review of Books*, 9 March: 6–8.

Whitehead, A. (2004) *Trauma Fiction*, Edinburgh: Edinburgh University Press.

Wiesel, E. (1968) *Legends of Our Time*, New York: Schocken Books.

——(1970) *One Generation After*, New York: Random House.

Wilkomirski, B. (1996) *Fragments: Memories of a Childhood 1939–1948*, trans. Carol Brown Janeway, London: Picador.

Williams, L. (1993) 'Mirrors without Memories: Truth, History and the New Documentary', *Film Quarterly* 46/3: 9–21.

Wilson, E. (2003) *Cinema's Missing Children*, London: Wallflower.

——(2006) *Alain Resnais*, Manchester: Manchester University Press.

Wilson, J. P. (2006) 'From Crisis Intervention to Bosnia', in C. Figley (ed.), *Mapping Trauma and its Wake*: 245–58.

Wilson, J. P and T. A. Moran (2004) 'Forensic/Clinical Assessment of Psychological Trauma and PTSD in Legal Settings', in J. P. Wilson and T. Keane, *Assessing Psychological Trauma and PTSD*, London: Guildford: 603–36.

Wilson, M. (1993) 'DSM-III and the Transformation of American Psychiatry: A History', *American Journal of Psychiatry* 150/3: 399–410.

Wiltshire, J. (2000) 'Biography, Pathography, and the Recovery of Meaning', *Cambridge Quarterly* 29/4: 409–22.

Wolcott, J. (1997) 'Dating Your Dad', *The New Republic*, 31 March: 32–6.

Wolfsohn, J. M. (1918) 'The Predisposing Factors of War Psycho-Neurosis', *The Lancet* 2 February: 177–180.

Wood, D. (1991) 'Introduction: Interpreting Narrative', in D. Wood (ed.), *On Paul Ricoeur: Narrative and Interpretation*, London: Routledge: 1–19.

Woolf, V. (1978) 'A Sketch of the Past', in *Moments of Being*, London: Triad Panther: 71–159.

—— (1981) 'Middlebrow', *The Death of the Moth and Other Essays*, London: Hogarth: 113–9.

Worrell, M. (2003) 'Working at Being Survivors: Identity, Gender and Participation in Self-Help Groups', in P. Reavey and S. Warner (eds), *New Feminist Stories of Child Sexual Abuse*, London: Routledge: 210–25.

'Wounded Mind' (1915) *Times* 24 April: 5.

Wright, L. (1994) *Remembering Satan: Recovered Memory and the Shattering of a Family*, London: Serpent's Tail.

Yardley, J. (1997) '"The Kiss" of Death for Literature?', *Washington Post*, 10 March: B2.

Yealland, L. (1918) *Hysterical Disorders of Warfare*, London: Macmillan.

Young, A. (1995) *The Harmony of Illusions: Inventing Post-Traumatic Stress Disorder*, Princeton, NJ: Princeton University Press.

Young, J. E. (1988) *Writing and Re-writing the Holocaust: Narrative and the Consequences of Interpretation*, Bloomington, IN: Indiana University Press.

——(1993) *The Texture of Memory: Holocaust Memorials and Meaning*, New Haven, CT: Yale University Press.

Zelizer, B. (1998) *Remembering to Forget: Holocaust Memory through the Camera's Eye*, Chicago: University of Chicago Press.

Žižek, S. (1994) 'David Lynch, or, the Feminine Depression', in *The Metastases of Enjoyment: On Women and Causality*, London: Verso: 113–36.

——(2000) *The Art of the Ridiculous Sublime: On David Lynch's Lost Highway*, Seattle, WA: University of Washington Press.

——(2005) 'Against Human Rights', *New Left Review* 34: 115–31.

Legal cases

UK

Alcock v. *Chief Constable of South Yorkshire* 1992: 1 Appeals Cases 310
Bourhill v. *Young* 1943: Appeals Cases 92
Coultas v. *Victorian Railway Commissioners* 1888: 13 Appeals Cases 222
Dulieu v. *White* 1901: 2 King's Bench 669
Frost v. *Chief Constable of South Yorkshire Police* 1997: 3 Weekly Law Reports 1194
Hambrook v. *Stokes Bros* 1925: 1 King's Bench 141
McFarlane v. *EE Caledonia Ltd* 1994: 2 All England Reports 1
McLoughlin v. *O'Brian* 1983: 1 Appeals Cases 410
Page v. *Smith* 1996: 1 Appeals Cases 155
Sion v. *Hampstead Health Authority* 1994: 5 Medical Law Review 170
Vernon v. *Bosley No. 1* 1997: 1 All England Reports 577
White v. *Chief Constable of South Yorkshire* 1999: 2 Appeals Cases 455

USA

Commonwealth v. *Frangipane*, Massachusetts 2001: 433 Mass. 527
Daubert v. *Dow Pharmaceuticals*, Supreme Court 1993: 509 US Reports 579
Engstrom v. *Engstrom*, California 1997
Jane Doe et al. v. *A Joseph Maskell*, Maryland 1996: 342 Md 684
State of Rhode Island v. *Quattrocchi*, Rhode Island 1999

Index

Related titles from Routledge

Culture and the Real
Theorizing Cultural Criticism
Catherine Belsey

Series: New Accents

'Belsey is that rarest of birds, a tough-minded romantic, at once a close reader and a far-seeker. She has shown us all how it is possible to write with extraordinary methodological and theoretical sophistication, and at the same time to write clearly, gracefully and simply. Belsey demonstrates by example that criticism can go about its academic business and still demand the critic to examine and take position on issues that affect our lives.'

—Harry Berger, *Professor of Literature and Art History, University of California, Santa Cruz*

What makes us the people we are? Culture evidently plays a part, but how large a part? Is culture alone the source of our identities? Catherine Belsey calls for a more nuanced account of what it is to be human. In the light of a characteristically lucid account of their views, as well as their debt to Kant and Hegel, she takes issue with Jean-François Lyotard, Judith Butler and Slavoj Žižek. Drawing examples from film and art, fiction and poetry, Professor Belsey builds on the insights of her influential *Critical Practice* to provide not only an accessible introduction to current debates, but a major new contribution to cultural criticism and theory.

ISBN10: 0–415–25288–1 (hbk)
ISBN10: 0–415–25289–X (pbk)

IBSN13: 978–0–415–25288–1 (hbk)
ISBN13: 978–0–415–25289–8 (pbk)
ISBN13: 978–0–203–00144–8 (ebk)

Available at all good bookshops
For further information on our literature series please visit
www.routledge.com/literature/series.asp

For ordering and further information please visit:
www.routledge.com

The New Critical Idiom

Series Editor: John Drakakis, *University of Stirling*

The New Critical Idiom is an invaluable series of introductory guides to today's critical terminology. Each book:

- provides a handy, explanatory guide to the use (and abuse) of the term
- offers an original and distinctive overview by a leading literary and cultural critic
- relates the term to the larger field of cultural representation.

With a strong emphasis on clarity, lively debate and the widest possible breadth of examples, *The New Critical Idiom* is an indispensable approach to key topics in literary studies.

'*The New Critical Idiom* is a constant resource – essential reading for all students.'
—Tom Paulin, *University of Oxford*

'Easily the most informative and wide-ranging series of its kind, so packed with bright ideas that it has become an indispensable resource for students of literature.'
—Terry Eagleton, *University of Manchester*

Available in this series:

The Author by Andrew Bennett
Autobiography by Linda Anderson
Adaptation and Appropriation by Julie Sanders
Class by Gary Day
Colonialism/Postcolonialism – **Second edition** by Ania Loomba
Comedy by Andrew Stott
Crime Fiction by John Scaggs
Culture/Metaculture by Francis Mulhern
Difference by Mark Currie
Discourse by Sara Mills
Drama/Theatre/Performance by Simon Shepherd and Mick Wallis
Dramatic Monologue by Glennis Byron
Ecocriticism by Greg Garrard
Elegy by David Kennedy
Genders by David Glover and Cora Kaplan
Genre by John Frow
Gothic by Fred Botting
Historicism by Paul Hamilton
Humanism by Tony Davies
Ideology by David Hawkes
Interdisciplinarity by Joe Moran
Intertextuality by Graham Allen

Irony by Claire Colebrook
Literature by Peter Widdowson
Magic(al) Realism by Maggie Ann Bowers
Metre, Rhythm and Verse Form by Philip Hobsbaum
Metaphor by David Punter
Mimesis by Matthew Potolsky
Modernism by Peter Childs
Myth by Laurence Coupe
Narrative by Paul Cobley
Parody by Simon Dentith
Pastoral by Terry Gifford
The Postmodern by Simon Malpas
The Sublime by Philip Shaw
The Author by Andrew Bennett
Realism by Pam Morris
Rhetoric by Jennifer Richards
Romance by Barbara Fuchs
Romanticism by Aidan Day
Science Fiction by Adam Roberts
Sexuality by Joseph Bristow
Stylistics by Richard Bradford
Subjectivity by Donald E. Hall
The Unconscious by Antony Easthope

For further information on individual books in the series
visit: www.routledge.com/literature/nci

Routledge Critical Thinkers
Series Editor: Robert Eaglestone, *Royal Holloway, University of London*

Routledge Critical Thinkers is designed for students who need an accessible introduction to the key figures in contemporary critical thought. The books provide crucial orientation for further study and equip readers to engage with each theorist's original texts.

The volumes in the *Routledge Critical Thinkers* series place each key theorist in his or her historical and intellectual contexts and explain:

- why he or she is important
- what motivated his/her work
- what his/her key ideas were
- who and what influenced the thinker
- who and what the thinker has influenced
- what to read next and why.

Featuring extensively annotated guides to further reading, *Routledge Critical Thinkers* is the first point of reference for any student wishing to investigate the work of a specific theorist.

'These little books are certainly helpful study guides. They are clear, concise and complete. They are ideal for undergraduates studying for exams or writing essays and for lifelong learners wanting to expand their knowledge of a given author or idea.'
—Beth Lord, *THES*

'This series demystifies the demigods of theory.'
—Susan Bennett, *University of Calgary*

Available in this series:

Available at all good bookshops
For further information on individual books in the series, visit:
www.routledge.com/literature/rct

Related titles from Routledge

Religion, Terror and Violence
Religious Studies Perspectives
Edited by Bryan Rennie and Philip L. Tite

'*Religion, Terror and Violence* is a timely collection on an urgent set of issues. Paul Christopher Johnson's essay skillfully combining theory, intellectual history, ethnographic observation and social criticism is, by itself, more than worth the price of admission. Maureen Korp's descriptive meditation on art and artists in response to 9/11 extends the intense interest by a number of contemporary students of religion in memorialization and memory to include other media, along with the architectural ... a pioneering contribution, enriching this nascent field.'

—Jonathan Z. Smith, *Robert O. Anderson Distinguished Service Professor at the University of Chicago, USA*

In light of the continued shadow cast by 9/11 and the subsequent war on terror, *Religion, Terror and Violence* brings together a group of distinguished scholars to scrutinize the intimate link between religion and violence. A key theme in this collection is that both the violence and the reactions to those events were intimately linked to cultural and social authorizing processes that could be called 'religious'.

In twenty fascinating contributions, such themes as national identity formation, ritualization of traumatic events, artistic representations and cultural power contestations are scrutinized, along with reflections on the role of the public intellectual in such situations.

ISBN13: 978–0–415–44230–5 (hbk)
ISBN13: 978–0–415–44231–1 (pbk)

Available at all good bookshops
For ordering and further information please visit:
www.routledge.com